The 10th Kentucky
Volunteer Infantry in
the Civil War

The 10th Kentucky Volunteer Infantry in the Civil War

A History and Roster

DENNIS W. BELCHER

To D. J. and Wade

Dennis Belcher

McFarland & Company, Inc., Publishers

Jefferson, North Carolina, and London

LIBRARY OF CONGRESS CATALOGUING-IN-PUBLICATION DATA

Belcher, Dennis W., 1950–
The 10th Kentucky Volunteer Infantry in the Civil War :
a history and roster / Dennis W. Belcher.
p.   cm.
Includes bibliographical references and index.

ISBN 978-0-7864-4153-2

softcover : 50# alkaline paper ∞

1. United States. Army. Kentucky Infantry Regiment, 10th (1861–1864)
2. Kentucky—History—Civil War, 1861–1865—Regimental histories.
3. United States—History—Civil War, 1861–1865—Regimental histories.
4. Soldiers—Kentucky—Registers.   5. Soldiers—Kentucky—Correspondence.
6. Kentucky—History—Civil War, 1861–1865—Registers.
7. Kentucky—Genealogy.   8. United States—History—Civil War, 1861–1865—Registers.
9. United States—History—Civil War, 1861–1865—Campaigns.   I. Title.
E509.510th .B45   2009   973.7'469—dc22   2009016503

British Library cataloguing data are available

On the cover: *Battle of Mission Ridge,* 1863 Cosack & Co. lith.,
Buffalo & Chicago (Library of Congress)

Manufactured in the United States of America

*McFarland & Company, Inc., Publishers
Box 611, Jefferson, North Carolina 28640
www.mcfarlandpub.com*

For the memory of the men of
the 10th Kentucky Infantry.

For Nancy

Acknowledgments

I want to thank the numerous people who have made this project possible. In particular, I would like to thank Robert Preston, who keeps the 10th Kentucky Infantry alive today, for his support and willingness to share information. I would also like to thank Joni House and Kurt Holman at Perryville Battle State Historic Site. The local historians in central Kentucky have been of tremendous help, in particular Nash Hayes in Lebanon and Steven Wright in Elizabethtown.

The Kentucky Historical Society, the Filson Historical Society, University Press of Kentucky, and University Press of Kansas have been invaluable in their assistance. I also want to thank the national treasures where history is preserved—the Library of Congress, the National Archives in Washington, D.C., and the Abraham Lincoln Presidential Library, where Debbi Hamm was of great assistance. I can't thank T. Joseph Hardesty at the Louisville Free Public Library enough for his efforts in finding biographical information. I want to thank Jeff Patrick at Wilson's Creek National Battlefield for his efforts with the *National Tribune*. A huge "thank you" to Rick Baumgartner at Blue Acorn Press for sharing his photos of the 10th Kentucky.

Thanks to all the librarians who weave their magic every day.

I can't express my appreciation enough to those who agreed to read the sections of this book: Charlie Crawford, Georgia Battlefields Association; Kurt Holman, manager of Perryville Battlefield State Historic Site; Steve Adolphson, fellow author and expert on the Battle of Hartsville; Dr. Daryl Black, curator, Chattanooga History Center; and Brandon Slone, military historian, Kentucky Historical Society.

I also want to acknowledge and express my gratitude to Thomas Vought, Kansas State University, who worked tirelessly on constructing many of the maps for this book.

Table of Contents

Preface

Most people find their way to *Dyer's Compendium* when they start researching Civil War regiments. *Dyer's Compendium* has three short paragraphs about the 10th Kentucky Infantry and ends with a very short summary: "Regiment lost during service 2 Officers and 70 Enlisted men killed and mortally wounded and 5 Officers and 144 Enlisted men by disease. Total 221." This was the starting point for me in my quest for information about this regiment, but their story is so much more.

In November 1861, 867 simple men stepped into their uniforms and made a commitment to defend the unity of their country, and three years later fewer than 140 of these men walked bloody and battered off their last battlefield just south of Atlanta near Jonesboro, Georgia. The story of the 10th Regiment Kentucky Volunteer Infantry has two parts—the war in which they fought and the men who made up this regiment.

Their story includes massive heartbreak and high humor and includes such names as Chickamauga, Missionary Ridge, Chattahoochee River and Atlanta. It would be difficult to develop a work of fiction that encompasses the story that is included here.

The story of the 10th Kentucky Infantry has been a difficult effort to assemble because none of the ranking regimental officers were ever married or had children who could have preserved valuable information about the regiment. The history of the regiment was assembled with the aid of the memoirs of John Harlan, the first colonel of the 10th Kentucky, up to March 1863. After that time, the story relies primarily on letters and official documents. The letters of Seth Bevill, James Scott, Edward Mittler, Martin VanBuren Crouch, and Henry Davidson were critical in personalizing the activities of the regiment.

A few points need to be made about this book. First of all, Civil War records can be very, very complete; but likewise, there are many errors. One of the biggest problems with Civil War history is the poor spelling of the names of men. That was the state of Civil War records of the time. Secondly, there is often a total lack of information. For example, much, if not all, of the enlistment information for Company H of the 10th Kentucky Infantry has been lost. Finally, the 10th Kentucky Infantry is an underappreciated regiment that, fought for three years and participated in significant actions that helped define who these men were. These were just farm boys from Kentucky and many of the parents received letters like this: "It becomes my painful duty to inform you that your son Richard Roaler, that Brave, that Gallant Boy you loved, whom I loved, who we all loved is dead. He was mortally wounded by the enemy at the Battle of Chickamauga Creek...."

Let us not forget the actions of the "sons of the dark and bloody ground."

Sons of the Dark and Bloody Ground
Ye must not slumber there,
Where stranger steps and tongues resound
Along the heedless air.
Your own proud land's heroic soil
Shall be your fitter grave;
She claims from war his richest spoil,
The ashes of her brave.
—By Theodore O'Hara, "Bivouac of the Dead"

ONE

Organizing the 10th Kentucky

"We must rally now where the National flag invites us."—John Marshall Harlan

Civil War Comes to Kentucky

As the Civil War split the country, central Kentucky was one of the nation's most divided areas. This region harbored sympathies for both the Union and Confederacy. The 10th Kentucky Volunteer Infantry was formed primarily by individuals from west-central Kentucky, with half of its members coming from Washington and Marion Counties.

The people who joined came from a variety of occupations and locations, and their reasons for joining were just as varied. The initial leaders of the regiment were Colonel John Marshall Harlan, originally from Boyle County, and Washington Countians Lt. Colonel William H. Hays and Major Gabriel Caldwell Wharton. All three of the regimental officers and the regimental adjutant were lawyers. The lives of these three senior officers crossed during the war and their relationships carried on after the war. All three men survived the conflict and went on to live lives of service to their communities and country.

The situation in Kentucky in 1860 was tenuous. The presidential election of Abraham Lincoln and Hannibal Hamlin in 1860 dashed the final hope for many Southerners. Southerners perceived that this election would mean the end of slavery and their way of life. Kentucky was a truly divided state and Governor Beriah Magoffin and many state officers, while not openly declaring their support for secession, did not discourage a movement in support of secession. Governor Magoffin stated that "he would not furnish troops for the wicked purpose of subduing her sister Southern States."[1] Kentucky did not support Lincoln and only 1 percent of the votes cast in Kentucky were for him, totaling only 1,364. Of these, only five came from Fayette County, the home of his in-laws. Kentucky wavered between joining the Confederacy and staying loyal to the Union.

Congressional elections held in June 1861 helped clarify where Kentucky would stand after the shelling of Fort Sumter: nine of ten congressional districts supported Unionist candidates. These elections were followed in August with state legislature elections where the Unionists' majority over the Secessionists was 76 to 24 in the House and 27 to 11 in the Senate.[2] The people had cast their votes and Kentucky was going to stay in the Union.

In August 1861, President Abraham Lincoln authorized the establishment of recruiting camps in Kentucky, and Confederate President Jefferson Davis responded by authorizing similar camps for his government. The fragile neutrality in Kentucky was quickly being ripped by the two opposing factions.

Both Union and Secession sympathizers formed volunteer companies in 1861 to support their position in regard to the political division of the state. The purpose of these volunteer companies was self-protection from the potential violence of the opposition. Both sides sought

3

to educate the people of Kentucky on the "correct" way of thinking. Many families were split on which side they should align. As one historian noted, "Only in Kentucky did father fight against son and brother against brother on a massive scale."[3] The presidents of the two warring factions were both born in Kentucky.

Finally, neutrality was lost in late summer 1861. The Union and Southern factions in Missouri were positioning themselves, with open conflict soon to occur. The boot heel region of Missouri was openly sympathizing with the South and the importance of the Mississippi River was not lost on either side. The city of Columbus was strategically located on the Kentucky side of the Mississippi River. Union forces in Missouri were ordered to gain control of Cape Girardeau and then instructed to march to Belmont, Missouri, where they were to destroy the Confederate works and construct their own.

As a result, the Confederates, under command of General Leonidas Polk, were ordered to capture Hickman and Columbus, Kentucky, and gain control of the Mississippi River on the Kentucky side. General Ulysses Grant then moved his forces into Paducah, Kentucky, to insure that no further control by the Confederacy occurred along the Mississippi or Ohio Rivers. Thus, Kentucky was invaded and had armies from the North and South within its borders. Neutrality was no longer an option.

Kentucky had over 250,000 slaves in 1860; however, the preservation of the Union was an equally, or even a more important, factor in the decision for men to support the Union cause. Kentucky was now an "invaded" state and many within Kentucky began to choose sides overtly.

On October 4, 1861, John Marshall Harlan, a lawyer living in Louisville, with strong political support was granted permission to organize a regiment of infantry, and that regiment was to become the 10th Regiment Kentucky Volunteer Infantry. The regiment was to draw men primarily from Louisville to Danville. The men came from all walks of life, but they believed that the Union needed to be preserved at all costs.

Leadership of the 10th Kentucky Regiment

The regimental leadership consisted of three senior officers and a regimental adjutant who was also an officer. The regimental officers were colonel, lieutenant colonel and major. In addition, the regimental staff included quartermaster sergeants, commissary sergeants, musicians and the medical staff. For the 10th Kentucky, the initial regimental officers were Colonel John Harlan, Lt. Colonel William Hercules Hays, and Major Gabriel Wharton.

Although we don't know the reasons every member had for joining the Union cause, John Harlan's philosophy can serve as a model for many people joining the 10th Kentucky. He was pro-slavery, but strongly believed that the Union had to be preserved.

John Harlan was a native of Boyle County, Kentucky, and his family was slaveholders. He was born in 1833 into a politically active family and as he grew older, he became very ambitious himself. The family definitely helped mold John's outlook on the state of affairs at the beginning of the war and helped define what his role would be in the upcoming conflict.

John Harlan's father, James Harlan, was a two-term Whig representative from Kentucky and was a strong supporter of Henry Clay, a founder and progressive leader of the Whig party. He was said to have one of the most powerful law firms in Kentucky.

When James Harlan was asked to become the secretary of state, the family was moved to Frankfort, Kentucky. John was educated at Centre College in Danville, Kentucky, and studied law at Transylvania College in Lexington, Kentucky. He also read law and entered practice in the 1850s. In 1851, Governor John L. Helm appointed him adjutant general of Kentucky, giving him his first military experience at age 18. His brother had served in the Mexican War and probably served as a role model for his younger brother.[4] John Harlan's occupational activities in Kentucky prior to the war included private practice, Frankfort, 1853–1861; city attorney, Frankfort, 1854–1858; judge, County Court of Franklin County, 1858; and private practice, Louisville, 1861.

John Harlan ran for Congress in 1859 as candidate for the Old Whig or Know-Nothing Party but was defeated by William E. Sims. He had attracted national attention during the election; however, he decided not to pursue politics in 1860, but instead concentrated on his law practice. Although John Harlan opposed Lincoln, he supported the Union "at all hazards." He traveled throughout the state in the summer of 1861 "earnestly urging the people to stand by the union."[4] After the battle at Fort Sumter, Harlan felt that it was time to commit himself to the preservation of the Union. In July 1861, John Harlan and friends met in Louisville because they felt that action had to be taken to keep Kentucky from drifting toward secession. Harlan spent May, June and July 1861 literally, daily, standing on boxes addressing anyone who would listen about the need to preserve the Union.[5] He became recognized as one of the firebrands for the Union cause.

Colonel John Marshall Harlan was a native of Boyle County, Kentucky, and the son of a two-term Whig representative. At the time the 10th Kentucky Infantry was organized, he was a lawyer living in Louisville (Library of Congress).

During this time an armed military company was formed in Louisville, which was organized, as described by John Harlan, as needed for self-defense. Harlan joined Crittenden's Union Zouaves and was appointed to the rank of captain. He recorded, "The rebels formed similar military organizations in Louisville."[6] The second purpose of the Crittenden Zouaves was to show that the Unionists would not be intimidated, according to Harlan. He still had not committed to joining the newly forming Union Army, but his decision was made simple when his mother came to him and encouraged him to join. He agreed.

While a member of Crittenden's Zouaves, John Harlan met William T. Sherman for the first time. Harlan's men were ordered to serve as guards for Sherman's headquarters in Lebanon Junction, Kentucky. Sherman was known as a cigar smoker and asked for a loan of Harlan's cigar to light his own. Accomplishing the lighting of the cigar, Sherman threw Harlan's cigar away, proving once again the privilege of rank. It is likely Sherman threw away Harlan's cigar without thinking.

Later in 1861, he established his camp near Lebanon, Kentucky, and began recruiting the 10th Kentucky Volunteer Infantry. Harlan was first colonel of the 10th Kentucky Infantry and he remained a colonel until March 1863, when he resigned to become the state's attorney general.

The next senior officer in the 10th Kentucky was Lt. Colonel William Hercules Hays. William Hays was instrumental in organizing the unit, with the majority of the enlistment coming from his home county, Washington, and neighboring county, Marion. While Harlan was seeking political approval to form the 10th Kentucky, he still needed men for the regiment. William Hays, a strong and recognized leader from Springfield, was the man who brought him many of his recruits. William Hays was from a prominent local family and was a recognized political leader for this part of Kentucky. Hays was born on August 26, 1820, in Washington County to William, originally from Virginia, and Eleanor Hays, a Washington County native. His was one of the founding families moving from Virginia to central Kentucky[7]; William was the youngest of 9 children.[8]

William Hays was educated in Washington County and in 1843 began reading law in Elizabethtown, Kentucky, under James W. Hays. In 1845, he began practicing law in Springfield and was elected county judge of Washington County in 1851 and 1854. In 1861 he was elected as a representative to the state legislature, but when he joined the 10th Kentucky Infantry, he resigned this office.

Lt. Col. William Hercules Hays was a native of Springfield, Kentucky. He was a judge, lawyer and state legislator and was instrumental in recruiting soldiers for the Union cause (Frohne and Son Historic Military).

The final initial senior regimental officer was Major Gabriel Caldwell Wharton. He was born in Springfield, Kentucky, on June 13, 1839, the son of a farmer, John Wharton, and Sarah Caldwell Wharton. He was educated at public schools, including the Springfield Academy, before studying at the law department of the University of Louisville. He also studied law with R. J. Browne in Springfield. He began his law practice in 1860 just prior to the beginning of the Civil War. He had an "active and lucrative practice," and after his first year of law practice, he enlisted in the 10th Kentucky Infantry and was commissioned as major of the regiment.[9, 10]

Wharton was a devoted subordinate to William Hays and assisted in the recruitment and organization of the 10th Kentucky. Hays was Wharton's mentor, and the two men made a cohesive and effective pair of leaders throughout the war. Wharton appears to have been a social and active individual, enjoying interactions with others.[11] He later was promoted to the rank of lieutenant colonel at John Harlan's resignation in the spring of 1863 and served with the unit until the end of the war.

The final regimental officer of the 10th Kentucky Infantry was yet another attorney, William J. Lisle of Lebanon, Kentucky. Lisle held the rank of regimental adjutant. He was a native of Green County, Kentucky, and was born in 1837, the son of Thomas W. and Nancy Tate Lisle. His father was also a lawyer. Lisle read law under Aaron Hardin and in 1859 graduated from the law department of Louisville University; he was in active law practice at the beginning of the war when he joined the 10th Kentucky Infantry.[12]

Over nine hundred men were in the 10th Kentucky at its maximum strength. It is beyond the scope of this book to highlight everyone in the regiment, but some details of the unit can be found in the appendices. Biographical information will follow for the staff and regimental officers.

The 10th Kentucky Infantry would have four regimental surgeons and as many assistant surgeons and hospital stewards during the war, but the initial

Major Gabriel Caldwell Wharton, a lawyer from Springfield, Kentucky, the son of a prominent farmer, and loyal friend of William Hays and John Harlan (Blue Acorn Press, Huntington, West Virginia).

medical staff was made up of Surgeon Dr. William Atkisson, Assistant Surgeon Thomas Knott, and Hospital Steward Richard Davenport. Thomas Knott was replaced by Charles Hardesty in 1862 as assistant surgeon.

Dr. Atkisson was one of two brothers who were physicians. He lived in Simpsonville, Kentucky, prior to the war and joined the 10th Kentucky when the unit was mustered into service. Dr. Atkisson was married on August 19, 1856, in Louisville to Mary Catherine Ewing. They had one son, George F., born in 1858.[13]

The remainder of the regimental staff consisted of a sergeant major and commissary sergeants, quartermaster sergeants and musicians. The regimental sergeant-major was initially Austin Maguire, but later that role was filled by Robert J. Smith, who enlisted at age 19 and was a farmer from Marion County. The regimental chaplain was Richard C. Nash, born on February 23, 1810, in Jefferson County, Kentucky. He was the oldest member of the officer-regimental staff and was on hand to handle the spiritual needs of the men of the 10th Kentucky. He was a Baptist minister. Reverand Nash was originally elected as captain for Company F, but was appointed regimental chaplain on November 13, 1861.[14]

The Beginning

The headquarters of the newly forming 10th Kentucky Infantry was at Camp Crittenden in Lebanon. The regiment was invited to a picnic on the fairgrounds in Springfield, and the event was described as follows: "On the day of the picnic the people, men, women and children from all parts of the county assembled in Springfield to welcome Colonel Harlan and his regiment of brave Kentuckians.... I started out [toward Lebanon] on my pony Flash to meet them.... I can never forget the impression ... one thousand men four abreast, came winding itself like some great monster along the road, with Colonel Harlan and his staff at their head.... I gave him the military salute, to which he gratefully responded with a smile."[15]

By October 12, 1861, the *Louisville Journal* reported that 275 men were already present at Camp Crittenden. Also in October, Colonel George Anderson established Camp John Graves, but there were not enough recruits to form a full regiment and many of these men became part of the 10th Kentucky. By November 21, 1861, the 10th Kentucky Infantry was able to muster about 870 men.

Once John Harlan committed himself to forming a Union regiment, he wrote an editorial and called for enlistment:

> To The People of Kentucky:
>
> I have been authorized to raise a regiment of infantry to be mustered into the service of the United States, and to form a part of the force under the command of General Robert Anderson. Companies will be received from any part of the State.
>
> Each company will be composed of not less than eighty-four nor more than one hundred and one men, rank and file, and will elect their officers.
>
> The cost of transportation to the place of rendezvous (which will be hereafter designated) as well as the cost of subsisting the troops previous to their being mustered into the service, will be paid by the Government. Lieutenant-Colonel, Major, and other regimental officers will be selected in due time. The regiment will be supplied with good arms.
>
> No written authority is necessary to raise companies. Let individuals organize themselves as rapidly as possible and report to me the names of the officers selected by the respective companies. Address me at Louisville, Kentucky.

And now I appeal to my fellow–Kentuckians to come forward and enroll themselves for service. Their invaded State appeals to them. Their foully-wronged and deeply-imperiled country appeals to them. The cause of human liberty and Republican institutions everywhere appeals to them. All that is most glorious in human government is now at stake, and every true man should come to the rescue.

The time, fellow-citizens, has come, and even the unpatriotic and the selfish should hasten to take up arms for the common defense of their State and country. Every consideration of enlightened self-interest calls us to the field. If our enemies triumph, all our trades, all our professions, all our avocations of whatever character, all our possessions of every description, become valueless. To save ourselves and our families from ruin, not less than to save our State and country from degradation and shame, we must rally now where the National flag invites us. Come, then, let us gird up the whole strength of our bodies and souls for the conflict, and may the God of battles guide home every blow we strike. For one, I am unwilling to see the people of my native State overrun and conquered by men claiming to be citizens of a foreign government. I cannot be indifferent to the issue which an unnatural enemy has forced upon Kentuckians.

John M. Harlan[16]

So recruitment now began in earnest and patriotic feelings surged throughout the countryside. A letter written by James P. Barbour of Washington County describes a recruiting session there on October 12, 1861:

Yesterday was a glorious day for old Washington. The loyal citizens of the country had purchased, in your city, a magnificent Union flag, and yesterday, by appointment, from the rotunda of the Court-house in Springfield, in the presence of a large concourse of the people, it was flung to the breeze, and, as it rolled forth in gorgeous beauty a shout went up from the multitude of spectators.... This was followed by speeches of great eloquence and power by Lieut. Col. Hays, Colonel Harlan, and the venerable and able Representative from this Congressional District, the Hon. C. A. Wickliffe.

The commanding officers of John M. Harlan, W. W. [W. H.] Hays, and G. C. Wharton, are the very pride of the State, to say nothing of the brilliant young men at the head of the companies already enlisted. No encampment in Kentucky has been commenced with more flattering auspices.[17]

The *Louisville Democrat* contained two such advertisements for the recruitment of the men who would become the 10th Kentucky Infantry.

The 10th Kentucky's regimental strength was 867 men in November 1861 when the unit formed. The regiment would never be able to bring that number of men to any engagement. It would add a total of 91 recruits over the next three years, but losses would greatly exceed the gains. While the 10th Kentucky was rallying around the flag, conditions within Kentucky were starting to intensify. Politically, Kentucky was now aligned with the North, but the sentiments within the state were anything but unanimous. Actions in east Tennessee, where residents opposed secession, caused concerns on both sides of the conflict. The Union would have liked nothing better than to have east Tennessee become a flaming ember in the side of the Southern government. The Secessionists recognized the importance of preventing any Union interference in the hotbed of resistance in eastern Tennessee.

In October 1861, Confederate General Felix Zollicoffer led an expedition into southeastern Kentucky to prevent the unwanted Union interference. On October 21, 1861, the ever aggressive General Zollicoffer attempted to take the Union works at Camp Wildcat, south of Mt. Vernon, Kentucky, but was repulsed. There were fewer than 80 casualties on both sides in the engagement, but any attempt for neutrality was being ground into the mud. Although the attack on Camp Wildcat was a relatively minor encounter, the need for fresh

Left: Enlistment advertisement for the "Grand Gathering" of the 10th Kentucky in Washington County; *right:* Enlistment advertisement for the "Mass Meeting" of the 10th Kentucky in Marion County (both from the *Louisville Democrat,* October 17, 1861).

troops to protect Kentucky was evident. The cry across the state of Kentucky was to rally around the flag.

Several regiments were being formed and there was competition to get enough men to have a fully staffed unit. So, along with local leaders exerting their influence within their communities, advertising became a way of increasing the enlistment. As the regiments were being formed, a camp of instruction was set up in Bardstown to train the officers on military conduct and affairs. Lebanon was a point of rendezvous for many of the regiments; it was specifically chosen to be visual to the populace. As many as 40,000 men had enlisted in the Union Army and 10,000 in the Confederate Army by the fall of 1861.

A Confederate military camp was established in Russellville, Kentucky, and those at this camp were resolved to take their state into the Confederacy. George W. Johnson of Scott County was even made governor in this Confederate civil government in Kentucky. Representatives were appointed and expected to attend the Confederate Congress.

One example of enthusiastic recruitment occurred in Washington County after the beginning of the war when a public meeting was held outside Springfield. Speakers included the ex-governor of Kentucky, Charles Wickliffe. As with many meetings in Kentucky, the session was opened with a prayer offered by "Brother" Sandusky: "Aid and comfort in the cause of the Union. We beseech Thee to go with and guide the armies of the Union in their battles against the rebels, who are striving to destroy our blessed Union of states; will Thou take each erring rebel by the nap of the neck and the seat of the breeches, and shake him over the fires of perdition...." When a member of the crowd yelled, "Give them hell, Bro Sandusky, give them hell," Brother Sandusky responded by saying, "And now, O, Lord, after Thost hast disposed of our enemies, and rebels of the South, which we know Thost will do in Thine own good time, we beseech Thee, O Lord, to turn Thy attention to some of our own friends. Teach them, we pray Thee, that there is a time and place for all things. Punish those who do not know how to keep quiet...."[18]

Flags

Flags in the Civil War were emotional symbols of country and home and were treasured items for which men would die. The flags for the 10th Kentucky Infantry appear to be lost in history and we may never completely know which design was used. Based on the style of the flags that were common to Kentucky infantry regiments, it might be surmised that the 10th Kentucky Infantry national colors would be similar to those of the 9th and 11th Kentucky Infantry Regiments that have been preserved by the Kentucky Historical Society.[19]

The design of the regimental standard might be more difficult to determine. The early Kentucky regiments had regimental standards made by Hugh Wilkins in Louisville. Some are preserved by the Kentucky Historical Society.

However, since Hugh Wilkins was commissioned by the state of Kentucky to supply flags to the Kentucky units (Union), it is likely that the 10th would have received flags similar to the ones pictured. Mr. and Mrs. Wilkins started delivering flags to federal units in

Left: 9th Kentucky Infantry national colors; *right:* 11th Kentucky Infantry national colors (Kentucky Historical Society).

Left: 3rd Kentucky Infantry Regimental Colors; *right:* 13th Kentucky Infantry Regimental Colors (Kentucky Historical Society).

January 1862 and some, like the 13th Kentucky, did not receive theirs until February 1862. The 10th Kentucky's colors were presented to the regiment on January 1, 1862. Some of the other Kentucky units may not have received the Wilkinses' flags until after the battle at Mill Springs. Presented by the "Loyal Ladies of Louisville Soldiers Association," the Hugh Wilkins national colors are generally distinguished by the light blue color of the cantons. The Wilkinses also made flags for some of the Indiana and Minnesota federal units.[20] Only one photo of the 10th Kentucky Infantry flag is known to exist.

The first Color Guard for the 10th Kentucky was appointed on December 28, 1861, and was made of corporals from the various companies. They included Phillip McGrath (Company B), William Gabheart (Company C), David White (Company D), George Enser (Company E), Charles Jarboe (Company F), Jeff Inman (Company G), Milton Earls (Company H) and Andrew Burger (Company K). Sergeant John Lee, Company K, was appointed regimental color sergeant.[21]

Corporal Orville Young with the 10th Kentucky Infantry national colors, presumably photographed later in the war (Blue Acorn Press, Huntington, West Virginia).

Mustering and Training of the 10th Kentucky

The 10th Kentucky was issued standard equipment including shirts, socks, blankets, tents, picks, mess kits, hatchets, spoons, tin cups, overcoats, pants, pillows and knives. They were also equipped with .69- and .71-caliber Prussian rifled muskets, but these were not the weapons that Colonel Harlan had hoped for. In a letter dated December 17, 1861, to John Tinnell, adjutant general for Kentucky, he states, "Please have us furnished at the earliest possible moment and if the whole regiment can be armed with the Enfield or Springfield rifles."[22] Approximately a month later, the 10th Kentucky Infantry was involved in its first clash with the Confederate Army. Colonel Harlan had hoped for more effective and modern rifles than these rifled muskets.

The men of the 10th came from a variety of counties with most originating from Marion and Washington, but Jefferson, Hardin and Nelson counties provided significant numbers. It is difficult to identify where all the men of 10th Kentucky were living, but the *Regiment Descriptive Book* does show where they were born. In addition to those mentioned, men were provided from 22 additional counties in Kentucky. Men of the 10th Kentucky were also native to several other states, including Ohio, Indiana, Pennsylvania, North Carolina, Maryland, Virginia, New York, Missouri, Tennessee and Alabama. Other countries also contributed men, including Ireland, which provided over 60 men, and England, Wales, Scotland, France, and Germany.[23]

The company regimental record book showed all men being between the ages of 12 and 51 years, but not everyone was truthful in their attempt to join the 10th Kentucky. Many too young to enlist lied about their ages. John "Roni" Sweeney, private, Company F, was only 16 when he enlisted. Both John and James Clarkson, brothers and privates in Company E, lied about their age to enlist in the 10th Kentucky. Pius Ignatius Higdon, private, Company G, was 17 when he enlisted. The youngest member of the 10th Kentucky was the four foot tall, 12 year old Robert Rea, Jr., a musician in Company K. Peter McLaine was 4'4", 15 years old and was a musician in the same company.

Traveling in Kentucky late in 1861 could be dangerous and sometimes embarrassing. It was reported in the *Louisville Daily Journal* in October 1861 that Colonel John Harlan and Captain Joseph Wilson had just escaped a trap set for them by rebel scouts when they were captured by their own army, by Colonel August Willich's 32nd Indiana Infantry sentries. Despite their appeals and explanations, they were taken at bayonet point on foot for three miles to Colonel Willich's headquarters at New Haven, Kentucky. Again, an appeal was made as to their identity, and finally the prisoners were identified by loyal citizens. "They spent the night with Colonel W., who gave them the freedom of his tent and the luckless colonel and his companions drowned their sorrows in a basket of Colonel Willich's Rhennish wine," the *Journal* reported.[24]

The 10th Kentucky was mustered into service on November 21, 1861, and was placed under divisional command of General George Thomas and brigade command of Colonel M. D. Manson. The regiment began training at Camp Crittenden in Lebanon, Kentucky, and then was stationed near Campbellsville in December 1861. After training for a little over a month, on December 31, 1861, the regiment marched toward Somerset, Kentucky, in anticipation of an attempt of the Southern forces to again attack southern and eastern Kentucky.[25] The 10th Kentucky was attached to the 2nd Brigade in General Thomas' division of the Army of the Ohio and were about to begin their long three-year march into history. One of the first assignments for the 10th Kentucky was outlined in Special Order 1, which sent Captain Henry G. Davidson and Company A to protect the railroad bridge on the Rolling Fork River.[26]

John Harlan summarized the feelings of those entering the Union cause at the beginning of the war:

> Kentucky was the first-born of the Union, and, despite the strong ties of kinship and business between them and the friends of secession, a large majority of its people held steadily to the view that if the Union ship went down, our State must be the last to desert it. That was the spirit in which the Kentucky Unionists rallied to the standard of the country in 1861, while some did not approve, indeed openly disapproved, many things done in the course of the war which were supposed injuriously to affect the institution of slavery, the Kentucky Unionists, all of them, clung unfalteringly to the idea that the dissolution of the Union was not a remedy for any evil, and that, cost what it might in men and money, the national authority, as derived from the Constitution, must be reinstated over every foot of American soil. To say nothing of the colored men in Kentucky who were mustered into the service of the United States towards the end of the war.[27]

By the end of 1861, barely six weeks after being mustered as a regiment, the 10th Kentucky was formed, trained and ready to meet the enemy. Unfortunately, the attrition of the Civil War began immediately after mustering. In November and December 1861, six men died and another seven deserted. This was just the beginning of the losses for the 10th Kentucky.[28]

Deaths and Desertions

	November 1861	December 1861
Died	Bland, Fletcher (A)	Price, William T. (D)
	Rodgers, James (C)	Walker, Richard (E)
		Voughn, William (F)
		Bayne, Patrick (H)
Deserted	McAnelly, William (K)	Waters, Charles (G)
	McAnelly, John (K)	White, William (H)
	Madden, Washington (K)	Yearns, John (H)
		McCardell, James (K)

(Letters in parentheses indicate the company of the individual.)

Companies of the 10th Kentucky

The 10th Kentucky Infantry was made up of ten companies, A–K, with J being excluded. For the most part, these companies were very similar, consisting of up to 100 men. The companies were commanded by a captain, a 1st lieutenant, a 2nd lieutenant and 5 sergeants.

Certain generalities can be made about the companies of the 10th Kentucky from the Regimental Record Book even though Company H's records have been lost. About half of the men of the regiment were from Washington and Marion counties, beautiful central Kentucky locations lying in the western part of the bluegrass area of the state. The counties were primarily agricultural, having excellent grasslands and forests on a rolling and hilly countryside. The next largest number of recruits were from Jefferson, Hardin and Nelson counties. Men were drawn from many areas in west central Kentucky, mostly farmers or sons of farmers.

For the most part the companies were very similar. Company A was highly concentrated with men from Jefferson County and Companies B–I were made up of men from the west-central counties. Distinctly different from the others was Company K, with a high percentage of foreign born and only a small number of farmers.

Pension records, census records and the 10th Kentucky Regimental Record Book offer the following on each company and its leadership.

COMPANY A

Company A was predominantly composed of men from Jefferson County and Louisville, but also included men native to other counties, states, and countries. The captain of the company was Henry G. Davidson, who was later promoted to the rank of regimental major. He was succeeded by William Lisle, an attorney from Marion County, for only a few months; he resigned due to medical reasons. Captain Lisle was replaced by Charles McKay from Bullitt County, who remained captain of company A for the rest of the war. Captain McKay was a doctor by profession. The enlisted non-commissioned men of Company A were primarily farmers and laborers. There were also a few blacksmiths, stone masons, carpenters, merchants, wagoners, and one cigar maker.

Henry G. Davidson, the original captain of Company A, was the son of merchant and banker William H. Davidson. Henry and his family were originally from Illinois, and Henry served as a clerk in Louisville before the war.

First Lieutenant Henry H. Warren was 5'9" with auburn hair and hazel eyes and a Louisville resident at the time of enlistment. He was born in Nelson County in 1841. Henry was originally a 2nd lieutenant and was promoted on May 25, 1863. He was a mechanic prior to his enlistment. First Lieutenant James Reynolds was born in 1836 and was 25 years old at the time of his enlistment. Lt. Reynolds would resign his commission in 1863.

PORTRAIT OF MAJOR HENRY G. DAVIDSON.

Captain Henry G. Davidson, Company A, was a native of Illinois and son of a merchant and banker in Louisville, Kentucky (Print Collection, Miriam and Ira D. Wallach Division of Art, Prints and Photographs, New York Public Library, Astor, Lenox and Tilden Foundation).

Second Lieutenant John W. Estes was born in 1839 and was 22 years old when he enlisted. He was born in Lincoln, Missouri, and was a carpenter and tobacconist prior to the war. He was 5'10" tall with black hair and gray eyes.

COMPANY B

Company B was heavily composed of men from Marion County, but had a few men from Washington, Nelson, LaRue and Taylor Counties. Captain John Milburn would be the

Captain John Milburn was instrumental in recruiting the men for Company B and served as captain throughout the war (Blue Acorn Press, Huntington, W. Va.).

only captain of Company B and Lieutenant William F. O'Bryan served as company lieutenant throughout the war. Lieutenant Robert Short resigned his commission in October 1862 due to illness and was replaced with Lieutenant John McCauley. The non-commissioned enlisted men were predominantly farmers, but there were a few laborers, blacksmiths, carpenters, stonemasons, painters, plasterers and a weaver.

Captain John Milburn was born in Lebanon, Kentucky, on October 14, 1839, and was 21 years old at the beginning of the war. He was the son of William and Ellen Milburn. Second Lieutenant William F. O'Bryan was born in 1841 and was the son of Robert and Cecelia O'Bryan. The family had lived in Louisville and was living in Chicago, Kentucky (Marion County), at the beginning of the war. He worked as a school teacher and clerked for his father prior to the war. William enlisted as a corporal and was promoted to 2nd lieutenant on September 13, 1862. He was promoted to 1st lieutenant after Robert Short's resignation.

First Lieutenant Robert S. Short was 6' tall. He was a farmer and was the son of Joseph and Mary Short, farmers from New Market, Kentucky. Second Lieutenant James Madison Davenport was born in Mobile, Alabama, in 1837. He moved to Frankfort, Kentucky, early in his life and was resident of Frankfort at the beginning of the war. He was officially promoted to the captaincy of Company G in September 1862. He was 5'10" tall with brown eyes and red hair, and his occupation before the war was school teacher.

COMPANY C

Company C also had only a single captain throughout the war and this was Edward Hilpp from Lebanon, Kentucky. He was ably supported by his two lieutenants, William Mussen and James Sallee. This group of officers served the entire war together in Company C.

While many of the enlisted non-commissioned men were from Marion County, this company represented many counties. Several soldiers were from LaRue, Taylor and Green counties. The occupations of the men of Company C were varied, but most were farmers. There were also painters, blacksmiths, a cigar maker, a school teacher, shoemakers, carpenters, a wagoner and a stonemason.

Captain Edward Hilpp was of German descent. He was Jewish and had two brothers, Adolph and Benjamin. The Hilpps lived Louisville in the 1850s, and in 1858 the family moved to Lebanon. Edward Hilpp was a master painter in Lebanon at the beginning of the war. Prior to joining the 10th Kentucky, Edward was a "recruiter," forming his own company in

Left: Captain Edward Hilpp of Company C was a master painter residing in Lebanon, Kentucky, at the time of the war (Nash Hayes). *Right:* Lt. William Mussen, Company C, was a farmer living in Marion County. "Billy" Mussen would serve with Company C throughout the war (Steven L. Wright Collection, U.S. Army Military History Institute).

Marion County. Once the 10th Kentucky was formed, Edward Hilpp's company became Company C and was made up primarily of men from his home county.[29, 30]

First Lieutenant William Mussen was a farmer from New Market, Kentucky. He was born on December 26, 1833, and was 26 years old at the time of enlistment. He was 5'5" tall with dark brown hair and blue eyes.[13]

Second Lieutenant James Sallee was born on May 27, 1837, and was the son of a farmer, Tom Sallee, in Marion County. He was a farmer at the time the 10th Kentucky was mustered into service. He was 5'8" tall and a robust individual.

COMPANY D

The county which supplied the largest number of men for Company D was Washington, but many men were also natives of Marion County. Captain George Riley was the only captain and James Mills served as lieutenant throughout the war. Lieutenants Stephen Dorsey and William Hupp were forced to resign due to medical problems and Lieutenant Edward Penick served as 2nd lieutenant for the remainder of the war.

The occupation of the noncommissioned enlisted men was almost totally that of farmer, but there were also 2 teachers, 5 blacksmiths, a carpenter, 2 laborers, a stonemason, and a shoemaker. One soldier listed his occupation as doctor and one soldier was a preacher at the time of his enlistment.

Captain George Riley was a Springfield, Kentucky, native. He was born on March 31, 1838. He attended Bethany College in Virginia and returned home to establish his law practice prior to the war. He was a 5'8" tall with black hair and gray eyes and commanded Company D throughout the war. Because of his legal training, he was called on to represent some of the soldiers who were court-martialed.

First Lieutenant William J. Hupp was a resident of Willisburg in Washington County, Kentucky. He had married Lucinda Curtsinger in October 1848. He was a veteran of the 4th Kentucky Infantry that had fought in the Mexican War and had broken his wrist in a fall from a wall during that conflict. He offered his services during the Civil War, but was forced to resign in 1862.

Second Lieutenant Stephen N. Dorsey was from Washington County and he was born in 1838. He was the son of Edward and Sarah Dorsey, farmers in Marion County. Prior to the war, Stephen was a working on the farm of Perry Lanham in Texas, Kentucky. He was 6'1" tall.

Captain George Riley, Company D, was a Springfield native and lawyer (Blue Acorn Press, Huntington, West Virginia).

COMPANY E

Company E was heavily made up of men from Washington County with only a few other counties represented. Seth Bevill served as company captain until September 1863, when he was replaced with Andrew Thompson. Clem Funk served at the company's 2nd and, later, 1st lieutenant.

Most of the noncommissioned enlisted men gave their occupation as farmer. There were also 5 laborers, a carpenter, 2 blacksmiths, a plasterer, carriage maker, and a cabinetmaker.

Captain Seth Bevill was from Washington County. He was born on September 6, 1840, and was

Lt. Clem Funk, Company E, worked as a farmer and lived with the James Champion family in the Mackville area of Washington County (Stephen Wright).

21 years old at the mustering of the 10th Kentucky. He was the son of the Springfield postmaster. He had three brothers and one sister. Seth was a deputy court clerk in Springfield, Kentucky, prior to enlisting in the 10th Kentucky. His sister would later marry William Lisle, captain of Company A, and one of his brothers enlisted with and fought for the Confederacy. Seth was never married.

First Lieutenant Andrew Thompson was mustered in as 1st lieutenant and promoted to captain. Thompson was a native of Washington County and was born on April 16, 1840. He was the son of Mitchell Thompson and educated in public schools in Washington County. He was a farmer during his early years. Second Lieutenant Clem Funk worked as a farmer and lived with the James Champion family in the Mackville area of Washington County, prior to the war.

COMPANY F

The county supplying the majority of the enlisted men for Company F was Marion, followed by Washington, but this company also had men native to Casey, Bullitt, Madison and Jessamine. Franklin Hill was the only captain of the company and his initial lieutenants were Joseph Adcock and Charles McKay.

The enlisted men were predominantly farmers but also included 9 laborers, 2 carpenters, 2 blacksmiths, 1 shoemaker and 1 student.

Captain Franklin Shannon Hill was born in 1821 in Washington County. He was a large man, approximately 6'1" tall, with a fair complexion and blue eyes, and was 40 years old at the time of the Civil War. His home was in Mackville, Kentucky, where he was a farmer and a constable in his area of the county. He was married to Diana Bogie on October 22, 1846.

First Lieutenant Charles McKay was a resident of Shepherdsville in Bullitt County and assisted in encouraging men from Bullitt County to enlist in the 10th Kentucky. He was 20 years old when he enlisted and he combined his men with those of Captain Franklin Hill to form Company F. The son of physician Samuel McKay, Charles attended medical school prior to enlisting in the 10th Kentucky. Charles McKay would later in the war assume the captaincy of Company A.

Second Lieutenant Joseph Adcock

Captain Franklin S. Hill, Company F, was a farmer and constable from Mackville (Blue Acorn Press, Huntington, West Virginia).

was born in Washington County on June 25, 1836, a son of Elijah and Jemimah (Clark) Adcock, natives of Kentucky. He attended public school in Washington County and in November 1861 enlisted in the Tenth Kentucky Infantry. He was a teacher.[31]

Company G

The men of Company G represented primarily three counties—Marion, Washington and Nelson—though most were from Marion. Captain William Hunter was the company's first captain and was succeeded by James Davenport. Lieutenants Charles Spalding and Edward Ferrill resigned and Edward Blanford was the only lieutenant appointed to succeed the previous officers. Blanford later was transferred to the Pioneer Corps; the company did not replace him.

The enlisted men had overwhelmingly been farmers but the ranks also included a carpenter, a blacksmith, a wagoner, a medical student, a distiller, a shoemaker and two school teachers.

Captain William Reynolds Hunter was born on May 28, 1841, near Bardstown in Nelson County. He was 5'7" tall with brown hair and hazel eyes. He was medical student at the time he was mustered into service.

First Lieutenant Charles Spalding was the son of Theodore and Mary Spalding of Springfield. He was a farmer and was 18 years old at the time he was mustered into service. Second Lieutenant E. C. Ferrill was a resident of Chicago, Kentucky, in Marion County. Edward was born in 1838 and was a farmer.

The Smith Brothers, William, Tom and Frank (left to right), are examples of how families enlisted in the 10th Kentucky. These three brothers enlisted as privates in Company G and Company A (Lisa Smith).

Company H

Unlike the other companies, the records for Company H are missing from the 10th Kentucky's Regimental Record Book and therefore, the information about occupations and birthplaces are not available.

Captain Buford R. Pendleton was born November 12, 1831, in Mearamak, Kentucky, and was living in Marion County at the beginning of the war. Buford was a farmer from a farming family. He was 6' tall with a dark complexion, dark hair and hazel eyes. He wasn't married before or during the war.

First Lieutenant William Thomas Shively was born in Taylor County, Kentucky, on March 8, 1830. William was one of six brothers who served in the Union Army.[32] William was educated in district schools of Taylor County. He began flat-boating on the Ohio and Mississippi rivers, traveling to New Orleans in 1850. In October 1853 he married and settled on a farm on Cloyd's Creek in Marion County, where he continued to live for five years. He then moved to Taylor County and bought a four hundred acre farm, where he lived at the outbreak of the Civil War.

Second Lieutenant Henry C. Dunn enlisted as commissary sergeant and was promoted to the rank of 1st lieutenant in December 1862. Lieutenant Dunn served on detached duty as topographical engineer in General James B. Steedman's division in 1863. Later he held the same position in General John Brannan's division until the Battle of Chickamauga.

Henry was 5'10½" tall with gray eyes and brown hair. He was born on May 6, 1835, at Mount Vernon, Ohio. He was the son of Jacob and Rosanna Dunn of Knox County, Ohio, and was one of 13 children. He was educated at Centre College in Danville and was a school teacher in Bowling Green, Kentucky, prior to the war.

COMPANY I

Israel Webster was the only captain of Company I and his only lieutenants were William Kelley and John Myers.

The enlisted men were predominantly farmers but the roster also included a miller, doctor, laborer, carpenter, shoemaker, stonemason, painter, gas fitter, and wagon maker, along with three blacksmiths and two teachers.

Captain Israel B. Webster was from Louisville, Kentucky, and lived there for most of his life. He was born in Plattsburg, New York, in 1826 and he and his brother moved to Evansville, where they opened a photography shop. The brothers had a photography shop

Captain Isreal B. Webster of Company I was born in Plattsburg, New York, and he was a photographer prior to the war (Blue Acorn Press, Huntington, W. Va.).

in Louisville from 1851 to 1860. He was married to Harriet Lemerle when he enlisted in the 10th Kentucky. For most of his life, he worked with his brother as a photographer. He also had a good voice and was skilled at playing the flute. Captain Webster was 5'10" tall with dark hair and blue eyes and was one of the older captains, 36 years of age at enlistment. He would contract a case of malaria in March 1862. Also, he would receive a back injury during the Hoover's Gap campaign that would plague him during and after the war.[33]

First Lieutenant William E. Kelley was only one of two officers of the 10th Kentucky who served in the Mexican War; he was a private in the 4th Kentucky Volunteers. He was born in Washington County on July 27, 1826. He married Elizabeth Chase in Marion County on July 6, 1854. William organized a company prior to the war as part of the Home Guards and participated in arresting and detaining Southern sympathizers. The unit disbanded and enlisted in the 10th Kentucky. William Kelley was a wheelwright before the war. Second Lieutenant John H. Myers was 21 years old when he enlisted and was a farmer living with James and Sarah Myers in Haysille, Kentucky, in Marion County prior to the war.

COMPANY K

The composition of Company K was far different from the rest of the 10th Kentucky units. Only 20 men were native Kentuckians and most were foreign born. Marion County and Jefferson County provided the majority of the Kentucky natives and one man each was provided by Bullitt and Casey counties. Others were from Ohio (8), Virginia (3), Maryland (2), Pennsylvania (2), Indiana (1) and New York (1). Company K had foreign born soldiers from Ireland (45), Germany (7), Wales (1), Scotland (1), France (2) and England (2).

William Tweddle was the original captain of Company K but resigned in 1862. He was succeeded by Captain Henry Waller and then Captain John Denton. James Watts was the company's lieutenant.

The men were primarily laborers but some were farmers, students, carpenters, stonemasons, merchants, cigar makers, painters, coopers, plasterers, shoe makers, wagon makers, clerks, tailors, and printers, along with one sailor, and one sculptor.

Captain William Tweddle was born in Askrigg, England, and was living in Louisville at the time of the formation of the regiment. He was one of the older officers of the regiment, being 43 years old when he was mustered into service. He was 6'1" tall with brown hair and blue eyes. He also had a great deal of experience because he spent 10 years fighting Indians, including in the Indian War of 1835. From 1856 to 1857 he worked as a clerk and bookkeeper for Joseph Metcalf, who was in the brewing business. From 1857 through 1861 he clerked for Thomas Anderson in the auction and commission business. He also sold dry goods as his own business.

First Lieutenant James R. Watts was called "Dick" by his friends. Watts, approximately 25 years old, was a resident of Louisville, Kentucky, at the time of enlistment. He was a printer and worked in the newspaper business prior to the war.

And so the command structure of the 10th Kentucky was set, but, by the very nature of the war, it was not destined to remain this way for long.

Two

10th Kentucky Infantry 1862

"I think to lose Kentucky is nearly the same as to lose the whole game."—Abraham Lincoln

After the 10th Kentucky was mustered into service in November 1861, the men spent the next five weeks getting supplied, trained, and doing guard duty. The regiment received their rifles and other equipment. The Union Army had an increasing number of clashes with the Confederates and positioning between the warring factions was taking place in Kentucky. The conflicts at Camp Wildcat in Laurel County, the Battle of Saratoga Springs in Lyon County, and the battle of Sacramento, Kentucky increased the awareness that conflict between the Union and Confederacy was to be a fighting conflict. On December 10, 1861, Kentucky was admitted into the Confederate States of America by the Confederate Congress, even though the Kentucky General Assembly had declared allegiance with the Union and remained intact. Events in Kentucky were moving forward at an increasingly alarming pace. John Harlan and his officers were developing their regiment into a cohesive fighting unit under the command of General George Thomas, the divisional commander, and Colonel M. D. Manson, the brigade commander.

General Thomas was to be a major part of the 10th Kentucky's existence from 1861 through 1864. Thomas was a native Virginian who entered West Point in 1836, graduating 12th in his class in 1840. He began his career in artillery and was involved in the Seminole War and the Mexican War. He taught at West Point and later participated in Indian warfare at Fort Yuma in 1855. When the Civil War began, he chose to stay with the Union, rejecting the action of his native state of Virginia. He was promoted to brigadier general of volunteers in 1861 at 45 years of age and became divisional commander of the Army of the Ohio.[1] He was to be a familiar face to the 10th Kentucky through the end of the war.

The 2nd Brigade was made up of 4 regiments reporting to Colonel M. D. Manson. Mahlon D. Manson, born in Piqua, Ohio, was the acting brigadier general of the second brigade. Manson had been elected regimental commander for the 10th Indiana before assuming command of the brigade. The 2nd Brigade comprised the 10th Indiana, 4th Kentucky, 14th Ohio and the 10th Kentucky. These four infantry regiments would spend the next three years together, through victory and defeat.[2]

Kentucky wavered between its allegiance to the Union and joining the rebellious states to the south. Kentucky also provided access to the Ohio and Mississippi rivers and it was strategic for controlling supplies and the potential access into western Tennessee and the rest of the mid-south. Kentucky also was a source of manpower and agricultural supplies needed for both armies. The morale value was tremendous if Kentucky would swing its support to either side; it therefore became a site of conflict throughout the war. The first real struggle occurred in January 1862. Abraham Lincoln summarized the importance of Kentucky by saying, "I think to lose Kentucky is nearly the same as to lose the whole game."[3] Jefferson Davis

The Battle of Mill Springs was the first major battle of the Civil War in Kentucky (Kentucky Historical Society, Martin F. Schmidt Collection).

felt that Kentucky had been lulled into a false sense of security and the state would soon be "subjugated" by the federal troops. Because the Union troops had seized strategic points in the state, the Confederate government felt that it must repel this invasion.[4]

The Battle of Mill Springs

Felix Zollicofer was the Confederate general in charge of occupying southern Kentucky and had been repulsed in his attack on Camp Wildcat in October 1861. However, Zollicoffer was an aggressive general and wanted to engage his northern foe. He knew that Union forces were concentrating in the area of Columbia, Kentucky, and began to move his forces to the west to be in closer proximity. By November 27, the Confederate forces decided to go into winter quarters at Mill Springs on the southern side of the Cumberland River. Aware of the presence of one another, the opposing armies naturally attracted each other and sparks began to fly. A Union force was located at Waitsborough on the north side of the Cumberland and a few miles north and east of Mill Springs. Zollicoffer decided to force the Yankees away from Waitsborough, and in early December the opposing forces shelled one another.

Although caution was exerted by both sides, it was becoming more and more difficult to keep the opposing forces at bay. In early December, Zollicoffer moved his forces to the north side of the Cumberland River and set up defensive works in an area called Beech Grove. This movement was designed to place his force in an offensive posture in regard to his northern foes, and also in a potentially disastrous defensive one. There was no way to retreat except by ferry from the northern side of the Cumberland River if the Confederates were forced to retreat.

General Don Carlos Buell commanded the Union forces in Kentucky and did not want to take the offensive against Zollicoffer, but others within the Union forces did. Both sides sought to engage the enemy but neither side forced a full blown battle. However, in late December 1861, General Buell decided that he would no longer allow Zollicoffer to remain on the north side of the Cumberland River and sent his forces, under command of General George Thomas, to move Zollicoffer back to southern side of the river.

In January 1862, General Thomas ordered his forces to march along the Cumberland River toward Mill Springs, where General Felix K. Zollicoffer's rebels had established their camp and fortifications. General Thomas marched through Campbellsville and Columbia. The 10th Kentucky and other regiments of the 2nd Brigade were located in the rear of Thomas' division. The march toward Zollicoffer's forces at Mill Springs was miserable. It was cold and rainy and the men

General George Thomas was a native Virginian who chose to be loyal to the Union (Library of Congress).

slogged through mud, which exhausted them. One report indicated that the march progressed only eighteen miles in three days.[5] On January 12, the rain continued to fall and the 2nd Brigade could only advance six miles. On January 16, Manson's brigade halted at the rear of Thomas's division while the cavalry scouted the terrain ahead.

Two days before the Battle of Mill Springs (January 17, 1862), General Thomas ordered the 14th Ohio and 10th Kentucky to camp approximately 10 miles to the rear of divisional headquarters near Cain's store for purpose of guarding his right flank. The remainder of Thomas' division moved to Logan's Crossroads to face the enemy. The next morning (January 18, 1862) these regiments were ordered to "march at once to the farm of one Tarter, on the Jamestown Road and about six miles off the main road to Columbia and engage two rebel regiments supposed to be there encamped."[6] They marched through the night in a rainstorm and returned the next day after finding no Confederates.

The two regiments returned to camp cold, wet and tired, and the next morning (January 19, 1862) a cavalryman hurried into camp communicating the need for the regiments to rush to the front to meet a rebel force that was gathering at Logan's Crossroads.

Captain Israel Webster, Company I, 10th Kentucky, remembered the morning of the 19th:

> We of the 10th Kentucky did not roll out very early the next morning, it being Sunday, and besides that, our side trip had been made during a heavy rain. Sunday morn found us preparing breakfast, generally with fires all through the camp, upon which the coffee was boiling, and around which stood the men drying their clothing, which had been thoroughly soaked the day and night before, chatting and chaffing in the customary way, when there came to our ears the boon of a big gun. All was hushed instantly, and only glances full of inquiry were exchanged. Then came another until there appeared scarcely a second's interim between them. During this time each man, as of one accord, secured the best cup of coffee he could, and while rushing for his gun and accouterments gulped down the boiling fluid, and thus was

ready to fall in at the command. In an incredibly short time the line was formed and was out upon the road, and we were marching in route toward the cannonading that had been the disturbing element in our camp.[7]

As the battle on January 19 reached a critical situation at Logan's Crossroads, the 10th Kentucky and 14th Ohio slogged toward the battle on ground that "was so muddy under them that their feet slipped at every step."[8] Columbus Harshfield, a private in Company F, reported, "I do not believe our clothing was thoroughly dry on the whole way."[9]

The cause of the rapid march forward was unknown to the men of the 10th Kentucky, but the Confederate Army, recently placed under the command of General George B. Crittenden, had attacked General Thomas at Logan's Crossroads. In mid–January 1862, General Crittenden assumed command of Zollicoffer's Confederate forces. His strategy included positioning 4000 men along the Cumberland River in a fortified position near the town of Mill Springs. "By the evening of the 17th, Crittenden was also convinced that his position at Mill Springs and Beech Grove had become a frozen Khartoum. He was now aware that his supply line from Nashville by way of the Cumberland River had been severed,"[10] a historical account said. The Confederates decided that it was time to make a preemptive strike against George Thomas' force at Logan's Crossroads.

On January 17, George Thomas' division reached Logan's Crossroads, a small community consisting of only a few modest homes and a post office, about 10 miles north of the Confederate camp. Crittenden knew the value of preventing the Union Army from resting, gaining position and concentrating its forces. At this early stage in the war, a victory in this part of Kentucky could garner support for secession and stabilize the shaky situation in east Tennessee, where the majority of the population opposed secession.

At midnight on January 18, Confederate Generals Zollicoffers and William Carroll were ordered to attack General Thomas' division camped at Logan's Crossroads. The Confederates force-marched nine miles through a cold, wet and muddy night to meet the Union Army. They arrived at daybreak and immediately encountered Union pickets. The pickets fired at the advancing Confederates and fell back to their defensive line held by Colonel M. D. Manson's 10th Indiana Infantry. The alarm was immediately sent to the Colonel Speed S. Fry's 4th Kentucky.

By the time the 4th Kentucky reached the 10th Indiana's defensive line, the line was involved in a desperate fight and was close to being broken by the overwhelming number of the enemy. A depression in front of the newly forming Union troops served as an ideal position for the Confederates to pour fire into the blue ranks. The 4th Kentucky Infantry was subjected to the same fire that had been directed toward the 10th Indiana. An enraged Colonel Speed Fry mounted the fence in front of his regiment, shouted to the Rebels, and "defied them to stand up on their feet and come forward like men."[11]

Fry rode to the right of his regiment to better see the battle; he noticed a single figure riding toward him and that figure was his adversary, General Zollicoffer. When another Confederate approached him, Fry decided to return to the safety of his line. As he turned to ride away, he fired his pistol. "At this time General Zollicoffer rode up to the Nineteenth Tennessee and ordered Colonel Cummings to cease firing, under the impression that the fire was upon another regiment of his own brigade. Then the general advanced, as if to give an order to the lines of the enemy within bayonet reach, and was killed just as he discovered his fatal mistake."[12] Fry's bullet had reached him.

General Thomas quickly assumed control of the Union battle and ordered the 10th Indiana to protect the 4th Kentucky's right. The tide of the battle began to shift as Union troops were positioned and moved into the fray. The Confederates were thrown into some confusion with Zollicoffer's death, but General Crittenden organized his troops and ordered General Carroll to attack with his brigade, again shifting the battle back in favor of the Southern Army.

The January battle was fought with vigor in horrible weather, cold and poor visibility. To complicate matters for the Union troops, the poor visibility neutralized the Union artillery superiority. The Union counter-attacked with the 2nd Minnesota from the left and the 9th Ohio from the right. The 9th Ohio's bayonet charge broke Carroll's line, which retreated in a disorganized manner. The counter-attack won the battle for Thomas. The Union Army then captured the Confederate supplies that were left on the field. Crittenden's comments summarized the battle from his perspective: "From Mill Springs and on the first steps of my march, officers and men, frightened by false rumors of the movement of the enemy, shamefully deserted, and, stealing horses and mules to ride, fled to Knoxville, Nashville, and other places in Tennessee."[13]

The 14th Ohio and the 10th Kentucky did not reach the battlefield until after the rebels were defeated. The 10th Kentucky and 14th Ohio joined in the pursuit of the rebels and even marched past the body of General Zollicoffer. At the end of the day of the battle, General Thomas' division had reached the rebel fortification at Beech Grove several miles south of Logan's Crossroads but did not attack them. He relied on caution rather than attack a heavily fortified position while his forces were yet concentrated. Colonel Harlan approached General Thomas after arriving the night of the battle and asked to be put in front of the line the next morning. Colonel Harlan felt he was denied an opportunity to engage the enemy after rather fruitless duty all day. General Thomas agreed that Colonel Steedman's 14th Ohio, along with the 10th Kentucky, would lead the assault the next morning.[14]

On the evening of the 19th, Harlan assigned Captain George Riley's Company D to establish pickets. "A squad of soldiers under Captain Riley and Lieutenant Davenport [Second Lieutenant James Davenport of Company B] went within 100 yards of the rebel works and near enough to hear the rebels curse the damn Lincolnites for the fight at Logan's."[15]

The next morning, the regiments marched forward to storm the fortifications only to find them abandoned. "There was much disappointment in the Union troops, but there was no help for it." The rebels had withdrawn in the night.[16]

Captain Henry Davidson's entire Company A pushed forward as skirmishers, along with a squad of men under Captain Franklin Hill of Company F. Sergeant Richard Boyle of Company E commented on the difficulty of gaining the rebel entrenchments while passing "over fallen timber, underbrush and other obstacles almost insurmountable, with the embrasures frowning down."[17] Colonel Harlan would write about the outcome of the battle, "Mill Springs was the first decisive Union victory of the war and made Thomas the hero of the hour."[18]

Thus the 10th Kentucky had its first opportunity to meet the enemy, and while bravely led, they sought a Confederate force that didn't materialize. The fortifications were vacated after the clash with Thomas' division the previous day. John Harlan reported on the first conflict for the 10th Kentucky: "But I do claim for the officers and soldiers of this regiment that, under circumstances the most discouraging, they made a march (18 miles in about six hours) which indicated their willingness, even eagerness, to endure any fatigue or make any sacrifice in order to meet on the field of battle those wicked and unnatural men who are seeking without cause to destroy the Union of our fathers."[19]

During the Battle of Mill Springs or Logan's Crossroads, Colonel John Harlan made his need to be in the middle of the fight known to General Thomas. He wanted his men to be

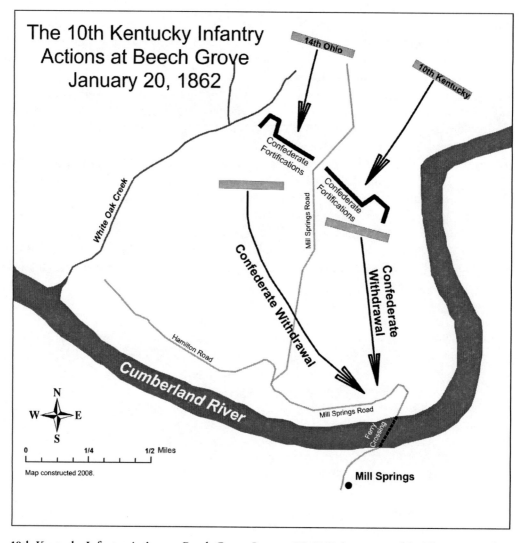

10th Kentucky Infantry Actions at Beech Grove, January 20, 1862 (map created by Thomas Vought).

involved and was not reticent about voicing this. The 10th Kentucky entered the battle with 625 effectives—600 enlisted and 25 officers. No causalities were recorded for the 10th Kentucky Infantry.[20]

Michael McMillen, Company F, was the first member of the 10th Kentucky killed in action. The details of this event are lost in history, but the Adjutant General's Report shows Private McMillen was killed at New Market, Kentucky, on January 1, 1862. In January 1862, one person was discharged, probably due to disability, four others died, five deserted and one person was transferred from the regiment.[21]

Shiloh and Corinth

The Army of the Ohio was reorganized in March 1862 with General Don Carlos Buell commanding. The 10th Kentucky was part of the First Division commanded by General

George Thomas and they were again part of the Second Brigade, now reporting to General Speed S. Fry, who previously commanded the 4th Kentucky Infantry and was recently promoted. From central Kentucky, the 10th Kentucky Infantry marched by the way of Stanford, Danville and Bardstown to Louisville. From Louisville it went by steamboat down the Ohio, then up the Cumberland to Nashville, and from Nashville it marched to Pittsburg Landing. It accompanied an expedition up the Tennessee River on transport to Chickasaw, where the troops landed and marched to Shiloh.[22]

Confederate General Albert Sydney Johnston, fearing the combined armies of Buell and Grant, decided to attack General Ulysses Grant's Army of the Mississippi by surprise. On April 6, 1862, General Johnston's army of more than 40,000 men attacked Grant at Shiloh, Tennessee. The attack was intended to weaken the Union Army, stop their reinforcements and advance in the south.

The daybreak attack took the Union Army totally by surprise and by mid-morning the Confederates seemed on the verge of complete victory. However, the Union right stiffened near Shiloh Church and the battle took a bloody turn as the Union organized and the Confederates continued to surge forward. Throughout the day, the Southern Army hammered the right side of the defenders, which gave ground but did not break. The fighting was fierce on both sides.

On April 6 and 7, the Battle of Shiloh ebbed and flowed, with one of the most important casualties being the Confederate General Johnston. The Army of the Ohio, with 22,000 men, began arriving on the evening of March 6 and entered the battle on March 7. With the reinforcements in place, at dawn, Grant attacked, pushing the exhausted Confederates steadily back until they finally began a retreat in the early afternoon that left the field to the Union forces.

When the Confederate Army was attacking Grant at Shiloh, the 10th Kentucky was with Thomas' division many miles away. They were ordered to move toward the battle with all possible speed. The regiment arrived at Pittsburg Landing late on the second day of the battle. Harlan's records state, "We arrived there about 9:00 o'clock and were immediately ordered to leave the boat and go into camp, as the boat was to go back to Pittsburg Landing for other troops. We thought at the time that it was a cruel order, as Thomas' troops had no wagons or tents with them and had nothing for their protection against bad weather, except the ordinary army blanket. But the order had to be obeyed, and the men were ordered to go out on the hillside, and make what provision for their comfort as they could."[23]

As soon as they made their bedding, the regiment fell fast asleep. In the early hours of the morning, it began to rain and became so unpleasant for the men that they had to get up to get out of the wetness. Then opportunity arrived. Harlan wrote, "Right before my eye was a large steamboat, brilliantly lighted, with no one occupying it except a few to guard it. I called my regiment into line and marched down to the boat, but my men were stopped at the plank way leading to the boat." The guards challenged Colonel Harlan and ordered him and the men to stop. Harlan's concern for his men overrode the guards' need to keep the regiment off the boat. Harlan ordered an unnamed captain and his company that if the guard prevented the 10th Kentucky from boarding the boat, "to pitch them into the river." The guard stepped aside and the 10th Kentucky boarded the steamboat and slept in a warm, dry place for the rest of the night. This action was punishable by the provost and "perhaps, to be shot," but the guards never reported Colonel Harlan and the 10th Kentucky proceeded to the Shiloh battlefield.[24]

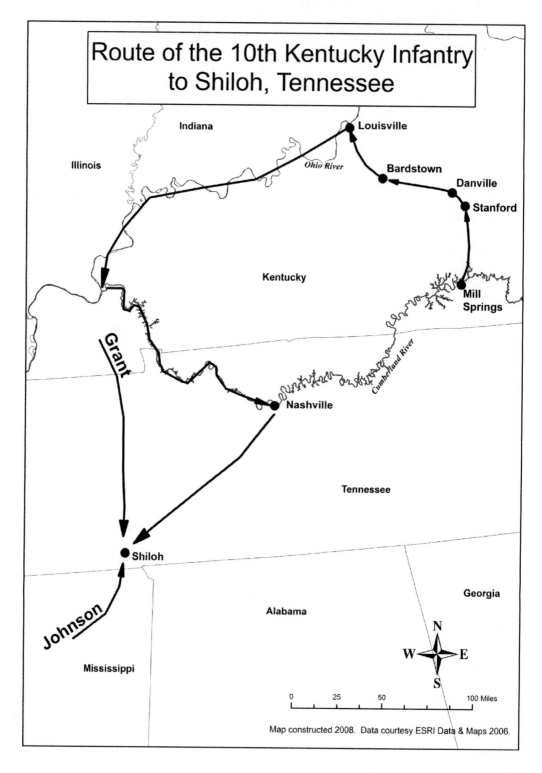

Route of the 10th Kentucky Infantry to Shiloh, Tennessee (map created by Thomas Vought).

The next morning the carnage of the battle was evident as the regiment marched through the battlefield. Colonel Harlan met General William T. Sherman on his march and was invited to meet with General Grant. The three officers met in General Grant's office on a boat at the river.

The 10th Kentucky marched with the Union Army from Shiloh to Corinth, Mississippi, but encountered no rebel soldiers. When they reached Corinth, they found no opposition. Then the Union Army split and Buell's Army of the Ohio occupied northern Mississippi and Alabama, and the 10th Kentucky was stationed in Eastport, Mississippi, for a time.

In a letter written to his parents on June 18, 1862, Sgt. James Scott, Company B, described the situation of the 10th Kentucky near Corinth. His 1st lieutenant was contemplating his resignation due to his extreme illness. (Lieutenant Robert Short would resign in October 1862.) He also described the poor marching conditions, including swamps, and said the men were attacked by scorpions and the ever ubiquitous mosquitoes. He speculated that 10th Kentucky would be moving back northward but gave up any hope of returning to Kentucky because the news around the camp revealed that Colonel John Harlan had been offered to return the regiment back to Kentucky, but he refused. Sgt. Scott also lamented the conditions of the citizens in Corinth. Although the 10th Kentucky had sufficient food, "it is pretty ruff and the citizens round here is bound to starve unless the government furnishes them something to eat." Sgt. Scott's impression was that the Confederate Army had foraged all the food from the local citizens and that the men were forced into the army. The 10th Kentucky was not destined to engage the enemy, and Sgt. Scott stated, "I think they have all gone home."[25]

Occupation and Death

For the next few months, the 10th Kentucky was stationed in northeast Mississippi and northwestern Alabama. In June, the 10th Kentucky was in Tuscumbia, Alabama, and it spent July in Eastport, Mississippi, and August in Winchester, Tennessee. While in occupation an interesting order was issued for the appointment of servants for the officers. As was the custom, the officers already had stewards or servants, but regimental records show the following appointments:

Bob, colored boy, servant to Col Jno. M Harlan
Daw, colored boy, servant to Lt Col. W H Hays
Peter, colored boy, servant to Adjutant W. Lisle
Dock, colored boy, servant to sutlery
Coleman, colored boy, servant to Capt H G Davidson
Harrison, colored boy, Sgt & 2 Mast S, Matlock, Samuel
James Murdey, white boy, servant to sutlery
A J Mussen, while male, servant to Capt E Hilpp[26]

A large number of deaths were recorded for the 10th Kentucky during the first four months of the year. This was due primarily to disease. Only one soldier died in battle, but at least 59 members of the regiment died during this period. An additional 18 members were discharged due to unfitness for duty. The peak period for deaths occurred in March, when 20 soldiers died. The adjutant general's report shows many deaths as unknown date or location. We know these figures to be the minimum losses. Fourteen soldiers also deserted during this period. Private William Jones of Company F was also listed as missing in action in

April. The slow attrition of the regiment, so common in the Civil War, continued to exact its toll during the first six months of 1862.

April took a toll on the medical staff of the 10th Kentucky; both Dr. William Atkisson and Assistant Surgeon Thomas Knott died in early April 1862. Dr. Atkisson died of pneumonia at Savannah, Tennessee, due to exposure experienced during the march. An exchange of letters in May 1862 between the Kentucky adjutant general and Mary Kate Atkisson, Dr. Atkisson's widow, showed the difficulty civilians experienced in obtaining loved one's remains. Colonel Harlan had tried to comply with the request to have Dr. Atkisson's body returned home, but was unable to find a suitable container and concluded to have the doctor's remains interred in Savannah, Tennessee. Mary Kate Atkisson's brother-in-law, Dr. Frances Atkisson, and a family friend attempted to physically go to Tennessee to retrieve the body, but were blocked from doing so by military authorities. She appealed to the Kentucky adjutant general for assistance and offered her appreciation and that "the widow and her fatherless boy will forever bless you."[27] Another letter, dated May 19, showed that the adjutant general agreed to help Mrs. Atkisson obtain the remains of her husband.

Another unfortunate story involves the Clarkson brothers from Springfield, Kentucky. James and John ran away from home to join the 10th Kentucky and were not old enough to enlist. A letter sent home said, in part: "It is near time for roll call. You must give my love to all the neighbors and keep a portion for yourself. You must write soon because I want to hear from you very bad and direct it to the Tenth Kentucky Regiment of the Volunteers Company E. You must write shore. We have no ink and I had to write in pencil."[28] Both brothers died in April 1862 of typhoid fever and were buried near Nashville, Tennessee.

Captain I. B. Webster wrote that his unit encountered typhoid fever at Mill Springs, and it proved to be worse than a battle with the Confederates: "I actually believe that our loss from that disease was greater than it would have been had they remained and kept us out of their camp."[29] Pension records of the officers showed that health problems were abundant in the regiment, and presumably the officers had a higher quality of life than the enlisted men.[30] According to the official records of the regiment, as many as 144 men of the 10th Kentucky would die of disease in early 1862. The first six months of the year would be a time of great hardship, so much that it was a significant event in the life of the regiment.

The records indicate that during March and April of 1862, Captains Webster, Milburn and Hill became very ill and Webster and Hill had to return to Kentucky for treatment and recuperation. Israel Webster developed a case of malaria and Captain Hill had what was possibly dysentery. Both officers returned to their units in May 1862. Captain Milburn became ill in February and did not return to his company until April 1862. Lieutenant Andrew Thompson was sick in February and absent from his company. Lieutenant William Kelley also contracted a "prolonged illness" in Tennessee in March 1862. Second Lieutenant John McCauley, Company B, also contracted dysentery, and entered the hospital in Louisville, and returned to the company in June 1862. It was during this time that Capt. William Tweddle, Company K, developed dysentery, but also lumbago, to such an extent that he was sent to the hospital and then returned to Louisville on the transport ship *Empress*. He would never return to his company due to the problems he developed during the march into Tennessee. Lieutenant Benjamin Smith became sick with dysentery and was left at Smithland, Kentucky, on March 2, 1862, and didn't return to the regiment until May of that year.

First Lieutenant William J. Hupp contracted a cold, then pneumonia after the Mill Springs campaign and was forced to recuperate. He then contracted a "persistent, chronic cough" and was forced to resign in June 1862. William Lisle, regimental adjutant, contracted a "fever" in April 1862. Second Lieutenant John Estes, Company A, and Lieutenant Robert Short both contracted illnesses that would ultimately cause these officers to resign their commissions. Lieutenant Charles McKay contracted a fever in February 1862 and did not return to the regiment until April 1862. Lieutenant James Watts contracted typhoid fever in March and later a second fever, "spotted fever," and was away from the company much of the summer of 1862.

The beloved Sgt. Jack Mills of Company I died at home in Bradfordville, Kentucky, of typhoid fever on March 13, 1862. Sgt. Mills was so well liked by his company that a resolution was passed and in part stated, "We, his Brethren in Arms, feel individually and collectively, this stroke from the Mighty hand of Death, and can only say, that as an officer, we respected and loved him, as a soldier, we honored him, and as a friend, we each and all were drawn towards him by the strongest ties of Friendship, and believe that his place in our Company will long remain unfilled."[31]

Changes in Officers

As a result of the ravages of disease, the face of the 10th Kentucky Infantry changed and the command structure also changed. Those officers who had organized and initially led the companies were now to be replaced by men who had demonstrated their qualities during the first six months of service.

COMPANY A

Second Lieutenant John Estes resigned in July 1862 and was replaced by Richard Grace. John developed typhoid pneumonia caused by exposure. He later developed chronic pleurisy in a convalescent camp near Gallatin, Tennessee, and was discharged.

Second Lieutenant Grace was born on June 24, 1844, in County Tipperary, Ireland, but moved to Springfield early in life and had been living in Washington County for 18 years by the beginning of the war. He was the son of James Grace and Anastasia Carcaran. Richard was a mechanic prior to the war. He was 5'10" and weighed 150 pounds. He had blue-gray eyes and auburn hair.

COMPANY B

First Lieutenant Robert S. Short resigned October 1862. He suffered from disease early in the war, beginning in February 1862. He was sent home in April to recuperate. He was again ill, and finally, in October 1862, he resigned his commission. Dr. Jabez Perkins, regimental surgeon, found Lieutenant Short incapable of performing his duties due to "incipient tuberculosis." Lieutenant Short attributed the onset of his illness to exposure while marching from Lebanon to Louisville. He "was taken with a kind of malarial fever.... It was accompanied by eruptions or breaking out on my face and hands which resembled measles so much that many of my comrades thought I had the measles, and I was not sure that it was not one form of that disease."

Second Lieutenant William O'Bryan was promoted to 1st lieutenant and John T.

McCauley was promoted to the rank of 2nd lieutenant. John McCauley was born on February 2, 1832, and was 29 years old when he enlisted. He was a farmer who lived in Raywick in Marion County. He was 6' tall with blue eyes and light hair. He was the son of Pius McCauley, a native of Ireland. John enlisted as a sergeant and was later promoted because "he did his duty well and was promoted to Lieutenant of said Co for efficiency, gentlemanly, meritorious and soldierly conduct in the service."[32]

COMPANY D

First Lieutenant William J. Hupp resigned June 12, 1862. William, a veteran of the Mexican War, contracted a cold that turned into pneumonia and was forced to recuperate after the Mill Springs engagement. He later contracted a "persistent chronic cough" and was forced to resign his commission in June of 1862. It appears that this chronic cough was tuberculosis. Lieutenant Hupp was replaced with James Mills.

First Lieutenant James Mills was born on July 16, 1839, in Hancock County, Kentucky, and was a farmer living at St. Marys in Marion County when he was mustered into the army. He was 22 years old at the time of his enlistment. He enlisted as a sergeant and was promoted to 1st lieutenant on September 21, 1862. He was 5'9" with gray eyes and black hair.

COMPANY G

Captain William Reynolds Hunter resigned June 16, 1862, at Corinth, Mississippi. Although records don't specifically address the illness that forced Captain Hunter's resignation, he was treated on March 6, 1862, and he resigned in June. Captain Reynolds was replaced with James Madison Davenport, previously an officer in Company B.

COMPANY K

Captain William Tweddle resigned April 17, 1862, after he developed dysentery and severe lumbago during the march to Pittsburg Landing in 1862. The condition was a result of being "exposed to lying upon the wet ground while sick ... that he was unable to move forward with his command." Henry Waller was named captain of Company K after William Tweddle's discharge. Henry was living in Dillsbourough, Indiana, prior to the war.

REGIMENTAL STAFF

After the death of Dr. Atkisson, he was replaced by James G. Hatchitt as regimental surgeon. James was born in Lunenburg County, Virginia, on August 10, 1824, and was married to Elizabeth D. Harlan on January 11, 1848. Dr. Hatchitt was the brother-in-law of Colonel John Harlan. Dr. Hatchitt and his wife lived in Harrodsburg and moved to Evansville, Indiana, before the war. He joined the 10th Kentucky in April 1862. He was promoted to brigade surgeon on June 26, 1862, and Dr. Jabez Perkins assumed his role as regimental surgeon. Dr. Hatchitt would hold numerous other positions during the war, including medical director for the 23rd Corps.

Dr. Jabez Perkins was born October 26, 1820, in Defiance, Ohio, At 18, he entered the Wesleyan University of Ohio, where he pursued his studies for two years, and then began his medical training with Dr. John Paul. After completing the first three courses of lectures in the medical department of the Western Reserve College at Cleveland, he began his practice at Springville, Michigan, and in 1859 took a course of lectures at the College of Physicians and Surgeons in New York City. After leaving college he made a trip through the South and, upon his return in 1860, resumed his practice. In July 1862, he was appointed surgeon of the Tenth Kentucky Regiment, and soon afterward was promoted to the position of medical director of the Twentieth Army Corps, which he held until October of the following year, when he was commissioned surgeon of volunteers. He remained in this position until October 1865. During that time he was a member of General Washington L. Elliot's staff and had charge of Hospital No. 19 at Nashville, Tennessee.

The final regimental surgeon for the 10th Kentucky Infantry was Dr. Charles Stocking, a native of Michigan and he was the son of a stone cutter. He was born in York, Michigan, on July 16, 1836, and was a medical student completing his baccalaureate degree at the University of Michigan prior to enlistment.

After the death of assistant surgeon Thomas Knott, Charles Hardesty was appointed assistant surgeon for the 10th Kentucky. Charles Hardesty was the son of Richard and Nancy Hardesty and was from Bullitt County. His family farmed and Charles was born in 1831.

The regimental losses continued for the 10th Kentucky from January through April 1862.

Regimental Losses January–April 1862

	January	*February*	*March*	*April*
Discharged		McBride, William (B)	Berry, William (E)	Troy, John (H)
		Seay, James (D)		Becker, Ulrick (K)
Died	White, David (D)	Rheule, Eincle (A)	Berry, James (A)	Mattingley, Wm. (B)
	Slayton, Marion (E)	Anderson, John (C)	Baumgarder, George (A)	Feather, John (C)
		Brackam, William (D)	Allen, Silas (C)	Clarkson, Jms (E)
		Crench, William (D)	Dye, Robert (C)	Clarkson, John (E)
		Lanham, James (D)	Puryear, Samuel (C)	McCullum, Wm. (F)
		Simms, Cornelius(E)	Sapp, Peter (C)	Atkissson, Wm.
		Hundley, Andrew (E)	Ripperton, William (D)	Knott, Thomas
		Hall, Joseph (E)	Shimmerhorn, Richard (D)	
		Rhodes, Thomas (E)	Smothers, Richard (D)	
		Richardson, William (E)	Toon, Peter (E)	
		Johnson, John (F)	Hiatt, Rueben (E)	
		Melton, David (H)	Baugh, Henderson (F)	
		Bell, Isaac (I)	Smith, Johnson (H)	
			Newton, Andrew (H)	
			Newton, Elias (H)	
			Marple, Jefferson (H)	
			Shively, Samuel (H)	
			Wright, Benjamin (H)	
			Mills, Jack (I)	
			Goodman, Frances (I)	
Deserted	Hall, William (F)	Murrell, Woods (A)		
	Steel, John (F)	Bryant, John (I)		
	Vanhorn, George (H)	Taylor. Eason (F)		
	Ceaver, Jesse (I)	Bowling, William (F)		
	Peters, John (I)	Gunter, Alexander (F)		
	Sadder, Thomas (I)	Enders, Michael (K)		
	Emms, Joseph (K)			

	January	*February*	*March*	*April*
Killed in Action				
	McMillen, Michael (F)			
Missing in Action				
				Jones, William (F)
Transferred Out				
	Kneibert, Jacob (K)			
Resigned				
				Tweddle, Wm. (K)

(Letters in parentheses indicate the company of the individual.)

In late spring of 1862 the 10th Kentucky "was ordered to march to Decherd, Tenn. and to take up duty to protect communication and transportation lines that were being threatened by the Confederate cavalry." This resulted in the 10th Kentucky marching alone, without outside support from other units, through hostile territory. As described by Colonel Harlan, this was a time when the 10th was experiencing a heavy amount of sickness that "had reduced the number of active soldiers in my regiment by several hundred. At least seventy-five were sick or were so weak from sickness that they could not carry a gun."[33]

On the first night of the march from Eastport, Mississippi, the 10th Kentucky crossed the Tennessee River and camped on the Alabama side. Two pickets per guard post were established to insure the safety of the men while in hostile territory. The pickets' instructions were to challenge anyone who approached the camp and if the person did not halt, then the guards were directed to open fire. About 2:00 A.M., one of the pickets fired and awoke the camp and then other pickets also opened fire. An Irish-American, Private Michael McNamara, Company C, was found to have been the guard who opened fire. He reported to the adjutant that he had ordered, "Halt!" and the person did not halt, and so he, did indeed, open fire. The next morning the intruder was discovered in the area in front of Private McNamara's post. It was found to be a "dead mule with a bullet through his forehead." Apparently, one of the regiment's mules had gotten loose in the night and had the misfortune of wandering in front of the picket line.[34]

The regiment next traveled toward Shelbyville, Tennessee, and a reminder of their purpose in the Civil War was shown in stark reality. They marched past two black men wearing Union uniforms who had been hanged by the roadside.

Colonel Harlan was faced with being in enemy territory with several sick men and he developed a successful strategy to protect his men.

> We reached Shelbyville about 11 o'clock, and as I was passing through the town I discovered about 30 or 40 well-dressed men in citizen's clothes, sitting quietly under the shade trees. It occurred to me, all at once, that there was a chance to protect my sick soldiers from rebel guerillas. I halted my regiment in the main street and sent one of my captains, with a squad of soldiers to where the crowd was, with orders to arrest about a half dozen of them and bring them to me. My orders were to select well-dressed, young men who appeared to be influential and well to do. Some of them wore pumps and white socks and seemed to be contented with their lot and with the situation. I then rode up, alone, to the crowd of citizens and said to them in substance: "It is proper to inform you as to what all this means. As we came along this morning we saw near here two Negroes, hung at the roadside and dead. They had on the uniform of the Union army and were hanged, no doubt, for that reason. Now, I warn you that for every soldier absent from my camp this evening, two of these arrested citizens will be shot by my orders." Of course, I did not really intent that this order should be executed literally.[35]

Captain Franklin S. Hill was the officer initially charged with capturing the civilian hostages. Colonel Harlan adopted this plan for every town his unit passed through. It was successful, but obviously, this did not endear the 10th Kentucky to the local citizenry.

Capture of Companies A and H

The Union plan for attacking the Confederate Army was a two-pronged approach—one prong was directed at the Mississippi River and the seemingly impregnable Vicksburg fortress, and the second prong was directed toward Tennessee with the ultimate objective being Chattanooga. Grant and Sherman would direct their efforts at Vicksburg and General Don Carlos Buell was to strike through Tennessee. Chattanooga was key for the Southern cause because of the control of the Tennessee River and, secondly, because the city was a railway center. In addition, eastern Tennessee had northern sympathies and an attack could yield benefits both political and military. Finally, the two-pronged attack would keep the southern forces from concentrating and threatening the north through an attack of their own.

Nashville, as a center of communications and supplies, was key to Buell's operations. Rail lines that ran from Nashville to Chattanooga would allow supplies to flow from Louisville to Nashville and eastward with his advancing army. So, one of the most important aspects of Buell's plan was to keep the rails in operation, and that was a part of the 10th Kentucky's activities in the summer of 1862. The various companies were dispersed throughout the area protecting specific sections of railroad, particularly bridges, because their destruction would result in lengthy repair periods.

In July 1862, the 10th Kentucky Infantry had the misfortune of having two companies captured by a larger Confederate cavalry force commanded by Brigadier General Frank Armstrong. Company A, commanded by Captain Henry Davidson, and Company H, commanded by Captain Buford R. Pendleton, had been sent to protect a railroad bridge in Courtland, Alabama. A small force of the 1st Ohio cavalry was also stationed to protect the bridge. The infantry companies had 97 men and the 1st Ohio cavalry had 35–40 men present. In General Armstrong's report, he indicated that the Confederate States of America (CSA) units involved totaled approximately 700 men.[36]

Colonel Harlan received news of the capture shortly after it occurred as he was traveling between Florence, Alabama, and Pulaski, Tennessee. He reported the incident immediately to Colonel Speed Fry and to General Don Carlos Buell, the Army commander.

Although Colonel John Harlan became aware of the capture of companies A and H shortly after it happened, he did not know the details of the event until he received a letter from Captain Henry Davidson, Company A, in early August. The companies were attacked by a combined cavalry force totaling 800, by Davidson's estimate, and the defenders quickly formed a defensive line behind a railroad embankment near a bridge. Although this position was selected to provide the best defense from such a large attacking force, the companies soon became surrounded. As the Confederates charged toward the surrounded companies, the 10th Kentucky released two volleys into their attackers. Davidson felt that they wounded several attackers and shot the horse of one of the ranking officers.

It soon became apparent that the attackers were gaining the rear of the 10th Kentucky. The companies abandoned the embankment, tried to escape by the creek, and assembled in gullies in a vain attempt to avoid capture. Captain Davidson ordered the men to fix bayonets, intending to attack through the weakest part of the Confederate line, but realized that the odds were greatly against him and that he had no chance to avoid being captured. Pendleton and Davidson decided the best course of action was to surrender.

Captain Davidson wrote of the exemplary conduct of the men "obeying every command with promptitude and alacrity and fighting gallantly until the last moment." Captain Pendleton, Lieutenant Reynolds, Lieutenant Barry and Lieutenant Shively were cited as "worthy of all praise for the brave and gallant manner in which they managed their troops." Private William Farmer, Company H, was killed, and Privates James Rogers, Mattis Cortes, and James Cable were all wounded in the incident.[37]

The capture of companies A and H was a significant event for the 10th Kentucky Infantry and was certainly an embarrassment for Colonel Harlan; it was a prize for the Confederacy but a much less significant event for them. General Frank Armstrong, commanding the Confederate forces at Courtland, Alabama, in his summary of the incident reported that he captured the companies of the 10th Kentucky with a small detachment of 1st Ohio Cavalry. The units attacking the 10th Kentucky were from General Armstrong's Brigade, additional cavalry from General Nathan Forrest, and two "partisan" companies. The cavalry reached Courtland and surprised the defenders by passing through the countryside without using any of the roads.

The cavalry was also successful in bringing long range artillery to use in capturing the Union forces. General Armstrong confirms Captain Davidson's account of the incident. The Confederates were within 500 yards of the defenders when they charged. When the 10th Kentucky was forced into the creek gulley they were protected from any attack on horseback, but the dismounted cavalry was able to surround and finally capture the men. General Armstrong would claim 133 prisoners, including eight commissioned officers, and two wagons, corn, arms, and camp supplies. Armstrong's men then destroyed the telegraph line and three parts of a railroad trestle. He also burned the depot and the bridge.[38]

Many stories tend to end at the capture, but we are fortunate to have the records of W. L. Curry of the 1st Ohio Cavalry. He described some of the hardships that resulted after capture of the 10th Kentucky and 1st Ohio Cavalry. He described the march to Moulton from Courtland, Alabama, as about 20 miles. The prisoners slept in a yard and were then quartered in the local courthouse, but were not furnished with blankets. The men were fed corn on the cob taken from the field with no additional food, and slaves assisted the prisoners with pots and the building of fires. The prisoners were very dissatisfied with their treatment and held a meeting to demand better conditions, but the cavalry rushed away to new operations and General Armstrong ordered, "Move those prisoners out on the road to Tupelo, Miss., on double quick." The prisoners were marched out at sundown with an escort of cavalrymen with drawn sabers, and the group marched from sundown to midnight without rest, food, or water as the temperature approached 100 degrees.[39]

By all indications the enlisted men were paroled, moved to Nashville and then on to Camp Chase, Ohio. The officers were retained by the Confederates and taken to Tupelo, Mississippi. The exchange of officers occurred on September 6, 1862, and the soldiers were returned to their units.

The capture of these companies had to be an embarrassment for Colonel Harlan and to make matters worse, General Don Carlos Buell, commander of the Army of the Ohio, sent a blistering correspondence to the officers:

Huntsville, Ala. July 26, 1862.
(Received July 27, 10.10 P.M.)

On yesterday the enemy's cavalry attacked the guards at several points on the road between Decatur and Tuscumbia; captured the one at Courtland; drove others into Decatur, and probably destroyed the bridge. These disgraceful and serious results are due to the neglect and disobedience of my repeated orders in regard to construction of stockades, and I shall bring every offender to trial. I am trying to make our lives secure against such occurrences, for they are fraught with the most serious consequences to an army operating on such long lines. I have requested General Grant to open the road again, for it is important to both of us.

D. C. BUELL.[40]

Needless to say, this correspondence greatly angered Colonel Harlan and the men of the 10th Kentucky to be so insulted by the commanding general. John Harlan was so outraged that he demanded a court of inquiry to address the actions of Captains Davidson and Pendleton, but no court of inquiry was ever convened. General Buell had made an enemy of a very powerful Kentuckian.

Men Taken Prisoner at Courtland

Company A		*Company H*	
Henry Davidson	Captain	Buford Pendleton	Captain
James Reynolds	1st Lieutenant	Henry Barry	1st Lieutenant
H. H. Warren	1st Sergt.	William Shively	2nd Lieutenant
Richard Grace	2nd Sergt.	Cornelius Abell	Sergt.
N. Herdel	3rd Sergt.	Joseph Shively	Sergt.
E. B. Lancaster	4th Sergt.	Stephen Shively	Sergt.
Jeremiah Arndt	5th Sergt.	William Wallering	Sergt.
Levi Arnold	Corp.	Thomas Wright	Sergt.
George Blandford	Corp.	B. F. Lyons	Corp.
Abe Herin	Corp.	William Swaney	Corp.
Harrison Roberts	Corp.	David Rice	Corp.
John Vanderheide	Corp.	Enoch Abell	Private
Simpson Arnold	Private	Addison Belton	Private
Gustave Asbeck	Private	M. Birmingham	Private
William Boyd	Private	Moses Campbell	Private
Robert Boyle	Private	J. P. Clements	Private
J. W. Bumgarder	Private	Zach Eades	Private
James Cable	Private, wounded in arm	John Farmer	Private
O. D. Casabon	Private	Joseph Farmer	Private
Henry Crutcher	Private	Moses Farmer	Private
Auguste Decker	Private	Nathaniel Farmer	Private
Nicholas Demarsh	Private	William Farmer	Private, killed in action
Stephen Demarsh	Private	Martin Ford	Private
Jacob Duffield	Private	Tandy Green	Private
Joseph Edmonson	Private	Isaac Harmon	Private
George Frank	Private	William Hart	Private
Peter Gaylock	Private	Perry Long	Private
Harvey Graham	Private	Elmore Marple	Private
Elias Harding	Private	Francis Murphy	Private
George Harding	Private	G. W. Murphy	Private
Conrad Hill	Private	John Murphy	Private
Aaron Jones	Private	Phil O'Connell	Private
William Jones	Private	D. A. Shively	Private
Joseph Jenkins	Private	James Sluder	Private
Frank Keeville	Private	John Sluder	Private
Blanden Kendall	Private	Michael Welch	Private
Culbraith Kendall	Private	William White	Private
Fred Kortz	Private		
John Kortz	Private		
Mathie Kortz	Private, wounded in cheek & arm		

Company A

William Kortz	Private
Ian Manly	Private
A. C. Mattingly	Private
Henry Mitchell	Private
John Mitchell	Private
Richard Mudd	Private
James Rogers	Private, wounded in thigh
Mike Ropp	Private
Fred Rosseles	Private
Fred Saal	Private
Anthony Shielly	Private
John Shielly	Private
William Shielly	Private
D. M. Shockley	Private
Lewis Shorten	Private
John Stoar	Private
A. F. Terry	Private
Frank Voclair	Private
John Watts	Private
Harry Weiser	Private
John Welsh	Private

First Presbyterian Church of Florence Incident

Corporal Robert Boyle, Company A. He and the men of companies A and H were captured at Courtland, Alabama (Bill Elswick Collection, U.S. Army Military History Institute).

While Companies A and H were being marched off to captivity for a few months, the rest of the 10th Kentucky was continuing with its duties of protecting transportation and communication lines. The regimental headquarters was located in Florence, Alabama. While the action at Courtland was serious, another lighter event was just about to begin on a quiet Sunday morning at church.

The 10th Kentucky was stationed at Florence, Alabama, and on July 27, 1862. Lieutenant Colonel Hays, Colonel Harlan and others attended services at the Florence Presbyterian Church. Approximately three-quarters of the congregation that Sunday were Union officers and soldiers. Dr. W. H. Mitchell, pastor, conducted the service. After reading the gospel, Dr. Mitchell said a prayer that caused a very unfavorable impression on the Union soldiers present. "He prayed in terms for the Confederate President, Congress and Cabinet, and asked God would smite to the earth their remorseless invaders. This was extraordinary language from a minister officiating within the military lines of a Division of the Union Army."[41]

After the prayer and before the sermon, many of the Union soldiers left the church. Colonel Harlan and other officers went to General Thomas' tent to explain what had occurred at the Presbyterian Church. When General Thomas heard the details, he said, "Go back and arrest the old scoundrel; no rebel preacher shall behave in that way in my lines." Even though Dr. Mitchell was still preaching his sermon, General Thomas reportedly said, "No matter, arrest him at once and deliver him to the 1st Ohio Cavalry with my order to send him at once to the north, not to return until the war is over."[42]

Colonel Harlan marched back into the church during the service and while Dr. Mitchell was still in the pulpit he stated, "Dr. Mitchell, I am here by the order of General Thomas to place you under arrest. You must have observed that a large majority of the congregation today were officers and soldiers of the Union Army. They came here in good faith to join with you and your people in religious services. You are within the lines of General Thomas. There is enough in religion about which a minister could pray and preach that would have been agreeable to all who heard you. Yet you prayed, in effect, that God would blast them and the Government which they represented. General Thomas regards your conduct as utterly inexcusable."[43]

Dr. Mitchell placed himself under Colonel Harlan's arrest. Colonel Harlan was confronted by a lady congregant and was called a Yankee. At this, Colonel Harlan said he wasn't a Yankee, but instead, was a Kentuckian. "She stamped her feet on the floor in rage and went off." Dr. Mitchell was transferred to the care of the cavalry and transported to the north, but was allowed to return home by October 1862.

A pro-Union newspaper, *Nashville Daily Union*, reported the event:

Traitor Clergyman Arrested.

On Sunday, the 26th ult., a large number of Union officers attended the Old School Presbyterian Church of the Rev. Dr. W. H. Mitchell at Florence, Alabama. So many of them were present that they constituted a majority of the congregation. After the usual opening hymn, the minister asked the congregation to unite in prayer, when, to their utter astonishment, the reverend traitor prayed for Jeff. Davis, for the success of the Confederate arms, and for the attainment of the independence of the Confederate people. The Union men were greatly indignant at this gross insult, but remained standing until the prayer was concluded, when they all left the church. After he had commenced his sermon, Col. Harlan returned to the church, walked up to the pulpit, arrested the preacher, and delivered him, in compliance with the orders of General Thomas, to a detachment of cavalry, which immediately conveyed him as a prisoner to Tuscumbia.[44]

The incident is presented from a different perspective in Doris Kelso's *History of the First Presbyterian Church*: "On Sunday morning, July 27, 1862, unawed by the military array before him, Dr. Mitchell prayed as usual for Jefferson Davis and for the success of the Confederate armies.... The scene that ensued can be better imagined than described. Amidst the tears and sobs of this flock, the undaunted pastor was taken from his pulpit."[45] There were those who felt this arrest was intended to subjugate and intimidate the local population.

Further Losses

Attrition continued to erode the 10th Kentucky, even though they had not been involved in any major conflict at this point.

Regimental Losses May–August 1862

	May	*June*	*July*	*August*
Discharged				
	Nelson, James (F)	Hogland, Isaac (C)	Ballou, John (C)	Davis, Nathaniel (D)
	Maloy, Daniel (K)	Smith, John (G)	Williams, Jesse (D)	Comfort, Thom. (D)
	Meckin, John (K)	Vessel, Walter (G)	McGhee, William (F)	Champion, Thom. (E)
	Carroll, John (K)	Newton, John (H)	Brown, Joshua (I)	
	Burger, Andrew (K)	Arnet Sr., John (K)	Temgate, William (I)	
		Burger, Andrew (K)		
		Lee, John (K)		
		Montrose, Joseph (K)		
		Sherman, Thomas (K)		
		Withrow, A. C. (K)		

	May	*June*	*July*	*August*
Died	Knott, Richard (B)	Mouser, William (D)	Farmer, William (C)	Boone, William (G)
	Simins, Thomas (B)	Weathers, James (E)	Hundley, Samuel (G)	Cabell, William (H)
	Dobson, James (C)	Carter, Joseph (F)	Raley, George (H)	Murphy, J. (killed) (K)
	Stillwell, Hattan (C)	Reagan, William (F)	Luster , James (I)	
	Hall, John (D)	Wise, John (H)		
	Montgomery, William (D)			
	Wakefield, William (D)			
	Hood, James (E)			
	Haydon, James (E)			
	Scott, Crow (F)			
	Baker, William (K)			
	Cox, Peter (K)			
	Cushin, Dennis (K)			
Deserted	Snow, William (I)		Whitehouse, Addison (G)	Kirkpatrick, Benjamin (C)
				Blandford, George (G)
				Newton, James (G)
				Smith, Pius (G)
Killed in Action			Farmer, William (H)	
Transferred Out		Hatchitt, James		
Resigned		Hupp, William (D)	Estes, John (A)	
		Hunter, William (G)	Fiedler, James (G)	
			Ferrell, Edward (G)	

(Letters in parentheses indicate the company of the individual.)

Battle of Perryville

In late summer 1862, the Confederacy realized that it must stop the Union's two pronged approach—Grant at the Mississippi and Buell in central Tennessee—into the heart of the south. Confederates also knew the importance of Kentucky and decided to risk taking control of this strategic area by invading into the state. The Confederate objective in this invasion was to march on Louisville, Lexington and other unspecified areas and to gain control of the Ohio River. Their hope was that thousands of Kentuckians would welcome their control of the state and join the Southern cause.

Confederate General Braxton Bragg's army moved north into Kentucky by way of eastern Tennessee, crossed the Cumberland River and marched

1st Lieutenant James Fiedler, Company G, resigned his commission July 19, 1862. He accepted the appointment of provost marshal of the 4th Congressional District in Kentucky (Steven Wright).

toward Glasgow. General Kirby Smith's cavalry was advancing before the infantry and by August the Confederates had moved to Big Hill near Richmond, Kentucky. On August 30, the advancing Southern Army slammed into the defending Union forces and then proceeded to advance northward. Lexington was the next target, and then Bragg's army moved throughout the state. Another clash between Union defenders and Bragg occurred on September 15 at Munfordville, Kentucky. On September 17, the bloodiest day of the Civil War was being fought in western Maryland at Antietam. Meanwhile, Bragg's soldiers were marching past Hodgenville, Lincoln's birthplace, and then camped in Bardstown.

The Kentuckians Prepare

The day-to-day duties for the 10th Kentucky were progressing into the summer of 1862 when General Bragg decided to invade Kentucky and shift the initiative from the Union armies threatening Mississippi and Tennessee. In August 1862, the 10th Kentucky, along with the rest of the Union Army of the Ohio, was ordered to return to Kentucky to prevent Bragg's army from capturing Louisville, Kentucky, Cincinnati, Ohio, and other key areas. At this time, the 10th Kentucky was part of the 3rd Army Corps commanded by General Charles Gilbert, General Albin Schoepf's division, Fry's brigade, being brigaded with the 4th Kentucky, 10th Indiana, 74th Indiana, and 14th Ohio. The 74th Indiana regiment was added to the brigade and remained part of the brigade throughout the war.

General Albin Schoepf was the commander of the First Division. He was born in Hungary in 1822 and received his military training in Vienna. He immigrated to the United States in 1851. He was appointed brigadier-general of volunteers in September 1861 and had experience facing Confederates at Wildcat Camp and also Mill Springs.

Organization of the Army of the Ohio

Army of the Ohio—Major General Don Carlos Buell, Major General George H. Thomas
Third Army Corps—Major General Charles C. Gilbert
  First Division—Brigadier General Albin Schoepf
    2nd Brigade—Brigadier General Speed Fry
      10th Indiana—Colonel William Kise
      74th Indiana—Lt. Colonel James Kerr
      4th Kentucky—Colonel John Croxton
      10th Kentucky—Lt. Colonel William Hays
      14th Ohio—Lt. Colonel George Este

On September 24, 1862, the first of General Don Carlos Buell's divisions began reaching Louisville. Buell knew that it was expedient to place his headquarters in Louisville to counter Bragg's threat. Mean-

General Charles Gilbert of the Third Army Corps (Library of Congress).

while, General Speed Fry's brigade moved by rail to the area near Munfordville in south central Kentucky, and

> was halted for some reason, and thus an opportunity was given for officers to confer with each other as to the possibility of an encounter by the Union Army with Bragg's forces. Some of the officers thought it was a great mistake not to hunt for and attack Bragg; for it was well known, that he was not far to the East, and was steadily moving in the direction of Louisville and central Kentucky. A few others predicted that Buell would not attack Bragg until after he had received reinforcements then being gathered in Louisville. Others inferred that Buell was untrue to his country and to his army, and would ultimately so manage his forces that Bragg would escape from the State and go back into Tennessee.[46]

Colonel Harlan spoke to a colonel from Ohio and stated that it was "distressing to think that we might, at any time, get into battle, under a commander, some of whose subordinate officers distrusted his fidelity; that if they really believed Buell to be untrue or unsafe as a commander, they should take active measures to have him put out of command."[47]

Not only were the commanders in the Army of the Ohio unhappy with the situation within the army, the common soldier was very dissatisfied because he was not paid. Both the 10th Kentucky and the 10th Indiana were not being paid. A near mutiny occurred in the 10th Indiana. Corps Commander General Charles Gilbert decided to punish the men by requiring them "'to stand to arms every morning from 3 o'clock until daylight' with all division and brigade commanders forced to circle their commands every thirty minutes to make sure the order was obeyed."[48] General Gilbert was despised throughout his corps. "As a Corps Commander, Gilbert proved to be petty, self-centered, and an unbending disciplinarian. The general possessed a colossal ego, one that seemingly required continual nourishment. This the soldiers quickly detected and strongly disliked."[49]

General Don Carlos Buell had command of the Army of the Ohio during the Battle of Perryville, but he was relieved shortly afterward (Library of Congress).

THE ACTION COMMENCES

The Battle of Perryville was fought on October 8, 1862, near Perryville, a small town of fewer than 500 people in the heart of Kentucky. Perryville possessed something that two tired and thirsty armies needed—water. The Chaplin River, Doctor's Creek, Bull Run and Wilson's Creek were all nearby. The Rebels arrived first in Perryville on October 6 after retiring from Bardstown and noticed that they were closely followed by blue-coated soldiers. There were three pursuers—Major General Alexander McCook on the left, Major General Thomas Crittenden advancing on the right from Lebanon, and General Charles Gilbert's corps in the center.

The first conflict began as the Union Army encountered Confederate cavalry and the general fighting began in an area around Peters Hill. The Battle of Perryville began in earnest the next day,

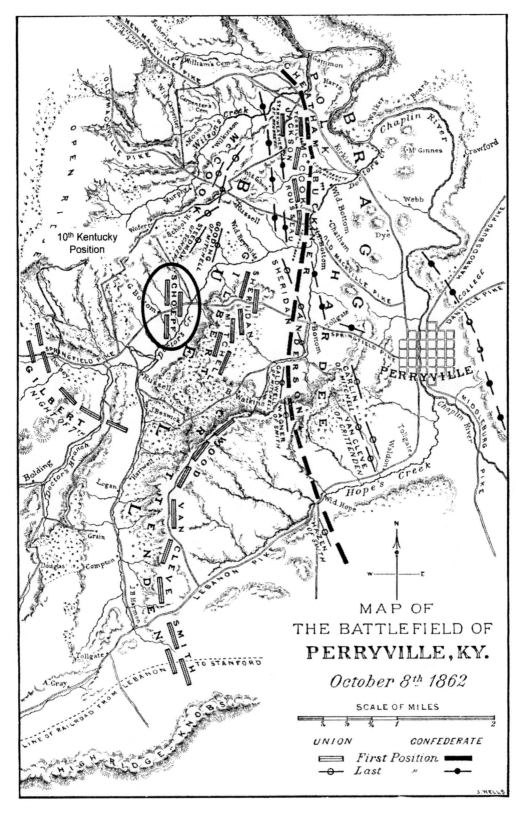

10th Kentucky, part of Schoepf's Division, at the Battle of Perryville (from *Battles and Leaders, Volume 3*).

October 8, 1862. At sunup, the fighting continued near Peters Hill and then stopped for a time as the Union Army fell into line across from the Confederate line. After noon, the Confederates attacked the left of the Union line, forcing it to fall back. More Confederates attacked but the Union line held and the Confederate attack was halted. The Union Army pursued the Confederates through the streets of Perryville after another Confederate attack along the Springfield Pike. After dark, fearing the Union reinforcements and being short of material and supplies, Bragg withdrew his army back into Tennessee.

THE 10TH KENTUCKY DURING THE BATTLE

The 10th Kentucky took no significant part in the battle even though they were relatively close to the action. The Battle of Perryville resulted in a strategic victory for the Union Army, because Bragg's Confederates were forced to abandon Kentucky. Many believe that General Buell missed the opportunity to destroy Bragg's army because only a small part of the Union Army was engaged in the battle. Buell reported that, even though he was close to the battle, he was unaware that it was taking place until later in the day. Buell's headquarters was located in an unusual acoustic shadow which prevented him from hearing the battle that raged a short distance away. Colonel Harlan stated he "was near one hundred yards of Buell's Headquarters during the whole time of the battle. At the time I was in command of a Brigade, and being about to march with my men for the purpose of joining the main body of our corps, Buell sent me an order to stay where I was until further orders, but holding my command ready for action, if any occasion therefore should arise."[50] The occasion did not arise which would cause Buell to move the 10th Kentucky toward the battle.

There are two recorded instances in which the 10th Kentucky men were involved in the Battle of Perryville. The first concerned Corporal Columbus "Ruck" Filiatreau of Company E, who was from Washington County. Ruck served as a battlefield nurse and was shot in the heel at the Battle of Perryville. The second event was the desertion of Private Royal Clark, who left the regiment during the battle. Private Clark would be the only man in the 10th Kentucky who would be charged with "cowardice in the face of the enemy." He would be court-martialed in November 1863. (See Chapter 5 for details of his court-martial).

RELATED EVENTS

Just prior to the Battle of Perryville, the army camped in central Kentucky and the 10th Kentucky camped on the Rolling Fork River near Lebanon, Kentucky. About 20 officers met in a country schoolhouse to discuss the actions of the recent battle. General Speed S. Fry was called to chair the meeting. Initially the officers directed their comments "against Gilbert, our corps commander. He was pronounced incompetent for this position and it was said that his removal was vital to the army."[51]

An officer from one of the Illinois regiments moved the focus of the discussion to General Buell. He said, "In my opinion, Buell is a traitor, is untrue to the army and untrue to the country." Colonel Harlan stated that he rose and then told the group that he did not agree with this evaluation of General Buell and would not support any action to remove him. The group did agree to send a telegram to the president, stating, "General Buell having lost the confidence of the Army of Ohio, we think that the public interests would be subserved by a change of commanders."[52] The telegram was never sent because President Lincoln had replaced General Buell with General William Rosecrans in the meantime. Likewise, the unpopular General Charles Gilbert was to be removed from contact with the 10th Kentucky. Although Gilbert was appointed to the rank of general prior to the Battle of Perryville, the U.S. Senate failed to confirm this appointment. He would serve the remainder of the war as assistant provost marshal in Hartford, Connecticut.

An interesting event occurred in one of the detachments of the 10th Kentucky Infantry operating in Washington County in October 1862. Corporal Martin Van Buren Crouch, Company D, had an identical twin, Richard, who remained in Kentucky during the war. Families were very close and Corporal Crouch's favorite sister, Sarah Jane, was seriously ill. A family member related:

> About that time, learning that Corporal Crouch's detachment would be marching through the country from Confederate held Frankfort, Richard rode to Springfield hoping to find his brother among the Union soldiers. Fortunately, Richard was able to spot his twin, and during a rest break, tell him of Susan Jane's illness. Corporal Crouch longed to see his sister, but the idea seemed impossible until a unique idea came to mind. Since the brothers looked exactly alike, why not exchange places temporarily? The exchange was made. Richard climbed into Martin's uniform and took his place when the rest break ended, and Martin, dressed in civilian clothes, rode to the family farm a few miles away. After spending a few hours with his sister, Papa was able to catch up with his detachment. Another exchange of clothing was made and Papa and Richard went their separate ways—Richard, back to the farm, and Corporal Crouch into the battle of Perryville.[53]

A side note in the history of the 10th Kentucky shows that Lieutenant Richard Grace deserted on October 10 but returned to the regiment in December. Lieutenant Grace challenged the desertion charge later in life and indicated that he was only absent without leave. No details of the event are available, but he was not subject to any confinement or other recorded punishment.[54]

Battle of Hartsville

After Bragg left Kentucky in October 1862, the Army of the Ohio pursued him into Tennessee. The 10th Kentucky was stationed near Gallatin, Tennessee. While occupying central Tennessee, the Union Army was harassed by the Confederate cavalry, which struck swiftly and then faded away. The cavalry of General John Hunt Morgan was to prove particularly worrisome over the next two months. The first event that peripherally involved the 10th Kentucky was the Battle of Hartsville, Tennessee.

HEADING TO EAST TENNESSEE

We know that Colonel Harlan was involved with the problems of marauding cavalry in November 1862 when he reported to Divisional Headquarters an incident that involved the capture and re-capture of a supply train near Rome. Lieutenant Colonel Hays and the 10th Kentucky were sent on November 29 to ward off any further raids in this area. Colonel Harlan praised Major Roswell Hill of the 2nd Indiana Cavalry for his efforts in recapturing the supply train. The cavalry pursued the Confederate raiders, and after a considerable skirmish, recaptured the entire supply train and returned it to the safety of the Union lines.[55]

Lt. Colonel William Hays wrote a letter to his father on November 17 while stationed at Hartsville, Tennessee. He related that he had been posted along the Cumberland River with the objective of supporting Union cavalry trying without success to engage General Nathan Bedford Forrest's Confederate cavalry, which was located a short distance away. While the 10th Kentucky and the 10th Indiana marched in support, both Union and Confederate forces moved away, leaving the foot-sore infantry to decide where to go next. Colonel Hays wrote that the 10th Kentucky was in good health and good spirits and that the brigade was posted at Gallatin, Tennessee. He wrote, "My position is much more laborious and my responsibilities are much greater since I have been in command of the regiment."[56]

Also on November 17, Lieutenant William Francis O'Bryan wrote to his father. In the letter, he related that the regiment force-marched 19 miles, which is another example of the difficulty of infantry regiments fighting cavalry. He expected that the 10th Kentucky was headed for eastern Tennessee, "sweeping the rebels as we go."[57]

In November and December 1862, John Harlan's brigade was responsible for guarding areas in central Tennessee. Harlan's headquarters was in Castalian Springs, Tennessee, and he assigned the protection of Hartsville to the 10th Kentucky's lieutenant colonel, William Hays, and Colonel John Croxton of the 4th Kentucky Infantry. These activities were especially important because General John Hunt Morgan's cavalry was located a few miles away. Harlan was particularly diligent in light of the capture of his two companies earlier in the summer.

The 10th Kentucky's brigade was subsequently replaced in Hartsville by the 39th Brigade of General Ebenezer Dumont's 12th Division of the Army of the Cumberland, commanded by Colonel Absalom Moore. Colonel Moore's brigade was 2500 strong and included the 104th Illinois (Moore's regiment), 106th Ohio, 108th Ohio and the 2nd Indiana Cavalry. Colonel Harlan commented that General Dumont, "without experience in the handling of soldiers, and knew [knowing] nothing of military or other discipline," was in command. "Information came to me at Castalian Springs, that he allowed his men to go around the country, at will, and in squads to farms, and commit depradations on the property and premises of non-combatants."[58]

ACTION IN HARTSVILLE

On the morning of December 7, 1862, volley fire was heard in Castalian Springs and Harlan's brigade hurried to Hartsville. On hearing the noise, Colonel Harlan sent couriers to determine the cause of the commotion:

> I followed immediately and rapidly after him with the Tenth Kentucky (Lieutenant-Colonel Hays) and the Seventy-fourth Indiana (Colonel Chapman), and four pieces of Southwick's battery, leaving the Fourth Kentucky (Colonel Croxton) and the Tenth Indiana (Lieutenant-Colonel Carroll), with two pieces of artillery, in a camp at Castalian Springs, to guard my own as well as Colonel Miller's camp, and to resist any attack upon that point. My intention was to go within 3 or 4 miles of Hartsville, and thus keep within supporting distance both of my own men, at the springs, and of Colonel Miller in his advance to Hartsville.[59]

When the unit arrived at Hartsville, dead and wounded were observed and the captured troops, about 2100 in number, were seen being hurried away about a mile away. It was immediately observed that the battle was over and "all had been lost."[60]

While the Union soldiers guarding Hartsville were captured and scurried off, their supplies for the most part remained and were collected by Harlan's men. Along with the supplies was a number of .577-caliber Enfield rifled muskets. These were the muskets that Harlan had hoped to receive at the beginning of the war and he now took this opportunity to supply his regiment with them. The weapons used by the 10th Kentucky prior to the capture of new arms were antiquated .69-and .71-caliber Prussian rifled muskets. He reported:

> The Tenth Kentucky Regiment, of my brigade, having arms which were, in many respects, very defective, and in some respects entirely useless to them, they were allowed to take out of the lot of recaptured guns 309, as well as 36,000 rounds of cartridges to suit them. That regiment turned over its old guns to the ordnance officer of the division, and will account to him for the guns retained, as above stated. This step was absolutely necessary, because there was no supply of ammunition on hand in the ammunition train of the division to suit the caliber of their guns (.71½), and because my brigade at the time was ordered to Hartsville, at which point there were reasons to apprehend that we would be attacked by the rebels. The exchange will add, in my judgment, one-third to the efficiency of that regiment in battle. If this step is not approved, the regiment will return to the proper officer, if ordered, all the guns thus received, and take such others as will be given them. The balance of the ordnance stores recaptured have been turned over to the ordnance officer of the division.[61]

Colonel Harlan reported that the Union units in Hartsville were having their breakfast when they were attacked and no pickets were posted. However, other sources clearly show that pickets had been posted. However, Moore's command was taken by surprise by General John Hunt Morgan's cavalry before it could manage a proper defense. Colonel Harlan reported that he noticed among the dead Confederates a man who was posing as a farmer a few days before, selling chickens in the Union camp. Harlan also related that he found a Confederate-clad man working with the wounded. Harlan asked the man what he was doing and the man replied, "Colonel Harlan, I know you—I am a Kentuckian, and I am doing what I can for these unfortunate wounded. I was left behind for that purpose." Harlan asked him, "Are you attending impartially to both sides?" He answered, "Yes." Harlan then told him to consider himself under arrest but to continue working with the wounded. The soldier was the Rev. Joseph Pickett, chaplain in the Confederate Cavalry. Reverend Pickett asked for and was granted a return to Kentucky after he attended to his duty. After the war he was elected a superintendent of public instruction.[62]

Morgan's strategy was to capture the garrison in Hartsville within an hour, because he knew that was length of time it would take Harlan's brigade to arrive. The Battle of Hartsville was a major defeat for the Union Army, which lost virtually the entire 39th Brigade with 2096 men killed, wounded, or captured, while the Confederates lost 139 men.

But not all was pleasant within the brigade while Colonel John Harlan was in command. The following is a section of a letter from a soldier in the 74th Indiana who was writing from Gallatin, Tennessee, in mid–December 1862, presumably referring to Colonel Harlan's anti-foraging policy. "Col. Harland commanding 2nd Brigade is down on the 74th but they are to sharp for him. He is partial to the Ky. Regt. they are the meanest damd Sunze Biches that ever was. I hate them more than I do the Rebels.—Helim Hatch Dunn, Co, D, 74th Indiana."

The Pursuit of Morgan During the Christmas Raid

At the close of 1862 the 10th Kentucky Infantry was involved in the pursuit of the Confederate cavalry in what was to be called "Morgan's Christmas Raid." While the Army of the

Cumberland was pursuing Braxton Bragg's army into Tennessee, the Confederates saw an opportunity to create havoc to communications, supplies and morale by raiding into Kentucky using their cavalry, which could strike fast and disappear before Union troops could react. The Confederate intent was to isolate Union forces and keep the Union Army from initiating a new campaign in Tennessee. The L&N Railroad at Muldraugh Hill was the target that would cause the greatest impact on supplies for Rosecrans' army.

The Confederate cavalry was under overall command of General John Hunt Morgan, an Alabama native who had close ties to Kentucky. Colonel Basil Duke, his brother-in-law, commanded the 1st Brigade of Morgan's cavalry. John Hunt Morgan was born in Huntsville, Alabama, and was the grandson of John Wesley Hunt, an early founder of Lexington, Kentucky. Morgan attended Transylvania College for two years but was suspended in 1844 for dueling. He enlisted as a private in the U.S. Army cavalry during the Mexican War. Afterwards, he became a hemp manufacturer and took over his grandfather's mercantile business in Kentucky. In 1857, Morgan raised an independent infantry company known as the "Lexington Rifles," and in September 1861, Morgan took his militiamen to the Confederacy. Initially, he was promoted as colonel of the 2nd Kentucky Cavalry, and he had just been promoted by Jefferson Davis, personally, to the rank of brigadier general on December 11, 1862. John Hunt Morgan was certainly having a good month, because three days later he was married to Martha Ready. What could be better? He was even married by Episcopal Bishop and Confederate General Leonidas Polk.

By Christmas 1862, Morgan and his 3900 troopers had reached Glasgow, Kentucky, and began their grim task of disrupting Union transportation and communications. The Union forces in Kentucky and also in Tennessee immediately knew of Morgan's presence. Morgan's first clash with blue-coated soldiers occurred near Cave City, Kentucky, and next Morgan burned the railroad bridge near Munfordville. General Thomas ordered Colonel Harlan to load his brigade onto the rail cars of the L&N Railroad at Gallatin, Tennessee, and travel north to prevent Morgan's cavalry from continuing their activities, particularly preventing them from reaching the city of Louisville. Harlan was soon to find that chasing cavalry with infantry was a frustrating task.

General John Hunt Morgan and wife, Martha. Morgan's Christmas Raid into Kentucky was pursued by the 10th Kentucky Infantry and resulted in a skirmish on the Rolling Fork River (Library of Congress).

Morgan's first raid into Kentucky took place in August 1862 when he destroyed railways, trestles, and telegraph lines. He became a celebrity in the South because of this successful raid. Morgan now moved into Kentucky with a large number of horsemen and seven pieces of artillery. So, on December 26, with another opportunity to cause havoc for the Union, he began his second raid into Kentucky. This raid was a classic example of brother vs. brother that so characterized the Civil War in Kentucky. Over 90 percent of Morgan's cavalry were Kentuckians and one Confederate remarked, "Tonight we camped on the sacred soil of Old Kentucky and it fills my heart with joy."[63]

Another example of the conflict between Confederate Kentuckians and the 10th Kentucky was the fact that Basil Duke, 1st Brigade commander of cavalry, and John Harlan shared the same alma mater—Transylvania University. Basil Duke, born in Georgetown, Kentucky, on May 28, 1838, studied law before the war and was practicing in St. Louis, Missouri, when it began. He soon returned to Kentucky, where he enlisted in Morgan's Lexington Rifles. Duke was promoted to the rank of full colonel of the 2nd Kentucky Cavalry at the same time that John Hunt Morgan was promoted to brigadier general.[64]

On December 26, Morgan burned L&N railroad bridges at Bacon Creek and Nolin, and then rode toward Elizabethtown. Morgan's cavalry burned crossties and rails and destroyed whatever was in their sight, including culverts and cattle guards. Morgan reached Elizabethtown on December 27. Here the Confederate raiders captured the town and bagged 652 Union soldiers.

John Harlan and his brigade were located at Castalian Springs when the call to head north was received. From the beginning, problems set in. The 10th Kentucky and the remainder of the 2nd Brigade were loaded onto a train that had a faulty locomotive. After a series of stops, starts and delays, Harlan threatened the railroad men, and a new locomotive was attached to the train. They finally reached Munfordville, Kentucky, about dark. At midnight, the brigade set out and marched 34 miles to Elizabethtown, which they reached at 7:00 A.M. Morgan's handiwork on the railroad forced Harlan's brigade to set off in pursuit by foot. The Union troops could get little information about the activities or location of Morgan's cavalry. "The rebel citizens did not wish us to know and the Union citizens were afraid to tell us anything," Harlan recounted.[65] While the Union troops were trying to locate the Confederate cavalry, Morgan's men were torching and burning the Muldraugh Hill bridge.

Colonel Basil Duke of John Hunt Morgan's command was wounded during the skirmish on the Rolling Fork River (Filson Historical Society, Louisville, Kentucky).

On December 27, 1862, Harlan surmised that the best route to intercept Morgan would be a country road to the Rolling Fork River at Johnson's Ferry. Harlan's

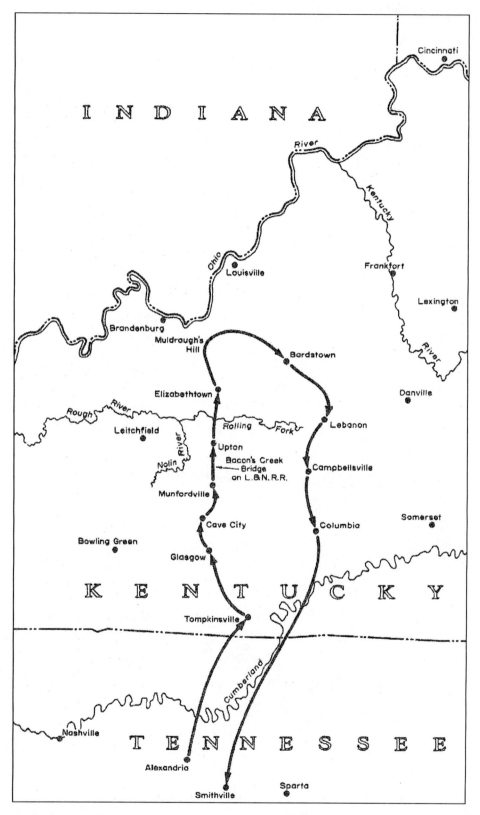

Morgan's Christmas Raid (by permission of the University Press of Kentucky, from *John Hunt Morgan and His Raiders* by Edison Thomas, 1985).

brigade was supplemented with Southwick's artillery and part of the 11th Kentucky Infantry, totaling about 3,000 men. Colonel Shanks' 11th Kentucky attached to the brigade found a portion of Morgan's cavalry resting near the Rolling Fork River and ordered the artillery to fire on them.

Once the firing began, Harlan's infantry marched forward and formed a battle line to meet their foe. The Confederates took cover in trees and on the bank of the Rolling Fork. The cavalrymen needed to cross the ford of the Rolling Fork, which could be seen a short distance away, but the artillery under John Harlan had targeted the ford and effectively cut the escape route without the loss of men and horses.

Colonel Duke was involved in the court-martial of Lt. Colonel Huffman, accused of violating surrender terms with prisoners, when he became aware that the Union forces were approaching his men. Duke ordered "Cluke's 8th Kentucky on the left, what was left of Stoner's 9th Kentucky on the right, and two companies of Gano's 3rd Kentucky in center" to hold the ford of the river. The Union forces greatly outnumbered the Confederates in this conflict by 2900 to 800 men.

As Harlan's men pressed forward, they hesitated in their assault, unsure of the size of the force they faced. This gave Duke an opportunity to withdraw his forces. "Just as Duke issued orders to execute his withdrawal plan, an artillery shell roared in and exploded with an ear-shattering bang. Two bleeding horses dropped in their tracks never to rise again and Duke tumbled to the ground with a serious head wound."[66]

The 10th Kentucky's role, under Lt. Colonel William Hays' command, was to support the section of Southwick's artillery located on a prominence to the right of the Union troops. Harlan recorded, "As the engagement developed, the Southern forces then made a diversionary attack to occupy an eminence upon the Union right. To meet this movement the Tenth Indiana (Colonel Carroll) was ordered to occupy that eminence, from which four companies were ordered to clear the woods on the right of my line. The Fourth Kentucky, Colonel Croxton; Fourteenth Ohio, Colonel Este; Seventy-fourth Indiana, Colonel Chapman, were ordered to form on the left of the Tenth Indiana. A section of the battery was ordered to occupy the eminence, and the Tenth Kentucky, Lt. Colonel Hays, ordered to support it."[67]

The deployment of Union troops came just as an attack from the Confederates was launched, which "silenced the artillery for about 30 minutes and this gave the Confederates additional time to cross the river." The Confederates then withdrew and escaped on horseback. Harlan chose not to continue his pursuit due primarily to the exhausted state of his troops. "My men were worn out and their rations exhausted, and in the swollen state of the river it would have been difficult for my infantry to cross. I feared, besides, that Morgan would whip around and make an attempt on this point."[68] He was also aware of damage to the Rolling Fork Bridge and set up a defensive position to protect the structure.

In his report of action, Colonel Harlan stated:

> I claim, for my command, that it saved the Rolling Fork Bridge, and most probably prevented any attempt to destroy the bridge at Shepherdsville, thus saving from destruction of property of immense value, and preventing the utter destruction of the line of railway, by which our army, near Nashville, was mainly supplied. And I submit whether the attack upon Morgan's forces, the timely arrival of my command at Rolling Fork, did not prevent a raid upon other important points in Kentucky. It is very certain that after my command drove the rebel chieftain across the Rolling Fork, in such a precipitate manner, he abandoned the railroad, and very soon thereafter fled from the State, hotly pursued by other forces.[69]

The skirmish at the Rolling Fork River was a small item for Confederate General Morgan, as he reflected in his official report on January 8, 1863:

> Just as the rear regiments were crossing Rolling Fork, a large force of the enemy consisting of cavalry, infantry, and several pieces of artillery, which had followed us from Elizabethtown— came up and began to shell the ford at which the troops were crossing. I immediately sent orders to Colonel Duke, who was in the rear, to send a courier to Colonel Cluke, ordering him to rejoin the command as rapidly as possible, and to hold the enemy in check until the entire command had crossed the ford. Colonel Duke, assisted by Colonel Breckinridge, placed seven companies from different regiments in position and held five in reserve. With this force he several times repulsed the enemy's advance, and very nearly succeeded in capturing two pieces of the enemy's artillery, when he fell from his horse, severely wounded by a shell. Colonel Breckinridge then took command, and maintained the position until Colonel Cluke's regiment had crossed the river, when I ordered him to fall back, which he accomplished in good order and without loss.
>
> In this affair only 3 men were hurt, on our side—Colonel Duke, Captain [V. M.] Pendleton [Company D, Eighth Kentucky Cavalry], (who was struck by a ball while gallantly leading a charge on the enemy's artillery), and a private slightly wounded. The enemy lost several officers and men killed and wounded.
>
> Meanwhile Colonel Chenault had captured and burned the stockade at Boston. He rejoined me that night at Bardstown. The force sent to burn the stockade at New Haven was not successful, and did not rejoin the command until the following night at Springfield....
>
> John H. Morgan, Brigadier-General[70]

Despite the failure of Harlan's brigade to "bag" Morgan's raiders, other Union units were rapidly converging on him. The Union objective, now, was blocking Morgan's route back to Tennessee. To confound Morgan's troubles, the weather was turning cold and unfavorable. On the evening of December 30, Morgan stayed at Bardstown and the next day moved southeast to Springfield, the home of many of the members of the 10th Kentucky.

A Union force moved to Lebanon, just south of Springfield, blocking his southern exit, but under the cover of darkness, Morgan by-passed Lebanon, and by the 31st he had reached Campbellsville. On January 1, Morgan made his way southward into Tennessee, ending his second successful raid into Kentucky. Despite Morgan's efforts, Union supplies were again steadily heading southward on February 1, 1863.

This effectively closed the book on 1862 for the 10th Kentucky.

Regimental Losses September–December 1862

	September	October	November	December
Discharged	Atkins, Lafayette (C)	Maurer, Francis (A)	Benedict, Edelen (H)	Allen, Samuel (C)
	Osborne, John (G)	Lamb, James (B)	Ainsworth, Henry (H)	Murphy, Benedict (H)
	Wright, Thomas (H)	Snider, James (D)	Goodman, Young (H)	Russell, Daniel (H)
	O'Connell, Philip (H)	Cain, Adam (D)		Wise, William (H)
	Wester, Michael (K)	Ratcliff, Joseph (F)		Farmer, Preston (H)
		Thomas, James (F)	Gunter, Henry (H)	
		Thompson, Lewis (G)		
		Wright, Samuel (H)		
Died	Worthington, Martin (H)	Peterson, Garrett (B)	Riggs, Thomas (C)	Millagan, Thomas (K)
	Willard, Hugh (I)	Oster, George (I)	Idoax , John (K)	
		Murphy, Burtley (K)		
Deserted	Durham, James (B)	Rhodes, William (B)	Hughes, Andrew (D)	Alvey, Alexander (B)
	Wade, John (B)		Brown, James (I)	

	September	October	November	December
Deserted (cont.)				
		Mills, Dennis (C)		McGinnis, James (K)
		Hall, Isaac (G)		Mordan, Patrick (K)
		Long, Perry (H)		
		Woolbridge, William (I)		
		Hicks, William (I)		
Missing In Action				
			Mosser, Henry (D)	
			William, Daniel (I)	
Resigned				
			Short, Robert (B)	
			Dorsey, Stephen (D)	
			Pendleton, Buford (H)	
Dismissed				
			Barry, Henry (H)	

(Letters in parentheses indicate the company of the individual.)

Leadership Changes within the 10th Kentucky

Many changes occurred during the first six months of 1862, but a few changes occurred during the second half of the year. The following are a summary of those changes, as compiled from Civil War pension records and the Kentucky Adjutant Generals Report (1866).

COMPANY D

Lieutenant Stephen Dorsey resigned his commission in Florence, Alabama, in November 1862 due to a disease of the throat. This problem was a "chronic inflammation of the throat and upper part of the trachea." He was replaced with Edward Y. Penick, 2nd lieutenant. Edward was born in 1838, son of R. N. Penick, a farmer in Marion County, and was 23 years old when he enlisted.

COMPANY G

First Lieutenant Charles Spalding resigned December 17, 1863, for an unspecified medical malady. In 1864 the unfortunate former lieutenant was shot to death in Washington County, Kentucky, by guerillas in an orchard near a friend's home. Also, 2nd Lieutenant Edward C. Ferrill resigned in August 1862 due to an unspecified problem.

First Lieutenant Edward O. Blanford would replace both the lieutenants who had resigned. Edward was a farmer and son of a farmer near Manton in Washington County. He was 20 years old when he enlisted and was the son of Thomas and Susan Blanford. He was a stout and able man at 5'10" and had brown hair and blue eyes. Edward served in Company G and was later detached to the Pioneer Corps for 2 years (December 1862 to August 1864).

A Dismissal in the Regiment

In 1862 Lieutenant Henry Barry, Company H, became the only "dismissal" within the regimental records during the war. Lieutenant Barry was a colorful individual and had many personal successes but would die early at 35 years of age. He was born in Schoharie County, New York, in April 1840 and was the principal of Locust Grove Academy in Louisville, Kentucky, at the time of the war. He was part of Company H captured at Courtland, Alabama, and was described as courageously facing the enemy. Lieutenant Barry was dismissed from the 10th Kentucky under Special Order No. 18 from Army of the Cumberland Headquarters on November 17, 1862. The order stated: "1st Lt Henry Barry, Co H 10th Kentucky Vols Infantry being reported as wholly inefficient as an Officer and absent without leave, is discharged the service of the United States from this date." It was signed by W. Sidell under General Rosecrans' orders.[71]

After leaving the 10th Kentucky, Henry Barry became the colonel of the Eighth United States Colored Artillery on April 28, 1864. He was promoted to brigadier general of Volunteers on April 13, 1865, and was mustered out May 11, 1866. After the war in 1867 he graduated with a law degree from Columbian College, which was later named George Washington University. He moved to Lowndes County, Mississippi, and became a U.S. representative from 1870 to 1875. He died unexpectedly in Washington, D.C., on June 7, 1875, of apoplexy.

Summary of 1862

Lt. Henry Barry in a photo made in 1875. He was dismissed from the 10th Kentucky "as wholly inefficient as an Officer and absent without leave" (Barnes Publishing Company Photo Archives: Georgetown University Library, Special Collections Division, Washington, D.C.).

The 10th Kentucky began the year and ended the year doggedly pursuing the enemy. Try though they may, they couldn't confront him. "Always too late" was their unofficial motto because they missed the enemy at Mill Springs, Shiloh, Corinth, Perryville, Hartsville and even during Morgan's Christmas Raid. While the 10th Kentucky was pursuing Morgan and protecting central Kentucky, the Battle of Stones River was developing, and again, the 10th would miss the opportunity to engage in battle, but a new wind was beginning to blow. This new wind would bring many changes in 1863.

Even though the 10th Kentucky was not involved in any major engagements, there were significant losses for the regiment. The first six months of the year resulted in major losses due to disease, but by the second six months, they were under control. However, the number of discharged men increased greatly during the last six months of 1862. The constant marching, movement, and sleeping out-of-doors took its toll on the men. Only two men were killed in action.

THREE

1863 Through Tullahoma

"Well it does seem that the "10th" will never have any hard fighting to do."
—Captain Seth Bevill, 10th Kentucky Infantry

In 1861 and 1862, the 10th Kentucky's lament was "Too late," but the regiment was in for drastic changes in 1863. General Rosecrans was now in charge of the Army of the Cumberland and his objective was to meet and destroy General Braxton Bragg's Army of Tennessee. The year began with a bang when Rosecrans' Army of the Cumberland met Bragg's Army of Tennessee near Murfreesboro, Tennessee, at the Battle of Stones River.

The Battle of Stones River was the first major engagement by the Army of the Cumberland, and it demonstrated that it could meet the Confederate Army and be successful, despite erratic performances by some commanders. The Army of the Cumberland had followed Bragg's army out of Kentucky after the Battle of Perryville and by winter had occupied Nashville. Going into battle, the Union Army had approximately 51,822 to Bragg's 51,132 men. The battle near Murfreesboro began on December 31, 1862, and continued through January 2, 1863. Fearing he was outnumbered, Bragg withdrew to the south to set up a new defensive line near Shelbyville and Tullahoma, Tennessee.

Because the Confederates withdrew, the battle is considered to be a Union victory. The estimated casualties were in excess of 22,000 total (Union 12,167; Confederate 10,000).[1] After this battle, the Army of the Cumberland remained in Murfreesboro for six months while it rested and refitted in preparation for the next attack on Bragg.

At the end of 1862, the 10th Kentucky and the other regiments in John Harlan's 2nd Brigade lay exhausted on the banks of the Rolling Fork in Central Kentucky after giving chase to John Hunt Morgan's cavalry. Prior to the 10th Kentucky's movement back to Tennessee, Sgt. Joseph Madison Buckman, Company G, deserted on the march on January 2, 1863, just after the 10th Kentucky's encounter with Morgan on his "Christmas Raid" into Kentucky. Joseph Madison Buckman was 24 years old, 5'8½" tall, with gray eyes and light hair and he was a carpenter from Marion County prior to his enlistment. There were several men who deserted from the 10th Kentucky, but Sgt. Buckman was one of two deserters who subsequently enlisted in the Confederate Army. He enlisted under the alias of John Bryan a little over a year later on March 1, 1864, in the 1st Tennessee Mounted Infantry. The 10th Kentucky also had a second member, Private William, alias Duncan, Bowling of Company F who was suspected to have deserted on December 28, 1862 and joined General John Hunt Morgan's cavalry. Private Bowling appears to have been captured by the Union Army in the summer of 1863.[2]

The 10th Kentucky rested, returned to Nashville, and then moved into central Tennessee in late January 1863 after the Battle of Stones River. The 10th Kentucky again found itself along with the 4th Kentucky and 74th Indiana fighting the Confederate cavalry, a task that was clearly difficult and one that the 10th Kentucky had been doing for the past few

Company G, 10th Kentucky Infantry (Ronald L. Smith).

months. The 2nd Brigade Headquarters were located in Lavergne, Tennessee, and the brigade was utilizing the services of the 1st Ohio Cavalry to provide scouting information on the enemy's actions. On the 25th of January 1863, Captain Cupp of the 1st Ohio Cavalry reported that a train had been attacked near Antioch, Tennessee, and two cars were burned and 55 prisoners taken; however, the locomotive and several other cars were saved. The cavalry force attacking the train was estimated to be about 2,000 strong.[3]

On January 26, 1863, a force of the 10th Kentucky, 4th Kentucky and 74th Indiana began a search for the Confederate cavalry, but no engagement occurred because the enemy withdrew. Again the pursuit took place in poor weather conditions and the regiment "suffered greatly from exposure to cold and rain."[4] Although remaining to guard the communication and supply lines, the 10th Kentucky rested and prepared for the next and more aggressive phase of the war.

On Ash Wednesday, February 18, 1863, the 10th Kentucky was camped at Lavergne, Tennessee. Lieutenant William Francis O'Bryan of Company B wrote to his family about the situation of the regiment. The weather was cold and cloudy. He reported that he had just recovered from a short illness, but had already recovered from a more serious illness earlier in the year. O'Bryan was a Roman Catholic and lamented his inability to go to confession but affirmed his trust in the Almighty. He was a teacher before the war and his family would be plagued with guerillas during the war. He ended his letter with this closing: "Dear Mother remember you poor soldier boy in your prayers. I remain you affectionate and Devoted Son."[5]

Another significant event in 1863 was Lincoln's decision to sign the Emancipation Proclamation. John Harlan's position prior to the war was the preservation of the Union, but opposition to the elimination of slavery. It is reasonable to believe that others of the regiment held the same belief, and the regimental records showed that black servants were assigned to some regimental officers. Lincoln's Emancipation Proclamation must have caused many in the regiment to examine their position with the Union Army; however, there is no evidence that this caused a significant problem for the 10th Kentucky.

After the Battle of Stones River, pressure from Washington was being exerted on Rosecrans' Army of the Cumberland to begin the offensive against Bragg in central Tennessee. Rosecrans delayed, first because of the poor weather, mud and poor roads. Later, he delayed because he insisted on a mounted offensive. He pressured General Henry Halleck to provide adequate mounts and units to mount them to finally neutralize the Confederate cavalry which had shown a propensity to ride circles around the infantry.

A letter by Sgt. James Scott, Company B, confirms the problems with the weather and describes the 10th Kentucky's situation in Tennessee. The 10th Kentucky was still garrisoned at Lavergne when Sgt. Scott wrote his letter in which he lamented not receiving letters from home. He also was concerned about Confederate raiders attacking into Kentucky by way of Mill Springs. He finished the letter complaining about the weather but confident that the 10th Kentucky could handle its Confederate adversaries. "Rosecrans is mud-bound so he cant move on after Bragg. We have built a fort here at Laverne that commands eighteen guns. We can whip all of Morgan's and Forest's forces if they come against us."[6] The letter shows more concern for the Confederate cavalry than for the infantry.

Harlan's Resignation

At Lavergne, Tennessee, on the 7th of March 1863, Colonel John Harlan resigned his commission as colonel of the 10th Kentucky Infantry. Colonel Harlan's father had recently died and he felt that he was required to return home to handle the family affairs. The law firm of James Harlan was one of the most powerful law firms in the state. Colonel Harlan's resignation letter is as follows:

> I deeply regret that I am compelled, at this time, to return to civil life. It was my fixed purpose to remain in the Federal army until it had effectually suppressed the existing armed rebellion, and restored the authority of the national government over every part of the nation. No ordinary considerations would have induced me to depart from this purpose. Even the private interests, to which I have alluded, would be regarded as nothing, in my estimation, if I felt that my continuance in, or retirement from, the service would, to any material extent, effect the great struggle through which the country is now passing.
>
> If, therefore, I am permitted to retire from the army, I beg the commanding general to feel assured that it is from no want of confidence either in the justice or ultimate triumph of the Union cause. That cause will always have the warmest sympathies of my heart, for there are no conditions upon which I will consent to a dissolution of the Union. Nor are there any conditions, consistent with a republican form of government, which I am not prepared to make in order to maintain and perpetuate that Union.[7]

A resolution was passed by the officers of the Second Brigade, Third Division, 14th Corps, which stated "that having been associated with Colonel Harlan for nearly eighteen months, during which time he has won the love and esteem of his whole command, by his amiable manners, unflinching integrity, and his indefatigable attention to his duties, we hereby extend to him a fond farewell, and express our sincere sorrow at his loss as a friend and companion in arms."[8]

With Colonel's Harlan's resignation, changes were in store for the 10th Kentucky. Colonel Harlan was the brigade commander and also the senior officer of the 10th Kentucky. The command of the brigade was officially given to General J. B. Steedman in July, but by August the new brigade commander was to be Colonel John Croxton of the 4th Kentucky Infantry and command of the 10th Kentucky became that of newly promoted Colonel William H. Hays. Major Gabriel Wharton who was made lieutenant colonel and Captain Henry Davidson, Company A, was promoted to regimental major.[9] The regimental adjutant, William Lisle, assumed the captaincy of Company A, but Captain Lisle would be forced to resign his commission in just a little over a month later on April 19, 1863, due to a medical problem. Lieutenant Charles McKay, serving in Company F and physician in civilian life, assumed the rank of captain in command of Company A.

Austin P. Maguire was appointed as the new regimental adjutant. Maguire, 25, enlisted as sergeant major and was promoted to the rank of 2nd lieutenant in Company A. Early in his life, Austin lived in Nelson County and later moved to Lebanon in Marion County prior to the war. Austin was the son of an Irish immigrant and his mother was Eliza Maguire, a Kentucky native. In 1860, Austin was living with Benjamin Spalding (a merchant in Lebanon) and Austin's occupation was that of clerk.[10]

The departure of Colonel Harlan may lead to speculation about his real reason for resignation—personal or political—but only he knew for sure what his intent was. Certainly, he had commanded a regiment for 18 months through various trials, but no major battles were destined while he commanded. He was very successful in his position as regimental, then brigade, commander. He was on the list of "To Be Brigadier Generals" published in Washington.[11]

Colonel Harlan was nominated and was elected as the attorney general for Kentucky in 1863, re-elected in 1865, and later became a justice of the U.S. Supreme Court. The men of the 10th Kentucky signed a petition wishing Colonel Harlan well and giving their support to him. He was a very popular with the men of the regiment that he formed in 1861, even to the extent that some to the men named their children after him.

In a letter written by Captain Seth Bevill, Company E, on March 29, 1863, in Fort Lavergne, Tennessee, to his father in Springfield, he explained the situation after John Harlan's resignation:

Lt. Austin Maguire, 10th Kentucky Regimental Adjutant (Randall Osborne Collection, Blue Acorn Press, Huntington, West Virginia).

> You say we no doubt miss Colonel Harlan. I cannot tell how much. Since he left us, we have first been under command of one colonel and then another. Colonel Croxton who is now the Senior Colonel is sick and at home. Colonel Este of the 14th Ohio who ranks next is under arrest. And Col. Chapman of the 74th Indiana is now commanding the brigade. Without wishing the others any ill I wish that something may turn up so that Colonel Hays may get command of the Brigade. Everyone is well pleased in the regiment with him, and Colonel Harlan was never more popular in the regiment than Col. Hays is.[12]

It is fortunate that John Harlan recorded the first part of the history of the 10th Kentucky because he preserved his personal insights on the operations of the regiment from the perspective of the colonel. His descriptions of the activities of the 10th Kentucky continued until his resignation in March 1863. The firsthand accounts of the activities of the 10th Kentucky for the remainder of the war have to be found in other sources.

Guerilla Activity in Kentucky

While the men of the 10th Kentucky went about their daily activities in Tennessee, they worried about what was happening to their loved ones in Kentucky. Because Kentucky was so divided, conflicts became part of daily civilian life, regardless of the side people supported— Union or Confederate. From the Union point of view the problem was referred to as the "Guerilla Evil" and this was particularly a problem in central Kentucky. During the war, guerrillas, partisan rangers, and scoundrels (from both sides) plagued the families of the men of the 10th Kentucky. The Union response from troops and provost guards was, many times, retaliation. General S. C. Burbridge was in charge of maintaining the peace in Kentucky for some time. His orders were to capture guerillas who had killed Unionists, and transport them to the scene and have them executed. General Burbridge found Kentucky "overrun" with guerillas. Burbridge was succeeded by General John Palmer of Illinois, who was defined as being fairer in his enforcement of the law. From the Southern perspective, the authority of the provost was viewed as equally abusive.

1st Lieutenant Charles Spalding, Company G, was shot and killed by guerrillas outside the home of one of his friends, Tom Blandford. Private William Hall, Company B, was murdered by guerrillas in November 1864 near his home in Nelson County. Lieutenant William O'Bryan, Company B, was always concerned for his family in Marion County, and Sgt. James F. Scott wrote often of the concern of General John Hunt Morgan's raids into Kentucky.

The father of the six Shively brothers all serving in the Union Army, including Captain William Shively of Company H, was reportedly killed by Union soldiers over a slave issue. John Shively was killed on August 12, 1864, reportedly because he still owned slaves.

Violence touched those at home and it made life more difficult to soldiers who were away and worried about family and friends there.

COURTS-MARTIAL

While awaiting the offensive against Bragg, the Union Army was plagued with desertions. Rosecrans began a process to exert discipline within the ranks.

The National Archives contains 19 records of the courts-martial of men of the 10th Kentucky. Courts-martial were held in the spring and summer of 1863, October–November 1863, July 1864, and November 1864. During the time of the Tullahoma Campaign, charges were brought against several members of the 10th. Those who stood court-martial from March through August 1863 are:

James Sallee, Lt.	Company C	March 1863
Seth Bevill, Captain	Company H	March 1863
James Burnell, Pvt.	Company F	August 1863
Charles McKay, Captain	Company A	August 1863
Isaac Hicks, Pvt.	Company I	August 1863
Daniel Richardson, Pvt.	Company I	August 1863
Jefferson Perkins, Pvt.	Company F	August 1863
Tandy Greier, Pvt.	Company H	August 1863

Both Captain Seth Bevill and Lieutenant James Sallee were tried on March 23, 1863, for disobedience of orders that occurred on February 21, 1863. Captain Bevill was tried first and Lieutenant Sallee was tried immediately afterward. Lieutenant Colonel Gabriel Wharton was the president of the court-martial. Other members included Major Myron Baker, 74th Indiana, Captain Thomas Cobb, 10th Indiana, 1st Lieutenant Joshua Jacobs, 4th Kentucky, 1st Lieutenant Charles Mann, 74th Indiana, and 1st Lieutenant James Mills, 10th Kentucky.

The details of the charges specified that Captain Bevill, "having reported himself at the Headquarters of the Convalescent camps and Barracks as being en-route to rejoin his regiment, was ordered by Jarvis Blum Clerk at said Headquarters in the name and by the authority of Lieut-Col Cahill Command Convalescent camps and Barracks to report himself on the following morning at six o'clock to take charge of a detachment [of] Convalescent Soldiers to Murfreesboro Tenn. Which order he failed to obey. This at Nashville, Tenn. on the twentieth day of February Eighteen Hundred and sixty-three."[13]

Seth Bevill's counsel was Colonel William H. Hays, his regimental commander. In the court-martial record, it was revealed that Lieutenant James Sallee, Sgt. William Beglow and Lieutenant John Myers were all present at the time the order was given. It appears that Captain Bevill did not report at the ordered time, but reported to Lt. Colonel Cahill at 7:00 the evening before his ordered duty. He did not report at the ordered time because he could not get transportation for the soldiers to Lavergne, where the 10th Kentucky was located. Lt. Colonel Cahill said he could get transportation for the soldiers, but, in fact, the transportation was not available. Lieutenant Sallee testified that he did not hear any order given to Captain Bevill, even though he was standing beside him. Lieutenant Sallee testified that he and Captain Bevill reported at 6:00 A.M. and took charge only of 10th Kentucky convalescent soldiers and he (Sallee) took them to Lavergne. Major Henry Davidson, Colonel William Hays and Lt. Colonel Gabriel Wharton also testified on Captain Bevill's behalf.

He was found not guilty.

Lieutenant Sallee faced exactly the same charges as Captain Bevill and was also defended by Colonel Hays. Captain Bevill testified on James Sallee's behalf. After previously clearing Captain Bevill on the same charge, the court rapidly heard this case and also found Lieutenant Sallee not guilty.[14]

Captain Charles McKay was tried on August 3, 1863, for actions on May 16, 1863. He was also defended by the regimental commander, Colonel William H. Hays. The court was made up of Lt. Colonel Marsh Taylor, 10th Indiana, Major Henry Davidson, 10th Kentucky, Major Edwin Hammond, 87th Indiana, Captain James Hudnell, 4th Kentucky, Captain George Kirk, 14th Ohio, Captain William Stinebeck, 82nd Indiana, Captain John Moulton, 2nd Minnesota, 1st Lieutenant Owen Brown, 17th Ohio, and 1st Lieutenant Martin Bruner, 9th Ohio. McKay faced two charges.

First charge: "Conduct to the prejudice of good order and military discipline. Specification 1st. In this that Captain Charles W. McKay of Co A 10th Kentucky Vol. Infantry did on the night of the 16th of May 1863 insult and abuse the Picket Guard while the said guard was in the performance of his duty, telling him he had no right to criticize an officer and that he did not know what his duties were."

Second charge: Conduct unbecoming an officer and a gentleman. Specification 1st. "In this that Captain Charles W McKay of Co A 10th Ky. Vol. Infantry did on the night of the 16th day of May 1863 say to the officer of the Picket post 'I know a damned sight more than you do' and the said Captain Charles W McKay as he rode alone speaking to one of the officers said 'that Lieut of the Post is a damned fool if he was a commissioned officer.' All of which occurred on the Nashville & Murfreesboro Pike near Lavergne Tennessee."[15]

The situation appears to have been that 10 to 12 mounted officers and men from 10th Kentucky approached a 2nd Brigade picket around midnight. The picket, Private William Farley, 14th Ohio, stated that men of the 10th Kentucky should not have been riding so fast after they had been halted. Captain McKay stated that a picket had no right to criticize an officer in the manner he was riding. The lieutenant-of-the-guard was Lt. James McBride. Lt. McBride stated that if "he was on post he would have shot Captain Davenport" [Company A]. Captain McKay said the lieutenant "was a damned fool, if he was a commissioned officer."

Private William Farley, a picket in the 14th Ohio, was a witness and stated that on the night of May 16, 1863, Captain Davenport first passed the pickets and Captain McKay passed second "and afterward came other officers and men." Lt. Colonel Gabriel Wharton was also part of the group of 10th Kentuckians and testified on Captain McKay's behalf.

Brig. General James Steedman also testified on Captain McKay's behalf and stated that the matter had been handled in his tent on May 19 when he called Captains Davenport and McKay with Lieutenant McBride and apologies were exchanged. General Steedman stated, "I never intended to order those officers to trial, if I had been in command at the post. They were forwarded without scrutiny, with other paper that had accumulated. If my attention had been called, I would have disapproved of them."[16]

Charles McKay was found not guilty.

August 10–15, 1863, Courts-Martial

A second series of courts-martial were held on August 10–15, 1863, and the court was made up of Major Edwin Hammond, 87th Indiana, Captain James Hudnall, 4th Kentucky, Captain George Kirk, 14th Ohio, Captain William Stinebeck, 82nd Indiana, Captain John Moulton, 2nd Minnesota, Captain E. F. Abbott, 74th Indiana, 1st Lieutenant Owen Brown, 17th Ohio, and 1st Lieutenant Martin Bruner, 9th Ohio. Lt. Colonel M. B. Taylor of the 10th Indiana was the president and Lieutenant G. W. Wood, 2nd Minnesota, was the vice president of the court-martial. Captain George W. Riley was defense counsel.

Private Isaac Hicks of Company I was court-martialed on August 10, 1863, at Camp Thomas, Tennessee. Private Hicks was charged with desertion: "Isaac Hicks Private in Co I 10 Infty Regt Ky vols did one day in July 1862 (date not known) absent himself from his duty, he being then on detached duty as Brigade wagoner, without leave from his commanding officer and did remain absent until the 12th day of June 1863, on that day he was arrested in Hardin County, Ky., by a detachment of men under com. of Lieut Funk of Co E all of the Reg above mentioned and by them brought to the Reg. on the 9th day of July 1863. This is at Florence, Ala."[17]

Lieutenant William Kelley was called to testify for the prosecution. He said the company thought that Private Hicks had been captured or killed, but members of the regiment had received letters that stated that he was at home in Kentucky. The regiment was near Eastport, Mississippi, moving toward Florence, Alabama, when he deserted. Private James Roaler, Company I, was also called as a prosecution witness and stated that Private Hicks went into Florence, Alabama, and never returned. Corp Caleb Welch, Company F, accompanied Lieutenant Funk to arrest Private Hicks and testified that he was found wearing citizen's clothes and was arrested as he rode on horseback.

Private Hicks asked a question about the condition of his family when he was captured and revealed his wife was sick, being attended by a physician. The defense called Sgt. William Kirby (Curby), Company I, who testified that Private Hicks had shown him a parole from a "lieutenant colonel Jones" of the Confederate Army in the fall of 1862. Private Daniel Richardson, also testified for the defense, stated that he saw a parole from a Lt. Colonel from a Tennessee regiment. Another private, William Green, testified the same as previous defense witnesses.

Captain I. B. Webster, Company I, testified that he received a letter from a friend of Private Hicks, because Hicks couldn't read or write, requesting transportation to the regiment. Captain Webster testified that he responded that Hicks should report to Elizabethtown. Private Hicks was found not guilty of desertion, but was found guilty of being absent without leave and was ordered to pay one year of his pay and allowance.

The court-martial of Jefferson Perkins, Private, Company F, 10th Kentucky Infantry, took place on August 11, 1863, at Camp Thomas, Tennessee. The charge brought against Private Perkins was desertion: "In this—That Private Jefferson T Perkins Co F 10th Regt Ky Vol Infty on or about the 3rd day of January 1863 did desert the service of the United States, in which he had been duly enlisted. This near Lebanon Junction Bullitt Co Ky. And did thus remain absent until the 29th day of June 1863."[18]

Sgt. John M. Thompson, Company F, was a witness for the prosecution. He testified that as the regiment was leaving Lebanon Junction Private Perkins asked for permission to go to the town to get his overcoat on January 2 or 3. He was given permission and never returned to the regiment. Private Perkins was serving as a scout for Colonel Harlan. Lieutenant Benjamin Smith, Company F, testified for the prosecution that he had received notice that Private Perkins was in the Union barracks in Louisville in March 1863. He also testified that Private Perkins returned to the regiment on his own accord.

Private Perkins did not call any witnesses on his own behalf. He was found not guilty of desertion but he was found guilty of being absent without leave. He was ordered to forfeit three months' pay and allowances.

The court-martial of Daniel Richardson, private, Company I, 10th Kentucky Infantry, took place on August 14, 1863, at Camp Thomas, Tennessee. Private Richardson was charged with absence without leave: "In this—That he, the said Daniel L Richardson, Private in Co. I, 10th Ky Vol Infty having been detailed for the recruiting service, per Genl Order, and sent to Ky upon said service, under the command of Captain Hilpp of Co. C 10th Regt Ky Vol Infty in common with others of said Regt., he the said Daniel L Richardson being the 5th Sergt of Co I in said Regt failed to come up to the Rgt until the 12th of June 1863, at which time he presented himself voluntarily to his Co and Regt. He has been reported absent without leave since the 20th of Jan., 1863 and on the 31st day of March, his position of 5th Sergt was declared vacant and a successor was appointed to the place."[19]

Stephan Gray, Sergeant, Company B, testified that Private Richardson accompanied a group of recruiters to Elizabethtown during the winter, but left the group due to illness. Private Richardson's captain, I. B. Webster, was called as a witness for the prosecution. Captain Webster indicated that he was at Elizabethtown at the time Private Richardson left the company and was not contacted by the accused. In addition, he was never informed of a reason for his absence, but had received a letter from the accused indicating that he was sick. Captain Webster reported that Daniel Richardson voluntarily presented himself to his company on June 12. Captain Edward Hilpp was also called as witness for the prosecution.

Second Lieutenant Clem Funk, Company E, was called for the defense. He testified that he had been in Kentucky to apprehend absentees and was made aware of Daniel Richardson's illness from citizens in the area. He visited Daniel Richardson's home and was informed that he planned to return to the regiment once his illness was over. He indicated that Private Richardson returned to the regiment before Lieutenant Funk did. Private Daniel Richardson was found not guilty.

The Court Martial of Tandy Greier, private, Company H, 10th Kentucky Infantry took place on August 15, 1863, at Camp Thomas, Tennessee. Private Geier was charged with desertion: "In this—That said Tandy Greier a private of Co H 10th Regt Ky Vol Infty U S Army duly enlisted and mustered into said Company, did on or about the 30th day of April 1863, desert, and absent himself from his said Company, without leave, from his proper commanding officer, and did so continue to absent himself, until apprehended, and brought back by virtue of Military authority, on or about the 12th of July."[20]

First Lieutenant Henry C. Dunn, 2nd Lieutenant Clem Funk, and 1st Sgt. Joseph Shively all testified for the prosecution. They testified that on April 30, Private Greier was missing at roll call and an unsuccessful search was made for him. Lieutenant Clem Funk led the capture of the accused, who was found at his home in Kentucky in civilian clothes. He was arrested and returned to the regiment on July 9, 1863.

Captain William Shively was the only defense witness. Questioning by the defense suggested that Private Greier was between 17 and 20 years old and had been persuaded to return home for an unspecified reason. Private Greier was found not guilty of desertion and found guilty of being absent without leave. He was ordered to forfeit six months' pay. Private Greier was to permanently desert in January 1864.

Private James Burnell of the 10th Kentucky was court-martialed on August 11, 1863, at Camp Thomas, Tennessee. He was charged with desertion and violation of the 22nd Article. The court was made up of Major Edwin Hammond, 87th Indiana, Captain James Hudnall, 4th Kentucky, Captain George Kirk, 14th Ohio, Captain William Stinebeck, 82nd Indiana, Captain John Moulton, 2nd Minnesota, Captain E. F. Abbott, 74th Indiana, 1st Lieutenant Owen Brown, 17th Ohio, and 1st Lieutenant Martin Bruner, 9th Ohio.

The desertion charge read: "In this—That James Burnell a private in Co F, 10th Regt Ky Vol Infty being duly enlisted in the service of the United States, did absent himself without leave from the service of the United States, his said Company and Regiment, then and there being in constant expectation of battle. All this at or near Elizabethtown, Hardin Co., Ky on or about the 29th of December 1862. And the said James Burnell did remain absent until the 9th day of July 1863, when he was duly arrested and brought to his Regiment."[21]

His second charge was violation of the 22nd Article: "In this—That the said James Burnell, a Private in Co F 10th Regt Ky Vol Infty on or about the 4th day of April 1863, being a member of Co F, 10th Regt Ky Vol Infty having been duly enlisted in the service of the United States, did enlisted himself in Co H, 34th Regt Ky Vol Infty. This was at the City of Louisville, Ky."[22]

Lieutenant Benjamin R. Smith of Company F was a witness for the prosecution and stated that Private Burnell left the regiment on the 29th of December 1862 without leave. He was arrested by Lieutenant Funk from the 34th Kentucky Infantry and was returned to the regiment. The accused stated that he was fatigued from a hard march and was about 18 years old.

Private Burnell wrote of the causes for his actions to the court. He stated that he was "overcome with fatigue and left the march. I was exhausted and tired down so that I was unable to overtake the Regiment." He returned to his home. Later, he went to Louisville with several acquaintances and enlisted in the 34th Kentucky.

Private Burnell was found to be guilty on both counts and sentenced "to be shot to death by musketry, at such time and place as the commanding General may direct." The case was submitted to the president with a recommendation for mercy. President Lincoln commuted the sentence to a forfeiture of 6 months' pay and a return of the defendant to service.

Capture of Captains Bevill and Milburn

Both Captain Seth Bevill and Captain John Milburn had the misfortune to be captured on April 12, 1863, while traveling on a passenger train going from Murfreesboro to Nashville. Confederate cavalry commanded by General John Wharton and Colonel Baxter Smith attacked the train. The suddenness of the attack resulted in a weak defense by the guard, and all on board were captured. The Union losses included 6 killed and 13 wounded, 3 mortally. Confederate losses were 6 killed, 6 wounded, and 3 prisoners. About 70 prisoners were captured and paroled, except 12 officers who refused parole.[23] Captains Milburn and Bevill were taken as prisoners of war to Virginia. They were exchanged and returned back to their companies by mid–May 1863.[24]

Tullahoma Campaign

While the 10th Kentucky was disciplining wayward soldiers, the war in central Tennessee was on the verge of a new chapter. General Rosecrans' goal in preparing to battle Bragg was to have a fully trained, rested, and healthy army. Even though the Army of the Cumberland

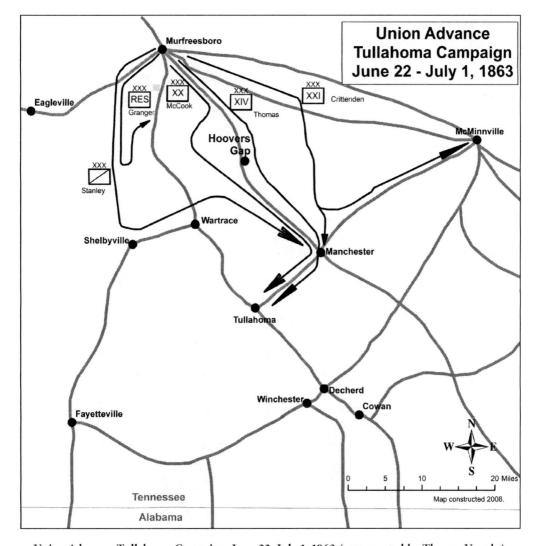

Union Advance, Tullahoma Campaign, June 22–July 1, 1863 (map created by Thomas Vought).

remained in place, it was involved with constant skirmishes with the enemy, particularly the Confederate cavalry. Rosecrans adamantly refused to advance on Bragg until he was ready. Finally, in June 1863, Rosecrans decided to begin his move southward. Rosecrans was to begin a campaign over the next month that was a classic in maneuver and positioning. Initially Rosecrans needed to determine where the weaknesses lay in the Confederate line. He began by probing with General D. S. Stanley's cavalry and General Gordon Granger toward Shelbyville, Tennessee, from his right flank, and ordered General George Thomas and General Alexander McCook's Corps to advance on the passes in the center of his lines; finally, General Crittenden was to probe toward McMinnville to the left.[25]

The Confederate base of supplies was established at Chattanooga. General Rosecrans recognized that the Southern cavalry was superior to his own and was causing major problems in maintaining his supplies and communications. In addition, he was advancing against an enemy which occupied superior position on the plateau of a range of rocky and rough hills in central Tennessee. The key in advancing against the enemy, with the objective being Tullahoma, was Hoover's Gap. Hoover's Gap controlled the Manchester Pike, the main thoroughfare to Tullahoma. This gap and all other passes were controlled by the Confederates. General Rosecrans fully expected the Confederates to bitterly contest any advance toward Tullahoma.

General Thomas' 14th Corps was intended as the main thrust through the center at Hoovers Gap. The famous attack by John T. Wilder, whose men had been furnished with 7-round Spencer "repeating" rifles and were mounted, overwhelmed pickets of Confederate General Stewart's infantry division, which was supported by General Joe Wheeler's cavalry. Wilder was able to advance rapidly through 12 miles of enemy territory, threaten General William Hardee's flank, and defend against a counterattack by Alexander Stewart's entire division while Thomas hurried through Hoover's Gap. Wilder's "Lightning Brigade" next threatened Manchester and forced Bragg away from Tullahoma. Colonel John Wilder was the First Brigade commander for Major General Joseph Reynolds's Fourth Division; the brigade was made up of the 98th Illinois, 123rd Illinois, 17th Indiana, and the 72nd Indiana.[26] On June 28, Hardee and Polk withdrew their forces from Tennessee and moved toward Chattanooga. While the victories at Gettysburg and Vicksburg were occurring, the Army of the Cumberland was passing Tullahoma in pursuit of Bragg's out-maneuvered army. The Tullahoma Campaign cost 586 Union casualties, which was mild by Civil War standards.[27]

During this campaign, the 10th Kentucky officially reported through General James Steedman, the brigade commander, and ultimately to Third Division Commander Brigadier General John Brannan, the new divisional commander for the 10th Kentucky. John Milton Brannan was born in Washington, D.C., on July 1, 1819. He entered the U.S. Military Academy in 1837 and after graduation was assigned to the artillery arm of the army as a 2nd lieutenant. Brannan served in the war with Mexico and was promoted to captain for his bravery in action. Brannan was appointed brigadier general of volunteers on September 28, 1861.[28]

Organization of the Army in Relation to the 10th Kentucky

Fourteenth Army Corps—Major General George H. Thomas.
Third Division—Brig. General John M. Brannan.
Second Brigade—Brig. General James B. Steedman.
10th Indiana—Colonel William B. Carroll.
74th Indiana—Colonel Charles W. Chapman.
4th Kentucky—Colonel John T. Croxton.
10th Kentucky—Colonel William H. Hays.
14th Ohio—Colonel George P. Este.

For the 10th Kentucky, the Tullahoma campaign was designed to focus the 14th Corps as a main thrust against the Confederate center, but the Lightning Brigade's success removed much of the formidable defense. On June 23, Brannan's Third Division moved from Triune to Salem, on the 24th it advanced to within a few miles of Millersburg, and on the 25th it reached Hoovers Gap. The advance for the 10th Kentucky through Hoovers Gap occurred on June 26; they were able to clear the gap and camp on the south side that evening. The maneuver by the 2nd Brigade, which was directed to the right of the Gap, was an attempt to turn the Confederate flank which occupied the heights over Garrison Creek. The brigade was thrown forward and succeeded in dislodging the Confederates; however, the defense was less than formidable.

General Brannan's recorded losses for the Hoovers Gap action are shown below[29]:

General William Rosecrans, as commander of the Army of the Cumberland, pursued Braxton Bragg into Georgia (Library of Congress).

Hoovers Gap Losses

Command	Enlisted men killed	Commissioned officers wounded	Enlisted men wounded
First Brigade:			
17th Ohio	3		21
31st Ohio	1		12
38th Ohio			6
82d Indiana			2
4th Michigan Light Battery	1		
Total First Brigade	4	4	41
Second Brigade:			
10th Kentucky			1
10th Indiana			1
74th Indiana			1
Total Second Brigade			3
Total Both Brigades	4	1	44

Note: Two horses killed.

On the 26th Captain Israel Webster, Company I, injured his back while preparing to advance through the gap. He was taken by ambulance to the field hospital. He quickly returned to his company.[30] On the 27th, the 10th Kentucky was moving forward again through Fairfield and onward until it occupied Tullahoma on July 1. On the 29th of June, General Brannan sent a one-sentence message from Crumpton's Creek. "I am pressing the enemy in front and right with more than one brigade."[31]

On June 30, the 2nd Brigade was again the advance unit and it was joined by the 38th Ohio. The units pushed to within 2 miles of Tullahoma. Webster wrote, "The rebels offered considerable resistance, occasionally bringing field pieces to bear upon our advancing forces."[32]

One additional casualty for the 10th Kentucky during this campaign was the loss of Assistant Surgeon Charles Hardesty of Bullitt County. Dr. Hardesty had joined the regiment in 1862 and during the Tullahoma campaign he contracted a "fever" and died in Nashville on July 7, 1863.[33]

Captain Seth Bevill summarized the 10th Kentucky's role in the Tullahoma campaign in a letter that he wrote to his sister on July 12, 1863, from a camp on the Elk River near Tullahoma:

> Well it does seem that the "10th" will never have any hard fighting to do. In the recent advance of the army, Gen'l (?) selected his old division, ours, and for three days when it was thought that every moment would bring a general engagement, held it in advance of his whole corps. And for two days before the evacuation of the rebel fortifications at Tullahoma, our Brigade was in advance and on the morning of the evacuation every man of us from the Major Generals down expected to have had a hard fought battle before gaining possession of the town. But the bird had flown, and we took quiet possession. And the 10th KY was not cut to pieces as I understand it was again reported, it only being on (?) skirmishing.
> We have been fasting here for several days, the road being in such terrible condition that our supply trains could not get to us; but all is right now as the cars are running to within five miles of us bringing any quantity of "crackers and bacon."
> You would probably have some curiosity to know when we will push on further south and I am sorry I cannot inform you; I would like to be enlightened on that point myself....
> No, the end is not yet. But God grant it may come as soon as the most hopeful expect it"[34]

This officially ended the Tullahoma campaign for the 10th Kentucky. What could have been a difficult fight at Hoover's Gap was averted by tactics and movement. Bragg withdrew his army in the direction of Chattanooga, which was a key supply and communications center for the south. And where Bragg went, Rosecrans was sure to follow. One of the most appropriate statements about the Tullahoma Campaign was written by General Henry Cist: "Brilliant campaigns, however, without battles, do not accomplish the destruction of an army. A campaign like that of Tullahoma always means a battle at some other point."[35]

One final reminder of the struggle many of the Kentuckians faced who had family and friends on different sides was expressed in Seth Bevill's letter to his sister regarding his brother, who was a soldier of Southern Army:

> Thinking of him has reminded me of something you wrote to me about not long since—that it had been hinted to you by some persons that you were not doing your duty to me as a sister by being so decided in your opinions in opposition to mine when I was in the army and by speaking so freely in my presence. No, my sister, if I thought for a moment that you could for one instant believe that I could think less of you, or love you the less, because you do not think as I do, or because you have been candid enough to tell me so, I would indeed be grieved. Am I more generous to my enemy on the battle field as a bad hearted man? Who that can (?) dispassionately and without prejudice think about this contest can for a moment think so. Am I to spurn my brother because he has espoused the cause he has, however much I may condemn him in it? Am I to have any the less brotherly affection from him, however much I may regret the action? You have always known how I have felt about this. I shall feel the same about it always. I would be glad if every one I loved could think as I do.[36]

Captain Bevill died within three months due to a gunshot wound from a Southern soldier.

In a letter written to his parents on July 27, 1863 from Winchester, Tennessee, Sgt.

James Scott showed his optimism of the war ending by Christmas; but like Captain Bevill, Sgt. Scott would die at Chickamauga. He wrote, "The boys is all well and harty and in good spirits. They all think we will be at home against Christmas. I hope it may be so for I wood like to spend next Christmas at home free from this infurnal rebellion. I do not suppose you will be interrupted by Morgan and his band much more. From all accounts he has plaid out. James F. Scott."[37]

Regimental Losses January–August 1863

	January	*February*	*March*	*April*
Discharged	Durbin, John C (A)	Wilson, Thomas (D)	Robinson, James (C)	Shipp, James (C)
	Gault, William (C)	Cussanger, James (D)	Hunt, Rueben (C)	Wade, George (C)
	Dawson, Martin (E)	Homan, David (D)	Slatterly, Patrick (C)	Wakefield, Squire (D)
	Reynolds, Francis (E)	Johnsey, William (D)	Bottoms, Bradford (D)	
		Southern, Charles (D)	Jackson, James (I)	
		Wicker, James (D)	Cooper, Philip (E)	
		Fields, Richard (E)	Filiatreau, William (E)	
		Gassalder, Arnold (E)	Lyns, Richard (E)	
		Darion, Simon (F)	Key, Thomas (F)	
		Hooper, Wesley (F)	Farmer, James (H)	
		Abell, Samuel (H)	Farmer, John (H)	
		Earls, Milton (H)	Painter, Aaron (H)	
		Raley, John (H)	Gegan, Patrick (K)	
		Jackson, Wm. (I)	Phibban, Patrick (K)	
		Phillips, Benjamin (I)		
Died		O'Bryan, John (F)		Sheultry, Cornel. (D)
		Smothers, John (I)		Ford, Martin (H)
				Roaler, Solomon (I)
				Stavton, John B. (I)
				Stoner, William (I)
Deserted	Gaylock, Peter (A)	Martin, Eugene (A)		Haman, Lee (D)
	Rogers, James (A)	Mitchell, John (A)		Broax, Alex. (K)
	Saal, Frederick (A)	Begals, John (I)		Carpenter, Chs. (K)
	Voclair, Frank (A)			
	Stoar, John (A)			
	Buckman, Jos. Madison (C)			
	Issac, Nathan (D)			
	Rhodes, Herod (E)			
	Foster, Larry (G)			
	Graham, David (G)			
	Turner, William (I)			
	O'Bryan, Paul (G)			
Transferred				Jasper, Abraham (I)
			Harlan, John M. (Staff)	Lisle, Wm. J. (A)

	May	*June*	*July*	*August*
Discharged	Sill, David (B	Graham, Mason (D)	Pickerel, Stephen (B)	Sapp, Cornelius (D)
	Woodrum, James (H)	Campbell, John A. to	Read, Philip (B)	Smothers, Wm (D)
	Hundley, James (K)	accept promotion (K)	Hundrix, William (D)	Goodman, Wm. (I)
	Kanleahy, Dennis (K)	Fox, James (K)	Clayton, Francis (G)	
	Garrison, John C. (Staff)		Linton, John (G)	
			Harshfield, Achilles (F)	
Died			Hardesty, Chas. (Staff)	Powers, Fran. (G)

	May	*June*	*July*	*August*
Deserted				
	Casabon, Oliver (A)	Mitchell, Jefferson (B)		
	Lawson, William (I)	Farmer, Thomas (H)		
Resigned				
	Reynolds, James (A)			

(Letters in parentheses indicate the company of the individual.)

FOUR

Chickamauga

"The fighting here was most terrific and bloody."—Major Henry G. Davidson, 10th Kentucky

The Army of the Cumberland was pursuing Bragg, and the strategic point for both armies was Chattanooga. Chattanooga was a railway hub and transportation center that controlled supplies and communication from Tennessee into Georgia. If this city fell into Union hands, then the Union Army could choose several different and vital areas of the South to attack.

As General Rosecrans concentrated his efforts on Chattanooga, it was vital for him to insure that he could supply his army. Much of his efforts in July and early August focused on stockpiling supplies and insuring an effective rail system for his army's needs. General Rosecrans had six objectives, as he pursued Bragg's army, designed to confuse the Southern Army as to his intentions: (a) he wanted to be sure that Bragg did not know where his army was located, (b) he wanted to repair the Nashville-Chattanooga Railroad without drawing the attention of the Confederates, (c) he wanted to disperse rations and establish a supply depot at Stevenson, Alabama, (d) he wanted to ensure that a bridge was established over the Tennessee River at Stevenson, (e) he waited until the corn was mature enough for consumption by the horses and (f) when the Army of the Cumberland crossed the Tennessee, Rosecrans wanted to maneuver Bragg away from Chattanooga.

The pressure was on Bragg in light of the Confederate defeats at Vicksburg and Gettysburg in July. The Southern Army needed a victory. Likewise, if the Union Army could defeat Bragg, this would be a devastating loss for the South and could signal that the war would soon be over.

For the rank and file of the Army of the Cumberland, life slowly moved forward. It appears that some of the officers of the 10th Kentucky had time to socialize with the southern ladies of Tennessee. In a letter that Captain Seth Bevill wrote, he states that "Col Hays finds some very attractive rebel ladies in Winchester, he goes there frequently."[1]

On August 12, 1863, the 10th Kentucky was located at Camp Thomas near Winchester, Tennessee. The time to move against Bragg was at hand, but the men were unsure of how this attack would proceeded. Captain Bevill wrote:

> We are under marching orders. Will certainly march tomorrow or the next day. Where I cannot tell, though the general impression is that we go in the direction of Bridgeport, AL, which is the point at which the Memphis and Charleston R. R. crosses the Tennessee River. General impressions in regard to the destination our army are as apt to be wrong as right. We are certainly going somewhere in two or three days and when we get there I can tell you with more certainty where we are....
>
> Genl Rosecrans reviewed our Division today. It is the first time many of us have seen him. I would have known him from the photographs I have seen of him, though he is rather heavier made than I had supposed. And is very pleasant in his manner. Genl McCook accompanied him, also Genl Jeff C Davis. These Genls and their staff, together with Genl Brannan (our commander) and his staff presented quite an imposing appearance."[2]

Advance at Chickamauga: Bragg attacks the Union Army in north Georgia (Library of Congress).

The Union Moves on Bragg

On August 15, the Army of the Cumberland was on the move. General Rosecrans did, in fact, split his army while moving toward Chattanooga. General Thomas directed General Joseph Reynolds and General John Brannan to take their 4th and 3rd Divisions down the Battle Creek Valley and begin crossing the Tennessee River. The other corps of the army moved by various routes toward their objectives.

General Brannan's division chopped down trees and made rafts to cross the Tennessee River. The 10th Kentucky advanced to the mouth of Battle Creek and their division began crossing the river on August 31, by swimming and using rafts. The unfortunate Private Patrick Mayland of Company K of the 10th Kentucky drowned on September 1, 1863, during the crossing.[3] But, the Union Army was able to surprise Bragg, and by September 9, the Confederate Army had abandoned Chattanooga. General Rosecrans believed that Bragg was retreating towards Rome, Georgia, and decided to pursue the rebel army. But as the days went by, and as the Army of the Cumberland pushed farther south and east of Chattanooga, the rebel resistance began to intensify. The general withdrawal toward Rome, Georgia, was slowing down. As it began to appear that a general engagement might take place, Rosecrans had the challenge of unifying his army, which was scattered in the mountains south of Chattanooga.

Major Henry Davidson, who was on leave in August, picked up the movements of the 10th Kentucky after leaving Winchester:

> I found my regiment about twelve miles above Bridgeport, Ala. on the Tennessee River on the first day of September. Our Division (the 3rd Division, 14th Army Corps) crossed the Tennessee, on rafts, constructed by our own men. A few days after we commenced crossing the

mountains, on the 14th of the month, we were in Lookout Valley, fourteen miles from Chattanooga completely flanking the enemy. While we were here Bragg evacuated the place, and right here, Gen Rosecrans committed his first error, instead of marching his army to Chattanooga, taking possession, & making it a base of operations, he divided his forces and went in pursuit of the enemy.[4]

The final movements that would ultimately become the Battle of Chickamauga began on September 9, 1863. General Rosecrans came to believe that the Confederates, demoralized, were retreating deep into Georgia. He was determined that his army would launch a general pursuit of Bragg and strike the Confederate Army before they slipped away. He ordered General McCook's 20th Corps, the southernmost corps of the Union Army, to proceed to the east and attack the flank of Bragg's Army. Thomas's 14th Corps was to cross the mountains near McLemore's Cove to attack Bragg's main force. McLemore's Cove lay just west of Pigeon Mountain and east of Lookout Mountain. The mobility within the area was limited and Bragg quickly realized that he could strike Thomas' divisions as they entered this valley with a superior Confederate force. Bragg developed a plan to attack Thomas' isolated divisions with strong forces under the command of General Pat Cleburne and General Thomas Hindman. As General James Negley's Division of the 14th Union Corps entered McLemore's Cove on September 10, the Confederate plan called for an attack on Negley's isolated division, but it did not occur because Hindman's forces were not in position to attack. Only Cleburne's troops were in place. The order on September 11 was again to attack the 14th Corps, which now included General Absalom Baird's Davison, which had joined Negley's.

General Thomas became aware that he was facing a strong Confederate force and ordered his remaining two divisions, Reynolds' and Brannan's, which included the 10th Kentucky, to join Negley and Baird. Before these divisions could reach them, Thomas withdrew his forces from the Confederate trap. It was clear that General Bragg and his commanders had decided that it was time to take the initiative after being pushed southward for the past year. The 10th Kentucky's march to join Negley and Baird began at 12:30 A.M. on September 12 and ended at noon. After resting for two hours they were marched another two miles to go into a defensive line to prepare for an anticipated attack.

As the Union forces scrambled to unite, Bragg planned to cut Rosecrans from Chattanooga by massing his army to the north and east of the Union forces. But the Union commanders became aware of this move on September 17 and moved to face the threat on the left flank, and support was thrown to the left of the army. Bragg felt that he was better positioned and could engage Rosecrans' left flank with a superior force with General John Pegram's, General Thomas Hindman's, General Benjamin Cheatham's and General William Walker's divisions.

Major Henry G. Davidson gave an account of the 10th Kentucky at Chickamauga in a letter (U.S. Army Military History Institute).

Battle of Chickamauga

The Battle of Chickamauga began on September 18 when Colonel Robert Minty's 1st Brigade cavalry (General George Crook's 2nd Division) engaged General Nathan B. Forrest's Confederate cavalry. This resulted in a request for reinforcements, as the Union cavalry saw the long lines of General H. T. Walker's Division of Confederates. Colonel Minty's cavalry and the Chicago Board of Trade artillery held the Confederate advance until mid afternoon. But at 3:00 P.M., the Confederates had moved to the west side of the Chickamauga Creek.[5]

Meanwhile, Colonel John T. Wilder's 1st Brigade (14th Corps, 4th Division) engaged Brigadier General St. John Liddell's brigades commanded by Colonel Daniel Govan and Colonel Edward Walthall at Alexander's Bridge south of Minty's position.[6]

Colonel Dan McCook, commanding the 2nd Brigade in the 2nd Division of Major General Gordon Granger's Corps, captured some Confederates on the evening of September 18. He concluded, erroneously, that a Confederate brigade was cut off and trapped on the west side of the Chickamauga Creek, and he dispatched his men to burn Reed's Bridge. Then he prepared to gobble up the brigade with a morning attack. The 14th Corps began arriving on the left side of the line on the evening of September 18 and General Rosecrans ordered McCook to withdraw. But before withdrawing, Colonel McCook told General Thomas and Colonel John Croxton about the alleged trapped Confederate brigade.[7]

During the evening of September 18, 1863, Confederate Brig. General H. B. Davidson's brigade of cavalry took up the position where the marooned brigade was supposed to be. A surprise was in store for the units that attacked the next morning.

THE TENTH KENTUCKY INFANTRY AT THE BATTLE OF CHICKAMAUGA

For two days in September 1863, the mettle of the 10th Kentucky would be tested and all their training during the past two years would be needed to survive the fury yet to come. The 10th Kentucky had done extensive marching up to this point in the war, but they had never participated in a hard-fought struggle with the enemy. Their time had come.

Organization of the Army of the Cumberland in September 1863

Fourteenth Army Corps—Major General George H. Thomas.
Third Division—Brig. General John M. Brannan.
  Second Brigade—Colonel John Croxton.
    10th Kentucky—Col. William H. Hays.
    4th Kentucky Volunteer Infantry—Lieut. Col. P. Burgess Hunt.
    14th Ohio Volunteer Infantry—Lieut. Col. Henry D. Kingsbury.
    10th Indiana Volunteer Infantry—Col. William B. Carroll.
    74th Indiana Volunteer Infantry—Col. Myron Baker.

General John Brannan guided his regiment through two days of fierce combat at Chickamauga (U.S. Army Military History Institute).

The 2nd Brigade of the 3rd Division of the 14th Corps was one of the first engaged in the Battle of Chickamauga on Saturday, September 19, 1863, and would have extensive combat throughout the next two days. The result was significant losses in number of men wounded, missing or killed. In fact, the 2nd Brigade lost 938 men over the 3 day battle, one of the highest percentage losses in the Union Army for this battle.

General Thomas ordered General John Brannan to advance and put the Union Army in an attack posture just as Bragg was trying to seize that initiative himself. John Milton Brannan was West Point graduate in the class of 1841 and his experience was in artillery. He was originally from the District of Columbia and was residing in Indiana before the war and he now commanded the 3rd Division for General Thomas.[8]

The first day of combat for the 10th Kentucky would be a full blown battle with the forces of Nathan Bedford Forrest's cavalry and Walker's corps of infantry. It was the 2nd Brigade, 10th Kentucky, and four sister regiments that were called to action while preparing for breakfast on the 19th at approximately 7:00 A.M. when they received orders to move against the perceived, lone Confederate brigade. Captain I. B. Webster, Company I, describes the call-to-arms for the 10th Kentucky:

> At break of day, Sept. 19, 1863, the order came down the line "Halt! Close up: stack arms and prepare and eat breakfast as rapidly as possible." This was the morning succeeding the memorable night of September 18, during a great part of which the whole heavens were lighted up by the fires kindled along the line of march. The halt was made near a running brook, and in a very short space of time many little fires were burning, around each of which were gathered small groups of men eagerly watching the coffee boiling while they toasted slices of bacon on the end of a stick.
>
> Just at this inopportune moment, Boom! Boom!! Boom!!! Came the sound of cannon from the direction in which we had been marching, and at no great distance from us.[9]

The 2nd Brigade had marched into the night during the evening of the 18th to be properly positioned the next morning. The 10th Kentucky began its march at 5 P.M. on September 18 and arrived a few minutes before it was marched quickly into battle down a farmer's lane mistaken for Reed's Bridge Road. The men of the 10th Kentucky, tired and hungry, grabbed whatever they found to eat on their way to the Confederate army. The lane on which the brigade marched actually paralleled the intended route. The 4th Kentucky was deployed on the left, the 10th Indiana took the center and the 74th Indiana was positioned on the right. The 10th Kentucky and the 14th Ohio followed as the reserve units. The 10th Indiana provided skirmishers. The 2nd Brigade had mustered a total effective force of 2164 men, excluding artillery going into the morning of September 19.[10]

Captain I. B. Webster's accounts shows that the brigade was still expecting to easily capture a Confederate brigade, but was quickly in for a surprise of their own:

> We had not far to go to find the enemy. The Major of our regiment [Davidson] rode down the line, and in a confidential manner said to me: "Captain, we have a soft snap here. A rebel brigade has crossed the creek to this side and our forces have destroyed the bridge behind them, and we are going to gobble them up." With that he rode off. Company A (Capt. Charles W. McKay), 10th Ky., was sent to the front after our line of battle had been formed, and deployed as skirmishers to cover the front of the 10th Ky. and 14th Ohio. Company A was not out very long before it was forced back to us in a hurry; and to use Capt. McKay's expression when asked the why of his sudden return, "It was too hot out there."
>
> Here to this time and at this place fell the first soldier [of the regiment], mortally wounded. His name was [Daniel] Stewart, a private in Company D. His arms went up, his gun flew far from him, and he fell in his place with a death wound in his groin."[11]

The skirmish line found the Confederate units ahead. The skirmishers quickly hurried back to their lines followed closely by their quarry, which was none other than Nathan Bedford Forrest's Confederate Cavalry commanded by General H. B. Davidson. Davidson's command was made up of five regiments and a contingent of artillery. The cavalry was stopped and sent scampering back toward its lines by a volley from the 10th Indiana. Then skirmishers were re-deployed and the advance continued.[12]

Croxton's brigade engaged the 6th Georgia, 10th Confederate Legion and 1st Tennessee Legion, and threw them into confusion by striking the left side of the Confederate line. General Nathan Forrest and General John Pegram, along with the officers of the Confederate Cavalry, restored their line after the 2nd Brigade attacked. Forrest formed a line of resistance and the 2nd Brigade's advance was halted; and, then, it was Forrest who sent an urgent plea for assistance.[13]

Colonel John Croxton was a very able commander of the second brigade. Although he had fairly recently assumed command of the 2nd Brigade after John Harlan's resignation in March, he was well respected by the corps commander. Croxton was the son of farmer in Paris, Kentucky, and had graduated from Yale in 1857. Like Harlan, Hays and Wharton, he also was a lawyer.

Croxton sent word to General Brannan of the increasing number of Confederate troops that he was facing and Brannan responded by dispatching Colonel Ferdinand Van Derveer's 3rd Brigade forward to support Croxton's brigade. Van Derveer's 3rd Brigade was made up of the 9th Ohio, 35th Ohio, 2nd Minnesota and 87th Indiana Infantry. The 10th Kentucky during this time was still in a reserve role along with the 14th Ohio. It was quickly learned that "instead of confronting an isolated brigade, Croxton was facing two strongly posted Confederate divisions."[14] Croxton's brigade continued to hotly exchange volleys with the Confederate cavalry to their front.

10th Kentucky at Chickamauga, Morning, September 19, 1863 (original map adapted from *This Terrible Sound: The Battle of Chickamauga*, copyright 1992 Board of Trustees. Used with permission of the author and the University of Illinois Press).

The request for assistance from Forrest resulted in Colonel Claudius Wilson's brigade (25th, 29th, 30th Georgia regiments and the 4th Louisiana Battalion with the 1st Georgia Sharpshooters) from Major General William H. Walker's Division and Colonel George Dibrell's Tennessee brigade (4th, 8th, 9th, 10th and 11th Tennessee Cavalry) part of Forest's Cavalry, being sent toward the action. At 9:00 A.M., Dibrell threw his troops into battle line and deployed them into a line that extended far beyond Croxton's left. Dibrell's position caused Croxton to deploy the 10th Kentucky to the left of the 4th Kentucky to meet the new Confederate assault. The 14th Ohio was sent to the right of the 74th Indiana.[15]

As the 10th Kentucky was deployed to the left flank of Croxton's brigade, it was slammed by George Dibrell's Confederates, who fired a volley into the defenders with the greatest losses occurring in Company B and Company K. As Hays took up his defensive position, the Confederates caused heavy losses in the 10th Kentucky, but the 10th Kentucky gave as good as they received, stiffly holding their line.

This was the first major conflict for the 10th Kentucky and the disposition of men became apparent, particularly that of the regimental Colonel, William Hays. His personality on the field was to fight. Hays, immediately faced with angry Confederates attacking his left, responded by ordering the first of two bayonet charges of the day for the 10th Kentucky. "Seeing the enemy about to turn my left flank, I ordered a charge and drove them in confusion some 200 yards, when I was compelled to fall back to the crest of the hill originally occupied by me," he wrote.[16]

Captain Israel Webster described the situation that the 10th Kentucky was facing before Colonel Hays' charge into Dibrell's troops:

Colonel John Croxton was a very able commander of the 2nd Brigade and had previously commanded the 4th Kentucky Infantry (Library of Congress).

Just at his time Capt. [John T.] Milburn of Company B (extreme left company) notified Col. [William H.] Hays that a large force was approaching our left flank at exactly right angles to us. The orders to "Left face, forward; double-quick, file left," came in rapid secession, and away we went to meet the new attack. This for the enemy detected our move to change front and poured a heavy volley into our left, which those two companies caught. We hustled the "Confeds" away from there, and then took our wounded off the field. We had no time to care for the dead because of the advance of the enemy upon what at first was our right, but just then was our rear.[17]

Major Henry Davidson described the actions of the morning: "The whole brigade stood like a solid wall, and although many a gallant spirit fell, we drove the enemy back not only holding our ground but advancing upon and occupying theirs."[18]

Intense fighting took place in the dense woods. According to Colonel Hays, "We met the enemy in force and had a hotly contested fight, Company B alone, of my regiment, losing in one hour 20 men killed or wounded."[19] During this battle Sgt. James Ewing, Company D, received two wounds, so hotly was the battle occurring, one in his side and the other in his arm. Seeing Ewing's injuries, Lt. Colonel Gabriel Wharton quickly jumped off his horse and allowed Ewing to be carried to the rear on his horse.

But Dibrell's men were no match for Croxton's infantry. Dibrell then tried to flank Croxton and find his rear, but in this attempt, he withdrew and ran directly into Van Derveer's brigade hurrying in support. This clash occurred about 400 yards to the left and rear of the 10th Kentucky. Also, Brannan, through Colonel John Connell, wisely positioned the 31st Ohio in the rear of the 2nd Brigade should assistance be required.

When Dibrell ran into Van Derveer's units, Croxton was then able to turn his attention to the units in his front, those of General H. B. Davidson. As the second Brigade pushed forward, Davidson's' cavalry was pushed off their ridge three times, only to return. Over one-third of Davidson's brigade was lost, killed or wounded in this defense. Forest desired to hold the 2nd Brigade in check until Colonel Claudius Wilson's infantry reinforcements could take over.[20]

Shortly after 9:00 A.M., Colonel Claudius Wilson's Georgia infantry brigade moved across Brotherton Road toward Croxton's right. Wilson's infantry struck Croxton's right flank less than 100 yards way. The undergrowth was so dense it was impossible to see other units in the vicinity. Wilson's infantry had immediate success and the right side of the line was thrown back toward Lafayette Road.[21]

To counter this move the 10th Kentucky was moved at double quick time from the left to the right to quickly meet the new challenge. Their volley into Wilson's Georgia infantry momentarily stopped the Georgians. The 74th Indiana quickly reformed and moved to the right of the 10th Kentucky. Croxton, realizing the immediate threat was from Wilson's infantry, disengaged the brigade from Davidson's cavalry and turned to meet Wilson's five regiments. But after three hours of continuous fighting, Croxton's brigade began to slowly fall back under the pressure of the new Georgia regiments. The brigade was forced back about 400 yards. This was approximately 10:30 A.M. and the 2nd Brigade had been fighting most of the morning with Forest's cavalry and now with Wilson's infantry, and their ammunition was all but depleted. Colonel William Carroll, 10th Indiana Infantry, was mortally wounded and left behind as the line moved backward.

During this conflict, Dr. Charles Stocking, the 10th Kentucky regimental surgeon, very nearly lost his life. He was spotted by Company I treating a wounded soldier after the 10th Kentucky had moved to his rear. He later said that he was not thinking of anything except caring for the wounded soldier; he was able to make a narrow escape.[22]

Colonel George Dibrell commanded the Confederate attack on the left flank of the 10th Kentucky on the morning of September 19, 1863, at Chickamauga (Library of Congress).

Colonel John Croxton, though heavily engaged, did not lose his sense of humor. It is often quoted that Croxton now sent word to Thomas asking him which of the four or five brigades he faced was he supposed to capture.

The increased firing convinced Thomas that a major situation was developing and as a result he sent Absalom Baird's 1st Division, 14th Army Corps, to relieve Croxton's 2nd Brigade. Baird's division not only relieved Croxton but also positioned his units to take Wilson in his left flank. Brannan sent the 31st Ohio forward from its reserve position to support Croxton. The 31st was inserted on the right of Croxton's line—to the right of the 74th Indiana. Croxton was running out of ammunition when help began to arrive in the form of Brigadier General John King's regular army brigade (15th, 16th, 18th, and 19th U.S. Infantry Battalions). Next came Colonel Benjamin Scribner's 1st Division, 1st Brigade, striking Claudius Wilson in the left flank. General John Starkweather's 1st Division, 2nd Brigade, acted in reserve behind King and Scribner.[23]

Thomas's relief for Croxton arrived with not a moment to spare. General John King's regular U.S. Army Brigade arrived behind Croxton's brigade. The First Battalion, U.S. Infantry, conducted one of the most difficult maneuvers on a battlefield when it filed through the right side of Croxton's line and opened up on Wilson's Georgians. Scribner and Starkweather's brigades allowed Croxton's brigade to fall back to replenish their ammunition. At approximately 11:00 A.M., the 2nd Brigade had been in action for over four hours, but the day was not over for the 10th Kentucky and the rest of the 2nd Brigade.

Colonel Benjamin Scribner's 1st Division, 1st Brigade, took Wilson's Georgians in the left flank, but he was prevented from decimating the Confederates for fear of firing into their own men. Scribner's position on Wilson's left and King in his front made Wilson's position untenable, and he withdrew across Jay's Mill Road with nearly half his men dead or wounded on the field. The morning, so far, was costly indeed for both sides and both armies fell silent and were glad for the moment to disengage.

Croxton's brigade withdrew to rest and replenish their ammunition after being in the line since early morning. General John King, Colonel Starkweather and Colonel Scribner of Absalom Baird's Division had dealt with Wilson's Brigade, which fell back toward Jay's Mill Road, but Wilson's men were soon to be replaced with two brigades—one of Arkansasians commanded by Colonel Daniel Govan and General Edward Walthall's Mississippians—all part of Brigadier General St. John Liddell's division in General William Walker's corps. The 10 regiments of Confederates in a battle formation crossed the Brotherton Road to strike Scribner's four right regiments. A desperate and bloody struggle ensued but the Southern units began to roll up the Union regiments one by one. Walthall and Govan rolled over Scribner, Starkweather and King.[24]

As these fresh Confederate brigades pushed steadily forward, they were soon to be halted by a stout Union defense. Colonel Ferdinand Van Derveer's 3rd Brigade and Colonel John Connell's 1st Brigade were ready for Walthall and Govan's Confederates and opened a volley into them at 40 yards, which stopped the advance. Again, a desperate battle took place.

To stem the success of Colonel Edward Walthall and Colonel Daniel Govan, Croxton's 2nd Brigade, freshly re-supplied, was, again, ordered back into the fray. Croxton now had control of six regiments, including the 31st Ohio. He ordered them into battle line and exchanged fire with Arkansas regiments for about 30 minutes. Croxton had divided control of the brigade, with Colonel Chapman of the 74th Indiana being in charge of one half. The line going into battle was, from left to right, 14th Ohio, 4th Kentucky, 74th Indiana, 10th Indiana, 10th Kentucky, and 31st Ohio.

While Govan was preparing a charge into the 2nd Brigade, the 2nd Brigade made a charge of its own. Having success earlier in the day in repulsing Dibrell's Confederates, Colonel William Hays returned to the tactic that worked so well earlier that morning. According to Hays, "Finding the enemy very stubborn, my men being shot in large numbers, and seeing what I supposed to be a battery of artillery in post ahead of me, I ordered a bayonet charge, which was received with loud cheers by my men; the Tenth Indiana and Thirty-First Ohio both came gallantly to my assistance, and we completely routed the rebels."[25]

Major Henry Davidson wrote of action:

> He [Col. Hays] ordered a bayonet charge, which was performed in a style never surpassed and scarcely ever equaled, there three Regiments, charged, Walker's whole Division of rebel Arkansasians and Mississippians, driving them in the wildest confusion, actually running clear through their lines, capturing many prisoners, and light pieces of artillery. One piece was dismounted, and had to be left in the field. All the artillery horses but one had been killed, forming a line of battle to meet the enemy who had been rallied and were advancing upon us evidently determined to retake their cannon. We determine to keep them or die. A detail was made from each regiment and they went to work with a will, and carried every piece off the field by hand. The fighting here was most terrific and bloody, our loss was very heavy at this time.[26]

CSA Colonel Govan reported in his after action summary: "A heavy column of the enemy moved on my left flank. The left regiment, according to my instructions, changed front so as to meet it, while the other regiments of the brigade engaged him in front. The overwhelming force which attacked my left flank and had gained my rear forced me to retire."[27]

Brannan's counterattack with Croxton resulted in the capture of the ground taken by Walthall and Govan and also the recapture of Baird's artillery lost earlier. Govan's Arkansas regiment was beaten and "broke in confusion" a few minutes before noon. The fighting again paused in this area of the field and the 10th Kentucky was eventually withdrawn from the line to re-supply, rest and reorganize.

New Union units moved forward to man the line where the morning's battle had taken place. By 2:30 P.M., Brannan's division was stationed along the north of the battlefield along Alexander Bridge Road to rest and re-supply. At 4:00 P.M. Major General Alexander Stewart's Division had success penetrating the center of Rosecrans' line, and Brannan's division was moved to support and positioned itself for the upcoming events on the 20th.

By no means was the Battle of Chickamauga, on September 19, isolated to the area where the 10th Kentucky Infantry was located. The morning battle began with the units in the northern part of the battlefield and worked south throughout the day. The afternoon battles were savage. The next phase included the Union division commanded by General Richard Johnson of Dan McCook's 20th Corps, and his Confederate adversary, General Benjamin Cheatham. As Johnson was advancing, completing the attack on Walthall and Govan, Cheatham slammed in his troops. The battle continued as fresh troops from both sides advanced into the battle until mid-afternoon, when the Southern forces had success pushing back the center of the Union line. As Bragg's army was pushing back the Union line, the 10th Kentucky was again ordered to move in anticipation of further fighting in the afternoon, but no further action was in store for the regiment.

Colonel Hays described his afternoon: "Upon being relieved I fell back as ordered about one-half mile in a southwesterly direction and rested until 4:00 P.M., when I received an order to march with the brigade. We proceeded in a southwest course until we struck the main Georgia State road, near which we took a position about 3 miles from the first position occupied by the regiment. Here we remained quiet until dark, when, by order of Colonel John T. Croxton, I moved my men to the rear three-quarters of a mile and camped for the night."[28] The afternoon movement of the division was important in halting the Confederate advance and stabilizing the Union line at the close of the day.

Major Henry Davidson summarized September 19 for the 10th Kentucky:

"The rebels attacked us again, and again without success, for the last two hours Gen Thomas was with us in person—at 2 o'clock P.M. we were relieved by Gen Johnson's division having fought, seven hours, without rest. You can judge how hard we fought, when I tell you that one hundred and twenty one of the brave men of my regiment were either killed, or wounded, a terrible-terrible thing, but the enemy had suffered far more than we had."[29] Records show that Captain Franklin Hill was injured in his hand but remained with the regiment. Captain James Davenport was shot in the right leg and Captain John Milburn was also wounded during the day's fighting.

The end of the first full day of fighting at Chickamauga was described by the *New York Times*:

> That was indeed a night of awful suspense which settled around us [after] the last gun had been fired on Saturday. It was very chilly and cold, and much suffering amongst the wounded was occasioned thereby. Those who were still alive and well, although they too were exposed to the numbing cold, thought but little of their physical condition. True, no warm fires kept the influence of the frost from their limbs, for fires were strictly forbidden. No blazing light helped to cheer their minds, and dispel gloomy images therefrom. But still, as they sank down in the darkness upon the hard, cold ground, they entirely forgot their bodily deprivations as they strove to imagine what might be the result to themselves, the country and the cause, of the gigantic struggle which might ensue on the morrow.[30]

The evening of the 19th of September had two armies facing each other along a north-south line along Lafayette Road. Rosecrans' strategy for the next day was defense, believing that he was outnumbered and deep in enemy territory. While both armies had battered themselves into a standstill, the Union Army was prepared to face the assault that was sure to come the next morning.

Day Three of the Battle

The day began early on Sunday, September 20, for the 10th Kentucky. Captain I. B. Webster described it: "At 3 o'clock am Sept 20 we were aroused, ordered into line and soon took up the march, destined we knew not where nor for what. However, we did not travel far until a line of battle was formed. Everything was shrouded in darkness. The morning air was cold, and the grass and foliage damp with the heavy dew of night, causing great discomfort. Fires were not allowed, and very few of us had blankets and none had overcoats. From that time until daylight seemed very long and felt very uncomfortable."[31]

During the early morning, the 10th Kentucky and Croxton's brigade were moved into the battle line just to the west of Lafayette Road about a quarter mile north of the Brotherton House. The Confederates began a general attack of the Union line around 9:00 A.M. on September 20. Confederate Major General Pat Cleburne's and Major General A. P. Stewart's attack was repulsed. The 10th and 74th Indiana infantries were in the primary battle line and fought back the Confederate attack by General John C. Brown's five Tennessee units: the 18th and 23rd battalions, 26th, 32nd, and 45th regiments. The 10th Kentucky, 4th Kentucky and 14th Ohio formed the reserve line on the morning of September 20, and even though they were not involved in the battle along the primary battle, they suffered from the secondary affects.

Captain Webster wrote of that morning's action: "Several of our men got shot in the top of the shoulder as they lay hugging close down in the little ravine with their heads toward the front and their heels high up on the other side of the ravine. Some got shot in the leg as they thus lay. All we could do was closely embrace Mother Earth and wish the enemy would quit throwing such ugly things at us."[32]

Forming the battle line south of Croxton's Brigade were four brigades of the 21st Army Corps command by General Thomas Wood. Immediately north of those brigades was Brannan's 1st Division, 1st Brigade, commanded by Colonel John Connell, then Croxton's brigade, and then next were Colonel Edward King's 2nd Brigade, and General John Turchin's 3rd brigade from Major General Joseph Reynolds' 4th Division. These were followed by General William Hazen's 2nd Brigade and General Charles Cruft's 1st Brigade, both under the command of General John Palmer.

One of the most important events in the Battle of Chickamauga was the controversial movement of General Wood's division out of the Union line from 10:30 to 11:00 A.M. By General Rosecrans' order, General Thomas Wood pulled his four brigades out of line just as nearly 11,000 Confederate soldiers received the order to advance against that same section. It has been estimated that the gap in the Union line was 500 yards wide. Wave after wave of Confederates poured through the Union line on the right and Croxton's 2nd Brigade had the misfortune to be only one brigade removed from this massive hole through which thousands of enemy troops streamed. All along the southern part of the Union line, the defenders were thrown back in confusion.

Colonel William Hays wrote, "The battle opened on our front about 9:00 A.M. and continued until about 10:30 or 11:00."[33] The 10th Indiana and 74th Indiana were in the Union line facing east throughout the morning while the 10th Kentucky, 4th Kentucky and 14th Ohio were in reserve positions. The two Indiana regiments were involved with the early engagements with the enemy that morning. Colonel Hays said that as the Confederates stormed through the resulting hole, "when the troops on our right gave way the enemy completely [flanked] us on the right in a large force. I immediately formed my regiment by filing to the right on a line perpendicular to the one just occupied, but held this position but a few minutes."[34]

Brannan, on Wood's left, was struck in front and flank. His right was thrown back; his left remained in position. Brannan said "the rebels took advantage of with great rapidity, intercepting and breaking the line of battle of the army at that point."[35] North of the gap, Brannan's division found itself assaulted in the flank and rear but resisted stoutly for a time before giving way and joining the rapidly developing rout. Major Henry Davidson explained the situation as the Confederates swarmed through the line: "We held our ground manfully, at this time, a Division to our right was moved to the left, leaving a gap between us and McCook's Corps, the enemy taking advantage of this forced us to change our position, and fall back."[36]

Colonel John Connell commanded the doomed position adjacent to the north of the hole vacated by Wood. He saw what was happening and sent word to Brannan. The sheer force of the Confederate breakthrough and the confusion that resulted from Connell attempting to shift his front led to the inevitable. As the battle heated up, the 10th Kentucky was moved into a primary firing position in the front line and stood behind a wooden fence. Brannan ordered Croxton to pull in his right flank and the 10th Kentucky filed to the right side of the 1st Ohio Light Artillery. The 4th Kentucky and 14th Ohio were positioned to the left of the battery. Captain Webster was in the middle of the fight and described the effort to stem the flow of Confederates:

> It appeared that by some means the rail and log breastworks had caught fire, and before we could advance any distance the fire was under good headway, and we were forced to fall back to prevent being burned up or suffocated by the smoke. Our line was halted in due time, and the enemy had not yet passed the breastworks when we felt an enfilading fire from our right rear. Our attention was called in that direction, and we saw coming through a cornfield a large body of men marching in good form in line of battle with colors flying, apparently unconcerned as though passing in review. The word was passed down the line that the colors were Gen. McCook's battleflag. We were ready to believe this as, they were just in the rear of

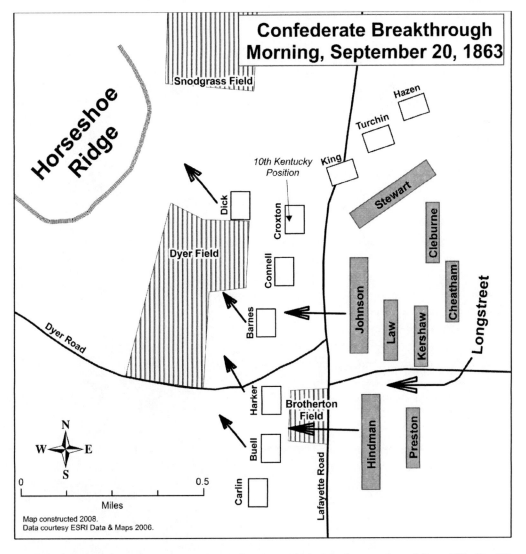

Confederate Breakthrough, Morning, September 20, 1863 (original map adapted from *This Terrible Sound: The Battle of Chickamauga*, copyright 1992 Board of Trustees. Used with permission of the author and the University of Illinois Press).

our line, and only a few moments before Gen. Baird had ridden up to and instructed one of our commanders to remain where they were and not change our position. His words were "Not yet; not yet.... One of my company turned around and responded very promptly, "Captain, they are shooting at us." I then told them to give to them thick and fast....

I found the forces of the enemy were fast getting into our rear, turning our right flank and doubling us up like an elbow, shortening the angle at every moment, thus enabling them to fire upon us from three directions. We were nearly annihilated when instructed to "come out of that," which we lost no time in doing. Our loss here was considerable, Capt Seth Bevill of Company E, 10th Ky, received a mortal wound from which he died [on September 21]. Second Lieut. John H Myers, Company I, was killed instantly and several others were killed.[37]

Croxton's Brigade tried to stem the flow of the Confederate attack, but they were in an indefensible position. They were now the extreme right of the broken Union line and without support on their right flank, which the Confederates were exploiting. Their defense could not last for long. Colonel James Sheffield's and General Henry Benning's Confederate brigades streamed through the ever-widening hole. Colonel Croxton was posted on the right when Benning attacked the line. The 2nd Brigade loosed a volley into Benning's Georgians (2nd, 15th, 17th, 20th regiments). Benning had closed to 40 yards when Croxton was shot in the leg. Facing Benning and Sheffield and being flanked, the brigade split in two. The 10th Kentucky retreated along with the 14th Ohio and 4th Kentucky. The 10th and 74th Indiana were led to the General Reynolds' line by Lt. Colonel Marsh Taylor, where they remained throughout the day.[38]

When Croxton was wounded, command was passed to Colonel William Hays for what remained of the 2nd Brigade. Colonel Hays tried to hold the brigade together without success. The collapse on Thomas's right was complete by 11:45 A.M. Colonel Hays wrote, "We were overwhelmed by numbers, and the enemy continued to flank us. Our loss at this point was very great. It was here that the gallant Captain Bevill fell mortally wounded. Colonel John T. Croxton, our brigade commander, was wounded at the same time. I then moved the regiment to the left, near the house on the hill, Colonel Croxton's wounds not permitting him to remain on the field, I took command of the brigade, and Lieutenant-Colonel Wharton took command of the regiment."[39]

General Brannan described the events occurring near Lafayette road at 11:00 A.M. "Wood being taken while marching by flank, broke and fled in confusion and my line actually attacked from the rear, was obliged to swing back on the right, which it accomplished with wonderful regularity under such circumstances (with, however, the exception of a portion of the First Brigade, which, being much exposed, broke with considerable disorder)."[40]

Colonel William H. Hays ordered two bayonet charges on the morning of September 19 (Blue Acorn Press, Huntington, West Virginia).

Having the ability to shoot from three directions into the 10th Kentucky, the attacking Confederates had an ideal situation for picking off their primary targets—officers. The 10th Kentucky suffered greatly from Confederate musket fire; as many a six officers were wounded in just a few minutes, including Lieutenant John Myers, Company I, and Captain Bevill of Company E, who was mortally wounded.[41] In addition, Lieutenant William Beglow was wounded in the left thigh and removed from the field.[42] Lieutenant Benjamin R. Smith was wounded in the left foot.[43] Lieutenant Henry Warren, with a gunshot to his left ankle that shattered the bone, was removed from the field.[44] Lieutenant James Sallee was also wounded.[45]

General Brannan was now faced with trying to reorganize what was left of his Division: "The line being now broken, and severely pressed at this point, and great confusion prevailing in the supports. I formed the remnant of my command.... in line to resist, if possible, the pressure of the now advancing rebels."[46]

Colonel Henry Kingsbury of the 14th Ohio described the event: "We were in this position when the line on our right was turned, and held the position until the right was so far driven back that the enemy held position in our rear, and were forced to retire." [47] What remained of the three regiments of Croxton's brigade fell back to a wood on elevated ridges about a half mile from their original battle line. General Brannan began organizing a second line of defense on what was to be named Horseshoe Ridge. The 10th Kentucky with the 14th Ohio and about 45 men of the 4th Kentucky would spend the next 5 to 6 hours on this hill. The defense of Horseshoe Ridge and Snodgrass Farm would become one of the legendary defenses of the Civil War. Regardless of the confusion and the great opportunities given and taken by both sides, the Army of the Cumberland refused to be destroyed and fought admirably under the control of General Thomas. This six-hour period led to Thomas' nickname "the Rock of Chickamauga." General Thomas established a defense around the Snodgrass homestead with the units he could find to form a line.

To the south of the Snodgrass homestead was a group of three hills, Horseshoe Ridge, which formed the southern defense of Thomas's line. Units were thrown into position to prepare to meet the Confederate Army. While the defense around the Snodgrass farm was being formed, General William Rosecrans returned to Chattanooga and left this area under General Thomas' control. By 12:45 P.M. the initial Union defenses around the Snodgrass farm were set.

After retreating, the 10th Kentucky, along with fragments of the 4th Kentucky and 14th Ohio, formed a line on Hill Two of Horseshoe Ridge. They were ordered to hold the enemy at all costs. Before September 19, the 10th Kentucky had fired very few volleys in anger at the Confederates, and in past two days they had faced legends of the Southern Army, including General Nathan Bedford Forrest and General Henry Benning. Now they were going to become acquainted with General Joseph Kershaw and his six regiments of South Carolinians.[48]

The 21st Ohio Infantry was given possession of Hill 3 on Horseshoe Ridge, while remnants of Croxton's brigade were given possession of Hill 2. The remnants of the 17th Kentucky, 17th Ohio and 31st Ohio were given control of Hill 1. Parts of the Union Army were beginning to form in a new battle line around the Snodgrass house and field where General Thomas decided to make his stand. At 1:00 General Joseph Kershaw's division moved against all threes hills of Horseshoe Ridge. According to one historical account, "The 3rd South Carolina Battalion and the 3rd South Carolina [Regiment] had come at Hill 2 by ways of the knoll in the Dyer Field.... [Once] upon its crest, the South Carolinians were exposed to a heavy fire from Brannan's Federals on Hill 2 ... two hundred yards to the north"[49]

The first coordinated attack on Horseshoe Ridge included the Kershaw Brigade and also

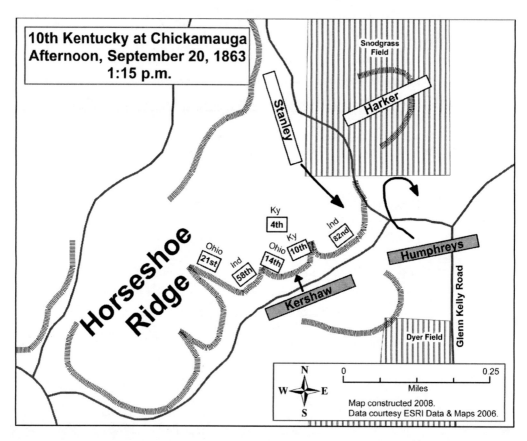

10th Kentucky at Chickamauga, Afternoon, September 20, 1863, 1:15 P.M. (original map adapted from *This Terrible Sound: The Battle of Chickamauga*, copyright 1992 Board of Trustees. Used with permission of the author and the University of Illinois Press).

the men of General Benjamin Humphreys' Mississippi Brigade. At about 1:15 Kershaw assaulted Hill 1, and the 82nd Indiana took the major thrust. Stanley's brigade rushed to stem the Confederate assault. At this time the 3rd South Carolina Battalion and 3rd South Carolina Regiment gained a toehold on the crest of Hill 2—held by the 14th Ohio, 4th Kentucky and 10th Kentucky—until forced off by enfilading fire from the 21st Ohio occupying Hill 3. The Confederates had been temporarily stopped but more Confederates were heading this way. Kershaw might have had more success if General Humphreys had joined in the attack. Humphrey's previous experience of attacks in such terrible conditions convinced him that the price would be too great to attack this ridge.

By all rights, the Union Army should have been disintegrating after the attack at 11:00 A.M. along Lafayette Road near the Brotherton house. In light of the overwhelming success of the Southern forces, it should have been as easy task to dislodge a smattering of regiments along a ridge; but the superior position of Horseshoe Ridge, the excellent leadership of General Thomas and others, and the basic nature of the men who were digging in on the ridge made the afternoon anything but easy.

By 1:30 P.M., however, Confederate commanders General Patton Anderson, Colonel Cyrus Sugg and Colonel John Fulton's troops arrived to attack the southern defenses along Horseshoe Ridge. Anderson had completely flanked the Union left flank. Luckily for the

Union Army, General James B. Steedman's brigades from General Gordon Granger's Reserve Corps began arriving on the Union flank that was just about to be attacked. Steedman arrived with not a moment to spare. General Steedman was ordered to take his troops forward to relieve those who had being carrying the battle and, reportedly, Steedman's only comment was, "Spell my name right in the obituaries."[50]

Steedman was a welcome sight and an old friend to the 10th Kentucky. He was able to extend the left flank of the Union line

General J. B. Steedman, *at right*, was divisional commander of the Reserve Corps. His charge on September 20 stabilized Thomas' flank (Library of Congress). *Below:* 10th Kentucky at Chickamauga, Afternoon, September 20, 1863, 2:15 P.M. (original map adapted from *This Terrible Sound: The Battle of Chickamauga.* Copyright 1992 Board of Trustees. Used with permission of the author and the University of Illinois Press.).

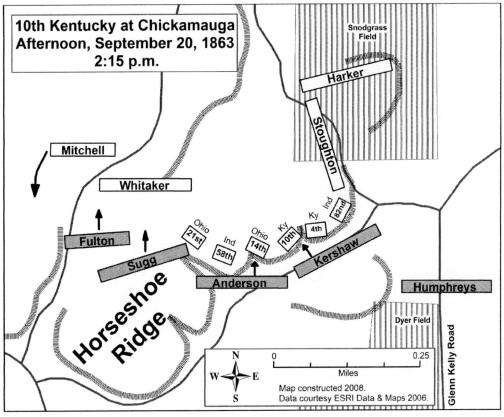

10th Kentucky at Chickamauga Afternoon, September 20, 1863 2:15 p.m.

and keep the rebels from getting behind the Union line. Anderson's assault at 2:15 P.M. was primarily directed at the 21st Ohio on Horseshoe Ridge Hill 3, which made one of the most dramatic stands in the war, but he also ran into Steedman's fresh troops. Brig. General Patton Anderson commanded six regiments of Mississippians and made the attack on the 21st Ohio. The 21st Ohio was armed with Colt repeating rifles and was able to repel the assault on Hill 3 until Steedman's reinforcements could arrive. Fighting was intense all along this line, but the Union line held.

While Anderson, Sugg and Fulton were attacking the left flank of the Union line, General Joseph Kershaw decided that it was time to launch another attack on Hills 2 and 3. This time the 2nd South Carolina Infantry made it to the crest of Hill 3 but was unsupported and was forced to withdraw. Kershaw's attack on Hill 2 was also repulsed, and again the Union line held along ridge.

General Brannan recorded, "My troops maintained their ground with obstinacy, evincing great gallantry and devotion in the most trying circumstances, until re-enforced about 3:30 P.M. by a portion of Granger's Reserve Corps."[51] General Gordon Granger's Reserve Corps was now poured into the fray and gave relief to the defenders of Horseshoe Ridge. Granger was a West Point graduate of 1845 and had the reputation of following rules and orders, and he insisted that he troops do the same. He had had the unexciting task of protecting the Rossville Gap while serving as a reserve for the army. He struggled with the decision to advance to relieve Thomas because of existing orders and the harassment by the ubiquitous Confederate cavalry. But the call to battle moved Granger's Corps forward and he arrived as Kershaw was attacking the center and left and Bushrod Johnson was attacking Thomas's right.

Major Henry Davidson expressed his relief when the reinforcements arrived: "General Thomas 'the noblest Roman of them all' is still with us, cheering us with his noble example & brave words. Now our ammunition is about to fail the men silently fix their bayonets without orders, resolved to hold the hill, or make it their grave, in good season General Gordon Granger arrives with part of the reserve corps, the enemy are driven back with great slaughter."[52]

The remnants of the 2nd Brigade were holding onto Horseshoe Ridge by their fingernails when fresh troops arrived. But prior to the arrival of the reinforcement, the suspense was intense, as a column of dust was seen approaching the 10th Kentucky's position on Horseshoe Ridge. Captain Webster expressed his feelings as the dust revealed blue uniforms:

> The moments passed; no noise in our front to give us an idea of where the enemy was or what he was doing. The silence was painful. One could hear the heart of this neighbor throb—all was so still. At last a faint sound. Soldiers exchanged inquisitive glances, seeming to ask, "What is that" The sound increased. It came near. It was in our rear. "Look, see those clouds? What is it?' The clouds thickened and rolled this way.... It was General Steedman (first Colonel of the 14th Ohio) coming to our relief. He was riding in front, and without a halt his whole line moved up the hill, passed over us, and descended the rebel side of the thicket, out of our sight in a twinkling. There was no confusion, no talking or cheering. It seemed as though every man thought he had a special errand down there, and it behooved him to get there as soon as possible. For a few minutes all was still. Then broke out a fusillade of musketry that was terrific."[53]

In fact, the relief for the 10th Kentucky came in the person of Colonel Ferdinand Van Derveer. Van Derveer arrived at Snodgrass farm at 3:00 P.M. and General George Thomas directed his troops to relieve the weary men along the crest of Hills 1 and 2 on Horseshoe Ridge.

At 3:30 P.M., Southern General Bushrod Johnson's troops launched another attack on the Union left flank with bloody results, but again the line held. By 4:00 P.M. General James Longstreet had taken control of the assault at Snodgrass farm and Horseshoe Ridge. He decided to commit his only unused units of General William Preston's reserve division—General Archibald Gracie's Alabama and Tennessee Brigade and Colonel John Kelly's Brigade. Gracie began his attack on Hill 1 and the southern aspect of the Snodgrass Farm with the assistance of some of Kershaw's regiments. Although the attack was designed to be coordinated with John Kelly's brigade, the attack started before Kelly was ready and he would not join until 10 minutes later. This final charge would be the beginning of the three attacks on Thomas's defenses. Gracie's men attacked the Snodgrass Farm but had no success; however, after a bloody struggle, the Confederates gained the crest of Hill 1 but could not push the Union forces back further; but neither could the blue-clad soldiers remove the Southerners from the crest. Kelly's men attacked Hills 2 and 3. It was at this time that the 10th Kentucky, filed to the left of Colonel Van Derveer's men, added their rifles to repulse the attackers. Kelly's men clung to the incline but could not advance and refused to return to the valley. Each side exchanged fire for the next hour. Now it was Bushrod Johnson's turn to attack the Union right flank again, but unlike the previous attacks, this one was successful and the Union line was thrown back. Finally, at 6:00 P.M. Colonel John Kelly's men surged over the sides of Hills 2 and 3 to gain the crest of the Horseshoe Ridge.[54]

According to Lt. Colonel Gabriel Wharton's description of the 10th Kentucky's activities on Horseshoe Ridge on the afternoon of the 20th, they held this position with only slight loss until 3:00, when Colonel Ferdinand Van Derveer's brigade relieved them. The 10th Kentucky was allowed to rest for about a half an hour and replenish their ammunition. Then Van

Battle of Chickamauga (Library of Congress).

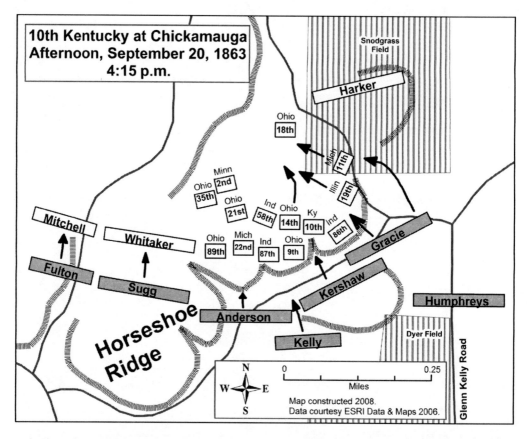

10th Kentucky at Chickamauga, Afternoon, September 20, 1863, 4:15 P.M. (original map adapted from
This Terrible Sound: The Battle of Chickamauga, copyright 1992 Board of Trustees. Used with permission of the author and the University of Illinois Press).

Derveer was "furiously assaulted" by Kelly's attack and the 10th Kentucky was ordered back
in line. Wharton recorded:

> The troops went forward with great determination at a double-quick, and took position behind
> a temporary fortification of rails, immediately on the left of the Third Brigade, Third Division,
> Fourteenth Army Corps, and poured a most destructive fire into the advancing columns of the
> enemy, which staggered them for a moment, but they rallied and advanced again and again. It
> seemed two or three times it would be impossible to hold our position, so overwhelming was
> the force of the enemy, but our troops, being partially screened by the rails, poured volley after
> volley into their masses, so well aimed that after three hours of most desperate fighting the
> enemy withdrew, just as our ammunition was exhausted and General Brannan had ordered the
> men to fix bayonets and receive the enemy on their points if they again advanced. During the
> whole fight the men never wavered or gave an inch, and the officers of my regiment were at
> their posts encouraging their men, several of them took the guns of their wounded men and
> shot away every cartridge in their boxes. The regiment suffered severely in this right.[55]

Gracie and Kelly would lose approximately half their men in this assault. Longstreet
would claim that there had been twenty-five separate charges that afternoon to overpower
the Union defense at Snodgrass Farm and Horseshoe Ridge.[56] By 6:00 P.M. the order to retire
was received and the 10th Kentucky moved to Rossville and then on to Chattanooga. The
Confederate Army now had control of Horseshoe Ridge and Snodgrass Farm.

The New York Times would describe the battles at Horseshoe Ridge:

The fight around the hill now raged with terror inexperienced before, even upon this terrible day. Our soldiers were formed in two lines, and as each marched up to the crest and fired a deadly volley at the advancing foe, it fell back a little ways, the men lay down upon the ground to load their guns, and the second line advanced to take their place! They, too, in their turn retired, and thus the lines kept marching back and forth, and delivering their withering volleys, till the very brain grew dizzy as it watched them. And all the time not a man wavered. Every motion was executed with as much precision as though the troops were on a holiday parade, notwithstanding the flower of the rebel army were swarming round the foot of the hill, and a score of cannon were thundering from three sides upon it. Every attempt of the enemy to scale it was repulsed.[57]

The 10th Kentucky's Private Richard Logsdon was mortally wounded late on the afternoon of September 20 defending Horseshoe Ridge. He lay wounded near his lieutenant, Clem Funk, and said, "Clem, do not desert your post, go to your boys. I am dying. Farewell."[58] Private Logsdon lived until October 16. Also during the defense of Horseshoe Ridge, Lieutenant William Kelley was shot in the hip and taken to a house for care and later captured by the Confederates.[59]

Late in the day on September 20, General Brannan sent his topographical engineer, Lieutenant Henry Dunn of the 10th Kentucky, to inform a regiment that they were firing on their own men. Unfortunately, the regiment turned out to be Rebels and they immediately captured Lieutenant Dunn. He was sent to Atlanta and then to Libby Prison in Richmond, where he assisted in making an escape with Colonel Thomas Rose and the men of the 77th Pennsylvania. He was recaptured after nine days less than a mile from the Union lines in Williamsburg and thrown in the dungeon with his fellow escapees in Libby Prison. He was then transferred to Macon, Georgia, then to Charleston, South Carolina, then back to Macon. He finally agreed to his parole and was sent to Washington, D.C. with his health severely impaired. His parole came one month after the expiration of his enlistment.[60]

General Brannan cited Lieutenant Dunn for "fearlessness and gallantry, carrying my orders under the severest fire, and using every effort to rally and encourage troops to return to their flag."[61] General Brannan also recognized Colonel William Hays, who "commanded such portion of the Second Brigade of my division as were mustered on the ridge ... and behaved most gallantly during the entire action, keeping his command to the crest of the hill when he had not a cartridge left."[62] Captain Webster described the end of the day for Company I: "We marched along in a narrow pass for quite a distance, and about 10 o'clock we halted and remained there during the night. Thus ended the second day's fighting. All our wounded, who were left at the house before mentioned, were captured the next day."[63]

Major Davidson summarized the losses for the 10th Kentucky during the last day of the battle: "The hill was covered with dead & wounded Rebels. Our loss was much lighter than on Saturday being protected by logs and rails. My regiment lost forty four men this day, making a total of one hundred and sixty five killed and wounded out of four hundred and fifty-two. It would be impossible for me to give you an accurate description of the battle this day—imagine two hundred pieces of cannon belching forth, and seventy five or eighty thousand muskets firing all at the same time. The grape shot canister, and bullets fell around thicker and faster than any hail storm you ever witnessed."[64]

Chickamauga was clearly a defeat for the Union forces, although the Confederate forces suffered greater losses. The Army of the Cumberland had successfully positioned Bragg out of central Tennessee, but was soundly defeated in north Georgia. The defeat meant the end of Rosecrans as the head of the Army of the Cumberland, but his replacement was another type of general, indeed.

The 10th Kentucky entered the engagement on the 18th with 421 men and by dark on the 20th, 256 remained. Over 166 were killed, missing, captured or wounded in the 3-day battle. The 10th Kentucky lost approximately 40 percent of its force in this fight. They were experienced soldiers going into the fight, but those who made it through this battle were changed men. September 19 took the greatest toll; the 10th Kentucky lost 120 men on the first day. They were thrown into the fight over and over and their final action was a bayonet charge that routed their foes. On September 20, they lost their brigade commander; Colonel Hays moved to replace him and command the brigade. They retreated when flanked by superior forces, but reformed and made significant contributions to holding Horseshoe Ridge Hills 1 and 2. They lost 46 men the second day, including 7 officers. The defense on Horseshoe Ridge was important in saving the Army of the Cumberland to fight another day. And that day would be two long, hard months in the future. General Henry Cist, *The Army of the Cumberland*, would write of George Thomas' defensive stand on Horseshoe Ridge, saying he "successfully resisted for nearly six long hours the repeated attacks of that same rebel army, largely re-enforced until it numbered twice his command, when it was flushed with victory and determined on his utter destruction. There is nothing finer in history than Thomas at Chickamauga."[65] And the 10th Kentucky Infantry was part of this.

10th Kentucky Infantry Losses at Chickamauga[66]

Killed in Action

McGrath, Philip J.	Sgt	Company B	Scott, James F.	Sgt	Company B
Fenwick, G.W.	Pvt	Company B	Mattingly, Joseph S.	Pvt	Company B
Blanford, Robert	Pvt	Company B	Blair, John T.	Pvt	Company B
Peterson, T. G.	Pvt	Company B	Thurman, James P	Pvt	Company C
Garrison, G. B.	Corp	Company D	Ewing, William T.	Pvt	Company D
Fowler, John J.	Pvt	Company E	Adams, Elisha M.	Pvt	Company E
Hundley, James	Pvt	Company E	Ash, Henry	Pvt	Company F
Tumey, William	Pvt	Company F	Myers, John H.	Lt	Company I
Roaler, Richard	Pvt	Company I	Wilkins, Edward	Sgt	Company K
Dugald, Campbell	Corp	Company K	Maloney, Daniel	Pvt	Company K
Mule, Stonemason	Pvt	Company K			

Mortally Wounded

Miles, Thomas	Pvt	Company B	Died 9-19-1863
Steward, Charles G.	Pvt	Company D	Died 9-19-1863
Hagan, John T.	Pvt	Company D	Died 10-1-1863
Bevill, Seth	Capt	Company E	Died 9-21-1863
Ensor, George W.	Corp	Company E	Died 10-20-1863
Noe, George A.	Corp	Company E	Recovered
Adams, William T.	Pvt	Company E	Recovered
Logsdon, Richard L.	Pvt	Company E	Died 10-16-1863
Corcoran, Philip	Pvt	Company E	Recovered
Campbell, John	Pvt	Company E	Died 9-19-1863
Cox, Micajah	Pvt	Company F	Died 9-24-1863
Ballard, Joseph	Pvt	Company G	Died 9-19-1863
Waters, Jas. R	Pvt	Company G	Died 9-23-1863
Clark, John M	Pvt	Company G	Died 12-4-1863
Welch, Michael	Pvt	Company H	Died 10-26-1863

Wounded and Subsequently Died

Phillips, John H.	Corp	Company D	Died 10-1-1863
Waters, Jack H.	Pvt	Company E	Died 10-4-1863
Woods, James	Pvt	Company F	Died 10-13-1863
Avis, Edward	Pvt	Company G	Died 10-24-1863
Eads, Zachariah	Pvt	Company H	Died 10-13-1864

Wounded and Subsequently Died (cont.)

Sluder, John M.	Pvt	Company H	Died 10-16-1863
Smothers, John	Pvt	Company I	Died 2-29-1864

Severely Wounded

Manly, Samuel	Sgt	Company A	Spraggins, Alexander W.	Pvt	Company E
Ropp, Michael	Pvt	Company A	Thompson, John B.	Pvt	Company E
Nash, Richard C.	Chaplain		Myers, William A.	Pvt	Company E
Warren, Henry H.	Lt	Company A	Cooley, Stephen	Pvt	Company F
Crutchett, Henry	Pvt	Company A	Sweeney, John	Pvt	Company F
Smith, Thomas M.	Pvt	Company A	Smith, Samuel	Pvt	Company F
Jones, William	Pvt	Company A	Troutman, Sebastian	Pvt	Company F
Harding, William	Sgt	Company B	Smith, Benjamin R.	Lt	Company F
Green, Francis	Pvt	Company B	Davenport, Jas. M.	Capt	Company G
Fenwick, Thomas	Pvt	Company B	Peak, Thomas	Pvt	Company G
Blanford, Edward	Pvt	Company B	Hayden, William	Pvt	Company G
Miles, Chas. Henry	Pvt	Company B	Ferrill, Francis L.	Corp	Company G
Whitfield, William	Pvt	Company B	Belton, Addison	Pvt	Company H
Fogle, William	Pvt	Company B	Campbell, Moses	Pvt	Company H
Butler, William	Pvt	Company B	Beglow, William	Lt	Company H
Meece, George W.	Corp	Company C	William Kelley	Lt	Company I
Mattingley, Martin V.B.	Corp	Company C	Brown, Thomas J	Sgt	Company I
Buckman, Mike	Corp	Company C	Mills, John F.	Pvt	Company I
Ewing, James C.	Sgt	Company D	Burchell, Jno.	Pvt	Company I
Luckett, Thomas A.	Pvt	Company D	Abel, Joshua J.	Pvt	Company I
Price, Thomas	Corp	Company D	Taylor, Henry	Pvt	Company I
Beaven, Chas.	Pvt	Company D	Rea, Robert Sr.	Sgt	Company K
Stines, Robert	Pvt	Company D	Welsh, Richard	Pvt	Company K
Dearing, John L.	Pvt	Company E			

Slightly Wounded

Herdel, Nicholas	Sgt	Company A	Shockley, Davis M.	Corp	Company A
Creagle, James	Pvt	Company A	Rossles, Frederick	Pvt	Company A
Milburn, John	Capt	Company B	Blair, David	Pvt	Company B
Mattingly, Walter	Pvt	Company B	Llewellyn, Elisha O.	Pvt	Company B
Sanders, James	Pvt	Company B	Sallee, James	Lt	Company C
Martin, James B.	Sgt	Company C	Buckman, J.	Pvt	Company C
Andrews, Albert T.	Pvt	Company C	Craig, John	Pvt	Company C
Hogland, John	Pvt	Company C	Beaven, Chas.	Pvt	Company D
Foster, Andrew J.	Sgt	Company D	Shockley, Robert G.	Sgt	Company D
Wells, Elbert S.	Pvt	Company D	Seay, Francis B.	Sgt	Company D
Leathers, Jesse M.	Pvt	Company D	Hughes, Thomas D.	Corp	Company D
Snider, Alfred	Pvt	Company D	Yocum, Richard B.	Pvt	Company D
Mouser, John W.	Pvt	Company D	Janes, Joseph A.	Pvt	Company E
Nix, George W.	Pvt	Company E	Courtney, John W.	Pvt	Company E
Sullivant, Patrick	Pvt	Company E	Dobson, William H.	Pvt	Company E
Nally, Thos. J.	Pvt	Company E	John Beasley	Pvt	Company F
Edwards, William M.	Pvt	Company E	Sutterfield, Edward H.	Pvt	Company F
Thompson, John M.	Pvt	Company F	Perkins, Jefferson	Pvt	Company F
Grant, Joseph	Pvt	Company F	Kelly, Wm. P.	Pvt	Company F
Harshfield, Columbus	Pvt	Company F	Litsey, Martin H.	Pvt	Company F
Cooley, Columbus	Pvt	Company F	Land, Squire	Pvt	Company F
Mattingly, Wm.	Pvt	Company F	McCabbins, Moses	Pvt	Company F
Williams, Thomas	Pvt	Company F	Kelty, Miles Pius	Pvt	Company G
Sluder, Alexander	Pvt	Company F	Right, Jonathan	Pvt	Company G
Blemford, James	Pvt	Company G	Shively, David A.	Pvt	Company H
Pennington, John	Pvt	Company G	Gaddis, William J.	Sgt	Company I
Hagan, James	Pvt	Company G	Munday, Silas	Pvt	Company I
Rice, David E.	Corp	Company H	Garvey, Charles	Corp	Company K
Roots, William	Sgt	Company I	Lee, John L	Sgt	Company K
Harrison, Samuel H.	Pvt	Company I	McVey, William	Pvt	Company K
Burk, Tobias	Corp	Company K	Rase, William	Pvt	Company K
Molim, Adam	Pvt	Company K	Buckley, John	Pvt	Company K
Cady, Michael	Pvt	Company K			

Missing

Frank, George	Pvt	Company A
Mitchell, Henry	Pvt	Company A

Missing (cont.)

Sapp, Burnet B.	Pvt	Company C	Died 10-29-1863
Walker, Robert B.	Pvt	Company E	Captured
Thompson, Edward A.	Pvt	Company E	
Weir, Henry	Pvt	Company F	
Mattingley, Nicholas	Pvt	Company F	Captured
Mattingley, Thomas	Pvt	Company F	Captured
Roots, William	Corp	Company H	Captured
Brown, Josiah	Pvt	Company I	Captured
Dunn, Henry	Lt	Company H	Captured[66]
		(Detached to Brigade)	

Additional 10th Kentucky Casualties— Kentucky Adjutant General's Report

Company B

Hall, William, Sr.	Pvt	Missing in action 9-23-1863, Chattanooga, Tenn.

Company C

Russell, David	Corp	Wounded at Chickamauga 9-19-1863

Company D

Yocum, James M.	Mus	Prisoner—Captured at Chickamauga 12-24-1863
Cronch, James P.	Pvt	Prisoner—Captured at Chickamauga 12-24-1863

Company E

Fenwick, Edward	Pvt	Died 10-9-1864 in Chattanooga

Company I

Harrison, William R.	Pvt	Wounded at Chickamauga 9-20-1863

Regimental Losses September–November 24, 1863

	September	*October*	*November to 24th*
Discharged			
	Hickey, Patrick (C)	Krahl, Conrad (A)	Askren, Samuel (A)
	Lawson, David (I)	Isaacs, John (I)	Perkins, Jabez (Staff)
	Smith, Hamilton (I)	Lawson, Lenox (I)	
Died			
		Garrison, Gideon (D)	Sapp, Burnet (C)
		Hagan, John (D)	Vestrees, Josiah (H)
		Ensor, George (E)	
		Waters, Jack (E)	
		Woods, James (F)	
		Eads, Zachariah (H)	
		Sluder, John M (H)	
		Welch, Michael (H)	
		Lane, Patrick A. (I)	
		Martin, Jesse (I)	
Killed in Action			
	McGrath, Philip J. (B)		
	Scott, James F. (B)		
	Blair, John T. (B)		
	Blanford, Robert (B)		
	Fenwick, George (B)		
	Mattingly, Joseph (B)		
	Miles, Thomas (B)		
	Peterson, Thomas (B)		
	Ewing, William T. (D)		
	Steward, Charles (D)		
	Bevill, Seth P. (E)		
	Adams, Elisha (E)		
	Campbell, John (E)		
	Fowler, John (E)		
	Hundley, James (E)		

	September	*October*	*November to 24th*

Killed in Action (cont.)

Logsdon, Richard (E)
Ash, Henry (F)
Cox, Micajah (F)
Tumey, William H (F)
Ballard, Joseph (G)
Waters, Jas. R (G)
Myers, John H (I)
Roaler, Richard (I)
Wilkins, Edward (K)
Dugald , Campbell (K)
Maloney, Daniel (K)
Mayland, Patrick (K)
Mule, Stonemason (K)

Missing

Hall, William, Sr. (B)

Transferred

September	October	November to 24th
Riley, John (C)	Whitfield, James (E)	Benningfield, John (C)
McCann, James (K)		

Captured

Thurman, James (C)
Yocum, James M. (D)
Cronch, James P. (D)
Walker, Robert (E)
Mattingley, Nicholas (F)
Mattingley, Thos. A. (F)
Dunn, Henry C. (I)
Brown, Josiah (I)

FIVE

Chattanooga and Missionary Ridge

"The gallant 10th Ky was laying down in line of Battle with all there
guns loaded when they rose up and sent a volley of Destruction
through there ranks"—Thomas Ireton, 89th Ohio

The day after the Battle of Chickamauga marked the beginning of two long months of incarceration in the city of Chattanooga for the 10th Kentucky Infantry. The men had lost 166 of their friends, relatives, and comrades that each had grown to know over the past two years. Colonel William H. Hays was the temporary brigade commander, taking command after Colonel John Croxton's leg wound on September 20, and Lt. Colonel Gabriel Wharton assumed the regimental command of the 10th Kentucky.

The 10th Kentucky suffered greatly in the previous battle. The official casualty list for the 10th Kentucky included one officer and 20 men killed in action, nine officers and 125 men wounded, and one officer and 10 men captured, for a total of 11 officers and 155 enlisted men.[1] The officers of the regiment were battered and bruised. John H. Myers, 2nd lieutenant, Company I, lay dead near the Brotherton cabin and Captain Seth Bevill, Company E, was wounded and died on September 21. William E. Kelly, 1st lieutenant, Company I, was shot on September 20 while in the center of the regiment bearing the regimental colors and encouraging the men.[2] He was wounded and taken to a house for care, but was left behind when the regiment withdrew and he was taken prisoner. He was paroled and moved to Louisville for care. Then he was moved to Camp Chase, Ohio, and returned to the regiment on May 19, 1864. Lieutenant Henry Dunn, General Brannan's topographical engineer, was captured and would remain a prisoner until after the 10th Kentucky was mustered out of service.[3]

Captain John Milburn, Lieutenant William Beglow and Lieutenant James Sallee would return to the 10th Kentucky in Chattanooga. First Lieutenant Benjamin R. Smith was shot in the foot and would not return to the regiment until November 1864, essentially missing the remainder of the war.[4] Lieutenant Henry Warren was wounded in the arm and ankle and would return to the regiment in June 1, 1864.[5] Captain James Davenport was wounded in his right leg and would return to the regiment after recuperating.[6] Captain Edward Hilpp received a flesh wound in his calf, but remained with his company. The enlisted men of the 10th Kentucky also suffered greatly.

For the companies, the following officers were available for duty on September 22: Capt. Charles McKay and 2nd Lt. Richard Grace (A); Capt. John Milburn, 1st Lt. William O'Bryan, and 2nd Lt. John McCauley (B); Capt. Edward Hilpp, 1st Lt. William Mussen and 2nd Lt. Wm Sallee (C); 1st Lt. James Mills and 2nd Lt. Ed Penick (D); Capt. Andrew Thompson, 1st Lt. Clem Funk (E); Capt. Franklin Hill, 2nd Lt. Joseph Adcock (F); 1st Lt. Charles Spalding (G); Capt. William Shively (H); Capt. I. B. Webster (I); Capt. Henry Waller, Lt. John Denton and Lt. James Watts (K).

Battle of Chattanooga (Library of Congress).

Although the initial list of casualties at Chickamauga indicated that only eleven members of the regiments were captured, the overall number was nineteen[7]: Company A, Lt. Henry Warren and Sgt. Samuel Manly; Company C, Pvt. James Thurman; Company D, Mus. James Yocum and Pvt. James Cronch; Company E, Pvt. Robert Walker; Company F, Pvt. Nicolas Mattingley and Pvt. Thomas Mattingley; Company H, Lt. Henry Dunn and Corp. William Roots; Company I, Lt. William Kelly, Pvt. Joshua Abel, Pvt. Josiah Brown, Pvt. John Burchell, Pvt. William Goodman, Pvt. William Harrison and Pvt. Silas Munday; and Company G, Corp. Francis Ferrill and Pvt. John Emery.

The number of men ready for duty was at its lowest of the war, except for the final battle. Many of the men captured were those who had been wounded and were left behind as the 10th Kentucky was forced to retreat from the Chickamauga battlefield.

One of the scourges of the war was the Confederate prisoner-of-war facility in Andersonville, Georgia. The name of this facility strikes fear and loathing in hearts even today. After Chickamauga, eleven soldiers were sent to this location and four would die there of disease and malnutrition by the end of the war.

10th Kentucky Men Sent to Andersonville

Pvt. Josiah Brown	Company I	Died in Andersonville 9-24-1864 of diarrhea
Pvt. Philip Brown	Company I	Died 4-28-1865
Pvt. James Cronch	Company D	Died in Andersonville 10-24-1864 of Scurvy
Pvt. John Emery	Company G	Died in Andersonville 6-27-1984 of typhus
Corp. Francis Ferrill	Company G	Exchanged, 1865
Pvt. William Goodman	Company I	Paroled
Sgt. Samuel Manly	Company A	Exchanged and returned to The 10th Kentucky 11-24-1864
Pvt. Nicolas Mattingley	Company F	Survived the war
Pvt. Thomas Mattingley	Company F	Survived the war
Pvt. James Thurman	Company C	Survived the war
Pvt. Robert Walker	Company E	Survived the war[8]

Lieutenant Henry Dunn was destined to be sent to various prisons, beginning with the Libby prison in Richmond, Virginia, until he was paroled in December 1864 with his health all but wasted. Lieutenant Kelly and Lieutenant Warren were captured and later paroled.

Chattanooga

On September 21, the 10th Kentucky slowly marched into Chattanooga, and on that day, Chattanooga was an occupied city. In 1860 Chattanooga had over 2500 occupants, but when the Union decided to occupy it, the populace had already moved out, anticipating this being a center of conflict. Chattanooga was now an abandoned railway village. The city, located in a beautiful river valley, was surrounded on three sides by mountains and on the other side was the Tennessee River.

After the Battle of Chickamauga, the men of the 10th Kentucky assumed that the Confederate Army would follow up their victory and move to attack Chattanooga. This sentiment was expressed by Major Henry Davidson: "We expected an instant attack. Everybody said let them come we are ready now, but they did not come, and the consequence was that in two weeks time, Chattanooga is simply impregnable."[9]

Fearing that the Confederates would attack his army with overwhelming reinforcements caused General Rosecrans to withdraw to Chattanooga and the defenses there. Also, the loss at Chickamauga caused Rosecrans to lose his confidence, and he sought safety for the remainder of his forces. His corps commanders had sent messages to him that they thought they could hold the mountains from the Confederates, but a Confederate prisoner gave information that suggested there were more Confederate reinforcements imminently expected. Therefore, Rosecrans made Chattanooga his fortress and it became besieged by the Confederate Army.[10] Rather than attacking the Union Army, Bragg decided that because of his high casualties, poor supply situation and the strong Union defenses, he would lay siege to Chattanooga and force the Union Army out through starvation. Bragg was now on the offensive for the first time since he attacked into Kentucky and was forced to retreat after the Battle of Perryville almost a year before.

The Union Army began to build their defenses and the city soon became an impregnable fortress. Battle lines extended around the city with breastworks established to make a frontal assault on the city virtually impossible.[11]

The Army of the Cumberland could stay in Chattanooga for 15 to 20 days with its current provisions. Supply trains were scheduled, but bad weather made roads almost impassable and the Confederate Cavalry began to take a heavy toll on the provisions expected to arrive in Chattanooga. On October 2, a successful raid on a Union supply train forced General Rosecrans to put the men on two-thirds rations. The loss of provisions also greatly reduced the number of horses that were serviceable, with as many as 250 horses dying of starvation. By October 25 10,000 animals were dead and the army was reduced to one-half rations.[12] The situation was going from hopeful optimism in September to near starvation in October. Starvation was not the only issue facing the men of the 10th Kentucky. They went into battle in September, but now autumn was creeping slowly toward winter and their clothing was no longer suitable for the conditions in Chattanooga which were cool days and even cooler nights.

The rains in September and the harassment of the supply trains by General Joe Wheeler's Confederate cavalry stopped the advance of reinforcements and supplies to Chattanooga. On October 8, General Bragg ordered Longstreet's troops into Lookout Valley, further tightening the noose around the city. Longstreet could now strike any Union troops on the south side of the Tennessee River between Bridgeport and Chattanooga. Major Davidson would reflect that the spirit of the Union Army was not broken, "but now a more fearful enemy than Gen. Bragg seemed about to attack us. Famine seemed to stare us in the face. But every man determined to hold Chattanooga, it had cost us too much to abandon it to the enemy again."[13]

Captain Israel Webster described the desperate food situation and also that the Confederates daily made their presence known by lobbing artillery shells into the city:

> Men without bread and mules without fodder for supplies had been tampered with; the former picking scraps of crackers out of the refuse pile in the corner on the floor of the commissary; while the latter stood tied to wagons, eating up the bodies thereof. We could get very little clothing, and, taken in all, were not contented and happy."[14]
>
> Nearly every day, and several times a day, would a shot or shell be sent over to us from that point [Lookout Mountain]. I have stood many a time, watch in hand, taking note of the time between the rising of the smoke, when the match was applied to the gun, and the boom of the report reaching me. Every time it made the distance five miles.[15]

Chattanooga from Lookout Mountain (Library of Congress).

There are many accounts of friendly interactions between the opposing armies throughout the war. As in other places, exchanges between Union and Confederates during the siege
of Chattanooga took place. Captain I. B. Webster describes one such exchange:

> Oh, Yank!
> Well, Johnny, what do you want?
> Say, have you got any coffee-e-e?
> Yes-s-s
> I'll give you some sugar for it.
> All right; come over.
> Will you let me go back?
> Of course, you can go back. Come on with your sugar.[16]

Captain Webster stated that exchanges of meager rations between the Union and Confederates went on for weeks. The 10th Kentucky's Corporal Columbus Filiatreau, Company

E, would later write of his experience in Chattanooga: "The next night fell back to Chattanooga and staid there for about 2 mo and liked to have starved. The enemy had our grub line cut off."[17]

For many of the unfortunate soldiers of the 10th Kentucky who fought at Chickamauga, the months following the battle were a life and death struggle. Many of the wounded did recuperate, but this was not the case for all. An example of the tragedy of Chickamauga and the arrival of the dreaded letter from the company commander was preserved in the case of Private Josiah Vestrees of Company H. Josiah's last action was at Chickamauga, where he fought throughout the battle but on September 23 felt ill and would later enter the hospital. His illness was due to his exhaustion and later turned into bronchitis. He died on November 9, 1863. His family received this letter:

> Chattanooga, Tenn
> November the 14th, 1863
>
> Dear Sir:
>
>   It is with pain that I write to inform you of the death of your son Josiah. He dyed the ninth of this month at the division hospital from exhaustion. He was with me in the Battle of Chickamauga and I am happy to inform you that he dun his duty on the battlefield. He was at his post all through the fight. He left 25 cts in postage currency and a pocket book and comb. He has not drawn any money since he came to the regiment. He borrowed twenty dollars from Isaac Harmon. Harmon is very sick and I think his recovery doubtful. Josiah went to the hospital three weeks before he died. He has never been stout since he came back. I sympathize with you and mourn your loss.
>
> Capt Wm Shively [Company H][18]

After Ulysses Grant's victory at Vicksburg he had remained essentially in place awaiting his next opportunity to strike the Confederate Army, but on September 23, he received a message ordering him to dispatch as many men as possible to the assistance of General William Rosecrans in Chattanooga. Grant immediately sent General William Sherman with part of two corps toward the east. "Fightin' Joe" Hooker was being sent from the Army of the Potomac with 15,000 men from the 11th and 12th Corps. Grant was then ordered to Louisville, Kentucky, where he met with Secretary of War Edwin Stanton and was made commander of the newly formed Military Division of Mississippi, which gave Grant control of most of the Union forces in the western theater. Rosecrans was also being removed as commander of the Union forces in Chattanooga. Grant made known his objective: "Hold Chattanooga at all hazards."[19]

On October 23, 1863, Major General Ulysses Grant arrived at Chattanooga and began his personal command of the Union Military Division of the Mississippi. Major General George Thomas, the hero of Chickamauga, was appointed as Rosecrans' successor effective October 20, 1863, to command the Army of the Cumberland.[20] The supplies began arriving to the army isolated in Chattanooga on October 30 and starvation of the Army of the Cumberland was averted. The rains that had begun in mid–October had stopped. The engineers of the army, under the command of General "Baldy" Smith, devised a plan to open up the supply route, and a "cracker line" was started. General Joe Hooker's troops were given the task of guarding this supply route and on October 29 fought a victorious battle at Wauhatchie. The battle insured that neither the ground nor river route to Chattanooga would be threatened thereafter.

Reorganization of the 14th Corps

With the promotion of the General Thomas to the command of the Army of the Cumberland, other changes were in store. The command of the 14th Corps fell to Major General John M. Palmer. General Palmer had previously served under Major General Thomas Crittenden as 2nd Divisional commander in the 21st Corps. The 10th Kentucky's old divisional commander, Brig. General John Brannan, assumed command of his first love, the artillery reserve. He was replaced with General Absalom Baird, 39 years old and a native of Washington, Pennsylvania. He commanded the 1st Division in the 14th Corps at Chickamauga, and he was a West Point graduate in the class of 1841. He was an instructor at West Point from 1852 to 1859. Later he was posted in Virginia and Texas. He had also served at the 1st Battle of Bull Run and the Peninsula Campaign.[21]

General John Palmer, 14th Army Corps Commander (Library of Congress).

With Colonel John Croxton's wound inflicted at Chickamauga, he was not able to resume his command of the 3rd Brigade, and Colonel Edward Phelps assumed Croxton's old command. Colonel Phelps was the regimental commander of the 38th Ohio, which had been assigned to the 1st Division after Chickamauga. Another change that resulted after the massive brigade losses at Chickamauga was the addition of the 18th Kentucky and 38th Ohio to increase the effective force of the 3rd Brigade. Colonel William H. Hays again assumed command of the 10th Kentucky with Lt. Colonel Gab Wharton as his second in command.[22]

Organization of the Army in Relation to the 10th Kentucky

Fourteenth Army Corps—Major General John M. Palmer.
Third Division—Brig. General Absalom Baird.
  Third Brigade—Colonel Edward H. Phelps
    10th Indiana—Lieut. Colonel Marsh B. Taylor.
    74th Indiana—Lieut. Colonel Myron Baker.
    4th Kentucky—Major Robert M. Kelly.
    10th Kentucky—Colonel William H. Hays.
    18th Kentucky—Lieut. Colonel Hubbard K. Milward.
    14th Ohio—Lieut. Colonel Henry D. Kingsbury.
    38th Ohio—Major Charles Greenwood.

Within the 10th Kentucky, 1st Lieutenant James "Dick" Watts, Company K, was removed from his duties. The wear of the war took its toll on Lieutenant Watts. He had been very ill and in October 1863 put in charge of the quartermaster duty for the regiment, in an attempt to try to improve his health. He remained in this capacity through the remainder of the war

Courts-Martial

In the months before and immediately after the Battle of Missionary Ridge, three additional courts-martial took place for privates of the 10th Kentucky Infantry.

In October 1863, Private Adam Arnold was tried on a charge of absence without leave: "Adam Arnold, Private Co A 10 Regt Ky vols having taken sick at Campbellsville, Ky on or about the 5th day of January 1862 was ordered to a Hospital at Lebanon, Ky at which he remained for a time in the charge of the surgeon attending. After the said Adam Arnold private Co A 10th Ky Vols, had recovered sufficiently to leave the Hospital, he went to his home where he remained without leave until arrested by the Provost Marshal of Louisville, Ky on the 9th day of October 1863 and sent to Chattanooga, Tenn. as a prisoner."[23]

He was found guilty and sentenced to forfeit all pay them due him and to be dishonorably discharged. The sentence was disapproved by the advocate general because of insufficient numbers of members on the court.

On November 28, 1863, Private Jerry Arnold was tried for desertion: "Jerry Arnold, a Private in Company A 10th Regt Ky Infantry having been captured and paroled by the enemy together with his company, at Courtland, Alabama on the 26th of July 1862 and in obedience with orders from Col Miller required to report to the military commandant at Louisville, Ky in which he neglected to do, and while on the cars with his company en route for Louisville, Ky on or about the 4th of August 1862, the said Jerry Arnold Private in Co A 10th Regt Ky vol Infty did get off of the car that contained his company at a station on the road, and proceed to his home in Jefferson County Ky. He has never reported to his regiment since that time."[24]

Lieutenant Richard Grace, Company A, was a witness for the prosecution and stated that Private Arnold left the company, returned home and complained about his health.

Private Arnold was found guilty and was sentenced to be "Shot to Death with Musketry." During the review of this case, it was determined that the court-martial was fatally defective for not being properly organized. The judge advocate having since died, it became impossible to correct these errors. As a result, the proceedings were disapproved and Private Arnold was released and returned to duty.

Private Royal G. Clark of Company B was tried for desertion and cowardice in the face of the enemy on November 20, 1863. The court was made up of Captain John Chase, 14th Ohio, Captain M. S. Turner, 4th Kentucky, John Crosson, 38th Ohio, Captain J. H. Cobb, 10th Indiana, Captain A. Moore, 14th Ohio, Captain E. M. Deuchard, 38th Ohio, and Captain R. S. Dye, 36th Regiment OVI (Ohio Volunteer Infantry), adjutant general.

The desertion change read: "In this that the said Private Royal G Clark, Co B 10th Regt Ky Vol Infty, did on or about the 7th day of October 1862 desert from his company & Reg then at or about near Perryville, Boyle County, Kentucky, and did remain absent then from until sometime in November 1862 when he was arrested by Sergt Gray of Co B 10th Ky Vol. Inft in Taylor County Kentucky."[25]

The charge read for cowardice in the face of the enemy: "In this that the said Royal G Clark Co B 10th Kentucky Vol Infty deserted from his company and Regiment on or about the 7th of October 1862 when said company and Regiment were in the presence of the enemy and forming a part of the reserve of the forces engaged in the fight at Chaplain Hill in that day."[26]

First Lieutenant William O'Bryan, Company B, testified that Private Clark started for a spring and never returned to the regiment. He was arrested in Taylor County and returned to the regiment. The prisoner stated to the court that he was sick at the time he left regiment and was sick in bed for five weeks. He stated that he still wasn't well enough to return to his regiment.

He was found guilty of the specification on the two charges and guilty of the first count. He was sentenced to forfeit all pay and allowance and to have his head shaved and be branded with the letter "D" and drummed through the camps of his division. He was also confined to hard labor for the remainder of his enlistment. The adjutant general overruled the requirement for branding and designated the military prison in Nashville as his place of confinement. All other aspects of the trial were upheld. Private Clark died in Nashville on May 26, 1864.

The Battle of Missionary Ridge

Prior to an attack on Missionary Ridge, General Grant ordered a demonstration by General Thomas' men for early in November, which would include the 10th Kentucky Infantry, but Thomas was able to get the order countermanded. Even though the 'cracker line' was working, the men of the Army of the Cumberland were in too poor condition to participate in a full battle.

Much has been written about Grant and his decisions regarding the battles of Lookout Mountain and Missionary Ridge. Clearly, General George Thomas and General Grant were less than excited about serving with one another. General Grant also had great confidence in General Sherman and his command, and he had a much lower opinion of the Army of the Cumberland. Therefore, when Grant formulated his plan of attack that began on November 24, he positioned General Joseph Hooker's and General Sherman's commands to take the action designed to force the Confederates off Missionary Ridge. Grant commanded about 80,000 men, which was roughly double that of Bragg, but Bragg had the better position.

A preliminary attack on November 23 was made on Orchard Knob, an elevated knoll occupied by Confederate pickets about half way from the Union lines and Missionary Ridge. General Thomas ordered 3 divisions—commanded by General Thomas Wood, General Phil Sheridan and General Absalom Baird (which contained the 10th Kentucky Infantry)—to advance from the defenses of Chattanooga to capture Orchard Knob. General Wood and General Sheridan's divisions captured their objective. As part of General Baird's Division, the 10th Kentucky probed ahead on the right of the other two divisions but had no fighting to do. The assault on Orchard Knob pleased General Thomas, who felt it was important for Grant to see that his command would fight.

Grant's overall success at Chattanooga on November 24 and 25 was notable, but the results, both positive and negative, were total surprises to him. On November 24, General Grant ordered Hooker's command on the right of the Union line to make a "demonstration" against Lookout Mountain, which resulted in the capture of the summit of the mountain. This weakened the anchor on Bragg's left. By the morning of November 25, Hooker's objective was taken and Grant's close friend, Sherman, began the day by moving into position to provide the blow that was to cripple and dislodge the Confederates on Missionary Ridge. Sherman was to attack from the north on the Confederate right flank and destroy the Confederate Army. Sherman got off to a bad start by assuming that he captured Tunnel Hill on November 24, the northernmost hill occupied by the Confederates, but he captured Lightburn Hill instead. So he awoke with his objective before him.

General Grant began his day by moving his command to Orchard Knob to better observe the day's actions. Sherman was to attack early on the 25th, but he delayed until 10:00 A.M., when he began, more due to Grant's demand for an attack, than personal initiative. The attack was beaten back by noon. The second attack began around 1:00 P.M. and after three hours of bloody, vicious combat, it was also unsuccessful. Sherman's delay and piecemeal attack, along with the excellent leadership of General Pat Cleburne, doomed Sherman to failure.

Missionary Ridge is a formidable geographic obstacle. It runs from the northeast of Chattanooga, almost beginning at the Tennessee River, and extends to the south of Chattanooga with very steep slopes, particularly in the area north of Rossville back toward the city. The Army of the Cumberland held the center of the Union Army and Grant's plan specified that they would remain in position, which would force the Confederates to keep their troops in position to repel an attack on the center of their line, thus allowing Sherman to overwhelm the flank. However, General Thomas, with General Grant's approval, ordered a limited advance on the Confederate center to take enemy rifle pits, thus relieving the pressure of Confederate reinforcements that might be sent to bolster the defenses against Sherman.

Four divisions in the Army of the Cumberland faced Missionary Ridge. General Baird's 3rd Division, 14th Corps, was on the left followed by General Thomas Woods' 3rd Division, 4th Corps, General Phil Sheridan's 2nd Division, 4th Corps, and General Richard Johnson's 1st Division, 14th Corps, lined from north to south. This force had over 23,000 men total. Their job was to capture the Confederate rifle pits directly in front of them. Once the advance began, both armies' artillery opened with barrages intended to overwhelm their opponents. As these ranks of blue-coated soldiers steadily advanced toward the rifle pits, the Confederates saw that they could not stop the flood of Union soldiers and scampered away toward their fortified line on Missionary Ridge. The ones who couldn't get away were captured by the advancing army.[27]

As the Army of the Cumberland captured these rifle pits, they found that they suffered miserably from the fire which poured on them from the ridge. Being in a position where they couldn't stay where they were and wouldn't retreat, they had one option and that was to attack up the hill of Missionary Ridge. To the surprise of all, the attack swept the Confederates off the ridge, giving the Union forces an outstanding victory. Although the Confederates had only 10,500 men on the ridge, their defenses had been considered impregnable.

One of the events that helped General Thomas' Army of the Cumberland's success in the Battle of Missionary Ridge was Hooker's victory on Lookout Mountain, which surprised the Confederate soldiers on the left flank. To panic them even more, General Peter Osterhaus, through Hooker's success, was able to gain the rear of the Confederate left flank, putting those defenders in weak position with the threat of being attacked on three sides by angry Yankees. So, when the Army of the Cumberland pushed forward, this end of the Confederate line was the first to weaken.

THE 10TH KENTUCKY AT MISSIONARY RIDGE

For the 10th Kentucky, their battle was to begin on the afternoon of November 25, 1863. The 10th Kentucky was only able to field 242 men that day. On the 23rd and 24th, the 3rd Brigade served as the reserve for their division. However, on the 25th, they were placed in line to the extreme left of the 14th Corps and the Army of the Cumberland. They had watched the Battle of Lookout Mountain on the 24th and they had watched Sherman's failed assault on the morning of November 25th. Captain Israel Webster would write that the 10th Kentucky's action began about 2:00 P.M. on November 25 when they were ordered to do some

Battle of Missionary Ridge. The 10th Kentucky's attack is in the foreground (Library of Congress).

marching to the north and then back to the south as a demonstration designed to keep the Confederates guessing as to their objective. Each time they marched north and then south, the Confederates, anticipating that they would turn to face them, followed along Missionary Ridge with men to thwart the anticipated attack. In fact, the 10th Kentucky had been ordered to march to the support of Sherman's attack on Tunnel Hill, which was not going well, but the brigade was recalled to the left of the Union line held by the Army of the Cumberland to make a demonstration against the Confederates on Missionary Ridge.

Grant became more and more concerned about his plan for Sherman to overwhelm the Confederate right flank, and he also saw that Hooker was not making the progress that he had hoped for on the Confederate left. General Thomas felt that Grant "was about to sacrifice what little of the Army of the Cumberland that he had left in a quixotic effort to salvage Sherman."[28] The 10th Kentucky, as part of Phelps's brigade, was positioned on the extreme left of the Army of the Cumberland and General Baird indicated that the interval between his left (Phelps's brigade) and Sherman was about two miles.[29]

Finally, about 3:00 P.M., the 10th Kentucky turned and began marching toward Missionary Ridge with their intent being to capture the Confederate rifle pits at the base of the ridge. They passed through a wooded thicket, hiding their movements from the Confederates, who had been dogging their movements for the last hour. The 10th Kentucky would have over two miles to march to their objective. Four divisions of the Army of the Cumberland were about to do battle with four Confederate Divisions and nine batteries of artillery.

Although given months to establish excellent defense on Missionary Ridge, it appears that the Confederate command only expected assaults on the flanks. Therefore the center of the Confederate line was not designed well and it wasn't until November 23 that the defensive work began on the center. In addition, the artillery was placed to shell Chattanooga and the plain before it, but the barrels of the cannon could not be lowered to shell the slopes of the ridge. No one had expected that anyone would be suicidal enough to attack up the steep slopes of Missionary Ridge. In addition, the morale of the Southern forces had been very low on November 25: Lookout Mountain had just been lost, Sherman was attacking their right flank and waves of blue coats were marching toward them.

The advance of the four divisions of the Army of the Cumberland would win the day for Grant. As at Chickamauga, the fate of the battle would result, this time in favor of the Union, on a confused order. In this case, the divisions would advance and take the Confederate rifle pits at the base of Missionary Ridge, but it was unclear what was to happen next. This lack of clarity of the order extended down to the regimental commanders.

The officers of the 10th Kentucky dismounted and walked with their men toward Missionary Ridge. The signal to attack sounded at 3:40 P.M., and then 23,000 blue uniformed men began what was to be the assault of Missionary Ridge. Captain Israel Webster gave this account of the 10th Kentucky's initial assault on Missionary Ridge: "When we emerged from this thicket we were about 300 yards from the Ridge, or its base, with a clear field before us. Our skirmishers passed on to the front, while we were ordered to lie down. About this time the Johnnies opened up their batteries, several of which were on the Ridge. They were so located that our position could be enfiladed by them. I well remember the place that fell to my lot...."[30]

Captain Webster noted the following experience with the regimental chaplain, Richard Nash, that happened while waiting for their turn to assault Missionary Ridge.

General Absalom Baird, the new divisional commander for the 10th Kentucky, replacing John Brannan after Chickamauga (Kentucky Historical Society).

Every instant was filled with startling scenes and sounds. Cannon-balls were coming in our midst, very close together, causing one to wonder where the next would strike. As yet none of our men had been hurt by them, nevertheless, the sound made by them while flying over head was not "sweet music" to our ears. Chaplain Nash, of our regiment, was sitting on a log under a large tree just in the edge of the woods we had passed through, holding the Colonel's and his own horse. One of these cannon-balls came shrieking over our heads, passed on, and then struck the tree over his head, making a frightful racket. I looked over that way, and was amused at what I saw. There sat the Chaplain shrinking down, into his soldier overcoat as low as he could get, his face turned toward me, upon which was a sickly smile, while he clutched the bridle-reins in a nervous grasp. The horses were prancing around frantically in their efforts to get away from there, and limbs and branches of various sizes were tumbling down among them from the tree. No one (man or beast) was hurt, but with every nerve at tension, one can readily conceive that it was rather a scary time."[31]

The Union Army marching toward the ridge must have been a spectacular sight from the crest. The Union Army marched forward through the woods and into the plain before the Confederate rifle pits. The march started, moved to quick-time, then double quick-time and finally some regiments ran to the rifle pits. As one historian described, "The air was sibilant with screaming shells."[32] As the Confederate pickets saw the sea of blue in front of them, they knew it was time to retreat to the apparent safety of their lines on Missionary Ridge, although some tried to hold their line and were engulfed. The sight of the butternut clad soldiers scurrying away exhilarated the attacking Union line. Only sporadic volleys from the Confederates slowed the advance. Many of the defenders were ordered away without even firing a shot.

The Confederate force on Missionary Ridge directly in front of Phelps's Brigade was General Alfred "A.J." Vaughn's Tennessee Brigade of Hardee's corps, made up of the 11th, 12th and 47th (combined), 13th & 154th (combined), and 29th Tennessee regiments. The regiment forming the skirmish line at the base of Missionary Ridge was the 12th and 47th consolidated Tennessee infantry, which withdrew in good order, being without support when the Alabamans on their left flank withdrew. General Baird remarked that the cannonade was very severe and the Division was caught in a cross-fire of artillery. The "atmosphere seemed filled with the messengers of death," he wrote.[33] Baird ordered his men past the rifle pits and to assault the ridge.

The Army of the Cumberland's success on Missionary Ridge resulted in their continued advance up the ridge. Colonel August Willich's brigade, of the 4th Army Corps, was the first regiment to run past the rifle pits and reach the crest of the ridge. Colonel Sam Beatty's brigade was next, and then came Colonel William Hazen. Before anyone could act, all four divisions were climbing the slopes. But still, the order was unclear on what had been intended. General Absalom Baird received a message just as his division reached the rifle pits that he was not to move past them, but the soldiers moved on. The assaults up the ridge lost any semblance of order. The fighting up and on the ridge was furious, with Confederate and Union lines forming a few yards from one another, but the seemingly never-ending supply of blue-coated soldiers moved up and onto the crest. Beatty, Willich and Hazen punched the first hole in the Confederate defense, forcing Colonel William Tucker's Mississippi brigade backwards. The gap in the Confederate line widened. Now a major weakness in the defense of Missionary Ridge became apparent—too much geography was being covered by too few men and there was an insufficient reserve to stop the Union troops from exploiting their advantage. Now Union soldiers began to file left and right along the ridge, turning the flanks of the defenders and allowing more Union regiments to reach the crest.

General Absalom Baird commanded the brigades of Beatty, Turchin, Van Derveer and finally Phelps, which would attack and gain control of the ridge from right to left. The 10th Kentucky, as part of Phelps's brigade, was among the last to attack and gain control of the Ridge. The Confederate left on Missionary Ridge was collapsing and Vaughn began sending regiments to try to stem the impending disaster. He first sent the 11th Tennessee, which ran into Turchin's brigade, which was rolling up the Confederate left. Next, Vaughn sent the 13th and 154th (combined) Tennessee to support his left. Finally realizing the location was no longer defendable, Vaughn pulled his brigade back from Missionary Ridge. Then Phelps' brigade was on the ridge.[34]

Lt. Colonel Gabriel Wharton described the charge up the hill to the crest of Missionary Ridge: "When the foot of the hill had been gained and ascent commenced, the line of battle was lost, the strongest men to the right of the regiment ... went first, and the weakest men formed the left of the regiment. Many fell going up the hill as if exhausted, but would rest a moment, take a sup of water from a mountain stream, and then forward again."[35] The assault up Missionary Ridge is almost unimaginable. The ridge was 400 to 500 feet higher than the plain of the city of Chattanooga and the incline is approximately 40 percent. The soldiers attacking up this ridge were at a decided disadvantage, but their two-month confinement in Chattanooga and their pride forced them upward into the muzzles of soldiers who had defeated this Army two months earlier. The Army of Cumberland would not be denied this day.

The assault toward the enemy was not without losses. Captain Webster noted: "As I started on again to catch up with the boys, my hat was blown off my head by the force of a passing shell, so near did it come to hitting me. By throwing up my hands I caught the hat, and following the directions of the ball's course with my eyes, I saw it strike the first file (Sergeant and four men) of a regiment on our right, marching by the right flank toward the Ridge. (I think it was the 9th Ohio.) Up flew their hands and guns, then down they all went. For an instant there was great confusion just at that spot. In a moment all was as before, seemingly, for the line moved right along as though nothing unusual had occurred."[36]

While Vaughn's troops were withdrawing, Van Derveer's and Phelps's brigades seized the opportunity to continue rolling up the Confederate left. Captain Webster describes the 10th Kentucky's actions:

> Our line soon formed, and away we go in line of-battle, in a left oblique direction. The ground descending and our march is short, when we came to a halt. At that moment the "ping" of a bullet was heard, followed closely by another, giving evidence of a near enemy and one that was ready to fight. I gave the command to my company to lie down, which they did in time to escape a volley of musketry fired at us just at that instant. Col. Hays came up to our rear just at this time and by his orders the whole regiment lay down. Load and fire as rapidly as possible was the next command. The men would load while down, then rise up and fire."[37]

Battle of Chattanooga (Library of Congress).

The 10th Kentucky had two men killed during the Battle of Missionary Ridge: Private John Garrott, Company C, and Private Stephen Nally, Company G. Captain Webster wrote:

> Two men of our regiment were killed upon the Ridge. I cannot recall their names, but one was of Co. C [Garrott]. He was just in front of me, and as he rose up to shoot, his gun fell out of his hands, he twisted his head and body around, looked at me in the face, his head leaned forward, his hat fell off his head onto the ground before him, his face dropped into his hands, and all fell into his hat, never to be moved again except by other power than his own. Never will I forget the pitiful expression upon his face as he looked into mine, nor the sight of his heart's blood as it oozed out of his mouth. I have often thought that he rose up to shoot just in time to save my life; for my head was in direct line with the range of that bullet, and by rising up before me he was struck in his heart. What might have been!"[38]

General Baird stated that as the division reached the summit it was directed to the left, where the enemy resistance was found.[39] Once reaching the top of the ridge, Phelps's brigade turned left and met Jackson's and Moore's brigades. General John Jackson commanded the 1st Georgia, 5th Georgia, 47th Georgia, 65th Georgia, 5th Mississippi, 8th Mississippi and 2nd Battalion of Georgia Sharpshooters. General John C. Moore commanded the 37th, 40th and 42nd Alabama. General Hardee observed the activity on Missionary Ridge and saw what was coming his way. Jackson's men "grew panicky" as the Union units approached to within 150 yards. After overrunning Vaughn's vacated entrenchments, Phelps extended the 10th Kentucky to connect the line with Van Derveer's flank. This allowed the 4th Kentucky to take the 10th Kentucky's place and place their flag on top of Missionary Ridge. The regiments in Phelps's brigade that attacked Missionary Ridge were aligned with the 10th Kentucky to the right of the first battle line, with the 4th Kentucky, 74th Indiana, and 38th Ohio extended to the left. The reserve positions were assigned to the 14th Ohio and 10th Indiana.[40]

The 10th Kentucky was able to offer a valuable service for the men of the 89th Ohio, as described by Thomas Ireton, a member of that unit, in letter to his brother:

> And up the Hill they come at us. It was then dark and our lines were in poor condition to receive a charge for every man was fighting on his own hook—but we stood our ground and give them the best we had in the shop until we was compelled by our broken ranks to fall back. We dropped back 20, or, 25 yards in good order where the gallant 10th Ky was laying down in line of Battle with all there guns loaded when they rose up and sent a volley of Destruction through there ranks which made them flee like so many sheep when the dogs get among them—That ended the fight on Missionary Ridge—we then went to work to prepare some coffee for supper and see to our killed and wounded."[41]

Lt. Colonel Gabriel Wharton described the 10th Kentucky's actions on the ridge:

> Col Hays rapidly formed the regiment on the right of Colonel Van Derveer's brigade, on an open field on a plateau, about 30 yards from a gorge which divided the ridge we were on and the one on which the enemy were posted, and opened on them a destructive fire, but they continued to advance, when the regiment was ordered to charge up the gorge, which it did in splendid style, which caused the enemy to waver. At the same moment the other regiment of our brigade, having gained the hill, charged down the ridge to the left of the Second Brigade and the enemy broke and fled perceptibly. This fight did not last more than twenty-five minutes, yet for that it was very hot. The officers and men behaved with great courage, many refusing to take cover when ordered to do so. The fighting closed at or near 5:30 P.M.[42]

Colonel Hays wrote that the charge to the summit was done at the "double-quick time" and once the unit reached the summit, it was only 25 to 30 yards away from the enemy on the left. Jackson's and Moore's units poured a "murderous fire" into the brigade. But the 14th

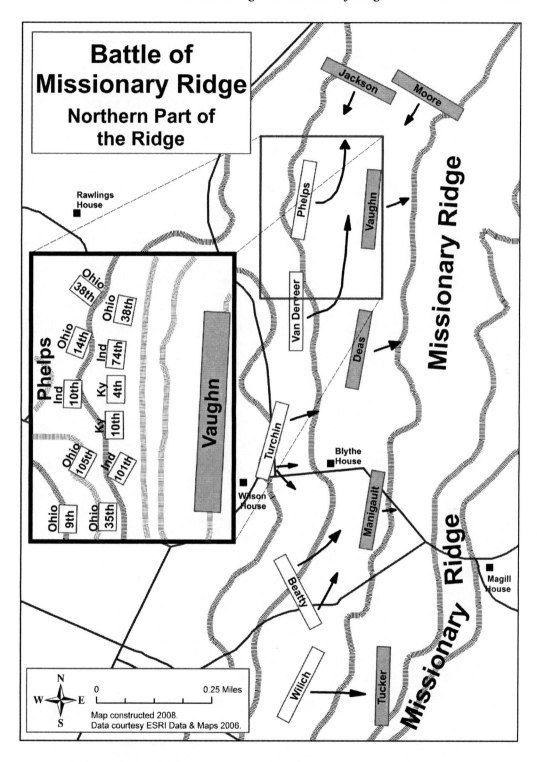

Battle of Missionary Ridge, Northern Part of the Ridge (original map adapted from *The Shipwreck of Their Hopes: The Battles of Chattanooga*, copyright 1994 Board of Trustees. Used with permission of the author and the University of Illinois Press).

Ohio and 10th Indiana came forward to engage the enemy and enabled the brigade to maintain its hold on the ridge.[43] Colonel Phelps was in the midst of his brigade encouraging them forward toward Jackson and Moore when he was shot and killed "a dozen yards from Jackson's line."[44] "The Gallant Colonel Phelps, commanding the Third Brigade, was shot dead after reaching the crest, in forming and directing his men," stated Absalom Baird.[45] Then the command of the brigade, just as at Chickamauga, fell to Colonel William H. Hays, and the command of the 10th was taken over by Gabriel Wharton.

The 2nd Brigade of Absalom Baird's division also focused and attacked Moore and Jackson's Confederates. Colonel Gustave Kammerling's 9th Ohio moved against Jackson's command and the 75th Indiana charged over the 9th Ohio (both regiments of Van Derveer's brigade) and broke Jackson's line, finally ending the battle near the 10th Kentucky. The lateness of the day, disorganization of units and exhaustion of the men effectively prevented any further pursuit of the enemy on the 25th. The Union had won a major victory and the door was open to Atlanta.

Major Henry Davidson summarized the Battle of Missionary Ridge in a letter to his aunt:

> On Wednesday Nov 25 we lay quiet until three o'clock P.M. when the word to advance was given. No soldiers ever went to battle in such splendid spirits. With one wild, loud, cheer the men went forward, up, up the steep rugged sides of Mission Ridge the soldiers go, each one as best he can. Mounted officers threw themselves from their horses, and climbed the steep ascent. The Rebels made a stand against our Brigade, our men made a furious assault, & the Rebel line is broken. They form again & endeavor to retake the Ridge. We charge then and scatter them to the winds, the fight is ended, the Rebels fly in disorder. The star & stripes wave over Mission Ridge, and the great victory of the war is won.[46]

CASUALTIES

The 10th Kentucky's losses were minor in the Battle of Missionary Ridge compared to Chickamauga. The casualty list for the 10th Kentucky includes no officers. Among enlisted men, two were killed, 10 were wounded, and none was captured.

Casualties by Company

Company C
Pvt John Garrott—killed
Pvt William Moore—wounded
Pvt David Allen—wounded
Pvt John Hoback—wounded
Company D
Pvt Alfred Snider—wounded
Pvt Benjamin Taylor—wounded
Company G
Corp Benjamin McCarty—wounded
Pvt Stephen Nally—killed
Pvt Richard Vessels—wounded
Company I
Pvt Benjamin Ellis—wounded
Pvt Isaac Hicks—wounded
Pvt Augustus Spencer—wounded

General Baird said the duty of Colonel William Hays "was handsomely performed."[47] The men of the 10th again performed well and began to look south for their next engagement.

Lincoln had earlier proclaimed that November 26, 1863, would be a "special day of thanksgiving and praise." [48] This was never truer than for the 10th Kentucky on the day after the Battle of Missionary Ridge. They had been only lightly affected, and with such a small number of men present for duty, they could not have suffered much more. The past two months had been a challenge for the regiment, but the men awoke on the 26th and were truly thankful that they were alive and victorious.

The 10th Kentucky bivouacked on Missionary Ridge after the battle and the next day they began to bury the dead and remove the wounded from the field. It wasn't until 3:00 P.M. on the 26th that they began the pursuit of the enemy. They marched about 8 miles to the Chickamauga Creek and camped for the night. On the 27th they marched to Ringgold, Georgia, and on the 28th they were employed in destroying four railroad bridges over the East Chickamauga Creek, and they destroyed about one mile of railroad. So began the assault on Georgia.

On the 29th of November they marched back to their old camp in Chattanooga to settle into winter quarters. One of the most interesting events of the Battle of Missionary Ridge occurred after the fighting. This was a tremendous success for the Union Army now under command of General Grant, but the success of the battle really resulted because of the action of the commanders of the four attacking divisions of Missionary Ridge who disobeyed Grant's orders about stopping at the rifle pits. Grant's order to Thomas was that the four divisions of the Army of the Cumberland would assault the rifle pits and stop. Grant was reported to have been very angry when he learned of the assault by the Army of the Cumberland on Missionary Ridge. The success of this action, however, put Grant in an awkward position of opposing the action that led to the great success of this battle. Arguments raged for years about this action, and in some cases history was re-written to capitalize on the success of the battle.

10th Kentucky Regimental Losses in November and December 1863

	November	*December*
Discharged		Skinner, Taleaferro (G)
		Birch, John H. (G)
		Belton, Addison (H)
Died	Hoback, Martin L. (C)	Pirtle, Isaac E. (A)
		Clark, John M (G)
Killed in Action	Garrott, John J. (C)	
	Nally, Stephen (G)	
Resigned		Spalding, Charles (G)
Transferred		Ballard, Shelby (G)
		Osborn, James (G)

(Letters in parentheses indicate the company of the individual.)

SIX

Atlanta Campaign

"It is the highest praise that can be spoken of them to say they
proved themselves worthy of the rank they bore and of the
men under them."—Colonel George Este, 14th Corps

After returning to Chattanooga in November 1863, the 10th Kentucky Infantry made
their winter quarters there, in much more comfort than they had had for the previous two
months. The supplies were still short but more plentiful than they had been in the prior
months. Now they were the victorious army ready to continue the war into the heart of the
South. The 10th Kentucky used the winter to rebuild the unit's strength; the regiment only
manned 242 men for the Battle of Missionary Ridge. Although the 10th Kentucky would
never again reach the numbers of men that were present early in the war, they were able to
field 436 men ready for duty in February 1864.[1]

Beginning 1864, the pendulum of the war was starting to swing in favor of the Union.
The previous year was a disaster for the Southern cause with major losses on the Mississippi
River, in Pennsylvania and finally at Chattanooga, but the South was, by no means, dead. The
Confederacy had to change its tactics from offensive to primarily defensive in strategy, but
was ready to lash out if the opportunity was present. In many cases, the Southern soldier was
even more determined to fight as he saw his sacred soil invaded by the Northern aggressor.

The Army of Tennessee, now facing the 10th Kentucky, had also changed since the Battle of Missionary Ridge. The army was now commanded by General Joseph E. Johnston, who
succeeded Braxton Bragg after his resignation on November 29 just after his defeat near Chattanooga. With Johnston in command of the Army of Tennessee, many of the problems inher-
ent under the old command were gone and the new army would prove to be a formidable
opponent in the next year.

The 10th Kentucky was preparing to enter a new phase of the war. This was the war that
would be waged on the South by General William Tecumseh Sherman. Despite Sherman's
lack of success at Missionary Ridge, he still had Grant's confidence, and when Grant was promoted in March 1864 to the rank of lieutenant general in charge of the entire Union forces,
he placed Sherman in charge of the Military Division of the Mississippi. Sherman and Grant
presented a new kind of warfare to the Confederacy. They were prepared to use their superior numbers and almost unlimited resources to grind the Southern Army down. Later, Sherman would realize the part the civilian played in supporting the Confederate Army, and he
would decide that even civilian property was not to be spared in what was to be total war
against the South.

On February 25, 1864, the 10th Kentucky was involved with the Federal Army in the
Battle of Rocky Face near Dalton, Georgia. The regiment remained with the General Absalom Baird's Division in the 14th Corps and was stationed at Ringgold, Georgia, until May
7, when the Union Army began its Atlanta campaign. The Atlanta Campaign is one of the

Siege of Atlanta (Library of Congress).

most difficult campaigns to describe in the whole Civil War, because it is a series of constant battles fought over four months involving numerous Union and Confederate forces over a variety of geographic locations. The 10th Kentucky was involved to various degrees in the Battles of Resaca, Adairsville, Calhoun, Kingston, Kennesaw Mountain, Chattahoochee/Vining Station, Atlanta, Utoy Creek, and finally Jonesboro.[2]

Dyer's Compendium shows the 10th Kentucky's activities from February 1864 through the Battle of Jonesboro as follows.

10th Kentucky Activities

Reconnaissance of Dalton, Ga.	February 22–27, 1864
Tunnel Hill, Buzzard's Roost Gap and Rocky Faced Ridge	February 23–25
Atlanta (Ga.) Campaign	May 1–September 8
Demonstration on Rocky Faced Ridge and Dalton	May 8–13
Buzzard's Roost Gap	May 8–9
Battle of Resaca	May 14–15
Advance on Dallas	May 18–25
Operations on line of Pumpkin Vine Creek and battles about	
Dallas, New Hope Church and Allatoona Hills	May 25–June 5
Operations about Marietta and against Kennesaw Mountain	June 10–July 2
Pine Hill	June 11–14
Lost Mountain	June 15–17
Near Marietta	June 19
Assault on Kennesaw	June 27
Ruff's Station	July 4
Chattahoochee River	July 5–17
Vining Station	July 9–11
Peach Tree Creek	July 19–20
Siege of Atlanta	July 22–August 25
Flank movement on Jonesboro	August 25–30
Battle of Jonesboro	August 31–Sept 1.[3]

The organization of the 14th Corps had also changed since the Battle of Missionary Ridge. General John Palmer again commanded the 14th Corps until August and then he was replaced with General Jefferson C. Davis. The death of Colonel Phelps, brigade commander for the Third Brigade at the Battle of Missionary Ridge, resulted in that position being filled by Colonel George Peabody Este, previously regimental commander of the 14th Ohio. Colonel Este was a New Hampshire native and graduated from Dartmouth College in 1846. He was practicing law in Toledo, Ohio, at the beginning of the war. He was the original lieutenant colonel of the 14th Ohio and was later promoted to command the regiment.[4]

Organization of the Army in Relation to the 10th Kentucky

Fourteenth Army Corps—Major
   General John M. Palmer.
      Third Division—Brigadier General Absalom Baird.
      Third Brigade—Colonel George P. Este.
         10th Indiana—Lieut. Colonel Marsh B. Taylor.
         74th Indiana—Lieut. Colonel Myron Baker.
         10th Kentucky—Colonel William H. Hays.
         18th Kentucky—Lieut. Colonel Hubbard K. Millard.
         14th Ohio—Major John W. Wilson.
         38th Ohio—Colonel William A. Choate.

Prior to beginning the Atlanta Campaign, the old scourge of the 10th Kentucky, disease, returned to plague the unit. A smallpox outbreak occurred in the late winter of 1863–1864. Captain Henry Waller of Company K died of small pox in March 1864,[5] and

The 10th Kentucky Infantry's Movements During the Atlanta Campaign (map created by Thomas Vought).

Colonel George Este, a New Hampshire native who was practicing law in Toledo, Ohio, at the beginning of the war (Blue Acorn Press, Huntington, West Virginia, L. M. Strayer Collection).

his successor, Captain John Denton, contracted smallpox but recovered. Captain Denton continued to serve as the only commissioned officer in Company K for the upcoming Atlanta Campaign.[6] Captain George W. Riley suffered a reaction from a smallpox vaccination that resulted in a two month confinement in the hospital. Captain Riley was serving as the topographical engineer for the division at this time and was not commanding Company D.[7] This was also a time that scurvy plagued many of the men of the 10th Kentucky.

As the war advanced, it became more and more difficult for the officers to maintain the men in the field. There appeared to be a process by which men could get a certificate of disability that would allow them to be discharged even though the disability did not exist. Two letters written by Major Henry Davidson to Edward Stanton, secretary of war, outlined the frustration experienced in the field. The first one read:

> March 21, 1864
> Ringgold, Gad
>
> Sir:
>
> I respectfully call your attention to the case of private Marcus Graham, Co "D" of my Regiment. Some time about the 1st of May, 1863, while the Brigade to which my Regiment is attached was stationed at Lavergne Tenn., his brother a citizen came to my camp and obtained permission for said Graham to accompany him to Nashville Tenn. for forty-eight hours; in less than a week official notice was received for hospital in Nashville that Marcus D Graham had been discharged from the service of the United States on account of physical disability. The man left the camp in perfect health, had never been sick from the time of enlistment. Fraud was so evident in obtaining his discharge that Col Wm H Hays commanding the regiment at that time made a statement of the case and forwarded it to Dept Headquarters asking an investigation and that the man be ordered back to duty.
>
> Nothing was ever heard afterward from the papers. I therefore renew Col Hays' request, and ask of you an order for this arrest and return to duty. He can be found in Marion County Ky near Lebanon."[8]

On the same day, Major Davidson sent a second letter to Edward Stanton on the same topic. This time the letter referred to discharges of Privates Danby Maxwell and Daniel Hughes, also of Company D. His concern in this case was "that through the influence of friends, and chicanery in the hospital, that both of these men have been transferred to the Invalid Corps at Louisville, Ky."[9] Major Davidson was concerned about the loss of men while the 10th Kentucky was trying to maintain its position at the front.

Regimental Losses January through April 1864

	January	*February*	*March*	*April*
Discharged				
	McDaniel, John (A)	Lynch, Robert (D)	Curd, Joseph (E)	
	Harmon, Isaac (H)			
	Purdy, William (I)			
Died				
	Davenport, Richard (Staff)		McVey, William (K)	Seay, John (E)
	Caniff, Elias (C)		Waller, Henry (K)	Caromed, Simon (K)
	Rose, James E. (I)			
Deserted				
	Grier, Tandy (H)			
Transferred				
	Norco, James (C)	Horsham, William (F)	Wells, Elbert (D)	Craig, John (C)
		Conway, Patrick (K)		Phillips, John (D)
		Durham, John (B)		Nix, George (E)

January	February	March	April

Transferred (cont.)

Rose, John C. (H)
Fitzgibbons, Pat. (H)

(Letters in parentheses indicate the company of the individual.)

It is apparent the toll of the war was great on all the men of the 10th Kentucky. Colonel Hays' account of the Atlanta Campaign up to August 24 is only a single page long. The soldiers were getting tired. Colonel William Hays' record of the 10th Kentucky's actions through mid–August is:

> HDQRS. TENTH KENTUCKY VOLUNTEER INFANTRY,
> Near Atlanta, Ga., August 24, 1864.

CAPTAIN: In compliance with orders, I have the honor to submit the following report of the operations of my regiment during the campaign:

The regiment left Ringgold, Ga., May 10, at 6 A.M., joining the division same day at 4 P.M. at Tunnel Hill. In the engagement around Buzzard Roost my command did not participate. Upon the arrival of the army in front of Resaca I was at the front line of the brigade, but had no engagement with the enemy. On the 13th of May moved to the right, and here had 1 man killed. My regiment from this time on never, until the 9th day of July, met the enemy as an organization. I was on the front line from the 2d of June until the evacuation of Kennesaw Mountain by the enemy, and consequently had some part of my command constantly upon the skirmish line, and shall therefore not try to make an extended report, but only give my losses and the date of their occurrence—May 15, 1 man killed; June 4, 4 men wounded; June 15, 1 man wounded; July 21, 2 men wounded. On the morning of the 9th of July I was ordered to support with my regiment a forward movement of the skirmish line. I moved out at 6 A.M., and followed the skirmishers at close supporting distance. They, meeting a largely superior force of the enemy, were compelled to fall back. As soon as they had rallied behind my line I opened a fire upon the enemy, which checked his advance. There being no connection on my left, and the enemy coming around on my flank, I was forced to fall back about 200 yards, where I compelled the enemy to halt, and the Tenth Indiana joining me, he fell back to his old position. That night the rebels evacuated that side of the river. This contest, although only lasting fifteen or twenty minutes, was very severe. My loss was 4 killed, 14 wounded, and 2 missing. Among the wounded were Lieutenants Warren and Grace, of Company A, who fell while gallantly discharging their duty. Since crossing the river parts of my command have again been daily on the skirmish line, and the following losses there occurred: July 20, 2 wounded; July 21, 1 wounded; August 4, 1 wounded; August 7, 4 wounded; August 13, 1 wounded; August 16, 2 wounded, making a total of 40 killed and wounded since the beginning of the campaign to the 16th instant.

I have the honor to be, captain, your obedient servant,

W. H. HAYS,
Colonel Tenth Kentucky Infantry.[10]

A summary of Colonel Hays' reports shows that once the Atlanta campaign began in May 1864, the 10th Kentucky had some action against the enemy, but the regiment was generally not a major participant in most of the conflicts. The Atlanta campaign was a series of battles over four months. Whether the Union won or lost the battles, the Confederates were slowly pressed south to the gates of Atlanta. As Sherman's armies pushed toward Atlanta, he kept the Confederate Army guessing what would be the next target. In mid May 1864, Sherman met the Confederate Army in a full engagement just north of Resaca, Georgia. The 10th Kentucky with the 14th Corps was positioned in the middle of the Union line facing Lieutenant General William Hardee's corps in the center of the Confederate line. The 10th Kentucky was in the front battle line at the Battle of Resaca and during the initial phase of the battle did not engage the enemy. However, one man of the 10th Kentucky, Private Bannister Skinner, Company G, was killed in action on May 15 as the regiment moved to the right.[11] The result of the Battle of Resaca was that General Sherman attacked the Confederates but was generally repulsed; but Sherman sent a force across the Oostanaula River which the enemy could not prevent, and the Southern Army was forced to retreat and fight another day. The estimated casualties were approximately 5500 men, with the Union and Confederates losing about the same number. General Absalom Baird stated in his official report that Lt. Colonel Gabriel Wharton of the 10th Kentucky Infantry was in charge of the skirmishers for the 3rd Brigade at the Battle of Resaca and that he was the first officer to enter the town.

On May 14, 1864, Sgt. James Champion received a severe concussion from an explosive shell which struck a tree. This would later be cited as the cause of a lifelong disability which would result in a determination of insanity. After the shell struck near him, he was found in an incoherent state. Lieutenant Clem Funk reported that Sgt. Champion was ordered to make a reconnaissance of the enemy near Resaca, Georgia. Lieutenant Funk stated that he found Sgt. Champion "talking very wildly" and speaking incoherently. Sgt. Champion was sent to the hospital, returned after a couple of days, and again began talking wildly. The officers of the regiment felt that he needed to be removed from the line and perhaps placed in an asylum. He would remain with the 10th Kentucky after his concussion, but he was not able to return to full duty and would not be sent to an "asylum without advice from his family."[12] He was placed under the watch of one of the other men of the 10th Kentucky throughout the campaign.

On May 27, 1864, the Union Army was dealt another setback by the Southern forces, this time at Pickett's Mill. The Union Army was to attack the seemingly exposed flank of the Confederate Army, but an uncoordinated attack led to a Union defeat. The Union Army lost approximately 1600 men to 500 lost by the Confederates. Corporal Aaron Jones and Private Mathie Kortz of Company A were wounded at Pickett's Mill, Georgia, in May 1864.

On June 4, four men (Aaron Jones, Company A, Terry Johnson, Company F, Joseph Browning, Company F, and Caleb Welch, Company F) were wounded in the actions around New Hope Church. In June, one man, Moses McCabbins, Company F, was severely wounded near Kennesaw Mountain. Some part of the 10th Kentucky was constantly on the skirmish line during the Battle of Kennesaw Mountain.

The Battle of Kennesaw Mountain was another setback for the Union Army. Kennesaw Mountain was north and west of Marietta, Georgia, and was strategic to the Southern plan to prevent the Union forces from penetrating deeper toward Atlanta. The Confederate Army had a superior defensive position. Again, this battle took a heavy toll on the Union Army, and one Illinois soldier wrote, "I tell you the men were mowed down like grass."[13] The Union would lose 3000 men to the Confederate's 1000. After the battle, Sherman was able to turn the Confederate flank and move steadily closer to Atlanta. The war was taking a tremendous toll on the 10th Kentucky and the men began to wear out. In February the 10th mustered more than 460 men; by the Battle of Kennesaw Mountain that number was down to 368 and by July 9 the number was further reduced to 268.[14]

A letter from Sgt. Edward Mittler, Company F, to his wife on July 2, 1864, gives a glimpse of the gruesome aspects of the war. The action to which he referred was probably the battle near Kennesaw Mountain: "and I think, that Sherman himself is not able to say how long we will yet remain in this position. Our fortifications are only 20 foot from those of the rebels. Last Monday, our whole line, made an attack upon the rebels, but did not gain much

The Union advances of Kennesaw Mountain (Library of Congress).

by it. We lost about 8–900 men which we buried Wednesday, which under a Flag of Truce. Our regiment was so fortunate as to be on the march,—in order to change position, therefore did not take part in this engagement."[15]

Sgt. Mittler barely missed being killed due to pure luck during one of the battles in June. He wrote to his wife, "You seem to be worried yet, on account of my wound, I can assure you, that is not necessary, as every sign of it, has disappeared. God has protected me—for, the ball passed through the filled water canteen of my neighbor to the left before it struck me, had the bullet struck me, without taking the course which, it did, I would surely not be able to write to you now."[16]

As the 10th Kentucky marched toward Atlanta, two additional soldiers were wounded on June 21; John Hogland, Company C, was severely wounded, and George Brady of Company B was slightly wounded.[17]

The next major engagement for the 10th Kentucky was an encounter on the Chattahoochee River, near Vining's Station. The Confederate line was constantly pulling back and selecting strategic opportunities to strike at Sherman's armies as they crept closer and closer to Atlanta. Atlanta was not going to be given up without a fight. One of the last natural barriers to Atlanta was the Chattahoochee River. The Union Army continued to probe, push, and engage the enemy.[18]

The result of one of the probes occurred on July 9, 1864, near Vining Station, Georgia, a small settlement with a ferry south of the town on the Chattahoochee River. A line of skirmishers was sent from the 10th Kentucky in advance of the Army of the Cumberland to protect the brigade. The 10th Kentucky Infantry was sent in support of the skirmishers that were probing for the enemy at 6:00 A.M.. The skirmishers found the enemy, in brigade strength, who lashed out against them, and as the 10th Kentucky fell into battle line to support them, found that along with the 10th Indiana they were two regiments facing a brigade of 4 or 5 regiments. As soon as the skirmishers were safely behind the 10th Kentucky, a volley was loosed into the pursuers. The 10th Kentucky was without contact with friendly forces on their flanks, and quickly found that they were being flanked by the Confederates. They fell back 200 yards to prevent this. The 10th Indiana quickly moved forward and loosed a volley into the Confederates, who decided that they had found the body of the Union Army and moved back to their original position.[19]

The Confederates who attacked the 10th Kentucky were probably one of General Walthall's brigades—Reynolds, O'Neal, or Quarles. Typically, O'Neal held the center position of Walthall's division and was probably the brigade that attacked the 10th Kentucky. Walthall punished the 10th for the mistake of losing support on their flanks. While the battle took only a few minutes, the toll was heavy on the 10th, with 4 men killed, 14 wounded and 2 missing, presumably captured. Two officers were wounded during the battle.[20]

The 10th Kentucky soldiers reported as missing were Sgt. Robert Clayton of Company C and Private Thomas Stewart of Company I. Both had been captured by the Confederates and sent to the dreaded Andersonville Prison. Private Stewart remained in Andersonville and was paroled in April 1865. Sgt. Clayton was exchanged from Andersonville in February 1865.[21]

Those who were killed in action were Charles Henry Miles, Company B, Joseph Buckman, Company C, John Mayes, Company E, and Tobias Burk, Company K. Among the wounded were Francis Murphy of Company G, Caleb Welch of Company F (who subsequently died), Nelson Southerland of Company F, John Curby of Company I, William Moore of Company C, Thomas Walstan of Company H, John Heaton, Company E, Tobias Burke, Company K, Scott Whitehouse, Company G, C. W. Mattingly, Company B, William Hall of Company B, William Cross, Company B, and Thomas Brown, Company K, whose right arm was amputated.[22]

One of the two injured officers was Lieutenant Richard Grace, who, on July 9, 1864, had a gunshot wound to his left thigh which missed the bone but caused severe injury to the muscles and resulted in severe lameness. He was treated at the divisional hospital, then sent to Chattanooga, and on to Nashville and then to Louisville. He was absent—"sick-in-hospital"—when the regiment was mustered out in December.[23] Lieutenant Henry Warren, Company A, was shot in the left leg about three inches below the knee July 9 at the Chattahoochee. This wound effectively ended the war for Lieutenant Warren. He recuperated but did not report back to his regiment until November 21, 1864.[24]

Colonel Este's report of the action is as follows:

> Moving out, the Tenth Kentucky Volunteers in support of the skirmishers, we soon engaged the rebel pickets, driving them at first a short distance with ease; but the skirmishers upon our left, having advanced within sight of the enemy's works, and meeting with a heavy and severe fire, fell back to their support. On being rallied and re-enforced by two additional companies of the Tenth Kentucky, they again advanced to the position they had before advanced to. The fire, however, of the enemy becoming very severe, and there being no connection on our left, the rebels meanwhile advancing in two lines of battle and endeavoring to gain our flank, the order was given to fall back, changing front to the left. The line was reformed about 150 yards in the rear, and the advance of the enemy checked, and they in turn retired, upon the coming of the Tenth Indiana, the fight lasting some fifteen minutes, and the fire was really very severe. Most of the officers and men behaved with the utmost gallantry, and did all under the circumstances the most exacting commandant could ask. The object of the advance was gained.

The enemy was found, and found, too, in uncomfortably strong numbers. That night they crossed the river, burning their boats and bridges behind them."[25]

Captain H. G. Neubert, 14th Ohio, reported in a letter published in the *Toledo Blade* that Colonel Este's brigade "fought with determined spirit and courage," but "by some misunderstanding our flank was exposed, which fact the wily enemy was not long in discovering and taking advantage of, for he immediately commenced a flank movement" and engaged the 10th Kentucky.[16]

The 10th Kentucky did not cross the Chattahoochee River until July 17 and then crossed over a pontoon bridge. The skirmishes and battles continued as the Union Army approached Atlanta. On July 17, 1864, Jefferson Davis relieved General Joseph Johnston of his command of the Confederate Army because of his inability to stop the Union Army from the slow march toward Atlanta. General Johnston was replaced with General John Bell Hood. General Hood decided to strike what he hoped was the exposed flank of the Union Army that would be crossing the Peachtree Creek. The Confederates under control of General William Hardee struck along a line that included the 14th Corps where the 10th Kentucky was posted, along with the 20th Corps and 4th Corps. Their target was to halt the 14th and 20th Corps and their intent was to strike the flank of the greatly outnumbered division of 4th Corps under

Union soldiers outside Atlanta (Library of Congress).

the command of General John Newton. The Confederates were repulsed, suffering enfilade fire as they attacked, and the Union Army was able to fight off their attackers.

The Southern attackers suffered greatly in this battle that cost 4,400 total casualties. The Union Army suffered 1,900 casualties compared to almost 2,500 losses for the Southern Army. The 10th Kentucky had 2 men wounded (Mathie Kortz, Company A, and Joseph Miles, Company E) on July 20 in this engagement along the Peachtree Creek. On the next day a soldier was wounded (James H. Brown, Company C) on July 21, which resulted in the amputation of his arm.

The Union Army pressed forward and began cutting railroad tracks into Atlanta in an attempt to demonstrate to Hood that the city could not be held. The Battle of Utoy Creek was an attempt by the Union Army to continue this strategy by destroying the railroad between East Point and Atlanta. Major General John Schofield's Army of the Ohio, supported by the 14th Corps, began its attack on August 5 and the engagements continued into August 7. The Union Army was initially successful in its assault, but reinforcements were thrown into the Confederate line. By the end of August 7, the Union Army stopped its assault and began digging trenches. During this battle the 10th Kentucky suffered one wounded (John Buckley, Company K) on August 4, and six wounded (Theo Masterson, Company G, George Riggs, Company G, Corp. James Higdon, Company E, James Johnson, Company B, and William Ferrill, Company G, who subsequently died on August 7). Another 10th Kentucky soldier was wounded on August 13 — William Dobson, Company C, who died of his wounds the next day. Three 10th Kentuckians from Company B (Lieutenant William O'Bryan, Private Charles Beavers, and Private John Martin) were wounded on August 16 in the siege and series of engagements during August southwest of Atlanta. Overall, the 10th Kentucky lost at least 40 men due to death, capture or wounding during the Atlanta campaign prior to the Battle of Jonesboro.[27]

The officer ranks were diminishing as were the number of men able to report for duty. Captain Franklin Hill developed scurvy during the campaign and he reported that several others in the regiment also suffered from this condition.[28] John T. McCauley, 2nd lieutenant of Company B, was hospitalized in mid July, 1864, during the Atlanta campaign with chronic diarrhea, lung disease (camp cough) and nervousness. This was due to hard and exhausting marching of the regiment. He returned to the regiment on August 24, 1864, just prior to the Battle of Jonesboro.[29] Captain Andrew Thompson was sent to the hospital from June 25 to July 14 due to chronic diarrhea.[30]

Courts-Martial

In April 1864, two 10th Kentucky privates, John Cooper of Company C and William Batman of Company K, stood general court-martial. Unlike the other court-martial records, which are very complete, there is little information about the legal events for these two soldiers. Private William Batman was tried for desertion and was fined $5.00 for the costs associated with his arrest, and fined the cost of one Prussian musket. Private Cooper was arrested and fined $10.00.

On July 5, 1864, Private Philip W. Brown, Company I, was court-martialed for absence without leave. His court was made up of Lt. Colonel M. Mudge, 11th Michigan, Captain S. E. Childs, 11th Michigan, Captain J. S. Curry, 21st Ohio, Captain Alex Semon, 69th Ohio,

1st Lieutenant John Silsby, 1st Wisconsin Heavy Artillery, and Captain I. B. Webster, 10th Kentucky.

The charge was absence without leave: "The said Philip W Brown, Pvt Co. I 10th Regt Ky Vol Infty, having been duly enlisted and mustered into the Service of the United States did on or about the 31st day of October 1862 while the Regt and Co to which he belonged was on the march, absent himself from his command without permission from his commanding Officers and did remain absent without leave until on or about the 9th day of February 1864 when he returned voluntarily to his company and reported for duty at Chattanooga Tenn., he has been doing duty ever since, this on the march from Kentucky to Tennessee and when the Regt was near Greensburg, Ky."[31]

Sgt. John F. Mills, Company I, testified for the prosecution that Private Brown was sick and was ordered to go back to the ambulance. When the ambulance came into camp, he was not in it and he was not seen again until February 1864. The accused offered no defense.

Private Brown was found guilty and sentenced to forfeit pay for one year and three months and that he make good the time he was absent to the government.

Above and opposite: **Rebel Defenses at Atlanta (Library of Congress).**

Regimental Losses May–August 1864

	May	*June*	*July*	*August*
Discharged	Oster, James (Staff)	Tarrill, Patrick (I)	Moore, George (A)	
Died	Clark, Royal G. (B)	Champion, Charles (E)	Livers, Samuel (B) Welch, Caleb (F)	Blair, James (B) Hayden, Andrew (B) Sallee, Thomas (C) Nix, William (E)
Killed in Action	Higdon, Alexander (E) Skinner, Bannister (G)		Miles, Chas. Henry (B) Buckman, Joseph (C) Mayes, John (E) Burk, Tobias (K)	Ferrill, William (G)
Captured			Clayton, Robert (C) Stewart, Thos. (I)	
Deserted				Cross, Richard (B) Miles, James M. (B)

May	June	July	August
Transferred			
	Crutcher, Henry (A)		

(Letters in parentheses indicate the company of the individual.)

The Battle of Jonesboro

The situation in Atlanta became a siege. The Union Army had pressed the Southern Army into a defensive role by pressing their attack on the golden city of the south—Atlanta— but both armies were entrenched and stalemated. To make things worse for the Union forces, 1864 was the year of the presidential election and Abraham Lincoln was not optimistic of his chance of winning. The momentum of the Union armies had ground to a halt. Lincoln's generals were stymied, not only in Atlanta, but also at Richmond and Petersburg, Virginia. Lincoln needed a victory. A complication to the situation in Atlanta was the harassment of the Sherman's long supply line that stretched to Atlanta by the Confederate cavalry under the command of General Joe Wheeler.[32]

The political arena was heating up with many pushing for peace instead of more, unending war. Too many families had been touched by high casualties of the Civil War for this not to be an unpopular conflict. George B. McClellan, ex-commander of the Army of the Potomac who had been relieved of command by Lincoln, had a high likelihood of being the presidential candidate for the opposing, Democratic party. Even those in Lincoln's own party felt that he should attempt to avoid a defeat in the election by opening negotiations with Jefferson Davis for peace.

The importance of the actions near Richmond and Atlanta could not be overstated for each side. A victory in Atlanta and Richmond for the Confederacy could mean salvation for the south and a new "peaceful" president. Likewise, a victory for the Union could mean that the war would soon be over and the country would still be under the guiding hand of Abraham Lincoln, who was determined to unify the country.

Under these pressures General Sherman had besieged Atlanta for over a month, and he knew the

General William Sherman commanded the military campaign on Atlanta (Library of Congress).

Union Army needed a win at Atlanta. General Sherman had been trying to find a way to push the Confederates out of Atlanta, a city which had become a heavily fortified island of Southern resistance. Frustrated in the attempts by the Union Army to take Atlanta, Sherman decided to swing west and south to cut railroad supplies from Mississippi and Macon, Georgia. General John Bell Hood realized Sherman's plan and swung the commands of Lieutenant General William Hardee, Major General Pat Cleburn and Major General Stephen Dill Lee to protect his supply route. On August 30, 1864, these forces converged on a little town south of Atlanta: Jonesboro.

On August 26, Sherman began moving his besieging army away from Atlanta to the south towards Jonesboro. On the 29th, the 14th Corps began an extensive destruction of the railroad south of Atlanta. Sherman ordered, "Let the destruction be so thorough that not a rail or tie can be used again."[33]

Thus the stage was set for the final conflict of the war for the 10th Kentucky Infantry, to occur on September 1, 1864, near the town of Jonesboro, Georgia. The regiment was at its lowest number of effective men in the entire war and their enlistment was to be over in November, about three months away. Fate truly had a hand in this final battle and the 10th Kentucky's actions were to prove significant.

Jonesboro became an important military target for Sherman's army because the Macon and Western Railroad ran through the town and was one of the last railroads supplying the Confederate Army in Atlanta. Sherman saw that cutting this railroad was his next step in gaining Atlanta. His plan was to send six corps, with greater than 60,000 men, to cut the last lifeline to the city and he wanted to do this before the Confederates knew his plan. Sherman left General Henry Slocum's 20th Corps to guard the Chattahoochee River bridge near Atlanta. On August 30 the Union Army's 16th, 15th, and 17th Corps moved toward Jonesboro and stopped for the night near Renfroe's Place or Plantation, just north and west of Jonesboro. The Confederates skirmished with General Oliver Howard's men and General John Bell Hood became aware of the specific target that Sherman had chosen. He knew that if Atlanta was to remain in Confederate hands, he had to protect the rail supply line. When Howard arrived at Jonesboro, he was unaware that the city was only lightly defended and could easily have been taken. Although the Union forces reaching the outskirts of Jonesboro were a major threat, it wasn't until the evening of August 30 that Hood realized the extent of the threat he was facing. He immediately began plans to reinforce the defenses there. He directed Generals William Hardee and Stephen Dill Lee to attack the Union Army at Jonesboro as soon as they could on the morning of August 31, and he felt that they should have no problem driving the Union forces away. Lee's and Hardee's men traveled through the night of August 30 to reach Jonesboro, but Lee did not complete his arrival until late morning on the 31st. So the morning attack was now out of the question. By the morning of the August 31 General John Logan's 15th Corps was a "mere eight hundred yards"[34] from the Jonesboro depot, but they watched as the Confederate reinforcements poured into the city.

General O. O. Howard's Army of the Tennessee got within cannon distance of Jonesboro on August 31 and they quickly realized that the Confederates had fortified the city in numbers too great for him to attack. Instead, he prepared his forces for a defensive battle because he believed that Hardee's and S. D. Lee's Corps would attack him. General Hardee was in overall command of the Confederate forces at Jonesboro. By the time the last of Lee's Confederate reinforcements arrived in Jonesboro, they were exhausted, but by 2:00 P.M. the Confederate lines began forming for the attack. The Confederate line stretched for about a

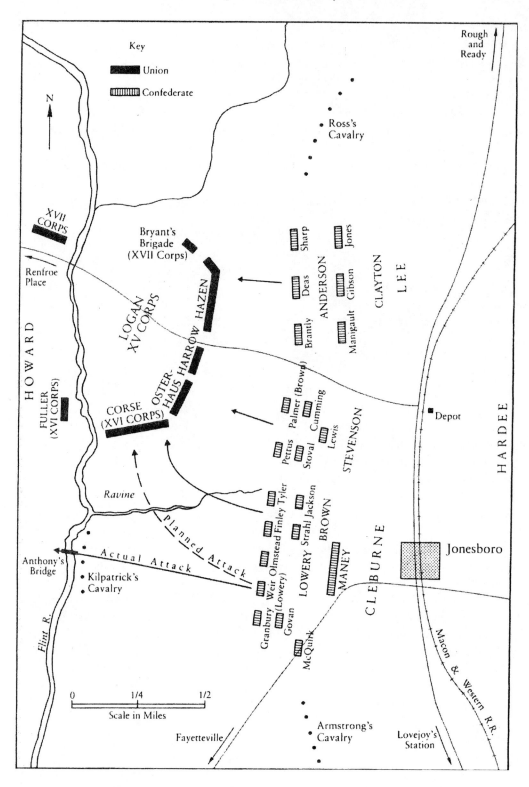

Battle of Jonesboro, August 30, 1864 (copyrighted and used with permission from the University Press of Kansas, from *Decision in the West* by Albert Castel, 1992).

mile and a half, roughly the length of Jonesboro, and officially contained about 26,000 men, but "no more than 20,000 of them are in line of battle."[35] On the afternoon of the 31st, the Confederate artillery began to pound the Union forces. Soon afterward, about 3:00 P.M., S. D. Lee's men charged toward General Logan's 15th Corps, which was supported by the 16th and 17th Corps, only to be stopped by volley after volley of fire unleashed into the attackers. Logan's corps had one division of the 16th Corps on his right flank at the time of the attack. General Pat Cleburne's men began their attack after Lee's attack ground to a halt, with some of his men being diverted toward Union cavalrymen away from the center of the fight. By the time the attack began, the defenders had almost an entire day to prepare their defenses, including preparing rifle pits and breastworks. The Union defenses, along with reserves, would total roughly the same number as the attackers. The well-aimed volleys and artillery of the entrenched defenders cut down the attackers. The Southerners could not mount an effective attack and were forced to withdraw to lick their wounds with losses of nearly 2200; men compared to 172 for the Union.

By 7:00 P.M. on August 31 Baird's division of the Army of the Cumberland reached the railroad north of Jonesboro and began to destroy the lifeline to Atlanta. During the day's battle, the 10th Kentucky and the 14th Corps were marching toward Jonesboro. Now, on September 1, 1864, the 10th Kentucky had 152 men ready for duty and 16 officers, barely one officer per company, and an average of 15 men per company. This small group of men was to have a significant an impact on the events in the engagement with the Confederates at Jonesboro. In this last battle of the war for the 10th Kentucky, the regiment was also to face the 9th Kentucky Confederates which included men from the same area of Kentucky as the 10th Kentucky, and they were to face the 6th/7th Arkansas, a regiment they faced about a year ago at Chickamauga.

SEPTEMBER 1, 1864, DAY 2

After Cleburne's and Lee's repulse on the 31st, General John Bell Hood began to realize that, at last, Atlanta could be lost and he might need to retreat toward Macon, Georgia. Hood still wanted to defend Atlanta and he was holding out for a miracle at Jonesboro. So Hardee was to be the instrument of this miracle. During the night, Confederate General William Hardee resolved to carry out General Hood's order to stand and fight the Union in an attempt to protect the railroad which provided the necessary supplies to maintain the defenses at Atlanta. General Hardee realized that he was vastly outnumbered, but must hold the Union Army to save his own. During the night, General Hood had ordered S. D. Lee's force back to Atlanta; therefore, Hardee was forced to stand alone. Although Hardee had experienced divisional commanders in General William Bate, General Pat Cleburne, and General Benjamin Franklin Cheatham, they were one corps facing several Union corps.

General Hardee constructed a defensive line, roughly running north and south, facing the Union forces. General Cleburne's Division, commanded by General Mark Lowery, was moved to the right; General John Brown's division would hold the Center. Cheatham's division, commanded by General John Carter, would defend the left of the Confederate line. Hardee would attempt to hold a two mile line with only 12,000 men. As September 1 began, the two armies began to position themselves for battle. The Union Army found itself in a reverse role of the action of the previous day. Now it would be attacking heavily defended positions. The Confederates began throwing up defensive works as the Union Army was preparing for its assault. General Jeff Davis's 14th Corps moved from the railroad destruction duties they were assigned overnight and went to the north of the Confederate line. General James Morgan's 2nd Division, 14th Corps, approached the Confederate defenses from the west. General Baird's division, with the 10th Kentucky, and General William Carlin's 1st Division, approached from the north. Orders were sent to Major General David Stanley to have his 4th Corps push toward the railroad, thus flanking the Confederate line by attacking from the north and east. This caused Hardee to move Cheatham's Division, which was entrenched on the southernmost part of the Confederate line, to protect against this new threat. The Confederates now were in the unenviable position of having the Yankees pressing them on two sides, the north and west.

At 4:00 P.M. on September 1, the armies were finally in position, and for the Confederates, it was stand and die. If they failed to hold the Union Army then the lifeblood of Atlanta was stopped and the city would have to be abandoned. For the Union, it was an opportunity to finally capture Atlanta and move on. They had the advantage and the position and needed to push the stubborn defenders away from the railroad to put an end to the fighting around Atlanta.

General James Morgan's division of the 14th Corps began the battle by pushing eastward toward General Daniel Govan's brigade's position. The Union Army decided to concentrate their forces to attack the apex of the arch of the southern defenses. Three brigades of Morgan's division pressed forward, along with two brigades of General William Carlin's division. Both divisions immediately ran into swampy ground, ditches and brushy terrain. As the 14th Corps advanced, they expected a simultaneous attack with General Stanley's 4th Corps, which did not materialize.

As the Yankees advanced, they came under tremendous musket fire and canister fire from the defenders. They continued to push forward, but were stymied. The first assault began with Carlin's two brigades striking the northern apex of the Confederate line. Major John Edie commanded one of the brigades which made it to within yards of the line of the 6th/7th Arkansas Infantry's position, but was forced to withdraw after losing too many man. At the same time, Colonel Marshall Moore led Carlin's second bridge but could not carry the works held by General Joseph Lewis' Kentucky brigade. The 14th Corps pushed forward without support and were ripped with volleys from entrenched defenders and subjected to enfilading fire from other Southern units.

As the brigades moved forward, the exact positions of the Confederates became apparent. General Jefferson C. Davis realized that the Confederate line was vulnerable and could be broken. He decided to add Colonel Este's brigade to the fight and try to break the point of resistance on the apex

Union General Jefferson C. Davis commanded the 14th Corps at Jonesboro and ordered the 10th Kentucky to attack the Confederates on September 1, 1864 (Library of Congress).

of the Confederate defenses. It was time for the 10th Kentucky to enter the fight. Este's brigade lined up about fifty yards to the rear of Major John Edie's 2nd Brigade of Carlin's 1st Division. Este had 1139 men ready for battle and at 5:00 P.M. he unleashed them on the Confederates, the 10th Kentucky and 38th Ohio in the front ranks supported by the 74th Indiana and 14th Ohio in the second ranks.

By now the 10th Kentucky was a veteran unit, even though they were few in number. Private George Terry of Company A explained the action as the 10th Kentucky fell into line: "We were hardly down when the sharpshooters got busy; the first shot falling short, striking, in front of our company, a man by the name of John Roudder a German. It knocked his hat off and stunned him a little. After brightening up he called for his hat, and someone called out to him. "John, you ought to be glad that you got your head." He replied: "Well, I haf mein headt, I vant my mein hatt."[36]

As the men moved forward they had to pass through a small valley and climb a ridge just in front of the Confederate defenders. Este ordered the men to fall on their stomachs as they gained the ridge, avoiding a murderous volley from the defenders by doing so. After the volley, the brigade was ordered to charge, and the men of Este's brigade drove forward into the Confederates. The 10th Kentucky and 74th Indiana charged the entrenchments that were occupied by the 6th/7th Arkansas Infantry and unloaded a volley into the Confederate lines. As the war progressed the losses within regiments became so great that they could not maintain the status of regiment. So, regiments were combined to produce enough men to be considered a regiment. This was the case with the 6th/7th Arkansas Infantry. As the 10th Kentucky and 74th Indiana charged forward again, they overwhelmed the 6th/7th Arkansas and thereby punched a hole in the Confederate line. The 38th Ohio and 14th Ohio had been stopped by Confederate defensive works. Colonel Este asked Colonel William Grower to send his 17th New York, 16th Corps, 4th Division, to push the line forward, which they did by moving to the left of the Ohio regiments and breaking through the works. Then the 38th Ohio, 14th Ohio, and the 17th New York drove into General Joseph Lewis' Confederates of Bate's division.

Colonel Este described the assault into the Confederate works: "Ordering bayonets fixed, the word 'forward' was given, and the command moved slowly and deliberately to the front with as much coolness and regularity as they ever had done on battalion drill. Ere reaching the crest of the hill and the edge of the woods, just beyond which the rebel line of works were constructed, I had ordered the lines to lie down whilst the first volley should be received, and then both lines to rush forward to the charge. The order was exactly executed, and the charge magnificently performed, and the first lines of the enemy's works carried as with a whirlwind. Still, their second and more formidable line remained."[37]

The Confederates now had major problems and focused their action on the Ohioans and New Yorkers. This allowed the 10th Kentucky and 74th Indiana to sweep behind Daniel Govan's brigade of Pat Cleburne's division. The mass of Union and Confederate soldiers clashed and the Confederates were swamped by the overwhelming numbers of Union soldiers attacking this part of the line. The Confederates had vowed to "to die or be captured in the ditches before they will leave them"[38] and they refused to retreat and were bayoneted and clubbed until they were dead or captured. General Daniel Govan was captured along with Captain Thomas Key's Arkansas battery.

Private G.W. Terry of Company A described the action as the 10th Kentucky engaged the 9th Kentucky Confederate Infantry, men from the same geographic area but on differ-

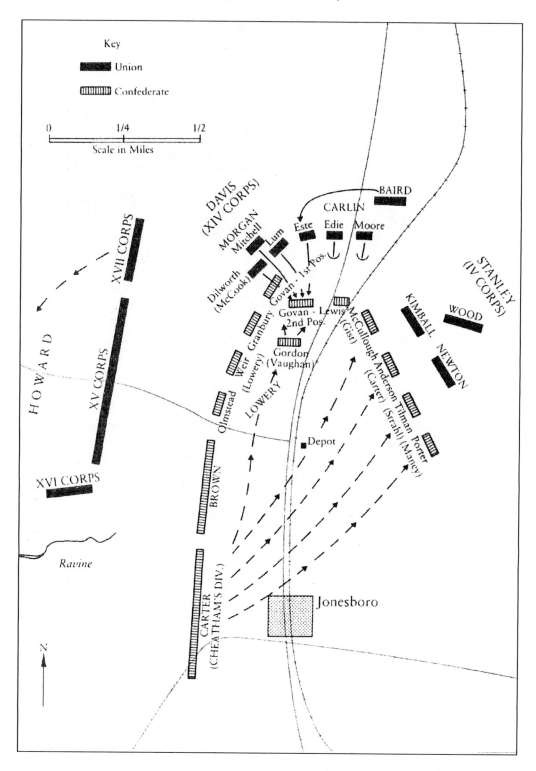

Battle of Jonesboro, September 1, 1864. The 10th Kentucky Infantry as part of Este's Brigade (copy-righted and used with permission from the University Press of Kansas, from *Decision in the West* by Albert Castel, 1992).

ent sides of the war. The irony of engaging men from the same hometown in their last battle of the war cannot be overlooked. Fighting neighbors seemed to intensify the conflict, not diminish it. "The next orders were from Col Phillip Lea, of the 9th Kentucky Confederate, lying in front of us. These were, 'Ready, aim, fire!' We dropped again to avoid the fire, and the next instant rose and gave them our compliments with bullets, bayonets, butts of guns and some fist work. Dick Welsh, an Irishman, did some of that. The regiment that we had struck was the 9th Kentucky Confederate...."[39]

Sgt. Major John Green, 9th Kentucky Infantry, Confederate, which was part of Major General William Bate's division of Hardee's corps, wrote in his diary:

> The Battle of Jonesboro was the fall of Atlanta. It was a matter of life & death to keep this horde of Yanks from advancing further because Gen Hood had not yet gotten his army safely out of Atlanta & this was our only road for retreat. General Hardee made a determined stand at this place, notwithstanding the disaster to part of his line. He massed several batteries & concentrated their fire upon that part of the enemy's line that had captured us. If the assistance of these batteries had come to us 15 minutes earlier our line would never have been broken, but they were the first of the troops falling back from Atlanta & after straining every nerve to get to us sooner were only able to get to our hard-pressed troops in time to save us from disaster.[40]
> The 10th Kentucky, by the queerest luck in the world, was matched against the rebel 9th Kentucky. The commanders of the two regiments were brothers-in-law and the men relatives, friends, acquaintances and schoolmates. They hated each other accordingly, and the fight between them was more bitter if possible, than anywhere else on the line.[41]

The 10th Kentucky engaged the 6th/7th Arkansas and the 9th Kentucky Infantry. Private Standard Harley of the 6th/7th Arkansas Infantry stated,

> As soon as I fired I squatted behind our little log works, got out another cartridge and looked up to insert it my gun above me—and there were two Federal soldiers standing above me with fixed bayonets and cocked guns. I was so frightened that I forgot that I had not loaded my gun, though I had started to do so. I jumped from under their bayonets, placed my gun near one's breast and snapped it, and did the rabbit act at a two-forty rate away from there. Five or six of us ran out, but only one was killed. It is miraculous how we escaped, under the circumstances. The only way I can account for it is that the greater part of the regiment surrendered, which occupied the attention of the men until we got, perhaps, 60 yards away through the thick saplings before they fired at us.[42]

The vicious hand-to-hand combat in this battle cannot be overstated. General Baird stated in his official report that he had never seen such extensive use of the bayonet in his career. He mentioned three Noe brothers of the 10th Kentucky who worked so effectively at this task that it reached his attention.

Captain H. G. Neubert, 14th Ohio, reported on the battle in a letter: "Gen. Baird was also in the very front of battle, inspiring the men to many deeds of bravery. His horse was also killed from under him. So stubborn were the rebels, that not until many were killed with the cold steel, would they surrender, but finally they succumbed and filed over the works to our rear, like sheep from a pen. This charge has never been equaled in this war, if in any other. We took nearly as many prisoners as we numbered.... I know no other instance where two lines of troops who fought as these did, were taken by lines with our disadvantages. This fact alone show what the fighting qualities engaged were."[43]

Once the Confederate line broke at the apex, then the 17th New York, 14th and 38th Ohio and Moore's 2nd Brigade, 1st Division, proceeded to roll up the Confederate line, including Lewis' brigade and Govan's brigade, taking hundreds of prisoners. Once the men of Este's brigade broke through the line, they swept both directions toward Lewis's Kentuckians and also behind Govan's men and opened the door for Morgan's division to sweep onto the Confederates.

General Pat Cleburne came to the rescue, sending Vaughn's Tennessee Brigade, commanded by Colonel George Gordon, to stem the Union success. Even though Baird had uncommitted troops, the frontal assault on the Confederate line had been a success. "They have made what until now no one has made during the entire campaign: a successful large-scale frontal assault," one historian recounted.[44] But where was Stanley's 4th Corps? During the assault they were "digging trenches and erecting breastworks as a precaution from being attacked."[45] Miscommunication resulted in a missed opportunity to cause greater damage to Hardee's corps. While clearly the Southern forces were outnumbered on paper, their defenses were formidable. It was the 14th Corps that carried the day at the Battle of Jonesboro. It was a great victory, but the opportunity to crush Hardee was lost. Hardee retreated with most of his corps intact. Hardee lost 1400 men at the Battle of Jonesboro with about 900 of those being prisoners. The Union Army primarily, the 14th Corps, lost 1271 men, killed, missing or wounded, and 330 of those came from Este's brigade, which had just slightly over 1100 men at the beginning of the battle.

Colonel William Hays' report of the action at Jonesboro said:

HDQRS. TENTH KENTUCKY VOLUNTEER INFANTRY,
Near Jonesborough, Ga., September 3, 1864.

CAPTAIN: I respectfully submit the following report of the part taken by the Tenth Kentucky Infantry in the assault upon the enemy's works on the evening of the 1st instant:

The regiment was on the right of the brigade in the front line, formed about 300 yards of the enemy's works, under the orders of Colonel Este, commanding the brigade. We fixed bayonets and moved forward to the assault about 5 P.M. The men reserved their fire until we reached the woods about thirty yards from the works of the enemy. Up to this time we had steadily advanced under a severe fire. As soon as we entered the woods the enemy, from behind their works, poured upon us a heavy volley of musketry, which, for a moment, caused the regiment to halt. We immediately returned the fire, and, with a shout, rushed on their works and captured a number of prisoners in their rifle-pits. The Seventy-fourth Indiana Regiment, which was in the rear line, closed up on us as we entered the works and gallantly charged the works with us. It being a larger regiment than mine, its right was some two companies farther to the right than ours. The enemy immediately in our front was the Sixth and Seventh Arkansas Regiments, of Cleburne's division, consolidated. We captured their flag, which has been sent to brigade headquarters. Private Henry B. Mattingly, of Company E, had the honor of capturing these colors. When we captured the works of the enemy, and for several minutes thereafter, our regiment and the Seventy-fourth Indiana had no support on our right, and the enemy fired up the line of works upon our right flank; but within some ten minutes the enemy was driven from our right flank by a well-directed fire from the Seventy-fourth Indiana and Tenth Kentucky Regiments. My regiment went into the fight with 152 guns. Our casualties will be annexed to this report. The officers and soldiers of my regiment behaved with great gallantry and courage. I would like very much to mention individual acts of officers and men, but in so doing I would have to mention so many names that it might seem to be a reflection upon those not mentioned. All, so far as I know or have information, nobly did their whole duty. Capt. James M. Davenport, of Company G, was gallantly leading his company, and while in the works of the enemy was severely wounded in the leg, which has since been amputated. Lieut. William E. Kelly, Company I, and Lieut. Joseph T. Adcock, Company F, were both severely wounded while gallantly leading their companies. Corpl. Orville B. Young, the color bearer, deserves special mention for the manner in which he discharged his duty when the regiment was checked by a murderous fire within twenty yards of the enemy's works. He ran forward with the flag, calling on his comrades to rally to it. It was the first flag placed on the enemy's works.

Respectfully, your obedient servant,

WM. H. HAYS,
Colonel Tenth Kentucky.[46]

Colonel Hays included his casualties at Jonesboro. The 10th Kentucky had 5 men killed in action, and 3 officers and 26 men wounded. Among the wounded were Lieutenant William F. Beglow, Company H, who was injured with a saber cut in the right breast.[47] Lieutenant William Kelley, Company I, who was wounded and captured at Chickamauga, paroled, was also wounded in the head at Jonesboro.[48] Captain James Davenport was shot in the same leg that was previously injured at Chickamauga and the leg was amputated on the field.[49]

Colonel Este wrote in his after-action report:

Colonel Hays, commanding Tenth Kentucky, gallantly assisted by Lieutenant-Colonel Wharton and Major Davidson, showed himself to be among the bravest of the brave, and, with his command, was among the first to reach the enemy's works. The amputated arms and limbs and torn bodies of the wounded officers—a list of whom is hereto attached—speak more eloquently than any poor words of mine can do their noble conduct. It is the highest praise that can be spoken of them to say they proved themselves worthy of the rank they bore and of the men under them.

Of enlisted men my especial attention has been directed by the regimental commanders to the gallant conduct of Corpl. Orville B. Young, Tenth Kentucky, color bearer, who, when the regiment was for a moment checked within twenty yards of the enemy's works by the murderous fire, rushed forward with the flag, and planting it on the works, called on his comrades to rally around it;

In conclusion, I cannot forbear giving expression to my feelings of pride and gratification at the manner in which the brigade upheld the honor of the division and corps upon that day, and to my belief that not an officer or private of my command went to the rear from the moment we formed for the assault without a good and sufficient reason.[50]

General Carlin, commanding the 1st Brigade of the 1st Division, pointed out the importance of the actions of breaking the Confederate line: "Had Este's brigade failed to carry the works, it is my opinion that a repulse along the whole line of the Fourteenth Corps would have been the result. By the confession of the enemy many of their men were killed with the bayonet in their own breast-works by the Tenth Kentucky Infantry, Colonel Hays commanding. I presume other regiments made use of the same weapon of the brave with equal effect."[51]

Private Orville Young received special recognition for rallying the 10th Kentucky and charging forward when

Captured Confederate flag of the 6th/7th Arkansas Infantry (National Park Service).

the regiment was close to the Confederate works and suffering greatly under the fire of the enemy. Another notable action was the capture of the flag of the 6th/7th Arkansas Infantry by Henry B. Mattingly. Private Mattingly, a Marion County native, was awarded the Medal of Honor for this action. He was the only member of the 10th Kentucky to receive this honor in the war. He received it in April 1865 for "gallantry in capturing rebel flags during the operations of the Army of the Cumberland."[52]

There were seven Confederate regimental colors captured at Jonesboro including the 6th/7th Arkansas flag captured by Henry Mattingly. Others included the 8th/19th Arkansas, 6th Kentucky, 3rd Confederate, 1st Arkansas, Key's Battery, and Swett's Battery.

The Battle of Jonesboro broke the back of the Confederate defense of Atlanta and ended an important phase in the Civil War. Late on the evening of September 1, General John Bell Hood ordered the evacuation of Atlanta. He also ordered the destruction of many of the Confederate supplies, which led to the famous fire scene depicted in *Gone with the Wind*. Hood's army slipped away from Sherman to fight another day, but the Union Army finally claimed Atlanta. This victory in Georgia was a significant step. It would help Lincoln to be re-elected, and the direction of the war would continue as it had for the past three years.

The official casualty report shows that the Confederates lost more men than the Union at the Battle of Jonesboro, but it was a hard fight for both sides. The charge on the Confederate works was very costly to Col. Este's brigade. Records show that the brigade lost 341 men, nearly one-third of its strength. This was the last action the 10th Kentucky Infantry would see. There were now fewer than 140 men remaining for duty.

It was time to go home.

10th Kentucky Infantry Casualty List—Jonesboro

Capt James Davenport, Co G	Severely wounded—leg amputated
Lt William Kelly, Co I	Severely wounded—head

Battle of Jonesboro (Library of Congress).

Lt Joseph Adcock, Co F	Severely wounded—side
Corp James Creigh, Co A	Severely wounded—left shoulder
Corp Gustave Asbeck, Co A	Severely wounded—right hand
Corp Frederick Kortz, Co A	Severely wounded—left shoulder
Pvt William Shielly, Co A	Severely wounded—right shoulder
Pvt John Ruder, Co A	Severely wounded—head
Pvt Joseph Edmonson, Co A	Severely wounded—leg
Pvt Frederick Rossles, Co A	Severely wounded—breast—mortal
Pvt Thomas Smith, Co A	Slightly wounded—side
Pvt George Terry, Co A	Severely wounded—leg
Pvt William Whitehouse, Co B	Killed in Action
Pvt Benjamin Hall, Co B	Slightly wounded—hip
Pvt William Fogle, Co B	Slightly wounded—hip
Pvt James Dunahoo, Co B	Severely wounded—forehead
Pvt John Boarman, Co C	Severely wounded—head
Pvt William Robinson, Co C	Severely wounded—shoulder
Pvt Andrew Elmore, Co C	Severely wounded—thigh
Pvt Thomas Willit, Co D	Severely wounded—arm amputated
Sgt Thomas Logsdon, Co E	Slightly wounded—thigh
Pvt James Young, Co E	Severely wounded—leg
Pvt J. Henry Grant, Co F	Killed in Action
Pvt Benjamin Estes, Co F	Severely wounded—thigh
Pvt Thomas Masterson, Co G	Killed in Action
Pvt August Fanvel, Co G	Severely wounded—thigh
Pvt James Campbell, Co H	Slightly wounded
Pvt Thomas Maston, Co H	Slightly wounded—back
Pvt John Averitt, Co I	Severely wounded—hip
Pvt John Willard, Co I	Killed in Action
Pvt General Goodman, Co I	Severely wounded—right side
Sgt William Wright, Co I	Severely wounded—hip and hand
Pvt John Wilcher, Co I	Severely wounded—elbow
Pvt Robert Squires, Co F	Killed in Action

Courts-Martial, November 1864

The 10th Kentucky was removed from the line after the Battle of Jonesboro and returned to Chattanooga. Courts-Martial were waiting for some of the men of the regiment.

In November 1864, Private Gerald Goodman was tried for desertion. The charge was "that the said Gerald Goodman, Private, Co I, 10th Regt Ky Vols did desert the said company and Regiment at or near Lavergne, Tenn. on or about the 25th day of May 1863 and did remain absent until the 20th day of September 1863, at which day he reported to Major H. G. Davidson at Chattanooga, Tenn."[53]

The charge was modified to change desertion to absent without leave. He was found guilty on the specification, but not the charge. He was sentenced to forfeit 4 months' pay.

Private William Goodman of Company I was court-martialed at Chattanooga on November 4, 1864. The court was made up of Major I. E. Callaway, 21st Illinois Infantry, Captain A. Pierce, 30th Illinois Infantry, Captain W. Pratt, 43rd Illinois Infantry, Captain W. Goeden, 15th Missouri Infantry, Lieutenant C. Scripture, 1st Ohio Artillery, and Lieutenant J. W. King, 44th U.S. Infantry. Captain I. B. Webster, serving as judge advocate, was absent. Also absent was Lieutenant J. T. McCauley, due to illness.

He was charged with being absent without leave. The 1st specification stated that Private William Goodman Co. I, 10th Ky Vol. Infty., while on at parole camp [Camp Chase Ohio] did obtain furlough from the first to the fifteenth day of March 1864, at the expiration of which period he failed to report as directed to his station then at Camp Chase Ohio." The 2nd specification said Private Goodman "in the month of May or June 1864, received

Officers of the 10th Kentucky Infantry after the Battle of Jonesboro (Blue Acorn Press, Huntington, West Virginia).

notice of his exchange by letter from Capt. I. B. Webster, Co I, 10th Ky Infty Vols. did remain absent from his Company and Regiment until the fifteenth day of September 1864 when he reported to his company for duty then at Atlanta, Ga."[54]

Private Goodman pleaded not guilty to all charges. Lieutenant William Kelly, Company I, served as a witness for the prosecution. Lieutenant Kelly reported that Private Goodman's character was excellent and he was one of the best men in the company. Lieutenant Kelly indicated that he knew of no reason for the Goodmans' absences. Sergeant Robert Rea, Company K, also served as a witness for the prosecution and also indicated that he did not know of any reason for Private Goodman's absence.

Private Elijah Noe, Company I, and Private Daniel Goodman, 21st Kentucky Infantry, were witnesses for the defense. Private Noe testified to the quality of Private Goodman's character. Daniel Goodman, uncle of Private Goodman, testified that William's stomach wound, inflicted at Chickamauga, caused him to be unable to return to the regiment. Captain I. B. Webster, Company I, submitted a letter to the court on behalf of Private Goodman.

Private Goodman was found guilty on all charges and ordered to forfeit his pay from March 15 through June 15, 1864, and to be honorably discharged at the end of his enlistment.

Corporal Thomas Jones, Company K, was also tried at court-martial on the same day as William Goodman before the same court. Corporal Jones was tried for desertion. The specification of the charge was: "Thomas A Jones corpl Co K 10th Ky Vol Infty, did desert the service of the United States at Louisville, Kentucky, on or about the first day of December 1862 and remain absent therefrom until the eleventh day of December 1863 at which time he was arrested and sent to his regiment.—All this done at Louisville, Ky."[55]

Corporal Jones entered the plea of not guilty. Captain John Denton, Company K, was a witness for the prosecution. He testified that Corporal Jones was left at the hospital in Columbia, Tennessee, in April 1862. He testified that an application for discharge was signed and forwarded to General Buell. The papers were never signed and ultimately lost. Corporal Jones was dropped from the company records due to desertion. Lee Johnston, quartermaster, was also a witness for the prosecution. He also reported that the discharge papers were never signed due to a "formality" and they were never forwarded again.

On the specification, Corporal Jones was found guilty of "without proper authority absent himself from his company and regiment." On the charge, he was found not guilty. He was required to forfeit his pay and clothing allowance from December 1, 1862, to December 11, 1863, and to be honorably discharged at the expiration of his enlistment.

Private Joseph Uptergrove, Company B, was tried on November 8, 1864 under the same court as the previous two trials. He was accused of desertion. The specification of the charge was: "Joseph Uptergrove private Co B 10th Ky Infty, did desert the service of the United States at Louisville, Ky on or about the 1st day of April 1862 and remain absent therefrom until arrested and sent to his Regiment on or about the 3rd day of March 1864. All this at or near Louisville, Ky."[56]

Second Lieutenant John T McCauley was the only witness in the trial and he testified for the prosecution. Lieutenant McCauley reported that the company was partially furloughed and allowed to return home. Private Uptergrove returned home to Nelson County because he was sick at the time. He did not return to his regiment until March 1864. Lt. McCauley stated that Private Uptergrove participated in the Atlanta-Jonesboro campaign and was excellent soldier in these actions.

Private Uptergrove was found guilty of "Did absent himself from his company and Regiment" and found not guilty of desertion.

The final record for men court-martialed with the 10th Kentucky Infantry occurred on November 26, 1864 in Louisville.

Private William Lawson, Company I, was accused of desertion. The specification of the charge was: "William Lawson private of Co 10th regiment Ky vol Infantry having been duly enlisted and mustered into the service of the United States, did desert the same on or about the 23rd day of May 1863 at Lavergne Tennessee, and remain absent therefrom, in Hardin County Ky, hiding from arrest and evading such men belonging to the company, as were in the said county on furlough, and making no effort to join his command, until he was arrested on or about the 15th day of Nov. 1864 and forwarded to Louisville Ky and on the 20th day of November 1864 sent to his regiment under guard."[57]

Private Lawson pled guilty to both the charge and the specification. His statement was as follows:

"My wife was sick having the catarrh, and was so lame in the hands that she could neither cook nor wash clothes.... I am a poor man and have five children. I thought I would go home. There was no one at home to help my wife.... I have got no learning myself and know nothing about military law at all.... the reason I stayed so long away, was because I was taken sick and lay there some three months...."

Private William Lawson, Company I, was sentenced to be transported to Camp Nelson, Kentucky, and be confined for one year, 5 months and 22 days to make good the time lost during which he was absent from his command. His sentence also stipulated that once every other month he was to have a ball and chain attached to his leg. At the end of his sentence, he was to have his head shaved and be drummed out of the service. These last two punishments may have been later deleted from his sentence.

Regimental Losses September–December 1864

	September	October	November	December
Discharged	Hahun, Samuel (E)	Clark, John (B)	Talmadge, Joseph (B)	Beavers, Wilford (D)
				Luckett, Thomas (D)
Died		Fenwick, Edward (E)	Hall, William, Jr. (B)	Sullivant, Patrick (E)
		Avis, Edward (G)	Fields, Henry (E)	
		Hays, Harrison (G)	Davidson, Henry (Staff)	
Killed in Action	Whitfield, William (B)			
	Grant, Henry (F)			
	Roberts, Squire (F)			
	Masterson, Thomas (G)			
	Willard, John (I)			
Transferred			Mills, John (B)	
			Newton, William (B)	
			Nolley, Wm. T. (B)	
			Hogland, John (C)	
			Noe, Elijah (I)	
			Hobbs, Levi A. (I)	
			Noe, Henry (I)	
			Saddler, Mathews (I)	

(Letters in parentheses indicate the company of the individual.)

Final Events

On November 6, 1864, General George Thomas issued Special Field Order No. 304 that relieved the 10th Kentucky Infantry of further duty and gave directions for their travel, first to Chattanooga, and then to Louisville to be mustered out of service.

The regiment was not to proceed past Chattanooga until it was confirmed that all the men had served their term of duty. It was also customary in the Civil War that regiments which were being mustered out had an opportunity to have those men who wished to continue in army service placed in a veteran corps. This does not seem to have been the case for the 10th Kentucky. Lt. Colonel Gabriel Wharton wrote about the slight that was made to these men who had fought so long in the service of their county:

> The veterans and recruits of the 10th Ky. Infantry were never properly assigned to any regiment after the discharge of the 10th. The descriptive rolls of these men were left with some officer at Chattanooga, who was careless enough to lose them. They were organized under a non-commissioned officer, and sent down on the road between Chattanooga and Atlanta to guard some post, and when Gen. Sherman cut the road and started on his march to the sea, they were left without orders or officers; some of them marched after Sherman and served under the old division commander, Gen. Baird, through that campaign; others came up and joined Gen. Thomas at Nashville, and fought through the war somewhat "on their own account." I have had much difficulty in having these men discharged and paid off because of the loss of their descriptive rolls for which they were not responsible. I am not sure as yet all these men have been discharged and paid. They were generally excellent soldiers, and have suffered grievous wrongs at the hands of their commanders.[58]

There were at least two melancholy incidents before the end of the war. One was the death of Major Henry Davidson. Major Davidson was the son of a banker and businessman in Louisville and he died in November 1864 when he contracted a "chill."[59] Davidson was such an integral part of the 10th Kentucky since its beginning and he was only a few weeks away from being mustered out. The other incident occurred when the regiment left Chattanooga and was transported to Nashville in November on open flat-cars. Captain John Denton contracted a severe fever and as result of this was in the hospital when the unit was mustered out.[60] It will probably never be known if this is where Major Davidson contracted his "chill."

The 10th Kentucky Regiment Volunteer Infantry after three long years was mustered out of service on December 6, 1864. The men, their families, and their country would never be the same. It is difficult to summarize the three years of the 10th Kentucky. The men were not from the most prosperous area of Kentucky and the majority were farmers and sons of farmers from around west central Kentucky, along with a good scattering of laborers and foreign born men. The 10th Kentucky was initially under the command of the benevolent, politically powerful John Harlan. When Harlan resigned to pursue his political career, the 10th Kentucky was left in the hands of the capable William H. Hays. William Hays was the guiding hand for the 10th Kentucky as the regiment went through the most difficult days in the war—Chickamauga, Missionary Ridge, Chattahoochee River and finally Jonesboro.

The regiment began with 867 good men whose goal was to preserve the Union and three years later had done just that. The 10th Kentucky was one of the first units engaged at Chickamauga and refused to be pushed off the field of battle on September 20, even when the full force of the Confederate Army was thrown at them on Horseshoe Ridge. The unit suffered a 40 percent loss of its men to death, capture or wounding. But the 10th rallied in Chattanooga and helped push Bragg off Missionary Ridge and helped march the Confederates back toward Atlanta. And the Battle of Jonesboro was legendary. The 10th Kentucky was down to its lowest effective force in the war and they knew that in three short months they could go home to their families, but in this last battle, those valiant men gave their last full measure. Atlanta was at stake and the 10th Kentucky's brigade was thrown into the battle as an attempt to break the Confederate line.

The 10th Kentucky and 74th Indiana charged into the Confederate line and received withering fire, and just as the line wavered, the color bearer ran ahead waving the colors and rallied the regiment. The 10th crashed into the 6th/7th Arkansas, the same unit they had routed at Chickamauga, and Private Henry B Mattingly would win the Medal of Honor for his capture of their colors. But then, the 10th turned their attack to their new foe, the 9th Kentucky CSA—men from their own hometowns. The 10th Kentucky and their comrades battered the weary Confederates into submission and helped bring about the fall of Atlanta and helped insure Lincoln's re-election.

The 10th Kentucky had done their job well.

Regimental Losses 1865

1865

Transferred

Arnold, Simpson (A)	Graham, Harvey (A)	Johnson, William (A)	Goodman, David (I)
Boyd, William (A)	Ham, Abram (A)	Shain, David (A)	Rea, Robert Jr. (K)
Duffield, Jacob (A)	Harding, Elias (A)	Watts, John R. (A)	Krival, Francis (C)
Frank, George H. (A)	Harding, George (A)	Abell, Cornelius (H)	

(Letters in parentheses indicate the company of the individual.)

Epilogue: Postwar Biographical Information for the Officers

"Life for the living, and rest for the dead"—George Arnold

As the Civil War ended, a profound change had occurred in the country. It was a time for rebuilding. The animosity between the North and South began a slow healing process. Those in both the Northern and Southern armies returned home to their lives, and they returned as changed men. Many returned to build their homes where they were reared and many were bitten by the "traveling" bug that had been their lives for the past three years. They moved from their home to new opportunities. Regardless of the pathway individuals took, they were part of the whole that was the nation and went on to contribute to building the nation during the latter part of the 19th century.

There are two parts to the story of the 10th Kentucky. One part is the actions of the regiment in the Civil War, and interwoven in that is the story of the men who made up the 10th Kentucky. The story of the men is extensive, because it includes who they were before the war, what role they played during the war, and what they became after. Some of the men were destined for greatness, like John Harlan, and some of the men were destined for tragedy and heartbreak, like Clem Funk. The final section of the history of the 10th Kentucky is a series of short biographies of the officers of the regiment.

Regimental Officers

We will begin with the colonel who had enough political influence to organize the 10th Kentucky and guide it until March 1863. John Harlan was probably the most famous of all the 10th Kentucky Infantry members. Kentucky is truly indebted to him and the role he played in the Civil War because of the efforts that he placed in aligning with the Union and identifying, organizing and leading the men of the 10th Kentucky. But duty called him into other arenas later in the war.

He was identified to be promoted to general in the volunteer army, and the promotion would surely have occurred based on Harlan's performance, popularity and position within Kentucky; but he chose another path. In 1863, he resigned from the regiment and was later elected attorney general for the state of Kentucky.

One of John Harlan's biggest contributions to the United States and civil rights was yet to come. He was a strong Unionist at the beginning of the Civil War, but he supported slavery. His attitude changed over time as he observed the way slaves were treated in the South. He had watched Southerners hang black men as a symbol of their defiance. During Reconstruction he again watched the defiance in the Southern states and recognized the need for civil equality. Harlan became a staunch supporter of the Kentucky Republican party, and in 1876, he played a crucial role in securing the presidential nomination for Rutherford B. Hayes. In 1877 Hayes rewarded him with an appointment to the U.S. Supreme Court. One historian described Harlan:

> Justice Oliver Wendell Holmes called his colleague John Marshall Harlan the last "tobacco chomping justice." Born in 1833 in Boyle County, Kentucky, Harlan not only chewed tobacco, but drank bourbon, played golf, loved baseball, and wore colorful clothing not often associated with Supreme Court justices. Although sometimes a terror to attorneys while on the bench, Harlan was approachable in person. A man of middle-class values, Harlan alone among the justices of his era was comfortable socializing with Hispanics, Negroes, and Chinese.
>
> Harlan is best known for his eloquent dissent in the 1896 case, Plessy vs. Ferguson, which upheld a Louisiana law requiring blacks and whites to ride in separate railroad cars. Harlan criticized the Court's adoption of the "separate but equal" doctrine in these memorable words: "Our Constitution is color blind and neither knows nor tolerates classes among citizens."[1]

John Harlan died in 1911 after a career of service and dedication to his country. At Harlan's memorial service, Attorney General George Wickersham said of him: "He was a student and disciple of Marshall, but among living men he could lead but he could not follow. Where others agreed with his views he would march with them, but when they differed he marched alone."[2]

After John Harlan's resignation, Colonel William Hays took control of the 10th Kentucky and guided the regiment through the most difficult days of the war. After the end of

Supreme Court Justice John Marshall Harlan. After leaving the regiment, he became Kentucky attorney general and later became U.S. Supreme Court justice (Library of Congress).

the Civil War, Colonel Hays remained a part of the army through 1866, assuming the role of state inspector general in 1865–1866. He dabbled in oil and gas after leaving the position of inspector general through 1867 but returned to his practice of law in his beloved Springfield, Kentucky, until 1879. Colonel Hays also was an unsuccessful candidate for Congress twice, in 1868 and 1872 as part of the Democratic Party. In 1879, he was appointed as judge to the U.S. District Court for Kentucky. He was confirmed in December 1879, but on March 7, 1880, he died of "heart disease" at the residence of E. L. Davison after a short illness.[3, 4, 5]

William Hays was a determined man, not one who would bring attention to himself, and in many ways as different from John Harlan as day and night. Harlan knew he had a place in history and worked at carving that place. William Hays knew he had a job to do when he joined the 10th Kentucky Infantry and was at least as popular with the troops as John Harlan. He was a steady hand for the men who served under him. He was called on to command his brigade during the heat of the battle, but always chose to return to the command of the 10th Kentucky. The men of the 10th Kentucky were from his county and he was dedicated to these men and the other men of the 10th Kentucky Infantry. His obligation was to them and history would take care of itself. One insight into the personality of William Hays was his actions at Chickamauga when, during his command in the first major battle of the regiment, he ordered two bayonet infantry charges into the enemy. It was said of Colonel Hays in his later life that he was well liked "on account of his high, honest and perfect good feeling."[6] He never married.

William H. Hays commanded the 10th Kentucky until the end of the war. He became state inspector general, practiced law, and served as judge to U.S. District Court for Kentucky (Nash Hayes).

Colonel Hays' partner in the command of the 10th Kentucky throughout the war was Lt. Colonel Gabriel Wharton. Gabriel Wharton resumed his law practice in Louisville after the war and in 1866 was appointed assistant United States attorney for the District of Kentucky. On the appointment of Benjamin H. Bristow as secretary of the treasury, Colonel Wharton succeeded to the post of district attorney, holding that office for ten years. In 1880 he opened an office in Washington, D.C., and, after two years' practice there, spent some time in Mexico in the interest of a railroad company that proposed linking Vera Cruz and Mexico City. Returning after a year's absence, he resided in New York City at the St. James Hotel, where he soon had a lucrative practice representing an Indiana car company.[7] His obituary said, "He was prominent in club life, was a sociable, gifted man, fashionable in attire and popular with men about the town. He was never married, though in his earlier days he was prominent in society."[8]

Gabriel Wharton was a gifted orator and he was also a close friend of President Ulysses Grant. It has been said of Gabriel Wharton that he put on his uniform and would sit in front of the Springfield courthouse after the war and talk to his friends.

He was on a visit to Louisville to see his brother when he died on February 22, 1887, while alone in his room at a hotel. He had fallen earlier in the day in front of his hotel. His health had been failing after his return from Mexico.

It was said of him: "In office, he was ever vigilant, faithful, urbane, and absolutely incorruptible. He was conspicuous for fidelity to public duty and to personal friendship—a very gallant, honorable, straightforward, and upright man.... A brave Federal soldier, he had no more attached friends than those who served in the Confederate Army. Clever in every sense, gentle and reliable. It is probable that not one of the thousands who knew him ever cherished an unkind thought of him. Welcome in every circle for his rare qualities as a conversationalist, he will be praised and mourned very sincerely by a large circle of friends."[9]

Of the other regimental officers, Major Henry Davidson is an example of tragedy. Henry Davidson was truly a man in the middle of it all. He was active in Louisville before the 10th Kentucky was mustered in. His company was skirmishers in the Battle of Mill Springs, he and his company were captured in Courtland, and he was involved in all actions through the end of the war, only to die at age 31 of a "congestive chill" on November 21, 1864, after the actions of the 10th Kentucky were over. His service was held at the Catholic Cathedral, and he was buried in the Catholic Cemetery in Louisville. He was the son of a prosperous family in Louisville, and it was sad, as with all the men of the 10th Kentucky who died, for him to die within three weeks of the regiment being mustered out of service.[10, 11, 12]

Adjutant Austin P. Maguire, the son of an Irishman, returned home and married Francis "Fannie" Jarboe in November 1865. He lived for a while in Athens, Alabama, in the late 1860s. He was a dry goods merchant in 1870 in his hometown, Bardstown, Kentucky, but late in 1870 he moved with his family to Osage Mission in Neosho County, Kansas. He had nine children and made Osage Mission, later re-named St. Paul, Kansas, home for the rest of his life. He was a long-time city clerk and also worked as a bookkeeper, and salesman for Colonel Williams' Store and later for Lake and Lake Dry Goods. In 1896, he was appointed justice of the peace. Austin survived his wife, Fannie, who died in 1902. Austin died at the age of 78 on October 20, 1914, and was recognized as one of the founders of Osage Mission and early businessman for the community.[13, 14]

Medical Staff

The medical staff of the 10th was transient, at best. Dr. William Atkisson was the first of the 10th Kentucky's four surgeons and fell victim to the diseases that ravaged the regiment during its first winter. He developed pneumonia due to the exposure that occurred during and after the Mill Springs campaign and died on April 8, 1862, near Savannah, Tennessee. He left a wife and a son.[15]

After the death of Dr. Atkisson, he was replaced with Dr. James G. Hatchitt. Dr. Hatchitt, John Harlan's brother-in-law, was also quickly promoted to positions in the army higher than those of regimental surgeon. In March 1864, Dr. Hatchitt, serving as medical director of the 23rd Corps, was granted a 30 day leave of absence due to diarrhea and general debility. James was promoted to rank of brevet lieutenant colonel in December 1865 and mustered out on December 8, 1865. After the war, Dr. Hatchitt moved to Frankfort and set up his practice. He served as the Frankfort postmaster. In the 1880s, he and his son went to Montana and established a horse ranch. President Harrison appointed him as agent to allot lands to Native Americans in the reservation.[16, 17]

He returned to Kentucky and was described "as a genial, whole soiled Kentucky gentleman of the old school." Dr. Hatchitt died on July 10, 1896, of chronic diarrhea in Newtown, Kentucky.

The surgeon's position fell to Dr. Jabez Perkins after Dr. Hatchitt's promotion, but Dr. Perkins, by all accounts a colorful and crusty physician, was rapidly promoted to greater responsibility within the Union Army. After being released from his army position, the doctor returned to New York City and spent eight months at the College of Physicians and Surgeons, and then moved to Owosso, Michigan, and engaged in general practice. He built up a reputation not only as a medical practitioner but also as a surgeon.

According to records, "While living in Lenawee County, Michigan, in 1858, Dr. Perkins was elected to the legislature, where he served one term greatly to the satisfaction and profit of his constituents, and to the credit of the Republican Party, which placed him in this honorable position. The doctor is a kind hearted and benevolent man, and does much for the unfortunate and needy, being ever ready to respond to the appeal of the distressed."[8]

He died in Owosso, Michigan, on November 7, 1907. One of his old-time patients commented: "He returned from the Civil War, bringing with him the white horse which he had used in his army service, and Dr. Perkins and the horse grew old together."[19]

A patient's daughter wrote of him: "He was very fond of children and devoted to these as to others in a large clientele. Many times when my father had typhoid fever he would come at midnight or later if he had been to see a patient, and stay all night with mother." He "was always gruff in manner," she continued, "but kindness itself although for many years crippled by rheumatism and necessitated to walk with two canes." 'Damn it, wouldn't I cure myself if I knew how,' he exploded to a woman who consulted him for this disease, pounding on the floor, the while, with both canes."[20]

The final regimental surgeon for the 10th Kentucky was Charles H. Stocking. Dr. Stocking took this position after Dr. Hatchitt's promotion and he served on a contract basis from 1863 to the end of the war. In 1865, he was appointed as surgeon for the 28th Regiment of Kentucky Volunteers.[21]

He married Matilde Breed on September 17, 1866, in Jamestown, New York. Dr. Stocking and Matilde moved to Freeport (Stephenson County), Illinois, six months after their marriage. The couple had two children.[22]

Charles purchased the interest in the drug business of Hicks & Treat in Freeport and became a druggist. He continued in this profession until the time of his death. He died on January 24, 1881, in Freeport and was buried in Tecumseh, Michigan. He died of complications of diseases produced by chronic diarrhea.[23] He would be referred to as "the pleasantest of social companions, the kindest and tenderest of husbands, and the most loving and indulgent of fathers."[24]

Company A

The final three officers in Company A survived the war and moved into productive lives. Captain Charles McKay returned to his home in Bullitt County and worked as a physician. He was the son of a doctor and became an excellent physician in his own right. While an officer in the regiment, he utilized his medical training and after each battle spent much of his time ministering to the wounded. In February 1862 he was taken ill with a fever and returned home to recuperate. He did not return to his regiment until April.

Charles married Ella Harris in June 1865 and the couple had three children. Ella died in 1877. Due to severe rheumatism, Captain McKay left Kentucky and moved to Hot Springs, Arkansas, in an attempt to improve his worsening medical condition. On October 3, 1881, he died in Shepherdsville, Kentucky, of heart failure at 40 years of age.

Captain Franklin S. Hill wrote that McKay "was a faithful soldier and a dutiful surgeon throughout the war and he died while in the prime of manhood." He also said, "There was never a better soldier mustered into the U.S. Service."[25]

First Lieutenant Henry H. Warren was injured twice, once on September 20, 1863, at

Chickamauga, when he was shot in the left arm, shattering the bone, and on July 9, 1864, at the engagement at the Chattahoochee, when he was shot in his left leg. After he was wounded at Chickamauga, he was captured and paroled. He recuperated and returned to the regiment in April 1864.[26]

He married Mary Catherine Chase on January 25, 1877, at St. Patrick's Church in Louisville, Kentucky. The couple had one son and resided in Louisville after the war. In 1880, he worked in a billiard room. He died in Jefferson County on May 6, 1911.[27]

Second Lieutenant Richard Grace was brevetted as captain later in the war and given temporary company command in the absence of the captain. He was wounded at the action on the Chattahoochee River on July 9, 1864. The gunshot wound to his left thigh missed the bone, but left Grace severely lame. He was treated at the divisional hospital, then moved to Chattanooga, on to Nashville and then to Louisville. He was absent, in the hospital, when the regiment was mustered out.[28]

After the war, Lieutenant Grace returned to Lebanon, Kentucky, and resided there until 1870 when he moved to St. Louis and onto Red Bud, Illinois. He returned to St. Louis in 1872. He moved to Jacksonville, Illinois, for two years and Chester, Illinois, for two years before returning to St. Louis where he died. He worked as a blacksmith, mechanic and coach and carriage manufacturer throughout his life.[23] He married Emily Faherty on May 27, 1873, at St. Patrick's Church in Ruma, Illinois. He and Emily had eight children who survived infancy. Two sons served in the First World War. He died of acute cardiac dilatation which resulted from broncho-pneumonia on September 8, 1925, in St. Louis. He was buried at Calvary Cemetery in St. Louis.

Three officers were discharged during the war due to physical disabilities. Captain William J. Lisle resigned in April 1863 due to a physical malady. He was originally a regimental adjutant and was promoted to captain of Company A in March 1863. Captain Lisle was a lawyer and made the city of Louisville his residence in 1873–77, during which time he was a member of the bar, and also secretary and treasurer of the Chesapeake and Ohio Railroad Company. In 1877 he formed a law partnership with R. H. Rountree, the oldest practicing lawyer of Lebanon. In 1862 Lisle married Ada McElroy, who died in 1877, leaving four children. In 1879 he married Mary (Mouring) Bevill and had two children. Mary Bevill was the sister of the late Captain Seth Bevill of Company E. Lisle died in Lebanon, Kentucky, on June 29, 1911.[29]

1st Lieutenant James Reynolds resigned his commission in May 1863. Lieutenant Reynolds was captured with his company in July 1862 in Courtland, Alabama, and he was paroled in Vicksburg, Mississippi, in September of that year. He resigned in May 1863 after suffering a severe skin condition, as described by Assistant Surgeon Charles Hardesty, "afflicted with 'Psoriasis' covering nearly the entire surface of his body and interfering with the free use of his body and interfering with the free use of his limbs, the flexion of which causing rupture of the cuticle at the joints. The disease is of 12 months standing and has not been benefited by treatment."[30]

Lieutenant Reynolds would never marry. He later worked in Louisville as a blacksmith and subsequently moved to the National Military Home in Marion, Indiana, as his health deteriorated. He died in 1901.

Second Lieutenant John W. Estes resigned in July 1862. He was honorably discharged in Nashville, Tennessee, on July 12, 1862, due to illness and replaced by Richard Grace. John developed typhoid pneumonia caused by exposure. He later developed chronic pleurisy in a

William Lisle (seated, front left) continued his law practice after the war (Georgeanne Edwards).

convalescent camp near Gallatin, Tennessee, and was discharged. After leaving the 10th Kentucky he lived in Bedford, Indiana (1864–1874), Washington, Indiana (1877 to 1886), Muhlenberg County, Kentucky (1886–1888), and then moved permanently to Louisville in 1888. After the war he became a tobacconist. John died on May 4, 1908. John was married twice, divorcing his first wife (Wanda Hamm), and later marrying Martha "Annie" McNichols on Nov. 10, 1892.[31]

Company B

Company B had only four officers throughout the war. After the war Captain John T. Milburn moved to Louisville, where he established a successful law practice on Jefferson Street. He remained in Louisville until his death. He maintained his connections with Marion County throughout his life. In 1868, he married Harriet "Haggie" Robertson of Springfield on October 29. He moved to Louisville and was elected to the school board, general council and the state legislature. He formulated and introduced the "Milburn Police Bill" while in the legislature. He resigned from the legislature on principle because "he could no longer remain in a body of which the members were supposed to be susceptible to taking bribes."[32, 33]

During the war John was sick, presumably with dysentery, from February 1862 until March 1862. He was captured near Antioch, Tennessee, in April 1863 and was a prisoner of war in Virginia until May 5, 1863, when he was exchanged and returned to his company. Later, he was wounded at Chickamauga. In December 1863 he was treated for bronchitis.

His health deteriorated in 1880s and on March 25, 1891, he died of uremic poisoning in Louisville and was interred in Cave Hill Cemetery.

First Lieutenant William Francis O'Bryan returned home to Louisville, where the family had moved to escape guerilla activities. His is also a story of tragedy because, unfortunately, he died on February 12, 1865, surviving the war by only a few months.

There were differences of opinion on the cause of death, and the exact nature of his death will never be known. The official cause was typhoid fever. During the war, however, William was wounded in the right thigh at an engagement at Utoy Creek, Georgia, on August 3, 1864, and his family believed that his death was directly related to this wound he sustained in the Atlanta Campaign. He was with Captain Milburn at the time he was wounded and within 3 weeks gangrene resulted. He was taken to the hospital in Nashville. He was furloughed on October 4, 1864, after leaving the hospital.[34]

Second Lieutenant John T. McCauley was sick during the war, first during the march from Nashville to Shiloh, presumably with dysentery. He was so ill that he had to be taken to the hospital in Louisville on the transport *Empress*. He entered the hospital on May 5, 1862, and was released on May 21, 1862. He was then furloughed home for further recuperation.

John Milburn established a successful law practice in Louisville after the war. He also was elected to the school board, general council and the state legislature (*The Courier-Journal*, Louisville, Kentucky, March 26, 1891).

He was hospitalized later during the Atlanta campaign with chronic diarrhea, lung disease (camp cough) and nervousness from the regiment's exhausting marches. He returned on August 24, 1864, just prior to the Battle of Jonesboro.[35]

When Lieutenant McCauley returned home after the war, he returned to farming, which was his occupation throughout his life. He married Mary Ann Browning on July 29, 1865, and had two children. In 1875, he moved his family to Loogootee, Indiana, and remained there for the remainder of his life. He died on March 22, 1905, of chronic bronchitis, lung and throat disease at the age of 73. He was buried at St. Mary's Cemetery in Loogootee.

First Lieutenant Robert S. Short resigned his commission in October 1862. He suffered from disease early in the war, beginning in February 1862, and he was sent home in April to recuperate. He was again ill and finally, Dr. Jabez Perkins, regimental surgeon, found Short had "incipient tuberculosis" and was unable to perform his duties. Lieutenant Short attributed the onset to exposure while marching from Lebanon to Louisville.

He became a farmer, teamster, and laborer and moved to Taylor County, Kentucky, then

Galesburg, Rio, and Ontario, Illinois. He married Elizabeth Handley on August 26, 1862, in Taylor County, Kentucky. Robert died on March 6, 1903, due to lung and heart disease. He was buried in the Linwood Cemetery in Galesburg, Illinois.[36]

Company C

Company C had only three officers during the war. Captain Edward Hilpp moved to Louisville after the war and worked with U.S. Internal Revenue Service as storekeeper-gauger. There are sources that say Captain Hilpp was born in three different locations, but his death certificate indicated that his birthplace was Kentucky. He died of "complication of disease," peritonitis, on April 9, 1908, and was buried in Cave Hill Cemetery on May 21, 1908.[37]

He was member of the Day-Night Lodge of Masons, Knights and Ladies of Honor. Captain Hilpp was originally married to Evanette Hite, but she died in 1894 in Lebanon, Kentucky. He subsequently married Lyte (Litie) Reynolds. At this death, he had one son, Roger. He was member of the East Baptist Church.[38]

First Lieutenant William "Billy" Mussen lived in New Market, Kentucky, and was a farmer. He was twice married, originally to Annie Freeman and later to Mary Porter. He outlived both wives and had no children. He died at the age of 89 on October 8, 1923, and was buried at the Presbyterian Church in New Market. The cause of death was an illness due to infirmities caused by his advanced age.[39, 40]

He was considered a "splendid citizen and was popular with everyone who knew him." He was also very charitable and generous to others, and he was a member of the Presbyterian Church. He lived his entire life at New Market, except for a short time in Perryville, Kentucky.

Second Lieutenant James E. Sallee was wounded on September 20, 1863, at Chickamauga and had detached duty in 1864 when he was placed in charge of an ambulance train for the 14th Corps. James returned home after the war. He settled in Buffalo in LaRue County and became a farmer again. He married Lucinda E. Hill in LaRue County on November 17, 1865. Sallee was one first of the people in LaRue County to work for the U.S. Internal Revenue Service. He worked for 35 years in his position with the IRS. James and Lucinda remained in Buffalo, Kentucky, into their 70s and had no children. James "Uncle Ned" Sallie died on July 27, 1914, at the age of 77; the official cause of death was senile debility. He was buried in the Buffalo Baptist Cemetery.[41, 42]

Company D

Captain George W. Riley was a lawyer and commanded the company throughout the war. Riley was lucky with his health throughout the war, until March 1864, when he was vaccinated for small pox. It was thought that he was treated with an impure dose of vaccine and had an allegoric reaction. He spent two months in the hospital recuperating from his vaccination and often had his arm in a sling.

George was not lucky in the affairs of the heart. He was married three times, first to Mary B. Edelen upon his return from the war, but they divorced in 1884. Next he married Georgiana Dunevan Miller in 1885 and divorced in 1901. His final wife was Melvina Rider Ramsey Holbrook, who also had been married twice before.

Although Captain Riley was lawyer, after returning from the war he became a school-teacher and lived in various locations, including Riley's Station, Kentucky, Litchfield, Kentucky, Denton, Texas, and then near Jacksonville, Illinois, from 1880 to 1909. He then moved to Los Angeles, where he remained until his death. He died at the Pacific Branch of Soldiers Home Hospital in Los Angeles, California, on February 2, 1918, of cerebral thrombosis.[43]

First Lieutenant James Mills returned to Marion County after the war and married Ellen "Alice" Hardesty on November 29, 1871. The couple had 13 children. James was injured during December 1862 when his horse fell as it walked on ice near Hartsburg, Tennessee, and he was unfit for duty until February 1863. He was left behind in Gallatin, Tennessee, while the regiment chased John Hunt Morgan during his Christmas raid. He also was absent due to fever and chronic diarrhea from August 30 through September 20, 1864.

He remained in St. Marys in Marion County until 1893, when he returned to Hancock County. He remained in Hancock County until his death on July 17, 1920, caused by heart disease and chronic gastritis. His captain, George Riley, wrote that "Mills was always a valiant and efficient officer."[44]

Second Lieutenant Edward Penick married Mary F. Neikirk on March 26, 1868. After the war he returned to Washington County and to farming.[45] Later Edward moved his family to Haysville in Marion County.

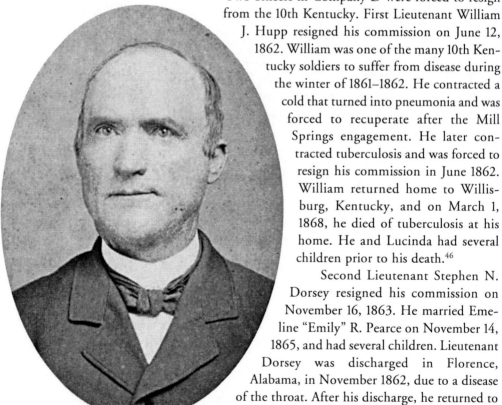

Two officers in Company D were forced to resign from the 10th Kentucky. First Lieutenant William J. Hupp resigned his commission on June 12, 1862. William was one of the many 10th Kentucky soldiers to suffer from disease during the winter of 1861–1862. He contracted a cold that turned into pneumonia and was forced to recuperate after the Mill Springs engagement. He later contracted tuberculosis and was forced to resign his commission in June 1862. William returned home to Willisburg, Kentucky, and on March 1, 1868, he died of tuberculosis at his home. He and Lucinda had several children prior to his death.[46]

Second Lieutenant Stephen N. Dorsey resigned his commission on November 16, 1863. He married Emeline "Emily" R. Pearce on November 14, 1865, and had several children. Lieutenant Dorsey was discharged in Florence, Alabama, in November 1862, due to a disease of the throat. After his discharge, he returned to Washington County and became a farmer for the rest of his life. Stephen died on March 24, 1895, in Springfield, Kentucky.[47]

George W. Riley, after returning from the war, became a school teacher and lived in various locations (National Archives).

Company E

There were only three officers for Company E. Captain Seth Bevill died at Chattanooga September 21, 1863, after being shot by a Confederate at the battle of Chickamauga. His death was due to "gunshot wounds through the body."[48]

Captain Andrew Thompson replaced Seth Bevill for the remainder of the war. Thompson returned to Washington County after the war and married Sarah "Alice" Harber early in 1866. Andrew's occupation after the war was that of farmer. Later he was elected to the position of county judge.[49]

Andrew Thompson and his wife had 2 children, and later the family moved to Louisville. Once in Louisville, he was elected to the state legislature from the first ward. He owned part of the Bourbon Stock Yards and was the president of the stockyard commission. Andrew died on October 15, 1899, of cerebral apoplexy, and he was buried at Pleasant Grove Cemetery in Springfield, Kentucky. "He was a man who made friends readily and was possessed of sterling integrity," an obituary said.[50]

First Lieutenant Clem Funk married Alice Duncan on November 15, 1865. After marrying, Clem moved to Nelson County, and in 1880 he was working as a United States storekeeper. He was killed on October 10, 1884, by Dr. T. D. Williams over a disagreement regarding money and insults. Clem met the doctor and an argument ensued that resulted in revolvers being drawn by both individuals, but Clem was shot and killed. The doctor was tried and acquitted.[51] Clem had three children and one was named John Harlan Funk in honor of the regimental colonel.[52]

Company F

The three officers of Company F returned from the war and reassembled their lives. Captain Franklin Shannon Hill returned to Washington County and was elected sheriff serving in 1870–1874. He farmed throughout his life and for four years in the late 1880s he worked with the Revenue Service. Except for the time working in the Revenue Service in Lebanon, he remained in the Mackville area in his occupation as a farmer.

Captain Hill developed dysentery during the 10th Kentucky's movement to Shiloh. Near Spring Hill, he left the regiment and returned to Kentucky to recuperate. He later returned to the regiment in May 1862. He was treated in the hospital in Louisville in December and January in 1864. He also developed scurvy in Ringgold Gap during the Atlanta campaign in April 1864.

After the war, he steadily lost the use of his right hand because of a hand and wrist injury he incurred at Chickamauga from a Minie ball or "hot ball." The injury resulted in "Dupuytren's contraction," which made his hand stiff and unusable.[53]

Captain Hill was working as a storekeeper at the Mattingly and Moore Distillery at the time of his death. Although he died in Nelson County, his residence was Mackville. He died at the age of 77 on October 26, 1898. "He was prominently connected and stood high in esteem of all who knew him," his obituary read.[54]

First Lieutenant Benjamin Smith suffered from dysentery and recuperated at home in May 1862. He received a gunshot wound in his left foot on September 20, 1863, and didn't return to the regiment until November 22, 1864. As he aged, the wound in the foot caused his ankle to contract and twist.

Benjamin returned to St. Marys, Kentucky, after the war and assumed his old occupation of carpenter and farmer. He married Sarah Talbott on January 31, 1866, at St. Joseph Church in Bardstown, Kentucky. The couple had nine children. Sarah died on January 31, 1886. His captain, Franklin S. Hill, wrote of him, "He was a first class soldier in every respect."[55]

Second Lieutenant Joseph Adcock received a gunshot wound at Jonesboro which disabled him for further service, was honorably discharged, and on recovering from this injury, moved to Macomb, Illinois, in 1865. He received a gunshot wound which fractured his eighth rib and entered his right lung. He established himself in the grocery trade, which he continued until his death. He died of pneumonia April 7, 1891, and was buried in Oakwood Cemetery. On September 13, 1866, Lieutenant Adcock married Nancy A. Pace, who was born in McDonough County, Illinois, and the couple had two children. He served as president of the school board for eight years. He was a member of the Methodist Episcopal Church in Macomb, where he was steward. He was also a member of the Masons. His obituary read, "The life of Mr. Adcock was beyond reproach. In business affairs he was diligent, upright and courteous. As a citizen he was public-spirited and useful, and the high esteem in which he was held by all who knew him attested the pure traits of his character."[56]

Company G

Company G lost all three of its initial officers to physical disabilities. Captain James M. Davenport finished the war in command of Company G but he had gone through a great deal of hardship in the battles that the 10th Kentucky had fought. James was wounded in the right leg on the first day of the Battle of Chickamauga on September 19, 1863, and unfortunately was wounded again, in the same leg, on September 1, 1864, during the Battle of Jonesboro. Both injuries were due to gunshot wounds and his leg was amputated about 3 inches above the knee in the field on the day of his second injury. In 1865, he re-enlisted and received a captaincy in the Veteran Reserve Corps. He was mustered out on June 30, 1866.[57]

He was married to Dora and had two children. After the war, he received an artificial leg and proceeded to travel to various locations. He may have re-entered his pre-war profession of school teacher after returning from the war. Then in 1866, he resided in Owensboro, Kentucky; in 1869 he was a clerk for the U.S. Treasury in Washington, D.C. In 1870–1874 he lived in Clinton, Kentucky; in 1877, in Erata, Mississippi; and finally, in 1883–1888 in Ennis, Texas. James M. Davenport died on January 10, 1888, at the age of 51 and was buried in the Myrtle Cemetery in Ennis.

First Lieutenant Edward O. Blanford returned home from the war and later moved to Kansas for a few years, but returned to Kentucky to become a farmer. He married Nannie Logsdon on September 16, 1873. After their marriage they moved to Missouri and then to Kansas, where he farmed, but health problems began to affect him. He returned to Kentucky in 1875 and began living with his father.

Lieutenant Blanford developed severe health problems after returning from the war. His problems began as headaches and then he began having nervous seizures and was confined to an asylum for the insane in Anchorage, Kentucky. He was later discharged, but was so severely ill that he was declared incompetent and guardians were appointed for him. He lived with different family members and institutions, including St. Vincent's Institute in St. Louis and

Lakeland Hospital in Kentucky, for the remainder of his life. Lieutenant Blanford died on Dec 18, 1907.[58]

Captain William Reynolds Hunter resigned his commission and was discharged on June 16, 1862, at Corinth, Mississippi. Although records don't specifically address the illness that forced Captain Hunter's resignation, he was treated on March 6, 1862. It was documented that disease of various types ravaged the men of the 10th Kentucky during this time.[59]

He married Maggie Ross in Louisville on May 17, 1862, and the couple had at least five children. After his discharge, he was involved in trading "all over the country" and in 1872 he moved to Louisville and became a policeman.[13] He died December 4, 1911, in Louisville of angina pectoris. He was buried at St. John's Cemetery in Louisville.

The hard luck of the officers continued with the retired 1st lieutenant of Company G, Charles Spalding. After Spalding resigned his commission on December 17, 1863, he returned to Washington County, Kentucky, where he was shot to death by guerillas in an orchard near his home in 1864.[60]

Second Lieutenant Ed C. Ferrill returned to Chicago, Kentucky, after he resigned his commission and made carpentry and blacksmithing his occupation.[61]

Company H

The four officers of Company H survived the war but all were touched by the three years of conflict. Captain William T. Shively lived on a farm in Taylor County, Kentucky, after the war but he sold it after a year. He then moved to Pottawattamie County, Iowa, in the summer of 1866 and worked in the milling business. In 1867 he worked in the steam sawmills near Avoca, Iowa, and later worked for a railroad. He then moved to Lemars, Iowa, where he homesteaded one hundred and sixty acres of land until 1882 and moved to O'Neill, Nebraska. In 1853, William was married to Teresa Hayden at St. Mary's church in Calvary, Marion County, Kentucky.[62]

First Lieutenant Henry C. Dunn served as topographical engineer for General Brannan at the time of the Battle of Chickamauga and was captured. Lieutenant Dunn spent time in a series of Confederate prisons and his health was drastically impaired. When Henry returned home he married Mattie E. Mahon on October 25, 1866, in Lebanon, Kentucky, and he had three children. Henry returned to his occupation as teacher, first in Bowling Green, Kentucky, then to Columbia, Kentucky; Perryville, Kentucky; Concord, North Carolina; and Rocky River, North Carolina. In 1895 he went to Rosebud, Texas. Once he finished his teaching career he became an insurance agent. Henry died of le grippe on March 8, 1911, in Rosebud, Texas.[63]

Second Lieutenant William F. Beglow received a gunshot wound to his thigh at Chickamauga and returned to the regiment. He also had a saber wound to his right breast at the Battle of Jonesboro. He developed lung disease while he was with the regiment, and his lung conditions continued to take a toll on him during the war.

William moved south (Alabama and Tennessee) immediately after the war and, in November 1865, he married Margaret Marshall. He worked in the railroad business immediately after the war, but his deteriorating health condition caused him to return to Louisville in 1869. His employment after the war was "clerk, bookkeeper and asst. assessor of the Int. rev. [Internal Revenue]."[64]

Unfortunately, at the age of 31, on April 11, 1872, William died of consumption in Louisville. Reports were that he returned after the war in a weakened health condition and he gradually deteriorated until his death in 1872. He was interred in Cave Hill Cemetery on April 12, 1872.[52] According to Corporal George Noe, "He was a favorite with everyone in the Regiment." According to I. B. Webster, "He was of a pleasant disposition, agreeable and gentle as a female. He was true and faithful as a soldier and an officer.... At the end of our service he was a mere shadow of his former self."[65]

Captain Buford R. Pendleton resigned his commission in November 1862. After his resignation, Captain Pendleton returned to farming and remained in Marion County for one year. He then moved to Rantoul, Illinois, and remained there for the next 27 years. Next he moved to Albany, Oregon, and then, later, to Lebanon, Oregon. During this time, he worked as a farmer and later lived on his pension. He died of cancer in Lafayette, Oregon, on October 27, 1909, and was buried in Masonic Cemetery.[66] He was never married.

Company I

Company I had the same three officers throughout the war. Captain Israel B. Webster left excellent written accounts of the battles of Chickamauga and Missionary Ridge in the *National Tribune*, a newspaper for Civil War veterans. He was married twice—in August 1846 to Harriet Lemerle, who died on December 29, 1873, of typhoid fever, and to Emma (Kirgivin) Keigwin of Philadelphia, Pennsylvania, on August 2, 1876. Emma died on November 25, 1914.

After the war, Israel B. Webster worked with his brother as a photographer in Louisville until 1878. He also joined the Masons after the war. In the 1880s, Webster was employed as a "special insurance agent" working for several companies. In 1894 he was elected magistrate of the Fourth District of Louisville. Captain Webster also worked as a stationery clerk in the office of the Revenue Service in Louisville for a few years before his death.[67]

Music was a key part of Captain Webster's life. He was said to be able to play every wind instrument. He was also the choir director for Christ Church Cathedral for many years. He worked with the choirs of the Second Presbyterian Church and the Broadway Methodist Church and was a member of the Mozart and Mendelssohn Societies.[68]

Captain Israel Webster died on March 18, 1902, in Louisville, Kentucky, of "tuberculosis of the bowels and senility." The cause of his death was later changed to complications resulting from an injury of the back which occurred during the Hoover's Gap campaign; the change allowed his widow to gain a pension. He was buried at Cave Hill Cemetery and shortly afterwards his body was moved to Jeffersonville, Indiana, for interment.

First Lieutenant William Kelley was wounded by gunshot in the right hip while rallying the regiment on September 20, 1863, at Chickamauga and was captured. He was paroled and moved to Louisville for care. Then he was moved to Camp Chase, Ohio, and returned to the regiment on May 19, 1864. He was also wounded in the head at the Battle of Jonesboro on September 1, 1864.

His wife, Elizabeth, died in 1868 and he subsequently remarried. He had a total of seven children. He moved to Lincoln County, Missouri, and became a farmer. He died in Argentville, Missouri (Lincoln County), on June 20, 1901, of urinary complications.[69]

Second Lieutenant John Myers was killed at Chickamauga. His record stated he "was a gallant and faithful officer, instantly killed at the Battle of Chickamauga Sept. 20, 1863. His body fell into the hands of the enemy."[70]

Company K

Company K had three captains during the war, none being from Kentucky. Captain Henry Waller was the captain throughout the Chickamauga and Mission Ridge campaigns, but unfortunately, he contracted small pox and died on March 13, 1864, in Chattanooga, Tennessee.

Captain Henry Denton, who succeeded Captain Waller, was very sick at the time that the 10th Kentucky was mustered out and was not present due to a "threat of Cerrebro Spinal Meningitis," but treatment averted the disease. His illness was said to be a result of riding in open box cars from Chattanooga to Nashville.[71]

Captain Denton returned home to Aurora, Indiana, after leaving service with the 10th Kentucky. He married Martha Cole on February 19, 1865. He worked in the Revenue Service, worked for William McHenry, lumber dealer, as a salesman, and also was postmaster of Aurora, Indiana. He died on October 10, 1893, of cancer. He left no children. The 1893 *Dearborn Independent* stated that "none knew him but to respect him."[72]

Israel B. Webster returned to photography after the war (Filson Historical Society, Louisville, Kentucky, Pettus-Speiden Family Collection).

First Lieutenant James R. Watts contracted typhoid fever early in the war and later had a second fever, thought to be "spotted fever," and was away from his company much of the summer of 1862. The wear of the war took its toll on "Dick." He became very ill, was taken out of line duty, and in October 1863 put in charge of the quartermaster duty for the regiment to try to improve his health. He remained in this capacity for the rest of the war. Lieutenant Watts returned to Louisville after the war. His first wife, Elizabeth, died on April 4, 1867, and he married Henrietta, his sister-in-law, on December 4, 1871.[73]

After the war Lt. Watts began working as a typesetter with the *Courier Journal* newspaper. He soon found that the gambling trade was more profitable. He owned several gambling establishments, including the Pearl Saloon, the Old Kentucky Club, and the Turf Exchange. Dick often traveled to various cities to gamble. He was reported to be very skilled at keno and faro. He had several other occupations including three terms in the lower board of the general council, employee of the post office and jailer for Jefferson County.[74]

Watts developed a form of rheumatism and a form of paralysis that caused him to become lame and affected his right side in the late 1870s. He died on January 17, 1898, in Louisville due to heart disease.

Captain William Tweddle resigned his commission on April 17, 1862. Captain Tweddle developed dysentery and severe lumbago during the march to Pittsburg Landing in 1862.

The condition was so severe that he was sent to the Louisville hospital, and he was never able to return to his company.[75]

After resigning, with a surgeon's certificate, William Tweddle worked in the Quartermaster Department through 1868. He was married to his wife, Mary, and they adopted a daughter. William moved to Colorado to work as clerk and assistant superintendent on a railroad connecting Kansas with Denver. He was forced to resign due to his lumbago problem and then was self-employed as a small-shop tobacconist.

William was living in the National Soldier's home in Virginia in 1890 suffering from lumbago. He moved to the Washington, D.C., area in 1891, and in 1892 he was married for a second time; his first wife died while traveling in Colorado in the early 1880s. William died on August 22, 1892, due to congestion of the brain. He was working as a watchman at the time of his death.

Finally, the spiritual leader for the 10th Kentucky, who was with the 10th Kentucky from beginning to the end, Rev. Richard C. Nash, died shortly after the regiment was mustered out of service in Hardin County Kentucky on February 4, 1865.

> "The muffled drum's sad roll has beat
> the soldier's last tattoo!
> No more on life's parade shall meet
> That brave and fallen few;
> On Fame's eternal camping ground
> Their silent tents are spread,
> And Glory guards, with solemn round,
> The bivouac of the dead
> By Theodore O'Hara, "Bivouac of the Dead"

Appendices

Appendix A. 10th Kentucky Roster from the Kentucky Adjutant General's Report, 1866

Regiment Staff	Rank	Comment
Harlan, John M.	Col.	Resigned March 6, 1863
Hays, William H.	Col.	Promoted March 11, 1863
Wharton, Gabriel C.	Lt. Col.	Promoted March 11, 1863
Davidson, Henry G.	Maj.	Died, Louisville 11-21-1864
Smith, Robert J.	Sgt. Maj.	Promoted 8-1-1862
Beglous, William F.	Q.M. Sgt.	Promoted to Lt. Co. H 3-11-1863
Johnson, Lee S.	Q.M. Sgt.	Promoted 1-26-1864
Lancaster, Edward B.	Q.M. Sgt.	Transferred to Co. A 7-31-1863
Matlock, Sam'l	Q.M. Sgt.	
Dunn, Henry C.	Com. Sgt.	Promoted to Lt. Co. H 12-11-1862
Garrison, John C.	Com. Sgt.	Discharged to 38th Ky. Inf. 5-28-1863
Moore, George W.	Com. Sgt.	Transferred to Co. D 6-1-1862
Newman, Nathan	Com. Sgt.	Prisoner of war
Lisle, Wm. J.	Adjts.	Promoted to Capt. Co. A 3-11-1863
Maquire, Austin P.	Adjts.	Promoted to Lt. and Adjutant 3-11-1863
Nash, Richard C.	Chaplain	
Arnott, John	Pr. Mus.	Promoted to principal musician 5-1-1864
Crutchett, Henry	Pr. Mus.	Transferred Co. A, 6-10-1862
Lennen, Joseph	Pr. Mus.	Promoted to principal musician 7-1-1862
Oster, James	Pr. Mus.	Discharged 5-9-1864, surgeon's certificate of disability
Atkisson, Wm.	Surg.	Died 4-14-1862
Hatchitt, James G.	Surg.	Promoted to brigade surgeon 6-26-1862
Perkins, Jabez	Surg.	Mustered out 11-18-1863 to accept commission in U.S. Volunteers
Stocking, Charles H.	Surg.	
Hardesty, Chas.	Asst. Surg.	Died July 1863
Knott, Thomas M.	Asst. Surg.	Died 4-5-1862
Davenport, Richard	Hosp.Stwd.	Died 1-17-1864
Leachman, Henry P.	Hosp.Stwd.	

COMPANY A

Name	Rank	Comment
Davidson, Henry G.	Capt.	Promoted to Major 3-11-1863
Lisle, William J.	Capt.	Resigned April 19, 1863
McKay, Charles W.	Capt.	
Reynolds, James	1st Lt.	Resigned May 4, 1863
Warren, Henry H.	1st Lt.	Wounded and captured at Chickamauga 9-20-1863, returned to regiment 6-1-1864, wounded at Chattahoochee River July 9, 1864
Estes, John	2nd Lt.	Resigned 7-19-1862
Grace, Richard	2nd Lt.	Wounded at Chattahoochee July 9, 1864, in hospital in Louisville
Maguire, Austin P.	2nd Lt.	Promoted to adjutant 3-11-1863
Arnold, Levi	Sgt.	
Blandford, George W.	Sgt.	

Name	*Rank*	*Comment*
Herdel, Nicholas	Sgt.	Wounded at Chickamauga
Manly, Samuel	1st Sgt.	Wounded and captured at Chickamauga, exchanged and returned to regiment 11-24-1864
Moore, George W.	Sgt.	Transferred 7-3-1865, mustered out
Burgess, Ray	Sgt.	Discharged for disability
Asbeck, Gustave	Corp.	
Boyle, Robert W.	Corp.	
Creagle, James	Corp.	Wounded at Jonesboro, Ga.
Jones, Aaron	Corp.	Wounded at Pickett's Mill, Ga.
Kortz, Frederick	Corp.	Wounded at Jonesboro
Krival, Francis	Corp.	Transferred 8-23-1865, mustered out
Roberts, Harrison	Corp.	
Shockley, Davis M	Corp.	
Mattingly, Alexander O.	Wagoner	
Arnold, Adam	Pvt.	
Arnold, Jeremiah	Pvt.	
Arnold, Simpson	Pvt.	Transferred 8-28-1865, mustered out
Askren, Samuel	Pvt.	Discharged for disability 11-9-1863
Baker, Samuel	Pvt.	Discharged for disability
Berhnes, Henry	Pvt.	Discharged for disability
Berry, James	Pvt.	Died Lebanon, Ky. 3-5-1862
Bland, Fletcher	Pvt.	Died Lebanon, Ky. 11-1861
Boyd, William	Pvt.	Transferred 8-15-1865, mustered out
Bumgarder, George W.	Pvt.	Died at home 3-2-1862
Bumgarder, John W.	Pvt.	
Cable, James	Pvt.	Wounded at Courtland, Ala.
Casabon, Oliver D.	Pvt.	Deserted 1-1-1863
Crutcher, Henry	Pvt.	Transferred to Vet Res. Corps 6-1864
Decker, August	Pvt.	Transferred to Vet Res. Corps
Demarsh, Nicholas	Pvt.	
Demarsh, Stephen	Pvt.	
Dennis, Frank	Pvt.	Discharged for disability
Duffield, Jacob	Pvt.	Transferred 8-28-1865, mustered out
Durbin, John C.	Pvt.	Discharged for disability 1-6-1863
Edmonson, Joseph	Pvt.	Wounded at Jonesboro, Ga.
Edmonson, Wilson W.	Pvt.	Discharged for disability
Frank, George H.	Pvt.	Transferred, mustered out
Gaylock, Peter	Pvt.	Deserted 1-1-1863
Graham, Harvey	Pvt.	Transferred 8-28-1865, mustered out
Ham, Abram	Pvt.	Transferred 8-28-1865, to make good time lost.
Harding, Elias	Pvt.	Transferred 8-28-1865, mustered out
Harding, George	Pvt.	Transferred 8-28-1865, mustered out
Hill, Conrad	Pvt.	
Jenkins, Joseph	Pvt.	
Johnson, John	Pvt.	
Johnson, William	Pvt.	Transferred 8-2-1865, mustered out
Jones, William	Pvt.	Wounded at Chickamauga
Kendall, Bladen A.	Pvt.	
Kendall, Culbraith	Pvt.	
Kortz, John	Pvt.	
Kortz, Mathie	Pvt.	Wounded at Pickett's Mill, Ga.
Kortz, William	Pvt.	
Krahl, Conrad	Pvt.	Discharged for disability 10-2-1863
Lancaster, Edward B.	Pvt.	
Martin, Eugene	Pvt.	Deserted 2-22-1863 Lavergne, Tenn.
Mattingly, John M.	Pvt.	
Mattingly, Thomas R.	Pvt.	Transferred to Co. F 2-1-1862
Maurer, Francis	Pvt.	Discharged for disability 10-2-1862
McDaniel, John	Pvt.	Discharged for disability 1-9-1864
Mitchell, Henry	Pvt.	
Mitchell, John	Pvt.	Deserted 2-22-1863 Lavergne, Tenn.
Mudd, Richard	Pvt.	
Mumford, Robinson	Pvt.	Discharged for disability
Murrell, Woods	Pvt.	Deserted 3-1-1862

Name	Rank	Comment
Pirtle, Isaac E.	Pvt.	Died at Chattanooga 12-1-1863
Rheul, Eincle	Pvt.	Died near Lebanon, Ky. 2-1862
Rogers, James C.	Pvt.	Deserted 1-1-1863
Ropp, Michael	Pvt.	
Rossles, Frederick	Pvt.	Wounded at Chickamauga, Ga.
Ruder, John	Pvt.	Wounded at Jonesboro, Ga.
Saal, Frederick	Pvt.	Deserted 1-1-1863
Shain, David	Pvt.	Transferred 10-18-1865, mustered out
Shielly, John	Pvt.	
Shielly, Anthony	Pvt.	To make good time lost
Shielly, William	Pvt.	
Shorten, Lewis	Pvt.	Discharged for disability
Smith, Thomas M.	Pvt.	Wounded at Chickamauga
Snawder, Joseph	Pvt.	
Stephens, Philip	Pvt.	
Steward, John	Pvt.	
Stoar, John	Pvt.	Deserted 1-1-1863
Terry, Arthur T.	Pvt.	
Terry, George W.	Pvt.	Wounded at Jonesboro, Ga.
Vanderheide, John	Pvt.	
Voclair, Frank	Pvt.	Deserted 2-22-1863, Lavergne, Tenn.
Watts, John R.	Pvt.	Transferred 2-25-1865, mustered out
Weiser, Harry	Pvt.	
Welsh, John	Pvt.	
Young, James	Pvt.	

COMPANY B

Name	Rank	Comment
Milburn, John T.	Capt.	
O'Bryan, William F.	1st Lt.	
Short, Robert S.	1st Lt.	Resigned 11-4-1862
McCauley, John T.	2nd Lt.	
Davenport, James M.	2nd Lt.	Promoted to Capt. Co. G, 6-16-1862
Gray, Stephen J.	Sgt.	
Harding, William	Sgt.	
Heinis, Ernst	Sgt.	
McCauley, Chas. B.	Sgt.	
McCauley, Thomas	Sgt.	
McGrath, Philip J.	Sgt.	Killed in Action 9-18-1863 Chickamauga, Ga.
Scott, James F.	Sgt.	Killed in Action 9-18-1863 Chickamauga, Ga.
Blair, David	Corp.	
Blanford, Edward	Corp.	
Cross, James	Corp.	
Cross, William	Corp.	
Fenwcik, Thomas	Corp.	
Llewellyn, Elisha O.	Corp.	
McBride, Wm. D.	Corp.	Discharged 2-24-1862 Bardstown, Ky.
Russell, John	Corp.	
Talmadge, Joseph	Corp.	Transferred 11-6-1864 Time unexpired
Vancleve, Samuel	Mus.	Absent—sick
Alvey, Alexander	Pvt.	Deserted 12-31-1862 New Market, Ky.
Blair, James	Pvt.	Died 8-30-1864 Chattanooga, Tenn.
Blair, John T.	Pvt.	Killed in Action 9-19-1863 Chickamauga, Ga.
Blanford, Robert	Pvt.	Killed in Action 9-19-1863 Chickamauga, Ga.
Brady, George W.	Pvt.	
Brady, Joseph	Pvt.	
Brown, D. Marcus	Pvt.	
Bullock, James G.	Pvt.	
Bullock, William	Pvt.	
Butler, William	Pvt.	
Cecil, John H.	Pvt.	
Clark, Edward	Pvt.	

Name	Rank	Comment
Clark, John	Pvt.	Discharged 10-19-1864 Washington, D.C.
Clark, Royal G.	Pvt.	Died 5-26-1864 Nashville, Tenn.
Cross, Richard M.	Pvt.	Deserted 8-1-1864 Louisville, Ky.
Caniff, George	Pvt.	
Donahoo, James	Pvt.	
Durham, James S.	Pvt.	Deserted 9-1-1862 Lebanon, Ky.
Durham, John S.	Pvt.	Transferred 2-11-1864 To Vet. Reserve Corps
Farris, Joseph G.	Pvt.	
Fenwick, Cornelius	Pvt.	
Fenwick, George W.	Pvt.	Killed in Action 9-19-1863 Chickamauga, Ga.
Fogle, William	Pvt.	
Green, Francis	Pvt.	
Greenwell, Francis	Pvt.	
Greenwell, John	Pvt.	
Hall, Benjamin	Pvt.	
Hall, William, Jr.	Pvt.	Died 11-10-1864 Marion County, Ky.
Hall, William, Sr.	Pvt.	Missing in action 9-23-1863, Chattanooga, Tenn.
Hayden, Andrew	Pvt.	Died 8-22-1864 Chattanooga, Tenn.
Howard, Edward	Pvt.	
Johnston, James	Pvt.	
Knott, Richard W.	Pvt.	Died 5-15-1862 Lebanon, Ky.
Lake, John B.	Pvt.	
Lamb, James R.	Pvt.	Discharged 10-24-1862 Louisville, Ky.
Livers, George	Pvt.	
Livers, Samuel	Pvt.	Died 7-5-1864 Nashville, Tenn.
Lucas, Henry	Pvt.	
Lucket, Thomas A.	Pvt.	
Maston, John E.	Pvt.	
Mattingly, Benjamin S.	Pvt.	
Mattingly, C. W.	Pvt.	
Mattingly, Henry B.	Pvt.	
Mattingly, John T.	Pvt.	
Mattingly, Joseph S.	Pvt.	Killed in Action 9-19-1863 Chickamauga, Ga.
Mattingly, Wm. B.	Pvt.	Died 4-5-1862 Nashville, Tenn.
Mattingly, Wm. L.	Pvt.	
McGavock, James W.	Pvt.	
Meadows, William	Pvt.	
Miles, Chas. Henry	Pvt.	Killed in Action 7-9-1864 Veining's Station, Ga.
Miles, Henry	Pvt.	
Miles, James M.	Pvt.	Deserted 8-1-1864 Louisville, Ky.
Miles, Thomas	Pvt.	Killed in Action 9-19-1863 Chickamauga, Ga.
Mills, John	Pvt.	Transferred 11-6-1864 Time unexpired
Mitchell, Jefferson B.	Pvt.	Deserted 6-30-1863 Louisville, Ky.
Newton, William	Pvt.	Transferred 11-6-1864 Time unexpired
Nolley, Wm. T	Pvt.	Transferred 11-6-1864 Time unexpired
Peterson, Allen	Pvt.	
Peterson, Garrett D.	Pvt.	Died 10-24-1862 Lebanon, Ky.
Peterson, John	Pvt.	
Peterson, Thomas G.	Pvt.	Killed in Action 9-19-1863 Chickamauga, Ga.
Pickerel, Stephen E.	Pvt.	Discharged 7-7-1863 Nashville, Tenn.
Read, Philip M.	Pvt.	Discharged 7-1-1863 Nashville, Tenn.
Rhodes, William M.	Pvt.	Deserted 10-31-1862 New Market, Ky.
Sanders, James	Pvt.	
Sill, David	Pvt.	Discharged 5-23-1863 Louisville, Ky.
Simins, Thomas A.	Pvt.	Died 5-27-1862 Lebanon, Ky.
Simms, Wm.	Pvt.	
Thompson, Richard G.	Pvt.	
Uptergrove, Joseph L.	Pvt.	Under arrest for desertion
Wade, Elijah	Pvt.	
Wade, John L.	Pvt.	Deserted 10-29-1862 New Market, Ky.
Whitfield, William	Pvt.	Killed in Action 9-1-1864 Jonesboro, Ga.
Wise, John	Pvt.	

COMPANY C

Name	*Rank*	*Comment*
Hilpp, Edward	Capt.	
Musson, William	1st Lt.	
Sallee, James E.	2nd Lt.	
Martin, James B.	1st Sgt.	Wounded at Chickamauga 9-19-1863
Buckman, Jos. Madison	Sgt.	Deserted 1-2-1863 on the march
Clayton, Robert H.	Sgt.	Prisoner Captured at Veining's Station 7-9-1864
Moore, William	Sgt.	
Nall, William H.	Sgt.	
Smith, Thomas G.	Sgt.	
Andrews, Albert T.	Corp	
Buckman, Jos. W.	Corp.	
Buckman, Joseph Mike	Corp.	Killed in Action Veining's Station, Ga. 7-9-1863
Craig, John	Corp.	Transferred to Vet. Res. Corps 4-30-1864
Hogland, Isaac	Corp.	
Mattingley, Martin V.B.	Corp.	
Meece, George W.	Corp.	Wounded at Chickamauga 9-19-1863
Robinson, James B.	Corp.	Discharged 3-1-1863 Lavergne, Tenn.
Russell, David	Corp.	Wounded at Chickamauga 9-19-1863
Dobson, James	Mus.	Died 5-5-1862 Louisville, Ky.
Hogland, Wm. H.	Wagoner	
Allen, David	Pvt.	
Allen, Samuel	Pvt.	Discharged 12-31-1862 Nashville, Tenn.
Allen, Silas W.	Pvt.	Died 3-23-1862 Nashville, Tenn.
Anderson, John	Pvt.	Died 2-11-1862 Marion County, Ky.
Atkins, Lafayette F.	Pvt.	Discharged 9-20-1862 Louisville, Ky.
Benningfield, John	Pvt.	Transferred to Vet. Res. Corps 11-1-1863
Ballou, John	Pvt.	Discharged 7-1-1862 Louisville, Ky.
Boarman, John	Pvt.	
Bright, William D	Pvt.	
Brown, James F.	Pvt.	Wounded at Peachtree Creek 7-21-1864—left arm amputated
Carum, James C.	Pvt.	
Cooper, John A.	Pvt.	
Caniff, Elias	Pvt.	Died 4-1-1864 Nashville, Tenn.
Dobson, William H.	Pvt.	Died Atlanta, Ga.
Dye, Robert T.	Pvt.	Died 3-3-1862 Lebanon, Ky.
Elmore, Andrew	Pvt.	
Farmer, William	Pvt.	Died 7-16-1862 Tuscumbia, Ala.
Feather, John H.	Pvt.	Died 4-17-1862 Taylor County, Ky.
Garrott, John J.	Pvt.	Killed in Action Mission Ridge, Tenn. 11-25-1863
Gault, William B. S.	Pvt.	Discharged 1-1-1863 St. Louis, Mo.
Gebhart, William H.	Pvt.	
Hickey, Patrick	Pvt.	Discharged 9-10-1863 Nashville, Tenn.
Hoback, James A.	Pvt.	
Hoback, John C.	Pvt.	
Hoback, Martin L.	Pvt.	Died 11-28-1863 Nashville, Tenn.
Hogland, Isaac, Sr.	Pvt.	Discharged 6-6-1862 Evansville, Ind.
Hogland, John B.	Pvt.	Transferred to Dept. of Cumberland 11-6-1864
Hogland, John	Pvt.	
Hunt, Rueben W.	Pvt.	Discharged 3-11-1863 Louisville, Ky.
Kirkpatrick, Benjamin R.	Pvt.	Deserted 8-1-1862 Hamburg Landing, Tenn.
Howell, James W.	Pvt.	
Hunt, Reuben W.	Pvt.	
Hunter, Francis M.	Pvt.	
Lake, Abraham	Pvt.	
McKenley, George W.	Pvt.	
McNamara, Michael	Pvt.	
Mills, Dennis	Pvt.	Deserted 10-12-1862 On the march
Moore, James R.	Pvt.	
Moore, William E.	Pvt.	
Newcomb, Thomas	Pvt.	
Newton, Joseph R.	Pvt.	
Noley, Edward B.	Pvt.	

Name	Rank	Comment
Norco, James	Pvt.	Transferred to Vet. Res. Corps 1-15-1864
Powers, George W.	Pvt.	
Puryear, Samuel J. B.	Pvt.	Died 3-27-1862 LaRue County, Ky.
Rice, John L.	Pvt.	
Riggs, Thomas	Pvt.	Died 11-6-1862 Marion County, Ky.
Riley, John	Pvt.	Transferred to Vet. Res. Corps 9-1-1863
Robinson, William W.	Pvt.	
Rodgers, Benjamin O.	Pvt.	Discharged 3-11-1863 Gallatin, Tenn.
Rodgers, James	Pvt.	Died 11-28-1861 Lebanon, Ky.
Sallee, Thomas J.	Pvt.	Died 8-18-1864 LaRue County, Ky.
Sapp, Burnet B.	Pvt.	Died 10-29-1863 Chattanooga, Tenn.
Sapp, Franklin	Pvt.	
Sapp, Jasper	Pvt.	
Sapp, Peter	Pvt.	Died 3-28-1862 Nashville, Tenn.
Shipp, Ambrose	Pvt.	
Shipp, James	Pvt.	Discharged 4-1-1863 Louisville, Ky.
Slatterly, Patrick	Pvt.	Discharged 3-1-1863 Lavergne, Tenn.
Stillwell, Hattan	Pvt.	Died 5-15-1862 Corinth, Miss.
Taylor, Thomas	Pvt.	
Thurman, James P.	Pvt.	Prisoner Captured at Chickamauga 9-20-1863.
Wade, George W.	Pvt.	Discharged 4-20-1863 Nashville, Tenn.
White, Wm. H.	Pvt.	
Wilson, Lafayette	Pvt.	
Wise, Chas.	Pvt.	

COMPANY D

Name	Rank	Comment
Riley, George W.	Capt.	
Hupp, William	1st Lt.	Resigned 6-16-1862
Mills, James J.	1st Lt.	
Dorsey, Stephen N.	2nd Lt.	Resigned 11-16-1862
Penick, Edward Y.	2nd Lt.	
Dunn, Henry C.	Sgt.	Transferred to non-commissioned staff 6-1-1862
Earing, James C.	1st Sgt.	Wounded Chickamauga 9-19-1863
Foster, Andrew J.	Sgt.	
Garrison, John C.	Sgt.	Transferred to non-commissioned staff 12-11-1862
Roberts, Marvis T.	Sgt.	
Seay, Francis B.	Sgt.	
Shockley, Robert G.	Sgt.	
Beaven, Chas.	Corp.	Wounded Chickamauga 9-19-1863
Crouch, Martin V.	Corp.	
Davis, Nathaniel W.	Corp.	Discharged for disability 8-10-1862
Garrison, Gideon B.	Corp.	Died. Atlanta. Wounded at Chickamauga
Hughes, Thomas D.	Corp.	
Murvill, Isaac H.	Corp.	
Phillips, John H.	Corp.	Transferred to Vet. Res. Corps 4-30-1864. Wounded at Chickamauga
Price, William T.	Corp.	Died, 12-3-1861
Seay, James A.	Corp.	Discharged for disability 2-4-1862
Snider, James A.	Corp.	Discharged for disability 10-10-1862
Wells, Elbert S.	Corp.	Transferred to Vet. Res. Corps 3-18-1864. Wounded at Chickamauga
White, David D.	Corp.	Died. 1-1-1862 Mill Springs, Ky.
Wilson, Thomas O.	Corp.	Discharged for disability 2-3-1863
Garrison, David R.	Mus.	
Yocum, James M.	Mus.	Prisoner—Captured at Chickamauga 12-24-1863
Shasson, Henry A.	Wagoner	
Abell, Benedict J. A.	Pvt.	
Beavers, Charles	Pvt.	Wounded Chickamauga 9-19-1863 and in Atlanta Campaign 8-16-1864
Beavers, Wilford	Pvt.	Discharged for disability 12-1-1864

Name	*Rank*	*Comment*
Beggley, Roland	Pvt.	
Bottoms, Bradford E.	Pvt.	Discharged for disability 3-8-1863
Brackan, William C.	Pvt.	Died 2-1862. Marion County, Ky.
Buckman, John G.	Pvt.	
Cain, Adam	Pvt.	Discharged for disability 10-1862
Compfort, Thomas	Pvt.	Discharged for disability 8-10-1862
Crench, Wm. W.	Pvt.	Died 2-18-1862. Washington County, Ky.
Cronch, James P.	Pvt.	Prisoner—Captured at Chickamauga 12-24-1863
Cussanger, James	Pvt.	Discharged for disability 2-5-1863
Ewing, William T.	Pvt.	Killed in Action Chickamauga. 9-19-1863.
Graham, Mason	Pvt.	Discharged for disability 6-11-1863
Hagan, James	Pvt.	
Hagan, John T.	Pvt.	Died 10-1-1863. Chattanooga, Tenn. Wounded at Chickamauga.
Hagerty, Richard	Pvt.	
Hahun, Samuel	Pvt.	Discharged for disability 9-19-1864 on account of wounds
Hall, John W.	Pvt.	Died 5-1862. Washington County, Ky.
Haman, Lee	Pvt.	Deserted 4-1863 in Marion County, Ky.
Hart, Thomas	Pvt.	
Homan, David	Pvt.	Discharged for disability 2-8-1863
Hughes, Andrew	Pvt.	Deserted 11-1-1862 South Tunnel, Tenn.
Hughes, David B.	Pvt.	
Hundrix, William	Pvt.	Discharged for disability 7-27-1863 On account of wounds
Hutchinson, William	Pvt.	
Isham, John W.	Pvt.	
Issac, Nathan	Pvt.	Deserted 1-1-1863. Rolling Fork Bridge, Ky.
Johnsey, William B.	Pvt.	Discharged for disability 2-7-1863
Lanham, James P.	Pvt.	Died 2-1862. Washington County, Ky.
Leankford, James A.	Pvt.	
Leathers, Jesse M.	Pvt.	
Lindsey, Buford	Pvt.	
Linnehan, James	Pvt.	
Luckett, Thomas A.	Pvt.	Discharged for disability 12-1-1864 on account of wounds—Chickamauga
Lynch, Robert N.	Pvt.	Discharged for disability 2-6-1864
Mattingly, Thomas	Pvt.	
Maxwell, Danby C.	Pvt.	
McHughes, Silas	Pvt.	
Milburn, William	Pvt.	
Montgomery, William	Pvt.	Died 5-1862. Washington County, Ky.
Mosser, Henry L.	Pvt.	Missing in action. 11-1-1862. Nashville, Tenn.
Mouser, John W.	Pvt.	
Mouser, William F.	Pvt.	Died. 6-10-1862. Corinth, Miss.
Parris, Thomas G.	Pvt.	Discharged for disability 6-29-1863
Ripperdon, Wm. D.	Pvt.	Died 3-1862. Washington County, Ky.
Sapp, Cornelius	Pvt.	Discharged for disability 8-24-1863
Sheultry, Cornelius	Pvt.	Died 4-17-1863 Nashville, Tenn.
Shimmerhorn, Richard	Pvt.	Died 3-1862. Mill Springs, Ky.
Smothers, Isaac	Pvt.	
Smothers, Richard	Pvt.	Died 3-8-1862 Lavergne, Tenn.
Smothers, Wm.	Pvt.	Discharged for disability 8-24-1863
Snider, Alfred	Pvt.	Wounded Chickamauga 9-19-1863 and Mission Ridge 11-25-1863
Southern, Charles	Pvt.	Discharged for disability 2-16-1863
Steward, Charles G.	Pvt.	Killed in Action. 9-19-1863 Chickamauga.
Stines, Robert	Pvt.	Wounded Chickamauga 9-19-1863
Taylor, Benjamin	Pvt.	
Wakefield, Wm. F.	Pvt.	Died 5-7-1862 Camp Dennison, Ohio
Wakefield, Squire H.	Pvt.	Discharged for disability 4-17-1863
Wells, John B.	Pvt.	
White, John N.	Pvt.	
Wicker, James T.	Pvt.	Discharged for disability 2-4-1863
Williams, Jesse R.	Pvt.	Discharged for disability 7-12-1862
Willitt, Thomas B.	Pvt.	Wounded Jonesboro, Ga. 9-1-1864

Name	*Rank*	*Comment*
Yocum, John R.	Pvt.	
Yocum, Richard B.	Pvt.	Wounded Chickamauga 9-19-1863

COMPANY E

Name	*Rank*	*Comment*
Bevill, Seth P.	Capt.	Wounded at Chickamauga 9-20-1863. Died at Chattanooga 9-21-1863.
Thompson, Andrew	Capt.	
Funk, Clem	1st Lt.	
Boyle, Richard	Sgt.	
Champion, James C.	Sgt.	
Cozine, John S.	Sgt.	Commissioned 2nd Lt. 9-22-1863, but never mustered
Higdon, Alexander B.	Sgt.	Died 5-27-1864 In the field
Janes, Joseph A.	Sgt.	
Logsdon, Thos. H.	Sgt.	
Champion, Thos. M	Corp.	Discharged 8-28-1862
Coomes, Burr	Corp.	
Dawson, Martin A.	Corp.	Discharged 1-13-1863 Louisville, Ky.
Ensor, George W.	Corp.	Died 10-20-1863. Chattanooga, Tenn.
Filiatrean, Columbus R.	Corp.	
Higdon, James A.	Corp.	Wounded near Atlanta 8-7-1864
Hundley, Andrew N.	Corp.	Died 2-27-1862 in Washington Co., Ky.
Leachman, Harrison P.	Corp.	Transferred to non-commissioned staff 5-1-1864
Logsdon, Ambr J.	Corp.	
Nally, Thos. J.	Corp.	
Noe, George A.	Corp.	Wounded at Chickamauga 9-20-1863
Noe, William T.	Corp.	
Thompson, Nathaniel P.	Corp.	
Hood, James K.P.	Mus.	Died 5-5-1862 In Springfield, Tenn.
Adams, Elisha M.	Pvt.	Died 9-19-1863. Chickamauga
Adams, William T.	Pvt.	Wounded at Chickamauga 9-20-1863
Berry, William G.	Pvt.	Discharged 3-10-1862 Louisville, Ky.
Bowles, George W.	Pvt.	
Campbell, John	Pvt.	Died 9-19-1863. Chickamauga
Carney, John	Pvt.	
Carroll, James	Pvt.	
Champion, Charles A.	Pvt.	Died 6-4-1864. Chattanooga.
Clarkson, James	Pvt.	Died 4-8-1862. Nashville, Tenn.
Clarkson, John	Pvt.	Died 4-30-1862. Nashville, Tenn.
Cooper, Philip	Pvt.	Discharged 3-18-1863 Louisville, Ky.
Corcoran, Philip	Pvt.	Discharged Nashville, Tenn.
Courtney, John W.	Pvt.	
Curd, Joseph	Pvt.	Discharged 4-27-1864 Camp Chase, Ohio
Dearing, John L.	Pvt.	Wounded at Chickamauga 9-20-1863
Dobson, William H.	Pvt.	Wounded at Chickamauga 9-20-1863
Edwards, John L.	Pvt.	
Edwards, William M.	Pvt.	
Fenwick, Edward	Pvt.	Died 10-9-1864. Chattanooga
Fields, Henry P.	Pvt.	Died in Louisville, Ky., 11-29-1864
Fields, Richard M.	Pvt.	Discharged 2-8-1863 Gallatin, Tenn.
Filiatreau, William T.	Pvt.	Discharged 3-16-1863 Louisville, Ky.
Foster, Benjamin	Pvt.	
Fowler, John J.	Pvt.	Died 9-19-1863. Chickamauga
Gassalder, Arnold	Pvt.	Discharged 2-2-1863, St. Louis, Mo.
Green, George L.	Pvt.	
Green, William	Pvt.	Discharged Nashville, Tenn.
Hall, Joseph	Pvt.	Died 2-26-1862 In Washington Co., Ky.
Haydon, James B.	Pvt.	Died 5-2-1862 In Washington Co., Ky.
Heaton, John W.	Pvt.	Transferred—Unexpired
Herbert, James P.	Pvt.	
Hiatt, Reuben	Pvt.	Died 3-27-1862 in Washington Co. Ky.

Name	Rank	Comment
Hundley, James R.	Pvt.	Died 9-19-1863. Chickamauga
Kating, John	Pvt.	
Logsdon, Richard L.	Pvt.	Died 10-16-1863. Chickamauga
Lyons, Richard	Pvt.	Discharged 3-9-1863 Louisville, Ky.
Mayes, John W.	Pvt.	Died 7-9-1864. Chattahoochee, Ga.
Miles, Joseph	Pvt.	
Murphy, Michael	Pvt.	Transferred—Unexpired
Myers, William A.	Pvt.	Wounded at Chickamauga 9-20-1863
Myers, William R.	Pvt.	
Nally, John H.	Pvt.	
Nix, George W.	Pvt.	Transferred to Vet. Reserve Corps 4-30-1864
Nix, William	Pvt.	Died 8-5-1864. Chattanooga, Tenn.
Peak, John F.	Pvt.	
Reynolds, Francis	Pvt.	Discharged 1-9-1863. Louisville, Ky.
Rhodes, Herod	Pvt.	Deserted 1-3-1863. Lebanon Junction, Ky.
Rhodes, Thos. D.	Pvt.	Died 2-25-1862 Crab Orchard, Ky.
Richardson, William S.	Pvt.	Died 2-25-1862 in Washington Co., Ky.
Savadge, Mathew	Pvt.	
Seay, John P.	Pvt.	Died 3-7-1864. Chattanooga, Tenn.
Simms, Cornelius	Pvt.	Died 2-15-1862. Somerset, Ky.
Slayton, Marion A.	Pvt.	Died 1-3-1862. Campbellsville, Ky.
Spraggins, Alexander W.	Pvt.	
Sullivant, Patrick	Pvt.	Died in Louisville, Ky., 12-4-1864
Thompson, Edward A.	Pvt.	
Thompson, John B.	Pvt.	Wounded at Chickamauga 9-20-1863
Toon, Peter	Pvt.	Died 3-12-1862 in Washington Co. Ky.
Walker, Richard R.	Pvt.	Died 12-15-1861 Lebanon, Ky.
Walker, Robert B.	Pvt.	Prisoner—Captured at Chickamauga 9-20-1863
Waters, Jack H.	Pvt.	Died 10-4-1863. Chattanooga, Tenn.
Weathers, James E.	Pvt.	Died 6-9-1862 Corinth, Miss.
White, Edward T.	Pvt.	
Whitfield, James	Pvt.	Transferred to Vet Reserve Corps 10-29-1863
Willis, Isaac T.	Pvt.	
Young, James R.	Pvt.	Wounded at Jonesboro, Ga. 9-1-1864

COMPANY F

Name	Rank	Comment
Hill, Franklin S.	Capt.	
McKay, Charles W.	1st Lt.	Promoted to Capt Co. A 5-24-1863
Smith, Benjamin R.	1st Lt.	Wounded at Chickamauga. 9-19-1863
Adcock, Joseph T.	2nd Lt.	Wounded at Jonesboro, Ga., 9-1-1864. Absent in hospital
Jarboe, Charles H.	Sgt.	
Johnson, Terry	Sgt.	
Maguire, Austin P.	Sgt.	Transferred to non-commissioned staff 11-21-1861
Mittler, Edward	1st Sgt.	
Robinson, Robert A.	Sgt.	
Thompson, John M.	Sgt.	
Asbeck, Gustave	Corp.	
Badgett, Hardin	Corp.	
Bottom, Calvin W.	Corp.	
Harshfield, Achilles	Corp.	Discharged 7-21-1863 Louisville, Ky.
Hocker, Jefferson	Corp.	
Newman, Mathew	Corp.	Transferred to non-commissioned staff 5-28-1863
Reagan, Levi N.	Corp.	
Smith, Robert J.	Corp.	Transferred to non-commissioned staff 8-1-1862
Southerland, Nelson	Corp.	
Sweeney, Carter	Corp.	
Webster, John W.	Corp.	
Welch, Caleb	Corp.	Died of wounds 7-24-1864
Young, Orville	Corp.	
Greenwell, Richard	Wagoner	
Ash, Henry	Pvt.	Killed in Action. 9-19-1863. Chickamauga

Name	*Rank*	*Comment*
Baker, John L.	Pvt.	
Baugh, Eli	Pvt.	
Baugh, Henderson	Pvt.	Died in Casey County, Ky., 3-6-1862
Bottom, Fidellar S.	Pvt.	
Bowling, William	Pvt.	Deserted 2-15-62 Stanford, Ky.
Browning, Joseph	Pvt.	
Burnell, James	Pvt.	
Carter, Joseph E.	Pvt.	Died in Washington County, Ky., 6-13-1862
Cooley, Cornelius	Pvt.	
Cooley, Edward	Pvt.	
Cooley, John B.	Pvt.	
Cooley, Stephen	Pvt.	
Cooley, William	Pvt.	
Cox, Micajah	Pvt.	Died of wounds 9-22-1863
Crouch, Stephen	Pvt.	
Cruse, Andrew	Pvt.	
Darion, Simon	Pvt.	Discharged. 2-20-1863 Louisville, Ky.
Estes, Benjamin	Pvt.	Wounded at Jonesboro, Ga., 9-1-1864. Absent in hospital
Gallagher, Wm. F.	Pvt.	
Gleason, Thomas	Pvt.	
Goldsmith, Maze	Pvt.	
Grant, Henry W.	Pvt.	Killed in Action. 9-1-1864. Jonesboro, Ga.
Grant, Joseph	Pvt.	Wounded at Chickamauga, 9-19-1863
Gunter, Alexander	Pvt.	Deserted 2-9-62. Mill Springs, Ky.
Hall, William	Pvt.	Deserted 1-6-62. Campbellsville, Ky.
Harshfield, Columbus	Pvt.	
Hooper, Wesley	Pvt.	Discharged. 2-20-1863 Louisville, Ky.
Howell, John G.	Pvt.	
Johnson, John	Pvt.	Died in Marion County, Ky., 2-9-1862
Jones, Samuel	Pvt.	
Jones, William	Pvt.	Missing in action. 4-1-1862. Columbia, Tenn.
Kays, Smith	Pvt.	
Kelly, Wm. P.	Pvt.	Wounded at Chickamauga, 9-19-1863
Key, Thomas P.	Pvt.	Discharged. 3-10-1863 Louisville, Ky.
Lampkins, Peter	Pvt.	
Land, Squire	Pvt.	
Lavey, Charles	Pvt.	
Lawson, Nimrod	Pvt.	
Lawson, Francis M.	Pvt.	
Linton, George M.	Pvt.	
Litsey, Granville	Pvt.	
Litsey, Martin H.	Pvt.	
Mattingley, Nicholas	Pvt.	Prisoner Captured at Chickamauga 9-19-1863
Mattingley, Thos. A.	Pvt.	Prisoner Captured at Chickamauga 9-19-1863
Mattingly, Wm.	Pvt.	Wounded at Chickamauga, 9-19-1863
McCabbins, Moses	Pvt.	
McCullum, William	Pvt.	Died in Marion County, Ky., 4-21-1862
McGhee, William	Pvt.	Discharged. 7-10-1862 Louisville, Ky.
McMillen, Michael	Pvt.	Killed in Action. 1-1-1862. New Market, Ky.
McMullin, John	Pvt.	
Mobberley, John W.	Pvt.	
Monroe, John	Pvt.	
Mullans, Wm. T.	Pvt.	
Mullin, Green Berry	Pvt.	
Nelson, James	Pvt.	Discharged. 5-31-1862 Louisville, Ky.
O'Bryan, John	Pvt.	Died in Lavergne, Tenn. 2-27-1863
Perkins, Jefferson	Pvt.	
Ratcliff, Joseph	Pvt.	Discharged. 10-1-1862 Louisville, Ky.
Reagen, Wm. H.	Pvt.	Died in Monterey, Miss. 6-10-1862
Roberts, Squire	Pvt.	Killed in Action. 9-1-1864. Jonesboro, Ga.
Russell, Ignatius	Pvt.	
Scott, Crow	Pvt.	Died in Corinth, Miss. 5-18-1862
Sluder, Alexander	Pvt.	
Smith, Samuel	Pvt.	Wounded at Chickamauga, 9-19-1883

Name	Rank	Comment
Steel, John V.	Pvt.	Deserted 2-19-62. Danville, Ky.
Sweeney, John	Pvt.	Wounded at Chickamauga, 9-19-1883
Sutterfield, Edward H.	Pvt.	
Taylor, Eason	Pvt.	Deserted 2-9-62. Mill Springs, Ky.
Thomas, James	Pvt.	Discharged. 10-2-1862 Louisville, Ky.
Thorp, Madison	Pvt.	
Troutman, Sebastian	Pvt.	
Tumey, William H.	Pvt.	Killed in Action. 9-19-1863. Chickamauga
Voughn, William	Pvt.	Died, Lebanon, Ky., 12-18-1861
Weir, Henry	Pvt.	
Williams, Thomas	Pvt.	
Winfield, John	Pvt.	
Woods, James	Pvt.	Died of wounds 10-13-1863
Horsham, William D.	Pvt.	Transferred to Vet. Res. Corps 2-15-1864
Young, Simon P.	Pvt.	Transferred—Unexpired

COMPANY G

Name	Rank	Comment
Davenport, Jas. M.	Capt.	Wounded at Chickamauga 9-19-1863, Lost leg at Jonesboro 9-1-1864
Hunter, William R.	Capt.	Resigned 6-16-1862
Blemford, Edward O.	1st Lt.	
Fiddler, James M.	1st Lt.	Resigned 7-19-1862
Spalding, Charles E.	1st Lt.	Resigned 12-17-1863
Ferrill, Edward C.	2nd Lt.	Resigned 7-19-1862
Bean, Benjamin	1st Sgt.	
Inman, Jefferson	Sgt.	
Nally, Robert	Sgt.	
O'Bryan, Peter	Sgt.	Discharged Nashville, Tenn.
Skinner, Taleaferro	Sgt.	Discharged Chattanooga, Tenn., 12-11-1863
Vessels, Henry	Sgt.	Under arrest, awaiting trial
Whitehouse, Mose	Sgt.	
Buckler, Willistan	Corp.	
Ferrill, Francis L.	Corp.	Wounded at Chickamauga 9-19-1863
McCarty, Benjamin	Corp.	
Phillips, Jonathan	Corp.	Absent—sick
Powell, John W.	Corp.	
Enbert, John	Wagoner	
Avis, Edward	Pvt.	Died 10-28-1864 Camp Joe Holt, Ind.
Back, Jefferson B.	Pvt.	
Ballard, Joseph	Pvt.	Killed in Action 9-19-1863 Chickamauga
Ballard, Shelby	Pvt.	Transferred to Vet. Res. Corps 12-9-1863
Ballard, William	Pvt.	
Birch, John H.	Pvt.	Discharged Louisville, Ky., 12-23-1863
Blandford, George H.	Pvt.	Deserted 8-31-1862 Lebanon, Ky.
Blemford, James	Pvt.	Wounded at Chickamauga 9-19-1863
Boone, William	Pvt.	Died 8-13-1862
Brothers, James M.	Pvt.	Died—Place and date unknown
Carrie, Anderson	Pvt.	Died—Place and date unknown
Caughlem, William	Pvt.	Died—Place and date unknown
Clayton, Francis S.	Pvt.	Discharged Louisville, Ky., 7-29-1863
Clark, John M.	Pvt.	Died 12-4-1863 Chattanooga, Tenn.
Emery, John W.	Pvt.	Died in Andersonville—Prisoner
Fanvell, Augustus S.	Pvt.	Wounded at Jonesboro 9-1-1864 Absent—in hospital
Ferrill, William	Pvt.	Killed in Action 8-11-1864 Atlanta, Ga.
Field, James	Pvt.	Died. Manton, Kentucky
Foster, Larry	Pvt.	Deserted 1-4-1863 Elizabethtown, Ky.
Graham, David	Pvt.	Deserted 1-4-1863 Elizabethtown, Ky.
Graves, Charles	Pvt.	Died—Place and date unknown
Hagan, John H.	Pvt.	Wounded at Chickamauga 9-19-1863
Hall, Isaac	Pvt.	Deserted 10-27-1862 Lebanon, Ky.
Hagan, William	Pvt.	Died—Place and date unknown

Name	Rank	Comment
Harman, Elias	Pvt.	
Havs, Nelson	Pvt.	Transferred to Vet. Res. Corps
Hayden, William	Pvt.	Wounded at Chickamauga 9-19-1863
Hays, Harrison	Pvt.	Died 10-7-1864 Nashville, Tenn.
Higdon, Pius	Pvt.	
Hundley, Samuel	Pvt.	Died 7-3-1862 Tuscumbia, Ala.
Kelty, Miles Pius	Pvt.	Wounded at Chickamauga 9-19-1863
Kelty, Thomas	Pvt.	Died—Place and date unknown
Lanlam, James.	Pvt.	Died—Place and date unknown
Linton, John E.	Pvt.	Discharged Louisville, Ky., 7-29-1863
Mahoney, William H.	Pvt.	
Masterson, Thomas	Pvt.	Killed in Action 9-1-1864 Jonesboro, Ga.
Mattingly, Albert	Pvt.	
Mattingly, John M.	Pvt.	Discharged Gallatin, Tenn.
McLain, James J.	Pvt.	
Mudd, Joseph	Pvt.	Mustered out 6-9-1865
Mudd, Valentine	Pvt.	
Nally, Stephen	Pvt.	Killed in Action 11-25-1863 Mission Ridge
Newton, James J.	Pvt.	Deserted 8-1-1862 Lebanon, Ky.
Newton, Robert	Pvt.	Died—Place and date unknown
O'Bryan, Paul	Pvt.	Deserted 1-4-1863 Elizabethtown, Ky.
Osborn, James	Pvt.	Transferred to Vet. Res. Corps 12-9-1863
Osborne, John F.	Pvt.	Discharged Nashville, Tenn. 9-11-1862
Peak, Thomas	Pvt.	Wounded at Chickamauga 9-19-1863
Pennington, John	Pvt.	Wounded at Chickamauga 9-19-1863
Phillips, Benjamin	Pvt.	
Powers, Francis	Pvt.	Died 8-1863 Nashville, Tenn.
Renhard, William	Pvt.	
Right, Jonathan	Pvt.	
Riggs, George	Pvt.	Wounded at Atlanta 8-1864
Skinner, Bannister	Pvt.	Killed in Action 5-15-1864. Resaca, Ga.
Smith, Frank	Pvt.	To make good time lost
Smith, John	Pvt.	Discharged 6-7-1862
Smith, Pius	Pvt.	Deserted 8-1-1862 Mill Springs, Ky.
Smith, William J.	Pvt.	
Spratt, John	Pvt.	
Tharp, Nathan	Pvt.	Died Crab Orchard, Ky.
Thomas, David	Pvt.	
Thompson, Lewis F.	Pvt.	Discharged 10-31-1862
Vessels, Richard J.	Pvt.	
Vessels, Walter	Pvt.	Discharged 6-1-1862
Waters, Charles D.	Pvt.	Deserted 12-23-1861 Lebanon, Ky.
Waters, Jas. R.	Pvt.	Killed in Action 9-23-1863 Chickamauga
White, George	Pvt.	Recruit, time unexpired
Whitehouse, Addison	Pvt.	Deserted 7-11-1862 Eastport, Miss.
Whitehouse, Scott	Pvt.	

Company H

Name	Rank	Comment
Pendleton, Buford R.	Capt.	Resigned 11-16-1862
Shively, Wm. T.	Capt.	
Barry, Henry W.	1st Lt.	Dismissed 11-17-1862
Dunn, Henry C.	1st Lt.	Captured at Chickamauga 9-20-1863 and exchanged. Honorably discharged 12-19-1864
Beglow, William F.	2nd Lt.	
Wright, Thomas R.	1st Sgt.	Discharged 9-17-1862 Louisville, Ky.
Edelen, Benedict	Sgt.	Discharged 11-11-1862 Louisville, Ky.
Shively, Joseph H.	1st Sgt.	
Shively, Stephen M.	Sgt.	
Swaney, William	Sgt.	
Waltring, William	Sgt.	

Name	Rank	Comment
Abell, Samuel	Corp.	Discharged 2-6-1863 Louisville, Ky.
Belton, Addison	Corp.	Discharged 12-11-1863 Lost left arm
Clements, James P.	Corp.	
Earls, Milton	Corp.	Discharged 2-9-1863 Gallatin, Tenn.
Lyons, Benjamin F.	Corp.	
Newton, Andrew J.	Corp.	Died Lebanon, Ky. 3-31-1862
Newton, Elias	Corp.	Died Nashville, Tenn. 3-15-1862
Rice, David E.	Corp.	
Roots, William	Corp.	Captured at Chickamauga 9-20-1863 and exchanged 7-31-1864.
Farmer, Joseph	Tmstr.	
Abell, Cornelius W.	Pvt.	Transferred—Mustered out 8-28-1865
Abell, Enoch	Pvt.	
Abell, George W.	Pvt.	
Ainsworth, Henry H.	Pvt.	Discharged 11-25-1862 Columbus, Ohio
Bayne, Patrick	Pvt.	Died Lebanon, Ky., 12-20-1861
Bermingham, Martin	Pvt.	
Brockman, James	Pvt.	
Cabell, William T.	Pvt.	Died Campbellsville, Ky., 8-28-1862
Campbell, James	Pvt.	
Campbell, Moses	Pvt.	Wounded at Chickamauga 9-19-1863
Campbell, William P.	Pvt.	
Crowell, James A.	Pvt.	
Eads, Zachariah	Pvt.	Died 10-13-1863 of wounds
Ellis, Benjamin	Pvt.	Transferred to Co. I 5-7-1862
Farmer, James	Pvt.	Discharged 3-12-1863 Louisville, Ky.
Farmer, John E.	Pvt.	Discharged 3-31-1863 Louisville, Ky.
Farmer, Moses	Pvt.	
Farmer, Nathaniel	Pvt.	
Farmer, Preston P.	Pvt.	Discharged 12-12-1862 Louisville, Ky.
Farmer, Thomas	Pvt.	Deserted in face of the enemy 6-30-1863
Farmer, William	Pvt.	Killed in Action 7-25-1862 Courtland, Ala.
Ford, Martin	Pvt.	Died 4-17-1863 Lavergne, Tenn.
Grier, Tandy	Pvt.	Deserted 1-1-1864 Chattanooga, Tenn.
Gunter, Henry	Pvt.	Discharged 12-15-1862 Louisville, Ky.
Hall, William	Pvt.	Transferred to Co. F 5-7-1862
Harbin, William	Pvt.	
Harmon, Isaac	Pvt.	Discharged 1-18-1864 Evansville, Ind.
Hart, William	Pvt.	
Kerr, Alonzo T.	Pvt.	
Key, Thomas P.	Pvt.	Transferred to Co. F 5-7-1862
Long, Perry	Pvt.	Deserted 10-5-1862 Camp Chase, Ohio
Marple, Elmore	Pvt.	
Marple, Jefferson	Pvt.	Died Nashville, Tenn., 3-15-1862
Martin, Thomas	Pvt.	
Melton, David	Pvt.	Died Crab Orchard, Ky., 2-25-1862
Murphy, Benedict J.	Pvt.	Discharged 12-29-1862 Louisville, Ky.
Murphy, Francis	Pvt.	Wounded at Chattahoochee 7-9-1864
Murphy, George M.	Pvt.	
Murphy, John A.	Pvt.	
Murphy, Thomas	Pvt.	
Newton, John S.	Pvt.	Discharged 6-5-1862 Gallatin, Tenn.
O'Connell, Philip	Pvt.	Discharged 9-20-1862 Columbus, Ohio
O'Donald, Jacob	Pvt.	
Painter, Aaron T.	Pvt.	Discharged 3-13-1863 Lavergne, Tenn.
Raley, George W.	Pvt.	Died. 7-3-1862 Tuscumbia, Ala.
Raley, John	Pvt.	Discharged 2-20-1863 Gallatin, Tenn.
Roberts, Squire	Pvt.	Transferred to Co. F 5-7-1862
Russell, Daniel J.	Pvt.	Discharged 12-1-1862 Louisville, Ky.
Shively, David A.	Pvt.	
Shively, Samuel	Pvt.	Died Taylor County, Ky., 3-10-1862
Sluder, James H.	Pvt.	
Sluder, John M.	Pvt.	Died 10-16-1863 of wounds
Smith, Johnson	Pvt.	Died Taylor County, Ky., 3-15-1862

Name	Rank	Comment
Spurling, James	Pvt.	
Troy, John	Pvt.	Discharged 4-25-1862 Nashville, Tenn.
Vanhorn, George S.	Pvt.	Deserted 1-5-1862. Campbellsville, Ky.
Vestrees, Josiah	Pvt.	Died Chattanooga, Tenn., 11-9-1863
Walstan, Thos. J.	Pvt.	Transferred to make good time lost
Welch, Michael	Pvt.	Died 10-26-1863 of wounds
White, William	Pvt.	Deserted 12-1-1861. Lebanon, Ky.
Wise, John R.	Pvt.	Died June 1862 on hospital boat
Wise, Samuel T.	Pvt.	Died Nashville, Tenn., 1862
Wise, William	Pvt.	Discharged 12-20-1862 Louisville, Ky.
Woodrum, Abner	Pvt.	
Woodrum, James	Pvt.	Discharged 5-28-1863 Lavergne, Tenn.
Woods, James	Pvt.	Transferred to Co. F 5-7-1862
Worthington, Martin T.	Pvt.	Died Nashville, Tenn. 1862
Wright, Benjamin	Pvt.	Died Nashville, Tenn. 3-10-1862
Wright, Samuel	Pvt.	Discharged 10-16-1862 Nashville, Tenn.
Wright, Thos. R.	Pvt.	
Yearns, John	Pvt.	Deserted 12-1-1861. Camp Crittenden, Ky.

COMPANY I

Name	Rank	Comment
Webster, Israel B.	Capt.	
Kelley, William E.	1st Lt.	Wounded, captured and paroled at Chickamauga 9-20-1863. Wounded at Jonesboro 9-1-1864
Myers, John H.	2nd Lt.	Killed in Action Chickamauga 9-20-1863
Brown, Thomas J.	Sgt.	Severely wounded at Chickamauga 9-20-1863
Curby, William J.	1st Sgt.	Captured and paroled near Huntsville, Ala. 8-8-1862
Giddis, William J.	Sgt.	Wounded at Chickamauga 9-20-1863
Jackson, Wm. H.	1st Sgt.	Discharged 2-27-1863 Lavergne, Tenn.
Mills, Jack E.	Sgt.	Died 3-2-1862 in Marion Co., Ky.
Richardson, Daniel L.	Sgt.	
Rose, James E.	1st Sgt.	Died 1-15-1864 in Marion Co, Ky.
Wright, William J.	Sgt.	Severely wounded Jonesboro 9-1-1863
Curby, John H.	Corp.	
Jackson, James N.	Corp.	Discharged 4-23-1863 Lavergne, Tenn.
Lawson, David	Corp.	Discharged 9-8-1863 Louisville, Ky.
Mills, Joel F.	Corp.	
Noe, Elijah	Corp.	Transferred to Dist. of Etowah 11-6-1864
Osburn, John A.	Corp.	
Purdy, Robt. L.	Corp.	
Rose, John C.	Corp.	Transferred to Vet. Res. Corps 4-1-1864
Turner, William	Corp.	Deserted 1-3-1863 Elizabethtown, Ky.
Osten, Jas.	Mus.	Transferred—non-com staff
Abel, Joshua J.	Pvt.	Captured and paroled near Decatur, Ala. 8-8-1862. Wounded, captured and paroled at Chickamauga 9-20-1863
Averrett, John D.	Pvt.	
Begals, John H.	Pvt.	Deserted 2-25-1863 Lavergne, Tenn.
Bell, Isaac	Pvt.	Died 2-1-1862 in Lebanon, Ky.
Brown, James W.	Pvt.	Deserted 12-27-1862 Bell's Tavern, Ky.
Brown, Joshua	Pvt.	Discharged 7-10-1862 Louisville, Ky.
Brown, Josiah	Pvt.	Prisoner Captured at Chickamauga 9-20-1863
Brown, Philip M.	Pvt.	Transferred—Mustered out 9-12-1865
Bryant, John H.	Pvt.	Deserted Nashville, Tenn. 3-5-1862
Burchell, Jno.	Pvt.	Captured and paroled near Decatur, Ala. 8-8-1862. Wounded, captured and paroled at Chickamauga 9-20-1863
Ceaver, Jesse M.	Pvt.	Deserted. 1-8-1862 Campbellsville, Ky.
Ellis, Benjamin	Pvt.	Wounded at Mission Ridge 11-25-1863
Fitzgibbons, Patrick	Pvt.	Transferred to Vet. Res. Corps 4-6-1864
Gaddis, Milton H.	Pvt.	
Goodman, David	Pvt.	Transferred—Mustered out 5-10-1865
Goodman, Francis M.	Pvt.	Died 3-10-1862 in Danville, Ky.
Goodman, General L.	Pvt.	Wounded at Jonesboro 9-1-1864

Name	Rank	Comment
Goodman, William	Pvt.	Wounded, captured and paroled at Chickamauga 9-20-1863
Goodman, Wm. H.	Pvt.	Discharged 8-4-1863 Louisville, Ky.
Goodman, Young	Pvt.	Discharged 11-8-1862 Louisville, Ky. Discharged 11-9-1863 Chattanooga, Tenn.
Green, William H.	Pvt.	
Gubehart, George W.	Pvt.	
Gunter, Alexander	Pvt.	Transferred to Co. F 2-1-1862
Harrison, Samuel H.	Pvt.	
Harrison, William R.	Pvt.	Wounded at Chickamauga 9-20-1863
Hicks, Isaac	Pvt.	Wounded at Mission Ridge 11-25-1863
Hicks, William M.	Pvt.	Deserted. 10-29-1862 Greensburg, Ky.
Hilton, Thomas R.	Pvt.	
Hobbs, Levi A.	Pvt.	Transferred to Dist. of Etowah 11-6-1864
Inman, Hardister	Pvt.	
Isaacs, James	Pvt.	
Isaacs, John	Pvt.	Discharged 10-6-1863 Louisville, Ky.
Jasper, Abraham	Pvt.	Transferred to Marine Brigade 4-4-1863
Lane, Patrick A.	Pvt.	Died 10-2-1863 in Chattanooga, Tenn.
Lawson, Lenox	Pvt.	Discharged 10-30-1863 Nashville, Tenn.
Lawson, William	Pvt.	Under arrest in Louisville awaiting trial for desertion. 5-25-1863 Lavergne, Tenn.
Litsey, Mastin H.	Pvt.	Transferred to Co. F 2-1-1862
Luster, James R.	Pvt.	Died 7-21-1862 in Tuscumbia, Ala.
Martin, Jesse	Pvt.	Died 10-24-1863 in Nashville, Tenn.
Miller, James C.	Pvt.	Discharged Nashville, Tenn.
Mills, James H.	Pvt.	
Mills, John F.	Pvt.	Wounded at Chickamauga 9-20-1863
Munday, Silas	Pvt.	Wounded at Chickamauga 9-20-1863
Noe, Henry H.	Pvt.	Transferred to Dist. of Etowah 11-6-1864
Noe, William B.	Pvt.	
Oster, George	Pvt.	Died 10-25-1862 in Nashville, Tenn.
Peters, John	Pvt.	Deserted 1-8-1862 Campbellsville, Ky.
Phillips, Benjamin	Pvt.	Discharged 2-5-1863 Gallatin, Tenn.
Purdy, William C.	Pvt.	Discharged 1-19-1864 Louisville, Ky.
Roaler, James	Pvt.	
Roaler, Richard	Pvt.	Died 9-19-1863 in Chickamauga, Tenn.
Roaler, Solomon	Pvt.	Died 4-27-1863 in Lavergne, Tenn.
Ross, John D.	Pvt.	
Saddler, Mathews	Pvt.	Transferred to Dist. of Etowah 11-6-1864
Saddler, Thomas	Pvt.	Deserted. 1-28-1862 Mill Springs, Ky.
Smith, Hamilton	Pvt.	Discharged 9-14-1863 Louisville, Ky.
Smothers, John	Pvt.	Died 2-29-1864 in Nashville, Tenn.
Snow, William J.	Pvt.	Deserted. 5-25-1862 Corinth, Miss.
Spencer, Augustus	Pvt.	Wounded at Mission Ridge 11-25-1863
Stavton, John B.	Pvt.	Died 4-21-1863 in Lavergne, Tenn.
Stewart, John	Pvt.	
Stewart, Thos.	Pvt.	Prisoner captured at Chattahoochee 7-9-1864
Stoner, William H.	Pvt.	Died 5-5-1863 in Gallatin, Tenn.
Tarrill, Patrick	Pvt.	Discharged 6-15-1864 Evansville, Ind.
Taylor, Henry	Pvt.	Wounded at Chickamauga 9-20-1863
Temgate, William A.	Pvt.	Discharged 7-27-1862 Florence, Ala.
Turpin, Levi	Pvt.	Discharged Nashville, Tenn.
Vessels, Philip M.	Pvt.	
Wilcher, John T.	Pvt.	Wounded at Jonesboro 9-1-1864
Willard, Hugh A.	Pvt.	Died 9-21-1862 in Nashville, Tenn.
Willard, John	Pvt.	Died at Jonesboro, Ga., 9-1-1864
William, Daniel	Pvt.	Missing Gallatin, Tenn., 11-11-1862
Woolbridge, William R.	Pvt.	Deserted. 10-29-1862. Greensburg, Ky.

COMPANY K

Name	Rank	Comment
Waller, Henry	Capt.	Died 3-13-1864 Chattanooga, Tenn.

Name	Rank	Comment
Denton, John H.	Capt.	
Tweddle, William	Capt.	Resigned 4-17-1862
Watts, James R.	1st Lt.	
Bellam, Richard R.	Sgt.	
Cox, Peter A.	Sgt.	Died 5-1862 Nashville, Tenn.
Garvey, Charles	1st Sgt.	
Johnston, Leroy S.	Sgt.	Transferred to non-com. staff 1-25-1864
Lee, John L.	Sgt.	
Rea, Robert, Sr.	Sgt.	
Richard, David	Sgt.	
Wilkins, Edward	Sgt.	Killed in Action 9-19-1863 Chickamauga
Baker, William	Corp.	Died 5-10-1862 Louisville, Ky.
Burger, Andrew	Corp.	Discharged 6-1862 Louisville, Ky.
Burk, Tobias	Corp.	Killed in Action 7-9-1864 Chattahoochee
Dugald, Campbell	Corp.	Killed in Action 9-19-1863 Chickamauga
Carroll, John C.	Corp.	Discharged 5-1862 Louisville, Ky.
Jones, Thomas A.	Corp.	Under sentence of court-martial for desertion
Lee, John F.	Corp.	Discharged 6-24-1862 Corinth, Miss.
Montrose, Joseph	Corp.	Discharged 6-1862 Louisville, Ky.
McLaine, Peter	Mus.	Transferred—recruit time—unexpired
Rea, Robert Jr.	Mus.	Transferred—mustered out 8-7-1865
Arnett, John Jr.	Pvt.	Transferred to non-com. staff 5-9-1864
Arnett, John Sr.	Pvt.	Discharged 6-24-1862 Corinth, Miss.
Batman, William	Pvt.	
Baugh, Eli	Pvt.	Transferred to Co. F 2-1-1862
Becker, Ulrick	Pvt.	Discharged 4-1862 Lavergne, Tenn.
Blair, John T.	Pvt.	Transferred to Co. B 2-1-1862
Broax, Alexander	Pvt.	Deserted 4-15-1863 Louisville, Ky.
Brown, Thos.	Pvt.	Wounded at Chattahoochee 7-9-1864 Right arm amputated
Buckley, John	Pvt.	
Cady, Michael	Pvt.	
Campbell, John A.	Pvt.	Discharged to accept promotion 6-9-1863
Cane, Adam	Pvt.	Transferred to Co. D 2-1-1862
Caromed, Simon	Pvt.	Died 4-12-1864 Ringgold Georgia
Carpenter, Charles A.	Pvt.	Deserted 4-15-1863 Nashville, Tenn.
Casey, John	Pvt.	
Conway, Patrick	Pvt.	In insane asylum at Washington, D.C., 2-22-1864
Cushin, Dennis	Pvt.	Died 5-8-1862 Louisville, Ky.
Cutsinger, James	Pvt.	Transferred to Co. D 2-1-1862
Dailey, Peter	Pvt.	
Dearion, Simon	Pvt.	Transferred to Co. F 2-1-1862
Dorsey, Morris	Pvt.	
Eady, Hugh	Pvt.	
Emms, Joseph	Pvt.	Deserted 1-25-1862 Mill Springs, Ky.
Enders, Michael	Pvt.	Deserted 2-27-1862 Mill Springs, Ky.
Fox, James	Pvt.	Discharged 6-20-1863 Louisville, Ky.
Fumbrell, Wm. M.	Pvt.	Transferred recruit time—unexpired
Gegan, Patrick	Pvt.	Discharged 3-6-1863 Paducah, Ky.
Hines, John	Pvt.	
Hines, Patrick	Pvt.	
Hundley, James	Pvt.	Discharged 5-26-1863 Louisville, Ky.
Idoax, John J.	Pvt.	Died 11-7-1862 Nashville, Tenn.
Kanleahy, Dennis	Pvt.	Discharged 5-18-1863 Louisville, Ky.
Kneibert, Jacob H.	Pvt.	Transferred to Miss. Marine Brigade 1-1-1862
Lee, Levi M.	Pvt.	
Lenihan, David	Pvt.	
Lennon, Joseph	Pvt.	Transferred to non-com. staff 3-6-1863
Madden, Washington	Pvt.	Deserted 11-1861 Lebanon, Ky.
Maloney, Daniel	Pvt.	Killed in Action 9-19-1863 Chickamauga
Maloy, Daniel	Pvt.	Discharged 5-1862 Louisville, Ky.
Mattingley, John B.	Pvt.	
Mattingley, John S.	Pvt.	Transferred to Co B. 2-1-1862
Mattingley, Nicholas	Pvt.	Transferred to Co F. 2-1-1862
Mattingley, Wm. H.	Pvt.	

Name	Rank	Comment
Mayland, Patrick	Pvt.	Drowned 9-1-1863
McAnelly, John	Pvt.	Deserted 11-1861 Lebanon, Ky.
McAnelly, Wm. T.	Pvt.	Deserted 11-1861 Lebanon, Ky.
McCann, James	Pvt.	Transferred to Vet. Res. Corps 10-29-1863
McCardell, James	Pvt.	Deserted 12-1861 Lebanon, Ky.
McGinnis, James	Pvt.	Deserted 12-1-1862 Nashville, Tenn.
McVey, William	Pvt.	Died 2-18-1864 Chattanooga, Tenn.
Meckin, John	Pvt.	Discharged 5-1862 Louisville, Ky.
Miles, Thos.	Pvt.	Transferred to Co. B 2-1-1862
Millagan, Thomas	Pvt.	Died 12-1862 Louisville, Ky.
Molim, Adam	Pvt.	
Montgomery, William	Pvt.	Transferred to Co. D
Mordan, Patrick	Pvt.	Deserted 12-29-1862 Bacon Creek, Ky.
Mule, Stonemason	Pvt.	Killed in Action 9-19-1863 Chickamauga
Mulloon, Patrick	Pvt.	Discharged Nashville, Tenn.
Munday, Patrick	Pvt.	
Murphy, Burtley	Pvt.	Died 10-21-1862 Nashville, Tenn.
Murphy, Jerry	Pvt.	Killed 8-1862
Murphey, John	Pvt.	Discharged Nashville, Tenn.
O'Donald, Jasper	Pvt.	
Phibban, Patrick	Pvt.	Discharged 3-11-1863 Lavergne, Tenn.
Philips, Jonathan	Pvt.	Transferred to Co. G 2-1-1862
Rase, William	Pvt.	
Roberts, Richard	Pvt.	
Sherman, Thomas B.	Pvt.	Discharged 6-1862 Louisville, Ky.
Sluder, Alexander	Pvt.	Transferred to Co. F 2-1-1862
Staffan, Joseph	Pvt.	
Stanton, John	Pvt.	Transferred to Vet. Res. Corps
Sutterfield, Edward	Pvt.	Transferred to Co. F 2-1-1862
Thomas, Jas.	Pvt.	Transferred to Co. F 2-1-1862
Welsh, Richard	Pvt.	
Wester, Michael	Pvt.	Discharged 9-1862 Nashville, Tenn.
Williams, Thomas	Pvt.	Transferred to Co. F 2-1-1862
Withrow, A. G.	Pvt.	Discharged 6-22-1862 Corinth, Miss.

Appendix B. 10th Kentucky Information from the Regimental Record Book

Regiment Staff	Rank	Age	Height	Eyes	Hair	Where Born	Occupation
Harlan, John M.	Col.	28				Boyle County, Ky.	Lawyer
Hays, William H.	Col.	41				Washington County, Ky.	Judge
Wharton, Gabriel C.	Lt. Col.	22				Washington County, Ky.	Lawyer
Davidson, Henry G.	Maj.	22				Illinois	Merchant
Smith, Robert J.	Sgt. Maj.						
Beglous, William F	Q.M. Sgt.						
Johnson, Lee S.	Q.M. Sgt.						
Lancaster, Edward B.	Q.M. Sgt.						
Matlock, Sam'l	Q.M. Sgt.						
Dunn, Henry C.	Com. Sgt.						
Garrison, John C.	Com. Sgt.						
Moore, George W.	Com. Sgt.						
Newman, Nathan	Com. Sgt.						
Lisle, Wm. J.	Adjts.						
Maquire, Austin P.	Adjts.	24				Nelson County, Ky.	Merchant
Nash, Richard C.	Chaplain	51				Jefferson County, Ky.	Minister
Arnott, John	Pr. Mus.						
Crutchett, Henry	Pr. Mus.						
Lennen, Joseph	Pr. Mus.						

Regiment Staff	Rank	Age	Height	Eyes	Hair	Where Born	Occupation
Oster, James	Pr. Mus.						
Atkisson, Wm.	Surg.					Simpsonville, Ky.	Doctor
Hatchitt, James G.	Surg.	37				Virginia	Doctor
Perkins, Jabez	Surg.	41				Defiance, Ohio	Doctor
Stocking, Charles H.	Surg.	25				Michigan	Doctor
Hardesty, Chas.	Asst. Surg.	30				Bullitt County, Ky.	
Knott, Thomas M.	Asst. Surg.	21				Marion County, Ky.	
Davenport, Richard	Hosp. Stwd.						
Leachman, Henry P.	Hosp. Stwd.						

COMPANY A

Regiment Staff	Rank	Age	Height	Eyes	Hair	Where Born	Occupation
Davidson, Henry G.	Capt.	22				Illinois	Merchant
Lisle, William J.	Capt.					Green County, Ky.	Lawyer
McKay, Charles W.	Capt.	20				Bullitt County, Ky.	Doctor
Reynolds, James	1st Lt.	24				Jefferson County, Ky.	Blacksmith
Warren, Henry H.	1st Lt.	20	5'9"	Hazel	Auburn	Nelson County, Ky.	Mechanic
Estes, John	2nd Lt.	22	5'10"	Gray	Black	Lincoln, Mo.	Carpenter
Grace, Richard	2nd Lt.	18	5'10"			Ireland	Mechanic
Arnold, Levi	Sgt.						
Blandford, George W.	Sgt.						
Herdel, Nicholas	Sgt.						
Manly, Samuel	1st Sgt.	18	5'8"	Light	Light	Baltimore, Md.	Merchant
Moore, George W.	Sgt.						
Burgess, Ray	Sgt.						
Asbeck, Gustave	Corp.	18	5'5"	Blue	Light	Jefferson County, Ky.	Farmer
Boyle, Robert W.	Corp.	18	5'7"	Light	Light	Washington County, Ky.	Farmer
Creagle, James	Corp.		5'9"	Blue	Light	Louisville, Ky.	Laborer
Jones, Aaron	Corp.	22	5'8"	Blue	Light	Jefferson County, Ky.	Farmer
Kortz, Frederick	Corp.	25	5'7"	Light	Chestnut	Jefferson County, Ky.	Farmer
Krival, Francis	Corp.		5'6"	Dark	Dark	Louisville, Ky.	Wagoner
Roberts, Harrison	Corp.	24	5'7"	Hazel	Chestnut	Bardstown, Ky.	Carpenter
Shockley, Davis M.	Corp.						
Mattingly, Alexander O.	Wagoner	21	5'7½"	Dark	Dark	Marion County, Ky.	Wagoner
Arnold, Adam	Pvt.	23	5'7"	Blue	Chestnut	Jefferson County, Ky.	Farmer
Arnold, Jeremiah	Pvt.	20	5'9"	Blue	Chestnut	Jefferson County, Ky.	Farmer
Arnold, Simpson	Pvt.	21	5'5"	Blue	Chestnut	Jefferson County, Ky.	Farmer
Askren, Samuel	Pvt.	19	5'8"	Blue	Chestnut	Marion County, Ky.	Farmer
Baker, Samuel	Pvt.	21	5'10"	Dark	Dark	Jefferson County, Ky.	Farmer
Berhnes, Henry	Pvt.	45	5'8½"	Blue	Chestnut	Jefferson County, Ky.	Farmer
Berry, James	Pvt.	18	5'9"	Dark	Dark	Jefferson County, Ky.	Farmer
Bland, Fletcher	Pvt.	21	5'10"	Dark	Dark	Marion County, Ky.	Farmer
Boyd, William	Pvt.	18	5'10½"	Dark	Dark	Jefferson County, Ky.	Farmer
Bumgarder, George W.	Pvt.	20	5'11"	Blue	Chestnut	Jefferson County, Ky.	Farmer
Bumgarder, John W.	Pvt.	18	5'8½"	Blue	Chestnut	Jefferson County, Ky.	Farmer
Cable, James	Pvt.	21	5'6"	Light	Light	Jefferson County, Ky.	Farmer
Casabon, Oliver D.	Pvt.	24	5'10"	Dark	Dark	Jefferson County, Ky.	Farmer
Crutcher, Henry	Pvt.						
Decker, August	Pvt.	44	5'7½"	Dark	Dark	Jefferson County, Ky.	Farmer
Demarsh, Nicholas	Pvt.	21	5'7½"	Black	Black	Jefferson County, Ky.	Farmer
Demarsh, Stephen	Pvt.	19	5'7½"	Black	Black	Jefferson County, Ky.	Farmer
Dennis, Frank	Pvt.						
Duffield, Jacob	Pvt.	31	5'8"	Dark	Dark	Jefferson County, Ky.	Farmer
Durbin, John C.	Pvt.	32	5'8½"	Dark	Dark	Bardstown, Ky.	Carpenter
Edmonson, Joseph	Pvt.	18	5'7"	Light	Light	Marion County, Ky.	Farmer
Edmonson, Wilson W.	Pvt.	45	5'10"	Light	Light	Marion County, Ky.	Farmer
Frank, George H.	Pvt.	18	5'6½"	Blue	Light	Louisville, Ky.	Laborer
Gaylock, Peter	Pvt.	19	5'6"	Blue	Light	France	Farmer
Graham, Harvey	Pvt.	19	5'7½"	Blue	Light	Louisville, Ky.	Farmer
Ham, Abram	Pvt.						
Harding, Elias	Pvt.	21	5'6"	Light	Light	Jefferson County, Ky.	Farmer

Regiment Staff	Rank	Age	Height	Eyes	Hair	Where Born	Occupation
Hardin, George	Pvt.	18	5'6"	Light	Light	Jefferson County, Ky.	Farmer
Hill, Conrad	Pvt.	21	5'10"	Dark	Dark	Jefferson County, Ky.	Laborer
Jenkins, Joseph	Pvt.	25	5'7"	Blue	Light	Jefferson County, Ky.	Farmer
Johnson, John	Pvt.	18	5'6½"	Blue	Light	Jefferson County, Ky.	Laborer
Johnson, William	Pvt.						
Jones, William	Pvt.	25	5'8"	Blue	Light	Jefferson County, Ky.	Farmer
Kendall, Bladen A.	Pvt.	24	5'11"	Light	Chestnut	Louisville, Ky.	Laborer
Kendall, Culbraith	Pvt.	21	5'9"	Light	Chestnut	Louisville, Ky.	Laborer
Kortz, John	Pvt.	25	5'7"	Light	Chestnut	Louisville, Ky.	Blacksmith
Kortz, Mathie	Pvt.	18	5'6"	Light	Chestnut	Louisville, Ky.	Farmer
Kortz, William	Pvt.	21	5'8"	Light	Chestnut	Louisville, Ky.	Farmer
Krahl, Conrad	Pvt.	33	5'8"	Dark	Dark	Germany	Stone Mason
Lancaster, Edward B.	Pvt.						
Martin, Eugene	Pvt.	24	5'9"	Black	Black	France	Brick Layer
Mattingly, John M.	Pvt.					Marion County, Ky.	Wagoner
Mattingly, Thomas R.	Pvt.	22	5'8"	Dark	Dark	Marion County, Ky.	Farmer
Maurer, Francis	Pvt.	27	5'10"	Hazel	Dark	Louisville, Ky.	
McDaniel, John	Pvt.	28	5'7½"	Blue	Sandy	Louisville, Ky.	
Mitchell, Henry	Pvt.	18	5'6½"	Hazel	Dark	Louisville, Ky.	
Mitchell, John	Pvt.	19	5'6½"	Hazel	Dark	Louisville, Ky.	
Mudd, Richard	Pvt.	18	5'9"	Dark	Dark	Marion County, Ky.	Farmer
Mumford, Robinson	Pvt.	35	5'10"	Black	Black	Germany	Laborer
Murrell, Woods	Pvt.	19	5'5½"	Dark	Dark	Louisville, Ky.	Merchant
Pirtle, Isaac E.	Pvt.						
Rheul, Eincle	Pvt.	18	5'7"	Blue	Light	Louisville, Ky.	Laborer
Rogers, James C.	Pvt.	18	5'8"	Blue	Light	Bardstown, Ky.	Farmer
Ropp, Michael	Pvt.	18	5'7"	Hazel	Chestnut		Farmer
Rossles, Frederick	Pvt.	24	5'10"	Light	Light		Cigar Maker
Ruder, John	Pvt.	30	5'8"	Light	Light	Germany	Farmer
Saal, Frederick	Pvt.						
Shain, David	Pvt.						
Shielly, John	Pvt.						
Shielly, Anthony	Pvt.						
Shielly, William	Pvt.						
Shorten, Lewis	Pvt.	42	5'7"	Dark	Dark	Louisville, Ky.	Laborer
Smith, Thomas M.	Pvt.						
Snawder, Joseph	Pvt.						
Stephens, Philip	Pvt.						
Steward, John	Pvt.						
Stoar, John	Pvt.						
Terry, Arthur T.	Pvt.						
Terry, George W.	Pvt.						
Vanderheide, John	Pvt.						
Voclair, Frank	Pvt.						
Watts, John R.	Pvt.						
Weiser, Harry	Pvt.						
Welsh, John	Pvt.						
Young, James	Pvt.						

COMPANY B

Regiment Staff	Rank	Age	Height	Eyes	Hair	Where Born	Occupation
MilBurn, John T.	Capt.	21				Marion County, Ky.	
O'Bryan, William F.	1st Lt.	20				Marion County, Ky.	Teacher
Short, Robert S.	1st Lt.					Marion County, Ky.	Farmer
McCauley, John T.	2nd Lt.	29				Marion County, Ky.	Farmer
Davenport, James M.	2nd Lt.					Alabama	Teacher
Gray, Stephen J.	Sgt.	30	5'7"	Gray	Black	England	Painter
Harding, William	Sgt.						
Heinis, Ernst	Sgt.	25	5'6"	Blue	Light	Germany	Weaver
McCauley, Chas. B.	Sgt.						
McCauley, Thomas	Sgt.	19	5'7"	Gray	Dark	Marion County, Ky.	Farmer

Regiment Staff	Rank	Age	Height	Eyes	Hair	Where Born	Occupation
McGrath, Philip J.	Sgt.						
Scott, James F.	Sgt.	24	5'10"	Blue	Dark	Marion County, Ky.	Farmer
Blair, David	Corp.	37	6'0"	Blue	Dark	Marion County, Ky.	Farmer
Blanford, Edward	Corp.						
Cross, James	Corp.	24	5'9"	Blue	Dark	Marion County, Ky.	Farmer
Cross, William	Corp.	29	5'7"	Blue	Dark	Marion County, Ky.	Farmer
Fenwick, Thomas	Corp.	35	5'6"	Blue	Black	Marion County, Ky.	Farmer
Llewellyn, Elisha O.	Corp.	21	5'5"	Blue	Dark	Indiana	Cooper
McBride, Wm. D.	Corp.	30	6'0"	Dark	Dark	Marion County, Ky.	Carpenter
Russell, John	Corp.	21	5'10"	Blue	Light	Marion County, Ky.	Farmer
Talmadge, Joseph	Corp.	18	5'6"	Blue	Dark	Alabama	Farmer
Vancleve, Samuel	Mus.	29	5'9"	Dark	Dark	Marion County, Ky.	Farmer
Alvey, Alexander	Pvt.	20	5'7"	Blue	Light	Marion County, Ky.	Farmer
Blair, James	Pvt.	25	5'11"	Blue	Light	Marion County, Ky.	Stonemason
Blair, John T.	Pvt.	23	5'11"	Blue	Dark	Marion County, Ky.	Farmer
Blanford, Robert	Pvt.	23	5'5'	Blue	Light	Marion County, Ky.	Farmer
Brady, George W.	Pvt.	23	5'7"	Blue	Dark	Marion County, Ky.	Farmer
Brady, Joseph	Pvt.	21	5'10"	Dark	Dark	Marion County, Ky.	Farmer
Brown, D. Marcus	Pvt.	18	5'5"	Brown	Dark	LaRue County, Ky.	Farmer
Bullock, James G.	Pvt.	18	5'8"	Black	Dark	Marion County, Ky.	Farmer
Bullock, William	Pvt.	20	4'11"	Black	Dark	Marion County, Ky.	Farmer
Butler, William	Pvt.	27	5'7"	Brown	Dark	Ireland	Farmer
Cecil, John H.	Pvt.	18	5'4"	Blue	Dark	Marion County, Ky.	Farmer
Clark, Edward	Pvt.	20	5'11"	Blue	Light	Ireland	Laborer
Clark, John	Pvt.	25	5'11"	Blue	Dark	Ireland	Laborer
Clark, Royal G.	Pvt.	37	5'10"	Brown	Light	Ireland	Laborer
Cross, Richard M.	Pvt.	18	5'4"	Blue	Dark	Marion County, Ky.	Farmer
Caniff, George	Pvt.	24	5'6"	Blue	Dark	Nelson County, Ky.	Cooper
Donahoo, James	Pvt.	28	5'9"	Blue	Dark	Nelson County, Ky.	Farmer
Durham, James S.	Pvt.	36	6'0"	Blue	Dark	Nelson County, Ky.	Farmer
Durham, John S.	Pvt.	18	5'6"	Blue	Dark	Nelson County, Ky.	Farmer
Farris, Joseph G.	Pvt.	19	5'5"	Blue	Light	LaRue County, Ky.	Farmer
Fenwick, Cornelius	Pvt.	43	5'9"	Light	Light	Marion County, Ky.	Farmer
Fenwick, George W.	Pvt.	22	5'7"	Dark	Black	Marion County, Ky.	Farmer
Fogle, William	Pvt.	21	5'7"	Light	Light	Nelson County, Ky.	Farmer
Green, Francis	Pvt.	26	5'7"	Blue	Red	Marion County, Ky.	Farmer
Greenwell, Francis	Pvt.	18	5'2½"	Brown	Light	Marion County, Ky.	Farmer
Greenwell, John	Pvt.	23	5'5"	Brown	Light	Marion County, Ky.	Farmer
Hall, Benjamin	Pvt.	18	5'8"	Gray	Red	Marion County, Ky.	Farmer
Hall, William, Jr.	Pvt.	18	5'8"	Gray	Light	Marion County, Ky.	Farmer
Hall, William, Sr.	Pvt.	20	5'10"	Gray	Light	Marion County, Ky.	Farmer
Hayden, Andrew	Pvt.	21	5'8"	Brown	Light	Marion County, Ky.	Farmer
Howard, Edward	Pvt.	42	6'2"	Brown	Black	Marion County, Ky.	Farmer
Johnston, James	Pvt.	24	5'5"	Blue	Light	Nelson County, Ky.	Farmer
Knott, Richard W.	Pvt.						
Lake, John B.	Pvt.	18	5'4"	Black	Dark	Marion County, Ky.	Farmer
Lamb, James R.	Pvt.	25	6'1"	Gray	Black	Taylor County, Ky.	Carpenter
Livers, George	Pvt.	24	5'7"	Gray	Dark	Marion County, Ky.	Farmer
Livers, Samuel	Pvt.	30	5'9"	Gray	Light	Marion County, Ky.	Farmer
Lucas, Henry	Pvt.						
Lucket, Thomas A.	Pvt.	20	5'6"	Black	Dark	Marion County, Ky.	Farmer
Maston, John E.	Pvt.	21	5'10"	Blue	Light	Marion County, Ky.	Farmer
Mattingly, Benjamin S.	Pvt.	22	6'0"	Gray	Light	Marion County, Ky.	Farmer
Mattingly, C. W.	Pvt.	18	5'6"	Gray	Light	Marion County, Ky.	Farmer
Mattingly, Henry B.	Pvt.	18	5'7"	Gray	Light	Marion County, Ky.	Farmer
Mattingly, John T.	Pvt.	23	5'7"	Brown	Dark	Marion County, Ky.	Farmer
Mattingly, Joseph S.	Pvt.	18	5'7"	Blue	Dark	Marion County, Ky.	Farmer
Mattingly, Wm. B.	Pvt.	18	5'8"	Brown	Dark	Marion County, Ky.	Farmer
Mattingly, Wm. L.	Pvt.	18	5'8"	Black	Dark	Marion County, Ky.	Farmer
McGavock, James W.	Pvt.	29	6'0"	Dark	Black	Virginia	Farmer
Meadows, William	Pvt.	37	5'9"	Blue	Light	Washington County, Ky.	Farmer
Miles, Chas. Henry	Pvt.	18	5'7"	Blue	Light	Marion County, Ky.	Farmer
Miles, Henry	Pvt.	19	6'0"	Gray	Black	Marion County, Ky.	Farmer
Miles, James M.	Pvt.	18	5'6"	Blue	Light	Marion County, Ky.	Farmer

Regiment Staff	Rank	Age	Height	Eyes	Hair	Where Born	Occupation
Miles, Thomas	Pvt.	22	5'7"	Brown	Dark	Marion County, Ky.	Farmer
Mills, John	Pvt.	18	5'4"	Blue	Light	Marion County, Ky.	Farmer
Mitchell, Jefferson B.	Pvt.	18	6'0"	Gray	Light	Nelson County, Ky.	Farmer
Newton, William	Pvt.	33	5'6"	Blue	Red	Marion County, Ky.	Farmer
Nolley, Wm. T.	Pvt.	32	5'5"	Blue	Dark	Taylor County, Ky.	Farmer
Peterson, Allen	Pvt.	22	5'10"	Blue	Light	Marion County, Ky.	Farmer
Peterson, Garrett D.	Pvt.	18	6'0"	Blue	Light	Marion County, Ky.	Brick Mason
Peterson, John	Pvt.	21	6'0"	Blue	Dark	Taylor County, Ky.	Blacksmith
Peterson, Thomas G.	Pvt.	25	5'7"	Blue	Light	Marion County, Ky.	Farmer
Pickerel, Stephen E.	Pvt.	26	5'10"	Blue	Red	LaRue County, Ky.	Farmer
Read, Philip M.	Pvt.						
Rhodes, William M.	Pvt.	18	5'8"	Gray	Dark	Marion County, Ky.	Farmer
Sanders, James	Pvt.	18	5'2"	Blue	Light	Taylor County, Ky.	Farmer
Sill, David	Pvt.	29	5'5"	Blue	Dark	Germany	Stone Cutter
Simins, Thomas A	Pvt.	35	5'11"	Blue	Brown	Marion County, Ky.	Farmer
Simms, Wm.	Pvt.	30	6'0"	Blue	Light	Marion County, Ky.	Plasterer
Thompson, Richard G.	Pvt.	26	5'7"	Blue	Light	Marion County, Ky.	Cooper
Uptergrove, Joseph L.	Pvt.	18	6'0"	Blue	Dark	LaRue County, Ky.	Farmer
Wade, Elijah	Pvt.						
Wade, John L.	Pvt.	18	5'3"	Blue	Dark	Taylor County, Ky.	Farmer
Whitfield, William	Pvt.	19	5'11"	Blue	Dark	Marion County, Ky.	Farmer
Wise, John	Pvt.						

Company C

Regiment Staff	Rank	Age	Height	Eyes	Hair	Where Born	Occupation
Hilpp, Edward	Capt.					Germany	Painter
Musson, William	1st Lt.	26				Marion County, Ky.	Farmer
Sallee, James E.	2nd Lt.	24	5'10"			LaRue County, Ky.	Farmer
Martin, James B.	1st Sgt	22	5'11"	Blue	Dark	Illinois	Miller
Buckman, Jos. Madison	Sgt.	23	5'8½"	Gray	Light	Marion County, Ky.	Carpenter
Clayton, Robert H.	Sgt.	20	5'8"	Black	Dark	Green County, Ky.	Farmer
Moore, William	Sgt.	21	6'½"	Gray	Light	Marion County, Ky.	Farmer
Nall, William H.	Sgt.	18	5'5"	Blue	Light	Taylor County, Ky.	Farmer
Smith, Thomas G.	Sgt.	28	5'8"	Blue	Sandy	Green County, Ky.	Brickmason
Andrews, Albert T.	Corp	21	5'9"	Blue	Light	LaRue County, Ky.	Farmer
Buckman, Jos. W.	Corp.	22	5'6"	Black	Light	Marion County, Ky.	Farmer
Buckman, Joseph Mike	Corp.	24	5'9½"	Gray	Light	Marion County, Ky.	Farmer
Craig, John	Corp.	22	6'3"	Blue	Light	Taylor County, Ky.	Farmer
Hogland, Isaac	Corp.	20	5'8"	Gray	Dark	Taylor County, Ky.	Farmer
Mattingley, Martin V.B.	Corp.	21	5'5"	Gray	Dark	Marion County, Ky.	Farmer
Meece, George W.	Corp.	30	5'10"	Black	Sandy	Pulaski County, Ky.	Cigar maker
Robinson, James B.	Corp.	20	5'10"	Blue	Dark	Taylor County, Ky.	Farmer
Russell, David	Corp.	21	5'10"	Dark	Dark	Marion County, Ky.	Farmer
Dobson, James	Mus.	26	5'6"	Blue	Dark	Green County, Ky.	Farmer
Hogland, Wm. H.	Wagoner	22	5'7"	Gray	Dark	Taylor County, Ky.	Farmer
Allen, David	Pvt.	18	5'5"	Blue	Dark	Marion County, Ky.	Farmer
Allen, Samuel	Pvt.	21	5'9"	Blue	Dark	Marion County, Ky.	Farmer
Allen, Silas W.	Pvt.	18	5'8"	Blue	Black	LaRue County, Ky.	Shoemaker
Anderson, John	Pvt.	29	5'10"	Brown	Dark	Marion County, Ky.	Farmer
Atkins, Lafayette F.	Pvt.	24	5'10½"	Blue	Dark	Tennessee	Teacher
Benningfield, John	Pvt.	18	5'0"	Blue	Black	Taylor County, Ky.	Farmer
Ballou, John	Pvt.	27	6'0"	Blue	Sandy	Green County, Ky.	Farmer
Boarman, John	Pvt.	19	5'4"	Blue	Dark	Marion County, Ky.	Farmer
Bright, William D.	Pvt.	20	5'9"	Black	Black	Marion County, Ky.	Farmer
Brown, James F.	Pvt.	23	5'5"	Blue	Light	LaRue County, Ky.	Farmer
Carum, James C.	Pvt.	18	5'0"	Blue	Black	Green County, Ky.	Farmer
Cooper, John A.	Pvt.	33	5'6"	Blue	Red	Marion County, Ky.	Blacksmith
Caniff, Elias	Pvt.	45	5'10"	Blue	Light	Virginia	Farmer
Dobson, William H.	Pvt.	23	5'6"	Blue	Sandy	Green County, Ky.	Farmer
Dye, Robert T.	Pvt.	25	5'8"	Blue	Dark	Hart County, Ky.	Farmer
Elmore, Andrew	Pvt.	21	5'4"	Blue	Sandy	Nelson County, Ky.	Farmer

Regiment Staff	Rank	Age	Height	Eyes	Hair	Where Born	Occupation
Farmer, William	Pvt.	37	5'7"	Black	Black	Taylor County, Ky.	Carpenter
Feather, John H.	Pvt.	19	5'11½"	Blue	Dark	Taylor County, Ky.	Farmer
Garrott, John J.	Pvt.	28	6'0"	Blue	Light	Marion County, Ky.	Farmer
Gault, William B. S.	Pvt.	19	5'9"	Blue	Light	Marion County, Ky.	Farmer
Gebhart, William H.	Pvt.	32	6'0"	Black	Dark	Green County, Ky.	Farmer
Hickey, Patrick	Pvt.	45	5'6"	Blue	Sandy	Ireland	Farmer
Hoback, James A.	Pvt.	28	6'1"	Gray	Black	LaRue County, Ky.	Farmer
Hoback, John C.	Pvt.	31	6'0"	Blue	Dark	LaRue County, Ky.	Farmer
Hoback, Martin L.	Pvt.	25	5'6"	Blue	Black	LaRue County, Ky.	Farmer
Hogland, Isaac, Sr.	Pvt.	45	5'7"	Black	Black	Green County, Ky.	Farmer
Hogland, John B.	Pvt.	45	5'11"	Blue	Sandy	Taylor County, Ky.	Farmer
Hogland, John	Pvt.	18	5'10"	Gray	Light	Adair County, Ky.	Farmer
Howell, James W.	Pvt.	18	5'6"	Black	Light	LaRue County, Ky.	Farmer
Hunt, Rueben W.	Pvt.	28	5'8"	Blue	Black	Taylor County, Ky.	Farmer
Hunter, Francis M.	Pvt.	19	6'0"	Blue	Dark	Marion County, Ky.	Farmer
Kirkpatrick, Benjamin R.	Pvt.	18	5'8"	Black	Black	LaRue County, Ky.	Farmer
Lake, Abraham	Pvt.	44	5'10"	Blue	Black	Adair County, Ky.	Farmer
McKenley, George W.	Pvt.	23	6'0"	Blue	Black	Marion County, Ky.	Farmer
McNamara, Michael	Pvt.	26	5'1"	Blue	Black	Ireland	Farmer
Mills, Dennis	Pvt.	23	5'9"	Gray	Dark	Marion County, Ky.	Farmer
Moore, James R.	Pvt.	18	5'5"	Black	Light	Marion County, Ky.	Farmer
Moore, William E.	Pvt.	18	5'6"	Gray	Light	Marion County, Ky.	Farmer
Newcomb, Thomas	Pvt.	18	5'0"	Blue	Dark	Marion County, Ky.	Farmer
Newton, Joseph R.	Pvt.	23	5'10"	Gray	Brown	Bullitt County, Ky.	Farmer
Noley, Edward B.	Pvt.	23	6'0"	Black	Black	Marion County, Ky.	Farmer
Norco, James	Pvt.	27	5'10"	Blue	Dark	Marion County, Ky.	Farmer
Powers, George W.	Pvt.	22	5'5"	Gray	Sandy	LaRue County, Ky.	Farmer
Puryear, Samuel J. B.	Pvt.	27	5'5"	Blue	Sandy	Taylor County, Ky.	Farmer
Rice, John L.	Pvt.	19	6'0"	Blue	Dark	Marion County, Ky.	Farmer
Riggs, Thomas	Pvt.	19	6'2"	Black	Black	Marion County, Ky.	Farmer
Riley, John	Pvt.	45	5'6"	Blue	Dark	Ohio	Farmer
Robinson, William W.	Pvt.	18	5'4"	Blue	Dark	LaRue County, Ky.	Farmer
Rodgers, Benjamin O.	Pvt.	45	5'5"	Black	Black	Adair County, Ky.	Farmer
Rodgers, James	Pvt.	18	5'5"	Gray	Light	Taylor County, Ky.	Farmer
Sallee, Thomas J.	Pvt.	25	5'10½"	Gray	Dark	LaRue County, Ky.	Farmer
Sapp, Burnet B.	Pvt.	42	6'0"	Blue	Black	Washington County, Ky.	Shoemaker
Sapp, Franklin	Pvt.	32	5'3"	Blue	Dark	Washington County, Ky.	Farmer
Sapp, Jasper	Pvt.	21	5'3"	Blue	Black	Marion County, Ky.	Farmer
Sapp, Peter	Pvt.	31	5'8"	Gray	Black	Marion County, Ky.	Farmer
Shipp, Ambrose	Pvt.	18	6'0"	Dark	Dark	Taylor County, Ky.	Farmer
Shipp, James	Pvt.	45	6'0"	Gray	Sandy	Taylor County, Ky.	Farmer
Slatterly, Patrick	Pvt.	40	5'9"	Blue	Sandy	Ireland	Farmer
Stillwell, Hattan	Pvt.	18	5'0"	Gray	Light	LaRue County, Ky.	Farmer
Taylor, Thomas	Pvt.	22	5'0"	Black	Dark	Marion County, Ky.	Farmer
Thurman, James P.	Pvt.	20	5'7"	Black	Sandy	Nelson County, Ky.	Farmer
Wade, George W.	Pvt.	22	5'11"	Blue	Light	Marion County, Ky.	Farmer
White, Wm. H.	Pvt.	32	5'8"	Gray	Light	Green County, Ky.	Wagoner
Wilson, Lafayette	Pvt.	18	5'10"	Black	Black	LaRue County, Ky.	Painter
Wise, Chas.	Pvt.	21	5'10"	Gray	Light	Green County, Ky.	Farmer

COMPANY D

Regiment Staff	Rank	Age	Height	Eyes	Hair	Where Born	Occupation
Riley, George W.	Capt.	23	5'8"	Gray	Black	Washington County, Ky.	Lawyer
Hupp, William	1st Lt.					Washington County, Ky.	Farmer
Mills, James J.	1st Lt.	22	5'8"	Gray	Black	Marion County, Ky.	Farmer
Dorsey, Stephen N.	2nd Lt.	23				Marion County, Ky.	Farmer
Penick, Edward Y.	2nd Lt.	22	6'0"	Gray	Black	Marion County, Ky.	Farmer
Dunn, Henry C.	Sgt.	24	5'11"	Gray	Black	Ohio	Teacher
Earing, James C.	1st Sgt.	29	5'11"	Black	Black	Marion County, Ky.	Farmer
Foster, Andrew J.	Sgt.	28	5'7"	Gray	Black	Washington County, Ky.	Farmer
Garrison, John C.	Sgt.	25	5'8"	Gray	Black		Farmer

Regiment Staff	Rank	Age	Height	Eyes	Hair	Where Born	Occupation
Roberts, Marvis T.	Sgt.	24	5'8½"	Hazel	Black	Marion County, Ky.	Farmer
Seay, Francis B.	Sgt.	30	5'9"	Gray	Black	Marion County, Ky.	Farmer
Shockley, Robert G.	Sgt.	33	6'0"	Black	Black	Washington County, Ky.	Farmer
Beaven, Chas.	Corp.	23	5'8"	Gray	Sandy	Marion County, Ky.	Farmer
Crouch, Martin V.	Corp.	22	5'8"	Gray	Light	Washington County, Ky.	Farmer
Davis, Nathaniel W.	Corp.	26	6'0"	Gray	Black	Washington County, Ky.	Farmer
Garrison, Gideon B.	Corp.	23	5'8"	Gray	Black		Farmer
Hughes, Thomas D.	Corp.	28	6'0"	Gray	Black	Washington County, Ky.	Carpenter
Murvill, Isaac H.	Corp.	34	6'0"	Gray	Black	Virginia	Farmer
Phillips, John H.	Corp.	18	5'8"	Light	Light	Marion County, Ky.	Farmer
Price, William T.	Corp.	22	5'8"	Light	Light	Marion County, Ky.	Blacksmith
Seay, James A.	Corp.	21	5'10"	Gray	Black	Washington County, Ky.	Farmer
Snider, James A.	Corp.	28	5'7"	Gray	White	Washington County, Ky.	Farmer
Wells, Elbert S.	Corp.	22	5'7"	Blue	Black	Nelson County, Ky.	Farmer
White, David D.	Corp.	23	6'2"	Gray	Black	Washington County, Ky.	Farmer
Wilson, Thomas O.	Corp.	39	5'8"	Gray	Black	Washington County, Ky.	Farmer
Garrison, David R.	Mus.	24	5'11"	Gray	Black	Ohio	Teacher
Yocum, James M.	Mus.	18	5'6"	Black	Black	Washington County, Ky.	Farmer
Shasson, Henry A	Wagoner	26	5'8"	Gray	Dark	Marion County, Ky.	Farmer
Abell, Benedict J. A.	Pvt.	32	5'8"	Black	Black	Marion County, Ky.	Farmer
Beavers, Charles	Pvt.	19	5'8"	Gray	Dark	Marion County, Ky.	Farmer
Beavers, Wilford	Pvt.	25	5'9"	Black	Black	Washington County, Ky.	Farmer
Beggley, Roland	Pvt.	42	6'0"	Gray	Sandy	Marion County, Ky.	Farmer
Bottoms, Bradford E.	Pvt.	35	5'8"	Black	Black	Marion County, Ky.	Doctor
Brackan, William C.	Pvt.	20	5'9"	Black	Black	Marion County, Ky.	Farmer
Buckman, John G.	Pvt.	23	5'11"	Gray	Black	Marion County, Ky.	Farmer
Cain, Adam	Pvt.	35	5'7"	Gray	Black	Marion County, Ky.	Farmer
Compfort, Thomas	Pvt.	45	5'6"	Gray	Gray	Ireland	Laborer
Crench, Wm. W.	Pvt.	20	5'10"	Black	Black	Washington County, Ky.	Farmer
Cronch, James P.	Pvt.	18	5'7"	Gray	Light	Washington County, Ky.	Farmer
Cussanger, James	Pvt.	18	5'7"	Light	Light	Washington County, Ky.	Farmer
Ewing, William T.	Pvt.	18	6'0"	Gray	Black	Washington County, Ky.	Farmer
Graham, Mason	Pvt.	18	5'8"	Gray	Black	Marion County, Ky.	Farmer
Hagan, James	Pvt.						
Hagan, John T.	Pvt.	19	5'8"	Gray	Dark	Marion County, Ky.	Farmer
Hagerty, Richard	Pvt.	35	6'0"	Gray	Sandy	Washington County, Ky.	Stone mason
Hahun, Samuel	Pvt.	35	5'7"	Dark	Dark	Nelson County, Ky.	Blacksmith
Hall, John W.	Pvt.	18	5'y7"	Gray	Light	Washington County, Ky.	Farmer
Haman, Lee	Pvt.						
Hart, Thomas	Pvt.	23	6'0"	Gray	Dark	Marion County, Ky.	Farmer
Homan, David	Pvt.	42	5'6"	Gray	Black		
Hughes, Andrew	Pvt.	33	5'7"	Dark	Dark	Marion County, Ky.	Shoemaker
Hughes, David B.	Pvt.	18	5'9"	Gray	Black	Washington County, Ky.	Farmer
Hundrix, William	Pvt.	25	5'8"	Black	Black	Washington County, Ky.	Farmer
Hutchinson, William	Pvt.	19	6'0"	Brown	Dark	Washington County, Ky.	Farmer
Isham, John W.	Pvt.	18	5'5"	Blue	Light	Washington County, Ky.	Farmer
Issac, Nathan	Pvt.	26	5'7"	Gray	Black	Marion County, Ky.	Farmer
Johnsey, William B.	Pvt.	24	5'9"	Dark	Dark	Marion County, Ky.	Farmer
Lanham, James P.	Pvt.	20	5'8"	Gray	Black	Washington County, Ky.	Farmer
Leankford, James A.	Pvt.	20	5'8"	Gray	Light	Marion County, Ky.	Farmer
Leathers, Jesse M.	Pvt.	18	5'11"	Gray	Light	Marion County, Ky.	Laborer
Lindsey, Buford	Pvt.	18	6'0"	Black	Black	Grayson County, Ky.	Preacher
Linnehan, James	Pvt.	18	5'5"	Gray	Light	Marion County, Ky.	Farmer
Luckett, Thomas A.	Pvt.	26	6'0"	Light	Light	Marion County, Ky.	Farmer
Lynch, Robert N.	Pvt.	20	5'6"	Black	Black	Virginia	Farmer
Mattingly, Thomas	Pvt.	20	5'5"	Dark	Dark	Washington County, Ky.	Farmer
Maxwell, Danby C.	Pvt.	18	5'8"	Black	Black	Marion County, Ky.	Farmer
McHughes, Silas	Pvt.	19	6'0"	Gray	Sandy	Washington County, Ky.	Farmer
Milburn, William	Pvt.	33	5'8"	Hazel	Sandy	Washington County, Ky.	Farmer
Montgomery, William	Pvt.	22	5'7"	Gray	Black	Washington County, Ky.	Farmer
Mosser, Henry L.	Pvt.	40	5'7"	Black	Black	Washington County, Ky.	Farmer
Mouser, John W.	Pvt.	22	5'9"	Gray	Light	Marion County, Ky.	Farmer
Mouser, William F.	Pvt.	23	5'8"	Gray	Black	Marion County, Ky.	Farmer
Parris, Thomas G.	Pvt.	22	5'6"	Dark	Dark	Grayson County, Ky.	Blacksmith

Regiment Staff	Rank	Age	Height	Eyes	Hair	Where Born	Occupation
Ripperdon, Wm. D.	Pvt.	21	5'6"	Black	Black	Washington County, Ky.	Farmer
Sapp, Cornelius	Pvt.	41	5'10"	Black	Black	Marion County, Ky.	Farmer
Sheultry, Cornelius	Pvt.						
Shimmerhorn, Richard	Pvt.	23	5'10"	Hazel	Light	Washington County, Ky.	Farmer
Smothers, Isaac	Pvt.	20	5'7"	Gray	Black	Marion County, Ky.	Farmer
Smothers, Richard	Pvt.	21	5'7"	Gray	Black	Marion County, Ky.	Farmer
Smothers, Wm.	Pvt.	41	5'10"	Hazel	Sandy	Marion County, Ky.	Farmer
Snider, Alfred	Pvt.	21	5'6"	Gray	Light	Washington County, Ky.	Farmer
Southern, Charles	Pvt.	32	6'0"	Gray	Black	Washington County, Ky.	Farmer
Steward, Charles G.	Pvt.	39	5'10"	Hazel	Light	Marion County, Ky.	Teacher
Stines, Robert	Pvt.	19	5'6"	Black	Black	Washington County, Ky.	Farmer
Taylor, Benjamin	Pvt.	23	5'7"	Dark	Black	Washington County, Ky.	Farmer
Wakefield, Wm. F.	Pvt.	20	5'10"	Dark	Black	Marion County, Ky.	Blacksmith
Wakefield, Squire H.	Pvt.	43	6'0"	Dark	Dark	Washington County, Ky.	Blacksmith
Wells, John B.	Pvt.	19	5'7"	Gray	Black	Nelson County, Ky.	Farmer
White, John N.	Pvt.	21	5'11"	Gray	Black	Washington County, Ky.	Farmer
Wicker, James T.	Pvt.	18	5'8"	Dark	Black	Washington County, Ky.	Farmer
Williams, Jesse R.	Pvt.	25	8'0"	Light	Light	Nelson County, Ky.	Farmer
Willitt, Thomas B.	Pvt.	45	6'1"	Dark	Sandy	Washington County, Ky.	Farmer
Yocum, John R.	Pvt.	19	6'0"	Dark	Dark	Washington County, Ky.	Farmer
Yocum, Richard B.	Pvt.	22	6'2"	Dark	Light	Washington County, Ky.	Farmer

COMPANY E

Regiment Staff	Rank	Age	Height	Eyes	Hair	Where Born	Occupation
Bevill, Seth P.	Capt.	21				Washington County, Ky.	Court Clerk
Thompson, Andrew	Capt.	21				Washington County, Ky.	Farmer
Funk, Clem	1st Lt.					Washington County, Ky.	Farmer
Boyle, Richard	Sgt.	25	5'9"	Blue	Light	Pennsylvania	Carriage Maker
Champion, James C.	Sgt.	25	5'6½"	Blue	Light	Washington County, Ky.	Carpenter
Cozine, John S.	Sgt.	22	5'10½"	Gray	Black	Springfield, Ky.	Farmer
Higdon, Alexander B.	Sgt.	23	5'10½"	Yellow	Dark	Washington County, Ky.	Farmer
Janes, Joseph A.	Sgt.	21	5'6½"	Blue	Light	Washington County, Ky.	Farmer
Logsdon, Thos. H.	Sgt.	20	6'2½"	Gray	Light	Washington County, Ky.	Farmer
Champion, Thos. M.	Corp.	35	5'8"	Gray	Dark	Washington County, Ky.	Farmer
Coomes, Burr	Corp.	18				Nelson County, Ky.	Farmer
Dawson, Martin A.	Corp.	44	5'8¾"	Hazel	Dark	Virginia	Farmer
Ensor, George W.	Corp.	23	5'2½"	Gray	Black	Washington County, Ky.	Farmer
Filiatrean, Columbus R.	Corp.	19					
Higdon, James A. .	Corp.	23	5'8"	Light	Black	Hardin County, Ky.	Farmer
Hundley, Andrew N.	Corp.	24	5'7½"	Yellow	Dark	Washington County, Ky.	Farmer
Leachman, Harrison P.	Corp.	20	5'7½"	Blue	Light	Washington County, Ky.	Farmer
Logsdon, Ambr J.	Corp.	18	6'1¼"	Gray	Sandy	Washington County, Ky.	Farmer
Nally, Thos. J.	Corp.		5'9¼"	Hazel	Black	Washington County, Ky.	Farmer
Noe, George A.	Corp.	22	6'0"	Gray	Black	Washington County, Ky.	Farmer
Noe, William T.	Corp.	21	6'0"	Blue	Dark	Washington County, Ky.	Blacksmith
Thompson, Nathaniel	Corp.	18	5'9¾"	Gray	Light	Washington County, Ky.	Farmer
Hood, James K.P.	Mus.	18	5'5"	Blue	Light	Washington County, Ky.	Farmer
Adams, Elisha M.	Pvt.	21	5'10"	Blue	Light	Washington County, Ky.	Farmer
Adams, William T.	Pvt.	22	5'11½"	Gray	Light	Washington County, Ky.	Farmer
Berry, William G.	Pvt.	30					Cabinet maker
Bowles, George W.	Pvt.	37	5'7"	Gray	Dark	Washington County, Ky.	Farmer
Campbell, John	Pvt.	24	5'7½"	Gray	Black	Ireland	Farmer
Carney, John	Pvt.	28	5'4½"	Blue	Sandy	Ireland	Laborer
Carroll, James	Pvt.	25					
Champion, Charles A.	Pvt.	23	5'4"	Blue	Sandy	Washington County, Ky.	Farmer
Clarkson, James	Pvt.	19	5'7"	Light	Light	Washington County, Ky.	Farmer
Clarkson, John	Pvt.	18	5'5"	Dark	Dark	Washington County, Ky.	Farmer
Cooper, Philip	Pvt.	25				Washington County, Ky.	Farmer
Corcoran, Philip	Pvt.	21	5'4½"	Gray	Black	Ireland	Laborer
Courtney, John W.	Pvt.	23	5'6"	Black	Black	Nelson County, Ky.	Farmer
Curd, Joseph	Pvt.	19					

Regiment Staff	Rank	Age	Height	Eyes	Hair	Where Born	Occupation
Dearing, John L.	Pvt.	27	6'2"	Gray	Sandy	Mercer County, Ky.	Farmer
Dobson, William H.	Pvt.	33	6'1½"	Hazel	Brown	Nelson County, Ky.	Farmer
Edwards, John L.	Pvt.	25	6'11¼"	Gray	Black	Washington County, Ky.	Farmer
Edwards, William M.	Pvt.	21	5'11½"	Gray	Brown	Washington County, Ky.	Farmer
Fenwick, Edward	Pvt.	19	5'7½"	Hazel	Brown	Washington County, Ky.	Farmer
Fields, Henry P.	Pvt.	26					
Fields, Richard M.	Pvt.	21					
Filiatreau, William T.	Pvt.	21					
Foster, Benjamin	Pvt.	22	5'6½"	Blue	Sandy	Washington County, Ky.	Farmer
Fowler, John J.	Pvt.	26	5'8"	Blue	Black	Washington County, Ky.	Plasterer
Gassalder, Arnold	Pvt.						
Green, George L.	Pvt.	44					
Green, William	Pvt.	18	5'5"	Black	Dark	Washington County, Ky.	Farmer
Hall, Joseph	Pvt.	18	5'9"	Dark	Dark	Anderson County, Ky.	Farmer
Haydon, James B.	Pvt.	18	5'8½"	Light	Light	Washington County, Ky.	Farmer
Heaton, John W.	Pvt.						
Herbert, James P.	Pvt.	28					
Hiatt, Reuben	Pvt.	19	5'11½"	Light	Light	Washington County, Ky.	Farmer
Hundley, James R.	Pvt.	21	5'11¼"	Blue	Black	Washington County, Ky.	Farmer
Kating, John	Pvt.	40	5'8"	Black	Black	Ireland	Laborer
Logsdon, Andrew	Pvt.	24	6'0"	Gray	Red	Washington County, Ky.	Farmer
Lyons, Richard	Pvt.	36	5'10"	Dark	Dark	Marion County, Ky.	Farmer
Mayes, John. W.	Pvt.	22	5'7"	Gray	Dark	Washington County, Ky.	Farmer
Miles, Joseph	Pvt.	18	5'5½"	Dark	Dark	Marion County, Ky.	Farmer
Murphy, Michael	Pvt.						
Myers, William A.	Pvt.	18					
Myers, William R	Pvt.	18	5'7¾"	Black	Black	Washington County, Ky.	Farmer
Nally, John H.	Pvt.	22	5'8"	Hazel	Black	Washington County, Ky.	Farmer
Nix, George W.	Pvt.	20	5'6"	Blue	Dark	Hart County, Ky.	Farmer
Nix, William	Pvt.	22	5'8½"	Blue	Light	Washington County, Ky.	Blacksmith
Peak, John F.	Pvt.	20	5'8"	Blue	Dark	Washington County, Ky.	Farmer
Reynolds, Francis	Pvt.	28	5'10"	Gray	Black	Ireland	Laborer
Rhodes, Herod	Pvt.	31	5'8¾"	Blue	Dark	Nelson County, Ky.	Farmer
Rhodes, Thos. D.	Pvt.	24	5'10"	Dark	Dark	Nelson County, Ky.	Farmer
Richardson, William	Pvt.	19	5'7½"	Blue	Light	Washington County, Ky.	Farmer
Savage, Mathew	Pvt.	30	5'6½"	Hazel	Black	Ireland	Farmer
Seay, John P.	Pvt.	22	5'6¾"	Gray	Dark	Washington County, Ky.	Farmer
Simms, Cornelius	Pvt.	30	6'0"	Dark	Sandy	Washington County, Ky.	Farmer
Slayton, Marion A.	Pvt.	19	5'9¼"	Dark	Dark	Marion County, Ky.	Farmer
Spraggins, Alexander	Pvt.	18	5'6"	Blue	Light	Washington County, Ky.	Farmer
Sullivant, Patrick	Pvt.	29	5'5¼"	Gray	Sandy	Ireland	Laborer
Thompson, Edward A.	Pvt.	19					Farmer
Thompson, John B.	Pvt.	25	5'6½"	Gray	Amber	Washington County, Ky.	Farmer
Toon, Peter	Pvt.	19	5'7"	Blue	Light	Washington County, Ky.	Farmer
Walker, Richard R.	Pvt.	19	5'9"	Blue	Sandy	Washington County, Ky.	Farmer
Walker, Robert B.	Pvt.	23	6'0"	Blue	Light	Washington County, Ky.	Farmer
Waters, Jack H.	Pvt.	18	5'7½"	Blue	Sandy	Washington County, Ky.	Farmer
Weathers, James E.	Pvt.	19	6'0"	Black	Black	Washington County, Ky.	Farmer
White, Edward T.	Pvt.	21	5'8½"	Blue	Dark	Marion County, Ky.	Farmer
Whitfield, James	Pvt.	44	5'7"	Blue	Dark	Marion County, Ky.	Farmer
Willis/Wells, Isaac T.	Pvt.	23	5'8½"	Dark	Dark	Washington County, Ky.	Farmer
Young, James R.	Pvt.	29	5'6"	Gray	Blue	Washington County, Ky.	Farmer

COMPANY F

Regiment Staff	Rank	Age	Height	Eyes	Hair	Where Born	Occupation
Hill, Franklin S.	Capt.	41				Washington County, Ky.	Farmer
McKay, Charles W.	1st Lt.					Bullitt County, Ky.	Doctor
Smith, Benjamin R.	1st Lt.	23	5'10"	Blue	Light	Marion County, Ky.	Carpenter
Adcock, Joseph T.	2nd Lt.	25				Washington County, Ky.	Farmer
Jarboe, Charles H.	Sgt.						
Johnson, Terry	Sgt.						

Regiment Staff	Rank	Age	Height	Eyes	Hair	Where Born	Occupation
Maguire, Austin P.	Sgt.						
Mittler, Edward	1st Sgt.						
Robinson, Robert A.	Sgt.						
Thompson, John M.	Sgt.						
Asbeck, Gustave	Corp.						
Badgett, Hardin	Corp.	24	5'7"	Blue	Light	Mercer County, Ky.	Farmer
Bottom, Calvin W.	Corp.						
Harshfield, Achilles	Corp.						
Hocker, Jefferson	Corp.						
Newman, Mathew	Corp.	27	5'9"	Blue	Light	Ireland	Farmer
Reagan, Levi N.	Corp.	18	5'7"	Dark	Dark	Madison County, Ky.	Farmer
Smith, Robert J.	Corp.						
Southerland, Nelson	Corp.						
Sweeney, Carter	Corp.	21	5'11"	Light	Light	Washington County, Ky.	Farmer
Webster, John W.	Corp.						
Welch, Caleb	Corp.						
Young, Orville	Corp.	29	5'11"	Light	Light	Clark County, Ky.	Farmer
Greenwell, Richard	Wagoner	21	5'10"	Light	Dark	Marion County, Ky.	Farmer
Ash, Henry	Pvt.	23	5'9"	Blue	Dark	Bullitt County, Ky.	Laborer
Baker, John L.	Pvt.	25	6'9"	Dark	Dark	Garrett County, Ky.	Farmer
Baugh, Eli	Pvt.	21	5'6"	Dark	Dark	Pulaski County, Ky.	Laborer
Baugh, Henderson	Pvt.	19	5'7"	Blue	Light	Lincoln County, Ky.	Farmer
Bottom, Fidellar S.	Pvt.	27	5'10"	Light	Light	Boyle County, Ky.	Farmer
Bowling, William	Pvt.	20	5'10"	Light	Light	Marion County, Ky.	Farmer
Browning, Joseph	Pvt.	27	5'9"	Dark	Dark	Washington County, Ky.	Farmer
Burnell, James	Pvt.	18	5'7"	Gray	Dark	Jefferson County, Ky.	Laborer
Carter, Joseph E.	Pvt.	30	5'11"	Blue	Sandy	Washington County, Ky.	Farmer
Cooley, Cornelius	Pvt.	18	5'7"	Light	Light	Marion County, Ky.	Farmer
Cooley, Edward	Pvt.	45	5'7"	Blue	Dark	Casey County, Ky.	Blacksmith
Cooley, John B.	Pvt.	21	5'8"	Dark	Sandy	Casey County, Ky.	Blacksmith
Cooley, Stephen	Pvt.	18	5'7"	Light	Dark	Marion County, Ky.	Farmer
Cooley, William	Pvt.	25	5'6"	Dark	Sandy	Marion County, Ky.	Farmer
Cox, Micajah	Pvt.	24	5'9"	Light	Sandy	Casey County, Ky.	Farmer
Crouch, Stephen	Pvt.	18	5'7"	Blue	Light	Oldham County, Ky.	Farmer
Cruse, Andrew	Pvt.	30	5'9"	Dark	Sandy	Marion County, Ky.	Farmer
Darion, Simon	Pvt.	22	5'10"	Light	Light	Marion County, Ky.	Farmer
Estes, Benjamin	Pvt.	23	5'11"	Blue	Light	Jefferson County, Ky.	Farmer
Gallagher, Wm. F.	Pvt.						
Gleason, Thomas	Pvt.	27	5'6"	Blue	Light	Ireland	Laborer
Goldsmith, Maze	Pvt.	21	5'10"	Blue	Sandy	Washington County, Ky.	Farmer
Grant, Henry W.	Pvt.	34	5'8"	Blue	Light	Jessamine County, Ky.	Farmer
Grant, Joseph	Pvt.	24	5'8"	Blue	Light	Jessamine County, Ky.	Farmer
Gunter, Alexander	Pvt.	23	6'3"	Dark	Dark	Casey County, Ky.	Farmer
Hall, William	Pvt.	20	5'10"	Light	Light	Marion County, Ky.	Farmer
Harshfield, Columbus	Pvt.	23	5'8"	Dark	Dark	Bullitt County, Ky.	Farmer
Hooper, Wesley	Pvt.	45	6'0"	Dark	Dark	Marion County, Ky.	Farmer
Howell, John G.	Pvt.	25	5'10"	Blue	Light	Bourbon County, Ky.	Laborer
Johnson, John	Pvt.	18	5'7"	Dark	Dark	Marion County, Ky.	Student
Jones, Samuel	Pvt.	21	5'8"	Dark	Dark	Nelson County, Ky.	Shoemaker
Jones, William	Pvt.	20	5'10"	Blue	Light	Boyle County, Ky.	Farmer
Kays, Smith	Pvt.	30	5'11"	Dark	Dark	Washington County, Ky.	Farmer
Kelly, Wm. P.	Pvt.	21	5'9"	Blue	Light	Washington County, Ky.	Carpenter
Key, Thomas P.	Pvt.	41	5'11"	Light	Light	Washington County, Ky.	Farmer
Lampkins, Peter	Pvt.	33	5'10"	Blue	Dark	Marion County, Ky.	Farmer
Land, Squire	Pvt.	43	5'7"	Dark	Dark	Marion County, Ky.	Farmer
Lavey, Charles	Pvt.	22	5'5"	Light	Light	France	Laborer
Lawson, Nimrod	Pvt.	18	5'6"	Light	Sandy	Washington County, Ky.	Farmer
Lawson, Francis M.	Pvt.	19	5'10"	Dark	Dark	Washington County, Ky.	Farmer
Linton, George M.	Pvt.	26	5'10"	Dark	Dark	Washington County, Ky.	Farmer
Litsey, Granville	Pvt.	24	5'7"	Dark	Dark	Bullitt County, Ky.	Farmer
Litsey, Martin H.	Pvt.	23	5'6"	Dark	Dark	Bullitt County, Ky.	Farmer
Mattingley, Nicholas	Pvt.	44	5'8"	Dark	Dark	Marion County, Ky.	Farmer
Mattingley, Thos. A.	Pvt.	21	5'10"	Dark	Dark	Marion County, Ky.	Farmer
Mattingly, Wm.	Pvt.	18	5'10"	Dark	Dark	Marion County, Ky.	Farmer

Regiment Staff	Rank	Age	Height	Eyes	Hair	Where Born	Occupation
McCabbins, Moses	Pvt.	21	5'6½"	Dark	Dark	Green County, Ky.	Laborer
McCullum, William	Pvt.	20	5'11"	Blue	Sandy	Marion County, Ky.	Farmer
McGhee, William	Pvt.	45	5'9"	Dark	Sandy	Marion County, Ky.	Farmer
McMillen, Michael	Pvt.	28	6'0"	Light	Dark	Marion County, Ky.	Farmer
McMullin, John	Pvt.	43	5'9"	Dark	Dark	Marion County, Ky.	Farmer
Mobberley, John W.	Pvt.	23	5'11"	Light	Light	Marion County, Ky.	Farmer
Monroe, John	Pvt.	18	5'7"	Light	Light	Bullitt County, Ky.	Farmer
Mullans, Wm. T.	Pvt.	25	6'0"	Dark	Dark	Marion County, Ky.	Farmer
Mullin, Green Berry	Pvt.	19	5'10"	Light	Dark	Indiana	Farmer
Nelson, James	Pvt.	31	5'10"	Dark	Dark	Nelson County, Ky.	Farmer
O'Bryan, John	Pvt.	35	5'5"	Dark	Dark	Ireland	Laborer
Perkins, Jefferson	Pvt.						
Ratcliff, Joseph	Pvt.	23	5'9"	Blue	Dark	Bullitt County, Ky.	Farmer
Reagen, Wm. H.	Pvt.	19	5'10"	Dark	Dark	Madison County, Ky.	Farmer
Roberts, Squire	Pvt.	18	5'6"	Dark	Dark	Washington County, Ky.	Farmer
Russell, Ignatius	Pvt.	23	6'0"	Light	Light	Marion County, Ky.	Farmer
Scott, Crow	Pvt.	26	6'2"	Blue	Sandy	Washington County, Ky.	Farmer
Sluder, Alexander	Pvt.	27	5'6"	Dark	Dark	Casey County, Ky.	Farmer
Smith, Samuel	Pvt.	18	5'11"	Light	Light	Marion County, Ky.	Farmer
Steel, John V.	Pvt.	22	5'11"	Dark	Dark	Boyle County, Ky.	Farmer
Sweeney, John	Pvt.	18	5'9"	Light	Light	Washington County, Ky.	Farmer
Sutterfield, Edward H.	Pvt.	18	5'8"	Dark	Dark	Adair County, Ky.	Laborer
Taylor, Eason	Pvt.	21	5'6"	Dark	Dark	Casey County, Ky.	Farmer
Thomas, James	Pvt.	25	5'7"	Dark	Dark	Washington County, Ky.	Farmer
Thorp, Madison	Pvt.	25	5'8"	Dark	Dark	Marion County, Ky.	Farmer
Troutman, Sebastian	Pvt.	19	5'10"	Dark	Light	Bullitt County, Ky.	Farmer
Tumey, William H.	Pvt.	20	5'10"	Blue	Light	Bullitt County, Ky.	Farmer
Voughn, William	Pvt.	21	5'7"	Blue	Dark	Maryland	Farmer
Weir, Henry	Pvt.	18	5'7"	Blue	Dark	Louisville County, Ky.	Farmer
Williams, Thomas	Pvt.	20	5'10"	Light	Light	Marion County, Ky.	Farmer
Winfield, John	Pvt.	28	5'7"	Dark	Dark	Missouri	Farmer
Woods, James	Pvt.	25	5'7"	Light	Light	Madison County, Ky.	Farmer
Horsham, William D.	Pvt.						
Young, Simon P.	Pvt.	27	5'11"	Light	Light	Clark County, Ky.	Farmer

COMPANY G

Regiment Staff	Rank	Age	Height	Eyes	Hair	Where Born	Occupation
Davenport, Jas. M.	Capt.	21	5'10"	Brown	Red	Alabama	Teacher
Hunter, William R.	Capt.	21	5'7"	Hazel	Brown	Nelson County, Ky.	Medical Student
Blanford, Edward O	1st Lt.	20	5'9"	Blue	Light	Washington County, Ky.	Farmer
Fiddler, James M.	1st Lt.						
Spalding, Charles E	1st Lt.	19	5'8"	Gray	Light	Washington County, Ky.	Farmer
Ferrill, Edward C.	2nd Lt.	23				Marion County, Ky.	Farmer
Bean, Benjamin	1st Sgt.	22	5'8½"	Black	Black	Nelson County, Ky.	Distiller
Inman, Jefferson	Sgt.	24	5'8"	Gray	Light	Marion County, Ky.	Farmer
Nally, Robert	Sgt.	21	5'9½"	Blue	Light	Marion County, Ky.	Farmer
O'Bryan, Peter	Sgt.	35	5'7"	Dark	Brown	Marion County, Ky.	Shoemaker
Skinner, Taleaferro	Sgt.	45	5'7"	Blue	Dark	Marion County, Ky.	Farmer
Vessels, Henry	Sgt.	25	6'1"	Gray	Light	Washington County, Ky.	Farmer
Whitehouse, Mose	Sgt.	28	6'0"	Black	Black	Marion County, Ky.	Farmer
Buckler, Willistan	Corp.	25	5'11"	Yellow	Black	Marion County, Ky.	Farmer
Ferrill, Francis L.	Corp.	22	5'9"	Hazel	Light	Nelson County, Ky.	Farmer
McCarty, Benjamin	Corp.	22	5'10"	Blue	Black	Marion County, Ky.	Farmer
Phillips, Jonathan	Corp.	20	5'11"	Blue	Black	Marion County, Ky.	Farmer
Powell, John W	Corp.	20	5'9"	Blue	Light	Nelson County, Ky.	Farmer
Enbert, John	Wagoner						
Avis, Edward	Pvt.	18	5'7"	Gray	Light	Nelson County, Ky.	Farmer
Back, Jefferson B.	Pvt.	19	5'9"	Hazel	Black	Marion County, Ky.	Farmer
Ballard, Joseph	Pvt.	20	5'9"	Gray	Dark	Marion County, Ky.	Farmer
Ballard, Shelby	Pvt.	18	5'5"	Gray	Light	Marion County, Ky.	Farmer
Ballard, William	Pvt.	30	5'10"	Black	Black	Marion County, Ky.	Farmer

Regiment Staff	Rank	Age	Height	Eyes	Hair	Where Born	Occupation
Birch, John H.	Pvt.	22	5'10"	Yellow	Black	Marion County, Ky.	Farmer
Blandford, George H.	Pvt.	21	5'9"	Gray	Black	Marion County, Ky.	Farmer
Blemford, James	Pvt.	18	5'0"	Blue	Light	Washington County, Ky.	Farmer
Boone, William	Pvt.	18	5'7"	Light	Black	Nelson County, Ky.	Farmer
Brothers, James M.	Pvt.	44	5'11"	Hazel	Dark	Marion County, Ky.	Farmer
Carrie, Anderson	Pvt.	43	6'0"	Yellow	Sandy	Marion County, Ky.	Farmer
Caughlem, William	Pvt.	18	6'0"	Blue	Light	Washington County, Ky.	Teacher
Clayton, Francis S.	Pvt.	16	5'5"	Gray	Light	Marion County, Ky.	Farmer
Clark, John M	Pvt.	18	5'6"	Gray	Light	Nelson County, Ky.	Farmer
Emery, John W.	Pvt.	27	5'10"	Black	Black	Marion County, Ky.	Farmer
Fanvell, Augustus S.	Pvt.	37	5'10"	Black	Black	Marion County, Ky.	Farmer
Ferrill, William	Pvt.	18	5'10"	Black	Black	Marion County, Ky.	Farmer
Field, James	Pvt.	36	5'10"	Black	Black	Washington County, Ky.	Farmer
Foster, Larry	Pvt.	18	5'9"	Black	Dark	Marion County, Ky.	Laborer
Graham, David	Pvt.	21	5'10"	Blue	Dark	Marion County, Ky.	Farmer
Graves, Charles	Pvt.	23	5'10"	Gray	Black	Washington County, Ky.	Farmer
Hagan, John H	Pvt.	26	6'0"	Blue	Black	Nelson County, Ky.	Farmer
Hall, Isaac	Pvt.	20	5'8"	Black	Black	Nelson County, Ky.	Shoe maker
Hagan, William	Pvt.						
Harman, Elias	Pvt.	20	5'6"	Blue	Light	Marion County, Ky.	Farmer
Havs, Nelson	Pvt.	18	5'10"	Gray	Light	Marion County, Ky.	Farmer
Hayden, William	Pvt.	18	5'5"	Blue	Curley	Washington County, Ky.	Farmer
Hays, Harrison	Pvt.	20	5'9"	Black	Black	Marion County, Ky.	Farmer
Higdon, Pius	Pvt.	18	5'9"	Blue	Light	Washington County, Ky.	Farmer
Hundley, Samuel	Pvt.	24	6'0"	Dark	Brown	Marion County, Ky.	Farmer
Kelty, Miles Pius	Pvt.						
Kelty, Thomas	Pvt.	25	5'9"	Blue	Black	Washington County, Ky.	Farmer
Lanlam, James.	Pvt.	20	5'11"	Blue	Light	Washington County, Ky.	Farmer
Linton, John E.	Pvt.	18	5'8"	Gray	Flaxy	Washington County, Ky.	Farmer
Mahoney, William H.	Pvt.	22	5'8"	Black	Black	Washington County, Ky.	Farmer
Masterson, Thomas	Pvt.	18	5'9"	Blue	Light	Nelson County, Ky.	Farmer
Mattingly, Albert	Pvt.	18	5'6"	Gray	Light	Washington County, Ky.	Farmer
Mattingly, John M.	Pvt.	18	5'11"	Red	Red	Washington County, Ky.	Farmer
McLain, James J.	Pvt.	24	5'11"	Yellow	Black	Washington County, Ky.	Farmer
Mudd, Joseph	Pvt.	20	5'9"	Gray	Light	Washington County, Ky.	Farmer
Mudd, Valentine	Pvt.	22	6'0"	Gray	Sandy	Washington County, Ky.	Farmer
Nally, Stephen	Pvt.	15	5'8"	Black	Dark	Washington County, Ky.	Farmer
Newton, James J.	Pvt.	22	5'10"	Black	Black	Nelson County, Ky.	Farmer
Newton, Robert	Pvt.	18	5'8½"	Black	Black	Nelson County, Ky.	Farmer
O'Bryan, Paul	Pvt.	30	5'8"	Blue	Gray	Marion County, Ky.	Farmer
Osborn, James	Pvt.	15	5'6"	Blue	Light	Marion County, Ky.	Farmer
Osborne, John F.	Pvt.		5'11"	Black	Dark	Washington County, Ky.	Farmer
Peak, Thomas	Pvt.	19	5'8"	Black	Black	Nelson County, Ky.	Farmer
Pennington, John	Pvt.	26	5'8½"	Blue	Light	Marion County, Ky.	Farmer
Phillips, Benjamin	Pvt.	18	5'8½"	Blue	Light	Marion County, Ky.	Farmer
Powers, Francis	Pvt.	18	5'6"	Blue	Black	Washington County, Ky.	Farmer
Renhard, William	Pvt.	19	5'0"	Blue	Black	Nelson County, Ky.	Laborer
Right, Jonathan	Pvt.						
Riggs, George	Pvt.	26	5'10"	Light	Light	Marion County, Ky.	Farmer
Skinner, Bannister	Pvt.	35	5'9"	Blue	Brown	Marion County, Ky.	Waggoner
Smith, Frank	Pvt.	22	5'11"	Brown	Black	Marion County, Ky.	Farmer
Smith, John	Pvt.						
Smith, Pius	Pvt.	22	5'10"	Blue	Flaxey	Nelson County, Ky.	Farmer
Smith, William J.	Pvt.	18	5'10"	Blue	Black	Marion County, Ky.	Farmer
Spratt, John	Pvt.	22	5'8½"	Blue	Flaxey	Marion County, Ky.	Farmer
Tharp, Nathan	Pvt.	35	6'0"	Black	Black	Marion County, Ky.	Farmer
Thomas, David	Pvt.	18	5'8"	Black	Black	Marion County, Ky.	Farmer
Thompson, Lewis F.	Pvt.	20	5'8"	Dark	Dark	Marion County, Ky.	Carpenter
Vessels, Richard J.	Pvt.	19	5'10"	Blue	Light	Washington County, Ky.	Farmer
Vessels, Walter	Pvt.	43	6'0"	Blue	Black	Washington County, Ky.	Farmer
Waters, Charles D.	Pvt.	22	5'9"	Black	Dark	Nelson County, Ky.	Blacksmith
Waters, Jas. R.	Pvt.	22	5'8"	Blue	Light	Nelson County, Ky.	Farmer
White, George	Pvt.						

Regiment Staff	Rank	Age	Height	Eyes	Hair	Where Born	Occupation
Whitehouse, Addison	Pvt.	21	5'10"	Blue	Dark	Marion County, Ky.	Farmer
Whitehouse, Scott	Pvt.	34	6'0"	Gray	Brown	Marion County, Ky.	Farmer

COMPANY H*

Regiment Staff	Rank	Age	Height	Eyes	Hair	Where Born	Occupation
Pendleton, Buford R.	Capt.	30				Marion County, Ky.	Farmer
Shively, Wm. T.	Capt.	31				Taylor County, Ky.	Farmer
Barry, Henry W.	1st Lt.					New York	Teacher
Dunn, Henry C.	1st Lt.	24	5'11"	Gray	Black	Ohio	Teacher
Beglow, William F.	2nd Lt.	20				Ireland	Clerk
Wright, Thomas R.	1st Sgt.						
Edelen, Benedict	Sgt.						
Shively, Joseph H.	1st Sgt.						
Shively, Stephen M.	Sgt.						
Swaney, William	Sgt.						
Waltring, William	Sgt.						
Abell, Samuel	Corp.						
Belton, Addison	Corp.						
Clements, James P.	Corp.						
Earls, Milton	Corp.						
Lyons, Benjamin F.	Corp.						
Newton, Andrew J.	Corp.						
Newton, Elias	Corp.						
Rice, David E.	Corp.						
Roots, William	Corp.						
Farmer, Joseph	Tmstr.						
Abell, Cornelius W.	Pvt.						
Abell, Enoch	Pvt.						
Abell, George W.	Pvt.						
Ainsworth, Henry H.	Pvt.						
Bayne, Patrick	Pvt.						
Bermingham, Martin	Pvt.						
Brockman, James	Pvt.						
Cabell, William T.	Pvt.						
Campbell, James	Pvt.						
Campbell, Moses	Pvt.						
Campbell, William P.	Pvt.						
Crowell, James A.	Pvt.						
Eads, Zachariah	Pvt.						
Ellis, Benjamin	Pvt.						
Farmer, James	Pvt.						
Farmer, John E.	Pvt.						
Farmer, Moses	Pvt.						
Farmer, Nathaniel	Pvt.						
Farmer, Preston P.	Pvt.						
Farmer, Thomas	Pvt.						
Farmer, William	Pvt.						
Ford, Martin	Pvt.						
Grier, Tandy	Pvt.						
Gunter, Henry	Pvt.						
Hall, William	Pvt.						
Harbin, William	Pvt.						
Harmon, Isaac	Pvt.						
Hart, William	Pvt.						
Kerr, Alonzo T.	Pvt.						
Key, Thomas P.	Pvt.						
Long, Perry	Pvt.						
Marple, Elmore	Pvt.						
Marple, Jefferson	Pvt.						

*The original records for company H were lost.

Regiment Staff	Rank	Age	Height	Eyes	Hair	Where Born	Occupation
Martin, Thomas	Pvt.						
Melton, David	Pvt.						
Murphy, Benedict J.	Pvt.						
Murphy, Francis	Pvt.						
Murphy, George M.	Pvt.						
Murphy, John A.	Pvt.						
Murphy, Thomas	Pvt.						
Newton, John S.	Pvt.						
O'Connell, Philip	Pvt.						
O'Donald, Jacob	Pvt.						
Painter, Aaron T.	Pvt.						
Raley, George W.	Pvt.						
Raley, John	Pvt.						
Roberts, Squire	Pvt.						
Russell, Daniel J.	Pvt.						
Shively, David A.	Pvt.						
Shively, Samuel	Pvt.						
Sluder, James H.	Pvt.						
Sluder, John M.	Pvt.						
Smith, Johnson	Pvt.						
Spurling, James	Pvt.						
Troy, John	Pvt.						
Vanhorn, George S.	Pvt.						
Vestrees, Josiah	Pvt.						
Walstan, Thos. J.	Pvt.						
Welch, Michael	Pvt.						
White, William	Pvt.						
Wise, John R.	Pvt.						
Wise, Samuel T.	Pvt.						
Wise, William	Pvt.						
Woodrum, Abner	Pvt.						
Woodrum, James	Pvt.						
Woods, James	Pvt.						
Worthington, Martin T.	Pvt.						
Wright, Benjamin	Pvt.						
Wright, Samuel	Pvt.						
Wright, Thos. R.	Pvt.						
Yearns, John	Pvt.						

COMPANY I

Regiment Staff	Rank	Age	Height	Eyes	Hair	Where Born	Occupation
Webster, Israel B.	Capt.	36	5'10"	Blue	Dark	New York	Photographer
Kelley, William E.	1st Lt.	35				Washington County, Ky.	Wheelwright
Myers, John H.	2nd Lt.	21				Marion County, Ky.	Farmer
Brown, Thomas J.	Sgt.	25	5'9"	Gray	Black	Meade County, Ky.	Farmer
Curby, William J.	1st Sgt.	25	6'0"	Gray	Dark	Illinois	Brick Mason
Giddis, William J.	Sgt.	24	5'8"	Blue	Black	Marion County, Ky.	Farmer
Jackson, Wm. H.	1st Sgt.	35	5'10"	Blue	Gray	N. Carolina	Farmer
Mills, Jack E.	Sgt.	24	5'5"	Black	Black	Marion County, Ky.	Farmer
Richardson, Daniel L.	Sgt.	36	5'10"	Blue	Brown	Hardin Co, Ky.	Farmer
Rose, James E.	1st Sgt.	20	5'10"	Blue	Brown	Marion County, Ky.	Farmer
Wright, William J.	Sgt.	19	5'11"	Blue	Light	Marion County, Ky.	Farmer
Curby, John H.	Corp.	18	5'9"	Blue	Dark	Hardin County, Ky.	Farmer
Jackson, James N.	Corp.	29	6'1"	Dark	Sandy	N. Carolina	Farmer
Lawson, David	Corp.	34	5'6"	Black	Dark	Hardin County, Ky.	Farmer
Mills, Joel F.	Corp.	19	5'4"	Dark	Dark	Marion County, Ky.	Farmer
Noe, Elijah	Corp.	22	6'0"	Gray	Red	Hardin County, Ky.	Farmer
Osburn, John A.	Corp.	24	5'11"	Gray	Auburn	Monroe County, Ky.	Farmer
Purdy, Robt. L.	Corp.	20	5'7"	Gray	Dark	Marion County, Ky.	Farmer
Rose, John C.	Corp.	18	5'6"	Blue	Light	Marion County, Ky.	Farmer
Turner, William	Corp.	24	6'2'	Blue	Black	Marion County, Ky.	Teacher

Regiment Staff	Rank	Age	Height	Eyes	Hair	Where Born	Occupation
Osten, Jas.	Mus.	44	5'11"	Blue	Gray	Hardin County, Ky.	Farmer
Abel, Joshua J.	Pvt.	35	6'2"	Hazel	Black	Marion County, Ky.	Farmer
Averrett, John D.	Pvt.	18	6'0"	Blue	Light	Marion County, Ky.	Farmer
Begals, John H.	Pvt.	25	5'9"	Gray	Black	Meade County, Ky.	Farmer
Bell, Isaac	Pvt.	19	5'4½"	Blue	Brown	Hardin County, Ky.	Farmer
Brown, James W.	Pvt.	19	5'10"	Blue	Light	Hardin County, Ky.	Farmer
Brown, Joshua	Pvt.	45	5'10"	Gray	Gray	Woodford County, Ky.	Doctor
Brown, Josiah	Pvt.	25	5'7"	Gray	Black	Hardin County, Ky.	Farmer
Brown, Philip M.	Pvt.	28	5'5"	Gray	Dark	Bullitt County, Ky.	Wagon Maker
Bryant, John H.	Pvt.	24	5'8"	Gray	Light	Casey County, Ky.	Farmer
Burchell, Jno.	Pvt.	24	5'8"	Dark	Dark	Marion County, Ky.	Farmer
Ceaver, Jesse M.	Pvt.	30	5'7'	Gray	Dark		Farmer
Ellis, Benjamin	Pvt.	20	5'8"	Blue	Light	Marion County, Ky.	Farmer
Fitzgibbons, Patrick	Pvt.	37	5'6"	Gray	Black	Ireland	Farmer
Gaddis, Milton H.	Pvt.	20	5'7"	Hazel	Brown	Marion County, Ky.	Farmer
Goodman, David	Pvt.	19	5'10"	Blue	Dark	Hardin County, Ky.	Farmer
Goodman, Francis M.	Pvt.	21	6'0"	Blue	Light	Hardin County, Ky.	Farmer
Goodman, General L.	Pvt.	22	6'0"	Blue	Light	Hardin County, Ky.	Farmer
Goodman, William	Pvt.	19	5'10"	Blue	Light	Hardin County, Ky.	Farmer
Goodman, Wm. H.	Pvt.	21	5'10"	Blue	Light	Hardin County, Ky.	Farmer
Goodman, Young	Pvt.	23	5'10"	Blue	Brown	Hardin County, Ky.	Farmer
Green, William H.	Pvt.	21	6'2"	Blue	Light	Hardin County, Ky.	Farmer
Gubehart, George W.	Pvt.	22	5'8"	Dark	Dark	Casey County, Ky.	Blacksmith
Gunter, Alexander	Pvt.		ND				
Harrison, Samuel H.	Pvt.	19	5'7"	Black	Black	Tennessee	Farmer
Harrison, William R.	Pvt.	18	5'7"	Gray	Light	Lincoln County, Ky.	Farmer
Hicks, Isaac	Pvt.	23	5'6"	Blue	Dark	Hardin County, Ky.	Farmer
Hicks, William M.	Pvt.	25	5'6"	Blue	Dark	Hardin County, Ky.	Farmer
Hilton, Thomas R.	Pvt.	25	5'6"	Blue	Dark	Hardin County, Ky.	Farmer
Hobbs, Levi A.	Pvt.	20	5'10"	Blue	Brown	N. Carolina	Farmer
Inman, Hardister	Pvt.	22	6'0"	Blue	Dark	Marion County, Ky.	Farmer
Isaacs, James	Pvt.	18	5'5"	Blue	Light	Marion County, Ky.	Farmer
Isaacs, John	Pvt.	40	5'10"	Blue	Gray	Marion County, Ky.	Farmer
Jasper, Abraham	Pvt.	25	5'9"	Blue	Light	Pulaski County, Ky.	Teacher
Lane, Patrick A.	Pvt.	18	5'7½"	Gray	Blue	Casey County, Ky.	Miller
Lawson, Lenox	Pvt.	43	5'11"	Blue	Light	Hardin County, Ky.	Farmer
Lawson, William	Pvt.	33	6'0"	Blue	Dark	Hardin County, Ky.	Farmer
Litsey, Mastin H.	Pvt.	23	ND				
Luster, James R.	Pvt.	19	5'7"	Blue	Light	Wayne County, Ky.	Blacksmith
Martin, Jesse	Pvt.	44	6'0"	Gray	Dark		Laborer
Miller, James C.	Pvt.	29	5'10"	Gray	Dark	Grayson County, Ky.	Farmer
Mills, James H.	Pvt.	21	5'11'	Blue	Light	Casey County, Ky.	Farmer
Mills, John F.	Pvt.	18	6'0"	Blue	Brown	Casey County, Ky.	Farmer
Munday, Silas	Pvt.	19	5'11"	Blue	Brown	Casey County, Ky.	Farmer
Noe, Henry H.	Pvt.	18	5'9"	Blue	Dark	Hardin County, Ky.	Farmer
Noe, William B.	Pvt.	29	5'11"	Blue	Brown	Hardin County, Ky.	Farmer
Oster, George	Pvt.	18	5'8"	Blue	Black	Hardin, Ky.	Farmer
Peters, John	Pvt.	28	5'10"	Hazel	Dark	Hardin, Ky.	Farmer
Phillips, Benjamin	Pvt.	38	5'11"	Black	Black	Marion County, Ky.	Carpenter
Purdy, William C.	Pvt.	25	5'9"	Gray	Light	Marion County, Ky.	Farmer
Roaler, James	Pvt.	22	5'10"	Blue	Black	Marion County, Ky.	Farmer
Roaler, Richard	Pvt.	18	5'10"	Blue	Dark	Marion County, Ky.	Farmer
Roaler, Solomon	Pvt.	21	5'9"	Hazel	Dark	Marion County, Ky.	Farmer
Ross, John D.	Pvt.	18	5'0"	Blue	Light	Grayson County, Ky.	Farmer
Saddler, Mathews	Pvt.	20	5'4"	Blue	Dark	Marion County, Ky.	Farmer
Saddler, Thomas	Pvt.	28	5'6"	Gray	Dark	Marion County, Ky.	Farmer
Smith, Hamilton	Pvt.	44	5'10"	Gray	Light	Woodford County, Ky.	Farmer
Smothers, John	Pvt.	18	5'5"	Blue	Light	Marion County, Ky.	Farmer
Snow, William J.	Pvt.	30	5'11"	Hazel	Black	Lincoln County, Ky.	Painter
Spencer, Augustus	Pvt.	23	5'7"	Blue	Dark	Grayson County, Ky.	Farmer
Stavton, John B.	Pvt.	28	5'10"	Blue	Dark	Marion County, Ky.	Farmer
Stewart, John	Pvt.	26	6'0"	Blue	Dark	Boyle County, Ky.	Blacksmith
Stewart, Thos.	Pvt.	18	5'6"	Gray	Dark	Boyle County, Ky.	Farmer
Stoner, William H.	Pvt.	17	5'9"	Dark	Black	Hardin County, Ky.	Farmer

Regiment Staff	Rank	Age	Height	Eyes	Hair	Where Born	Occupation
Tarrill, Patrick	Pvt.	44	5'7"	Hazel	Brown	Marion County, Ky.	Farmer
Taylor, Henry	Pvt.	19	5'11"	Gray	Light	Russell County, Ky.	Farmer
Temgate, William A.	Pvt.	28	5'10"	Blue	Light	Marion County, Ky.	Farmer
Turpin, Levi	Pvt.	18	5'5"	Gray	Dark	Casey County, Ky.	Farmer
Vessels, Philip M.	Pvt.	25	6'2'	Gray	Dark	Meade County, Ky.	Farmer
Wilcher, John T.	Pvt.	20	5'8"	Blue	Light	Lincoln County, Ky.	Farmer
Willard, Hugh A.	Pvt.	44	5'8"	Blue	Brown	Casey County, Ky.	Farmer
Willard, John	Pvt.	22	5'9"	Blue	Brown	Marion County, Ky.	Farmer
William, Daniel	Pvt.	22	5'3"	Blue	Brown	Missouri	Gas Fitter
Woolbridge, William R.	Pvt.	25	5'5"	Blue	Light	Hardin County, Ky.	Farmer

Company K

Regiment Staff	Rank	Age	Height	Eyes	Hair	Where Born	Occupation
Waller, Henry	Capt.					Indiana	
Denton, John H.	Capt.	20	5'6"	Blue	Light	Indiana	Merchant
Tweddle, William	Capt.	43	6'1"	Blue	Brown	England	Merchant
Watts, James R.	1st Lt.	25				Louisville, Ky.	Printer
Bellam, Richard R.	Sgt.	25	5'5¾"	Brown	Brown	Ireland	Printer
Cox, Peter A.	Sgt.	28	5'11½"	Hazel	Brown	New York	Printer
Garvey, Charles	1st Sgt.	42	5'8½"	Blue	Gray	Ireland	Plasterer
Johnston, Leroy S.	Sgt.	23	5'10"	Blue	Light	Ohio	Printer
Lee, John L.	Sgt.	24	5'7½"	Gray	Light	Louisville, Ky.	Clerk
Rea, Robert Sr.	Sgt.	38	5'8"	Black	Gray	England	Cooper
Richard, David	Sgt.	22	5'7"	Hazel	Brown	Scotland	Laborer
Wilkins, Edward	Sgt.	23	5'9"	Gray	Light	Louisville County, Ky.	Printer
Baker, William	Corp.	22	5'10"	Hazel	Black	Ohio	Printer
Burger, Andrew	Corp.	44	5'9"	Blue	Black	Germany	Tailor
Burk, Tobias	Corp.	36	5'11½"	Hazel	Black	Ireland	Farmer
Dugald, Campbell	Corp.	21	5'7½"	Blue	Light	Louisville, Ky.	Sculptor
Carroll, John C.	Corp.	45	5'7"	Blue	Gray	Ireland	Painter
Jones, Thomas A.	Corp.	40	5'4½"	Gray	Brown	Ohio	Printer
Lee, John F.	Corp.	44	5'8½"	Gray	Brown	Louisville, Ky.	Carpenter
Montrose, Joseph	Corp.	24	5'9½"	Hazel	Brown	New York	Cabinet Maker
McLaine, Peter	Mus.	15	4'4"	Brown	Light	Pennsylvania	Laborer
Rea, Robert, Jr.	Mus.	12	4'0"	Gray	Light	Pennsylvania	School Boy
Arnett, John, Jr.	Pvt.	17	4'6"	Brown	Brown	Virginia	Book Binder
Arnett, John, Sr.	Pvt.	42	5'10½"	Brown	Dark	Ohio	Carpenter
Batman, William	Pvt.	44	5'11"	Blue	Brown		Laborer
Baugh, Eli	Pvt.	21	5'7"	Dark	Brown	Boyle County, Ky.	Laborer
Becker, Ulrick	Pvt.	42	5'8"	Blue	Brown	Germany	Tailor
Blair, John T.	Pvt.	24	5'8"	Hazel	Auburn	Marion County, Ky.	Farmer
Broax, Alexander	Pvt.	24	5'9"	Gray	Brown	Louisville, Ky.	Laborer
Brown, Thos.	Pvt.	27	5'7½"	Hazel	Brown	Ireland	Laborer
Buckley, John	Pvt.	32	5'7"	Gray	Black	Ireland	Laborer
Cady, Michael	Pvt.	36	5'2"	Gray	Brown	Ireland	Laborer
Campbell, John A.	Pvt.	28	5'7"	Gray	Brown	Maryland	Marble Cutter
Cane, Adam	Pvt.	35	5'8"	Brown	Black	Marion County, Ky.	Farmer
Caromed, Simon	Pvt.	30	5'8"	Blue	Brown	Ireland	Laborer
Carpenter, Charles A.	Pvt.	27	6'2"	Gray	Black	Virginia	Laborer
Casey, John	Pvt.	37	5'11½"	Brown	Gray	Ireland	Laborer
Conway, Patrick	Pvt.	26	5'7"	Gray	Brown	Ireland	Laborer
Cushin, Dennis	Pvt.	40	5'7"	Black	Black	Ireland	Laborer
Cutsinger, James	Pvt.	ND					
Dailey, Peter	Pvt.	24	5'11"	Black	Black	Ireland	Laborer
Dearion, Simon	Pvt.	22	5'10"	Hazel	Black	Marion County, Ky.	Farmer
Dorsey, Morris	Pvt.	21	5'6"	Gray	Light	Ireland	Laborer
Eady, Hugh	Pvt.	36	5'7"	Blue	Brown	Ireland	Laborer
Emms, Joseph	Pvt.	29	5'7"	Brown	Black	Germany	Laborer
Enders, Michael	Pvt.	43	5'8"	Gray	Sandy	Germany	Carpenter
Fox, James	Pvt.	ND					
Fumbrell, Wm. M.	Pvt.	31	5'10"	Blue	Light	Maryland	Farmer

Regiment Staff	Rank	Age	Height	Eyes	Hair	Where Born	Occupation
Gegan, Patrick	Pvt.	37	5'10½"	Hazel	Dark	Ireland	Laborer
Hines, John	Pvt.	27	5'5½"	Blue	Brown	Ireland	Laborer
Hines, Patrick	Pvt.	30	5'6¼"	Brown	Brown	Ireland	Laborer
Hundley, James	Pvt.	30	5'8½"	Gray	Black	Ireland	Laborer
Idoax, John J.	Pvt.	31	5'8"	Hazel	Black	France	Wagon Maker
Kanleahy, Dennis	Pvt.	42	5'7"	Black	Black	Ireland	Laborer
Kneibert, Jacob H.	Pvt.	20	5'6"	Black	Brown	Louisville, Ky.	Merchant
Lee, Levi M.	Pvt.	18	5'4"	Light	Brown	Louisville, Ky.	Laborer
Lenihan, David	Pvt.	19	5'11"	Blue	Brown	Ireland	Laborer
Lennon, Joseph	Pvt.	30	5'7"	Brown	Brown	Ireland	Laborer
Madden, Washington	Pvt.	ND					
Maloney, Daniel	Pvt.	23	5'8"	Blue	Brown	Ireland	Laborer
Maloy, Daniel	Pvt.	42	6'0"	Blue	Brown	Ireland	Laborer
Mattingley, John B.	Pvt.	21	5'2"	Blue	Light	Marion County, Ky.	Farmer
Mattingley, Joseph S.	Pvt.	19	5'7"	Blue	Light	Marion County, Ky.	Farmer
Mattingley, Nicholas	Pvt.	43	5'7"	Dark	Black	Marion County, Ky.	Farmer
Mattingley, Wm. H.	Pvt.	20	5'1½"	Gray	Light	Marion County, Ky.	Farmer
Mayland, Patrick	Pvt.	26	5'5"	Blue	Dark	Ireland	Laborer
McAnelly, John	Pvt.	ND					
McAnelly, Wm. T.	Pvt.	ND					
McCann, James	Pvt.	38	5'7"	Blue	Red	Ireland	Cigar Maker
McCardell, James	Pvt.	44	5'7"	Black	Black	Ireland	Laborer
McGinnis, James	Pvt.	31	5'8"	Blue	Black	Ireland	Tinner
McVey, William	Pvt.	40	5'11½"	Blue	Black	Ireland	Laborer
Meckin, John	Pvt.	40	5'10"	Blue	Brown	Ireland	Laborer
Miles, Thos.	Pvt.	23	5'8"	Brown	Dark	Marion County, Ky.	Farmer
Millagan, Thomas	Pvt.	23	5'7"	Gray	Brown	Ireland	Laborer
Molim, Adam	Pvt.	18	5'2"	Dark	Dark	France	Laborer
Montgomery, William	Pvt.	ND					
Mordan, Patrick	Pvt.	21	5'4½"	Blue	Dark	Ireland	Laborer
Mule, Stonemason	Pvt.	39	5'7"	Brown	Brown	Germany	Laborer
Mulloon, Patrick	Pvt.	44	5'8"	Blue	Black	Ireland	Laborer
Munday, Patrick	Pvt.	22	5'9"	Gray	Fair	Ireland	Tailor
Murphy, Burtley	Pvt.	23	5'5"	Brown	Dark	Ireland	Laborer
Murphy, Jerry	Pvt.	35	5'7½"	Blue	Dark	Ireland	Laborer
Murphey, John	Pvt.	40	5'6½"	Blue	Gray	Ireland	Laborer
O'Donald, Jasper	Pvt.	36	5'7"	Gray	Brown	Ireland	Laborer
Phibban, Patrick	Pvt.	40	5'6"	Blue	Gray	Ireland	Laborer
Philips, Jonathan	Pvt.	22	5'10"	Dark	Dark	Marion County, Ky.	Farmer
Rase, William	Pvt.	35	5'7"	Hazel	Dark	Germany	Labor
Roberts, Richard	Pvt.	28	5'9"	Blue	Brown	Wales	Sailor
Sherman, Thomas B.	Pvt.	22	5'11"	Hazel	Dark	Indiana	Farmer
Sluder, Alexander	Pvt.	27	5'6"	Dark	Dark	Casey County, Ky.	Farmer
Staffan, Joseph	Pvt.	35	5'7"	Hazel	Auburn	Germany	Laborer
Stanton, John	Pvt.	43	5'5¾"	Blue	Gray	Ireland	Laborer
Sutterfield, Edward	Pvt.	ND					
Thomas, Jas.	Pvt.	20	5'6½"	Hazel	Brown	Marion County, Ky.	Farmer
Welsh, Richard	Pvt.	24	5'7½"	Hazel	Brown	Ireland	Laborer
Wester, Michael	Pvt.	27	5'7"	Blue	Black	Ireland	Laborer
Williams, Thomas	Pvt.	20	5'10"	Light	Light	Marion County, Ky.	Farmer
Withrow, A. G.	Pvt.	41	5'7½"	Gray	Brown	Virginia	Cooper

Appendix C. 10th Kentucky Men Buried at National and Soldiers' Cemeteries (Rolls of Honor)

Men of the 10th Kentucky Interred at Nashville National Cemetery

Soldier	Date of Death	Location
Silas Allen, Pvt.	March 23, 1862	Nashville, Tenn.
James Brothers, Pvt.	April 3, 1862	Nashville, Tenn.
Elias Cundiff, Pvt.	April 8, 1864	Nashville, Tenn.
James Clarkson, Pvt.	April 8, 1862	Nashville, Tenn.
John Clarkson, Pvt.	April 30,1862	Nashville, Tenn.
Royal Clark, Pvt.	May 26, 1864	Nashville, Tenn.
C. Colebuck, Pvt.	March 17, 1862	Nashville, Tenn.
Peter Cox, Sgt.	March 1862	Nashville, Tenn.
Zachariah Eads, Pvt.	October 11, 1863	Nashville, Tenn.
Charles Graves, Pvt.	April 15, 1862	Nashville, Tenn.
Charles Hardesty, Asst. Surgeon	July 7,1863	Nashville, Tenn.
Harrison Hays, Pvt.	October 7, 1864	Nashville, Tenn.
John Idoax, Pvt.	November 8, 1862	Nashville, Tenn.
Martin Hoback, Pvt.	November 28, 1863	Nashville, Tenn.
Samuel Livers, Pvt.	July 5, 1864	Nashville, Tenn.
Jesse Martin, Pvt.	January 24, 1863	Nashville, Tenn.
William B. Mattingly	March 31, 1862	Nashville, Tenn.
Burtley Murphy, Pvt.	October 22, 1863	Nashville, Tenn.
Elias, Newton, Cpl.	March 22, 1862	Nashville, Tenn.
George Oster, Pvt.	October 5, 1862	Nashville, Tenn.
Thomas Parris, Pvt.	July 4, 1863	Nashville, Tenn.
Francis Powers, Pvt.	August 1, 1863	Nashville, Tenn.
Peter Sapp, Pvt.	March 22, 1862	Nashville, Tenn.
John Smothers, Pvt.	February 29, 1864	Nashville, Tenn.
Cornelius Sheulty, Pvt.	April 17, 1863	Nashville, Tenn.
William H. Stoner, Pvt.	February 4, 1863	Nashville, Tenn.
Hugh Willard, Pvt.	September 21, 1862	Nashville, Tenn.
Samuel Wise, Pvt.	September 29, 1862	Nashville, Tenn.
Martin Worthington, Pvt.	June 13, 1862	Nashville, Tenn.
Benjamin Wright, Pvt.	March 21, 1862	Nashville, Tenn.

Men of the 10th Kentucky Interred at Chattanooga National Cemetery

Soldier	Date of Death	Location
J. J. Canott, Pvt.		Chattanooga, Tenn.
J. M. Clark, Pvt.	November 5, 1863	Chattanooga, Tenn.
Simon Cormody, Pvt.	November 12, 1864	Ringgold, Ga.
George Enos, Cpl.	October 19, 1863	Chattanooga, Tenn.
John T. Hagan	October 1, 1863	Chattanooga, Tenn.
Andrew Haden, Pvt.	August 22, 1864	Chattanooga, Tenn.
P. A. Lane	October 1, 1863	Chattanooga, Tenn.
William McVay	February 2, 1864	Chattanooga, Tenn.
William F Muller, Pvt.	May 19, 1864	Chattanooga, Tenn.
Stephen Nalley, Pvt.	November 25, 1863	Chattanooga, Tenn.
W. T. Price, Cpl.	December 8, 1863	Chattanooga, Tenn.
Isaace Perlte, Pvt.	December 3, 1863	Chattanooga, Tenn.
F. Roat, Pvt.	November 12, 1863	Chattanooga, Tenn.
B. B. Sapp	October 29, 1863	Chattanooga, Tenn.
J. M. Sludder, Pvt.	October 16, 1863	Chattanooga, Tenn.
John P Seay, Pvt.	May 7, 1864	Chattanooga, Tenn.
B. I. Skinner, Pvt.	May 15, 1864	Resaca, Ga.
Waller, Henry, Capt.	March 13, 1864	Chattanooga, Tenn.

Soldier	Date of Death	Location
M. Welch, Pvt.	October 26, 1863	Chattanooga, Tenn.
Caleb Welch, Cpl.	July 24, 1864	Chattanooga, Tenn.

Men of the 10th Kentucky Interred at Boyle County, Ky Cemetery

Soldier	Date of Death	Location
Francis M Goodman, Pvt.	March 2, 1862	Danville, Ky
Thomas Stallins, Pvt.	November 16, 1862	Danville, Ky

Men of the 10th Kentucky Interred at Soldiers' Lot, Franklin County, Ky., Cemetery

Soldier	Date of Death	Location
E. G. Curry, Pvt.	February 27, 1864	Frankfort, Ky.
Charles Gunn, Pvt.	March 1, 1864	Frankfort, Ky.

Men of the 10th Kentucky Interred at Marion County, Ky., National Cemetery

Soldier	Date of Death	Location
Isaac Bell, Pvt.	February 1, 1862	Lebanon, Ky.
James Berry, Pvt.	March 5, 1862	Lebanon, Ky.
Fletcher Bland, Pvt.	November 1861	Lebanon, Ky.
Robert T. Dye, Pvt.	March 3, 1862	Lebanon, Ky.
Richard Knott, Pvt.	May 15, 1862	Lebanon, Ky.
James McMillen, Pvt.	December 1862	New Market, Ky.
Andrew Newton, Cpl.	March 31, 1862	Lebanon, Ky.
Garrett Peterson, Pvt.	October 24, 1862	Lebanon, Ky.
Eincle Rehnl, Pvt.	February 1862	Lebanon, Ky.
James Rodgers, Pvt.	November 28, 1861	Lebanon, Ky.
Thomas Simins, Pvt.	May 27, 1862	Lebanon, Ky.
William Voughn, Pvt.	December 18, 1861	Lebanon, Ky.
Richard Walker, Pvt.	December 15, 1861	Lebanon, Ky.

Men of the 10th Kentucky Interred at Mill Springs National Cemetery

Soldier	Date of Death	Location
C. Simms, Pvt.	February 15, 1862	Vaught Cemetery
Richard Shimmerhorn, Pvt.	March 1862	Mill Springs, Ky.
David White, Cpl.	January 1, 1862	Mill Springs, Ky.

Men of the 10th Kentucky Interred at Marietta, Ga., National Cemetery

Soldier	Date of Death	Location
Joseph Mike Buckman, Cpl.	July 9, 1864	Vining Station, Ga.
Tobias Burk, Pvt.	July 9, 1864	Vining Station, Ga.
William H. Dobson, Pvt.	August 14, 1864	Atlanta, Ga.
William Ferrill, Pvt.	August 11, 1864	Atlanta, Ga.
W. J. Friell, Pvt.	August 1864	Atlanta, Ga.
Alexander B. Higdon, Pvt.	May 27, 1864	New Hope Church, Ga.
Henry Grant, Pvt.	September 1, 1864	Jonesboro, Ga.
Thomas Masterson, Pvt.	September 1, 1864	Jonesboro, Ga.
John W. Mayes	July 9, 1864	Vining Station, Ga.

Soldier	Date of Death	Location
Charles Henry Miles	July 9, 1864	Vining Station, Ga.
Squire Roberts, Pvt.	September 1, 1864	Jonesboro, Ga.
William Whitfield	September 1, 1864	Jonesboro, Ga.
John Willard	September 1, 1864	Jonesboro, Ga.

Men of the 10th Kentucky Interred at Atlanta, Ga., National Cemetery

Soldier	Date of Death	Location
G. B. Garrison, Cpl.	October 16, 1863	

Men of the 10th Kentucky Interred at Andersonville National Cemetery

Soldier	Date of Death	Location
Josiah Brown, Pvt.	February 4, 1864	Andersonville, Ga.
Philip Brown, Pvt.	April 28, 1865	Andersonville, Ga.
James Cronch, Pvt.	February 4, 1864	Andersonville, Ga.
John Emery, Pvt.	June 27, 1864	Andersonville, Ga.

Men of the 10th Kentucky Interred at Cave Hill National Cemetery

Soldier	Date of Death	Location
Anderson Carrie, Pvt.	July 7, 1862	Louisville, Ky.
William Caughlem, Pvt.	April 1, 1862	Louisville, Ky.
Dennis Cushing, Pvt.	May 8, 1862	Louisville, Ky.
James Dobson, Musician	May 5, 1862	Louisville, Ky.
William Fogle, Pvt.	December 5, 1864	Louisville, Ky.
John Wise, Pvt.	June 13, 1862	Louisville, Ky.

Men of the 10th Kentucky Interred at Corinth, Miss.

Soldier	Date of Death	Location
William Mouser, Pvt.	June 10, 1862	Corinth, Miss.

Men of the 10th Kentucky Interred at Shiloh National Cemetery

Soldier	Date of Death	Location
W. H. Reagan, Pvt.	June 10, 1862	Monterey, Tenn.

Men of the 10th Kentucky Interred at New Albany, In National Cemetery

Soldier	Date of Death	Location
Edward Avis, Pvt.	October 29, 1864	Jeffersonville, Ind.

Appendix D. Letters Written by the Men of the 10th Kentucky Infantry

Letter from Corporal Martin Van Buren Crouch, Company D, to his sister, used with permission from the Ollie Crouch Moore Collection. Courtesy of Eudora Gwinn Thompson Hahn.

Gallatin, Tenn.
Nov. the 14th 1862

Dear Sister again I am permitted to pen you a few lines to let you know where I am and how I am getting along. I am well as usual and the rest of the boys are well also with the exception of bad colds. When we left the Rowlingfork we continued our march until we reached Bowling Green and staid there three days out from their. We came to our present camp about two miles from Gallatin. The country is very good. It looks like the land about Harrodsburg and Lexington. We will not stay here more than a day or two and from here we will go to Nashville I expect. We are guarding the Louisville and Nashville Railroad. The rebels has torn it all to the south. Morgan is reported close to us but we can hear his being at a dozen different places at the same time. We heard from Jim Seay by a man who came from their. He said Jim wasn't entirely well yet. Tell Mother I got my cup knife apple towel and combs and everything she sent. Susan Jane write to me and tell Cricket and Dick to write. I will quit as Jim wants to write some. So nothing more but remain your brother until death.

M. V. Crouch

Letter written by Lt. Colonel William H. Hays to his father, used with permission from Nash Hayes.

November 17, 1862
Dear Father:

We are now stopping on the Cumberland River, we have been here two or three days, Our Regiment and 10th Indiana were ordered here to support some 1,500 cavalry that had been here a few days. They were threatened with an attack by Forest's cavalry, said to be in considerable force at Lebanon, Tenn., about 14 miles from here.

All the cavalry that we came here to support have been ordered from here to another point, and our regiment and the 10th. Indiana are left alone, We are about 17 miles from Gallatin where we have some forces, the nearest support we have.

Our regiment is in pretty good health and spirits, the other three regiments of our brigade are at Gallatin. Col. Harlan is there also.

I have been in pretty good health since I saw you. Tell Jim and Cyrus to write to me and give all the news of the country.

My position is much more laborious and my responsibilities are much greater since I have been in command of the regiment.

My regards to all and tell the boys to write to me often.

Truly Yours,
W. H. Hays (signed)

Letters Written by Lt. William Francis O'Bryan. These letters are located at the National Archives in Lt. O'Bryan's pension file.

Camp 12 Miles from Corinth
April 24th 1862
Dear Father

I take my pen in hand to let you know that we are generally well and hope these few lines may find you and all the rest of the family in the same good health that I am in now. Father, I have no news to write except that we have just been paid off. Father, I will enclose Fifteen Dollars which you can do what you please with it you have settled with Cole Blair. I want you to be sure and settle with him. Father, we only drew $26. This time and I would have sent more but the Captain said I had better retain $10. Dear Father, Edward Blandford encloses $30 and he wants you to send it to his mother. Father, give my love to all the family and retain a portion for yourself. Write as soon as you receive this. Direct your letter to me Co, B 10th Ky Regt General Thomas Division

    Nothing more at present from your affectionate Son,
W F O'Bryan

Camp Near Hartsville, Tenn
Nov the 17th 1862
Dear Father

As this is the first opportunity I have had of writing I thought I would write you a few lines to let you know how I am and how I am getting along. I am well at present and sincerely hope this may find you in the same good health. Dear Father, I have no news to write except we made a forced march of 19 miles yesterday after 12 Oclock to meet John Morgan but when we got here he was gone. Nobody knows where he is now, but Father, I can't tell whether we will stay here all winter or whether we will move tomorrow or not. We are upon an uncertainty. We are expecting an attack from Lebanon, Tenn and if there is one, we are prepared for it. Dear Father that is all I can write about that. My firm conviction is that we will go through East Tennessee and sweep the Rebels as we go. Dear Father, give my love to Mother and Mollie & all my brothers & Sisters & tell them to write to me as it is seldom I can get a chance to write for I am making out payrolls now and perhaps I will send home some money when I get paid. Dear Father, write and tell me something about Bettie's affairs,
Your Affectionate Son
W F O'Bryan

In Camp At Laverne Tenn
Febry 7th 1863
Dear Father

Your of the 3rd is at hand. It gratified me very much to hear from you and to hear that you were well. And more than anything else to hear that you had sent Mollie to school. The reason why this gratifies me so much is because I know it has been her desire to do to school for sometime before I left home. Dear Father you of course know your own business better than I could dictate. But undoubted you have in my estimation done the best thing you could have done. Because she is old enough now to know what she is going for. Dear Father answer this as soon as you receive it. Give my love to all my brothers and sisters and retain a portion for yourself and mother.

    I remain your affectionate son,
W. F. O'Bryan

P S
    Excuse my short letter as Milburn is on detached duty doing business for the company. I will do better in my next.
W. F. O'Bryan

In Camp At Laverne Tenn
Febry 18th 1863
Dear Mother

I received a letter from you a few days ago and was very glad to hear of your health being good. I am well at present and sincerely hope this may find you in the same good health. We have had a very wet spell of weather and there is a strong probability of its continuing wet. The weather is thick cloudy yet without any prospect of it clearing away. But thank God we are not marching. We can stay in our tents when it is raining and as we have plenty of wood handy. We can make ourselves very comfortable but not near so comfortable as if we were at home. I was always of a roving disposition but I am certain that my becoming a soldier will cure me of that entirely for I find that what you have so often told me is true. There is no place like home. Mother, you wanted to know whether I had been to confession or not since I left home. I have not and for there has been no priest with the Regiment since I left home. But I have not entirely forgotten the Almighty God above though placed in a situation that I cant go to church. Dear mother, I was sick all last week but I have got about well again. I thought that I was going to have another spell like the one I had at East Port and if it had turned our so I was coming home certain for you may be sure if I am sick very bad I will come home though it may cost me my commission. Mother, I expect we will be paid off in a few days as the Paymaster is here and you can tell Father I will send him some money as soon after I get paid and I can go to Nashville and send it by express. Give my love to all my relations and especially to Father and keep a portion for yourself. Dear Mother, remember your poor soldier boy in your prayers.

I remain your affectionate and devoted son,

Wm F O'Bryan

PS

Write soon and direct you letter to me Co. B. 10th Regt Ky Infantry 2nd Brigade 3rd Division Army of the Cumberland

W F O'Bryan

Dear Father

I now will speak something about business. It is impossible for me to collect from Gen Harlan what you have wrote for. Gen Harlan is in Kentucky now. And of course I cant collect anything from him. In regard to the other papers I think I can collect them and send the amount (with my own money) home. Father, you no doubt think me dilatory about sending money home but candidly I have never been paid since I saw you. Well now for something in regard to my taking command of Co. B. I told you in a letter that I expected Capt Milburn would resign but I am under the impression that it is a mistake. (Though Milburn may resign).

But Father, I hope he won't. You say that perhaps I would like to have my own way as I am 23 years of age. But Recollect. I know that I have a Father and I know that my Father is a capable of giving me advice. Therefore I will be governed by you except in political matters. For it is a candid fact, I cannot be biased in my opinion. Well now for a little of that (I cant say more for I have not room). But rest assured that I am a "Democrat," a True Douglas Democrat, and never no, never will I ever forsake the proud Banner of Democracy.

I think that is enough.

W F O'Bryan

Letters from Sgt. James F Scott. These letters are located at the National Archives in Sgt. Scott's pension file.

Camp near Corinth
June the 18, 1862
Dear Father and Mother

I have first received your kind and long looked for letter which gave me grate sadisfaction to hear that you was all well. I am well at present. I all so received a letter from T M Read. You note that you wanted to know whether I had got my business fixed up or not. I drawed my money yesterday. I drawed $73!! and 25 cts. I have sent you sixty dollars by express. It will be sent to Thomas Woods in Lebanon and he will send it to New Market. I expect it will get there before this letter. I want you to keep it or if you need it you can spend it or do as you like.

   Robert Short is here yet he is rite sick and has been for several days. He has sent in his res-ignation but has not received his discharge yet. We are down here in the black jack swamps where we can't see any thing but musketoes and scoripons. I don't know how long we will remain here. Colonel Harland wants to get based to Ky but I think it will be doubtful whether he gets the chance or not being that he had a chance when he was at Nashville and wouldn't accept it. We have plenty to eat down here but it is pretty ruff. The citizens round here is bound to starve unless the government furnishes them something to eat. The rebels has swept everything before them and forced all the men and boys in the army that was able to enroll. I haven't heard anything of the rebles for some time. I think they have all gone home. I know some of them has fun. I have saw several of them on their way home. They swore they didant intent to fight any longer. They say they was forced in the rebble served against their own will. They say that Beauegard intend to make a buly fight at Corinth but he couldn't get his officers and men to stand. They state that it took about half of his men to gard the balance from running off. I want you to send me some postage stamps for I can't get any of them here.

James F Scott

Camp at Lavergne Tennessee
February 25, 1863
Dear Father and Mother

I seat myself to write you a few lines to let you know that I am well at this time hopeing when these few lines reach your hands that they may find you both enjoying the same like blessings. I have wrote you four letters and haven't received a single one from you all. I can get news from all parts of Kentucky but I wood like to hear from home once and awhile. I got a paper yesterday stating that the upper part of Ky was full of rebbles and also that they was a large body crossing the Cumberland at Mill Springs. If that be true I woodant be surprised if we didn't have to come back again. They hasn't anything of importance going on out here at present. Rosecrans is mud-bound so he cant move on after Bragg. We have built a fort here at Laverne that commands eighteen guns. We can whip all of Morgan's and Forest's forces if they come against us.

   We drawed our money on the 21 and I started 50 dollars by express on the 23 day to you. William Meadows sent 45 dollars in the same letter to Noble in Lebanon and directed to New Market. Luellen sent 45 dollars in a separate letter directed to you to deliver that money. You make her and Meadow's wife give you a receipt for the amount so they be no difficulty here after and make them pay their part of the expenses for the expressing of it.

   I want you to write soon as you get this letter and let me no whether you received our money or not. I am going to send this letter by James Ship. He is discharged and going to start home this evening. So nothing more at present.

James F Scott

Camp Near Winchester Tenn
July the 22, 1863
Dear Father and Mother

I again seat myself to write you a few lines to inform you that I am well and harty at present hopeing when these few lines come to hand they may find you enjoying the same like blessing. I received your letter a few minnets ago dated July the 17 which gave me grate sadisfaction to hear that you are both well. I haven't any thing of interest to write at present. We are laying here in the hot sun. Got nothing to do only cook and eat we are getting tolerable plenty rations since the cars has got to running. I don't believe there is a rebel in fifty miles of here. I don't know how long we will stay here. There is some talk of Thomas' Corps going to Virginia but I hope it ain't so. I think the war is about plaid out. I have an idea that we will be at home against Christmas with out some grate blunder takes place, I just got a paper stating that they had captured Morgan and his hated (?) force. I hope it is so. They aught to hang him and all of his band. We have drawed money. I will send mine home as soon as they got the express office open at Dechard.

I want you to write as often as you can. Give my respects to all the friends. I will close this time.
James F Scott

Winchester, Tenn
July the 27, 1863
Dear Father

I seat myself this morning to inform you that I am well and harty. I am hopeing when these few lines come to hand they may find you enjoying the same like blessings. Father, I will send you $30 dollars in this letter by express. It will be directed to Ed Mahen, Lebanon ware you can pay the amount charged for expressing it
Yours truly
James F Scott

Winchester, Tenn
July the 27, 1863
Dear Father and Mother

I seat myself this morning to inform you that I am well and harty at present hopeing when these few lines come to hand they may find you enjoying the same like blessings. I haven't any thing of interest to write at present. Nothing transpired since I wrote before. We have awful hot weather down here. There is talk of this Corps being sent to Virginna. I don't know whether it will or not. They haven't anything to fight in Tenn nor nothing closer that Chatinuga. Old Hardee(?) is there with about ten thousand men to run quick as he finds we are comeing. I started 36 dollars by express this morning directed to Ed Mahon Lebanon, Ky where you will have to go to get it. The express will have to be paid. Make use of it as you please if you want to spend it any way you can do so. I will send a 2 dollar bill in this letter as a present. I want you to write as soon as you get this and let me know whether you have got it all or not.

The boys is all well and harty and in good spirits. They all think we will be at home against Christmas. I hope it may be so for I wood like to spend next Christmas at home free from this infurnal rebellion. I do not suppose you will be interrupted by Morgan and his band much more. From all accounts he has plaid out.

I will have to close by saying write soon
James F Scott.

Winchester, Tenn
August the 8, 1863
Dear Father and Mother

I seat myself his evening to write you a few lines to inform you that I just received you letter of the 6th which gave me grate sadisfaction to hear that was both tolerable well. You stated that you received my letter with the $2 dollars I sent you. I was afraid it wouldn't reach you but it is about as safe to send it in a letter as by express. I want you to write as soon as you get the 30 dollars I expressed. I was most afraid to reskit.

I have had my health first trate(?) for the last three months but I dread the march that we have before us. We have orders to march Monday morning towards Chatinuga. I suppose and dread the hot weather but we will make Rosecrans hop. I wood rather keep moving slowly along than to lay in camp if it wasn't so hot. You may listen to hear of some hard fighting in a few weaks if Bragg stays in Chatinnuga. I am glad to hear that the election has went off so well as it has.

I will have to close for it is so dark I can't see the lines.

James F. Scott

Transcripts of letters from Seth P. Bevill to his widowed father, Albert G. Bevill and sister. These letters are located at the National Archives in Capt Bevill's pension file and were transcribed by Paul Birkhead.

Fort Lavergne, Tenn March 29th 1863
My dear father

Your long expected letter came to hand this morning, only a few minutes ago. It was mailed on the 12th inst. So you see it has been some time coming. When I wrote to Mr. Booker I had not then received any letters but some came to hand a few days afterward; and when I wrote on the 18th I had received more in answer to my letter sent by express which also came to hand in a few days afterward. Tell Mary that I received hers of the 13th and wrote to her last Wednesday enclosing Ten dollars and sent by express to Phillips and Blandford requesting them to send it over to you. Let me know as soon as it comes to hand. I have been quite fortunate in receiving letters lately that have been mailed I suppose, coming to hand in due time.

I am glad to be able to inform you this morning that I am last released from arrest, having been honorably discharged by the sentence of a General Court Martial. I enclose the General Order. It is an official copy. I need not say that I feel considerable relieved, for although I felt confident that I would finally be honorably discharged from arrest. Yet it was so long before the trial came off, I could not help getting low spirited so long. I was under arrest five weeks before I got a trial.

I am sorry I neglected to enclose Parker (Herberts) descriptive list. I will enclose it in this. I had not heard of Wm. Filiatreau's discharge only through your letter. I have-omitted to say that I also received this morning Mary's letter of the 24 enclosing a short note from in regard to the (Possession) of Kentucky by the Confederates again. We have been very anxious here in regard to their intention and have anxiously awaited news in regard to it. From latest advises I think it will turn out to be only a Cavalry Raid at least I eamestly hope that it may be only this.

There is a good deal of talk in the Regiment now about our being mounted. Major Davidson saw Genl Rosseau in Nashville a day or two since, who told him he was on his way to see Genl Rosecrans about selecting eight or ten Kentucky Regiments to have them mounted to form a cavalry force to resist the invasion of the state by rebel cavalry. He said that he intended to call for the 10th Ky. He is direct from 'Washington, it is said, on this business. I am of opinion that he has no express orders from the authorities there but has been referred by them to Rosecrans and I think that the whole thing originated with Rosseau himself—in his ambition to get in some position where he would have more chance to keep his name before the people and distinguish himself, and I dont believe that he will succeed in getting his plans carried out. There are various opinions amongst the men—some wanting the change and some prefering infantry.

You say we no doubt miss Colonel Harlan. I cannot tell how much. Since he left us, we have first been under command of one colonel and then another. Colonel Croxton who is now the Senior Colonel is sick and at home. Colonel Este of the 14th Ohio who ranks next is under arrest. And Col. Chapman of the 74th Ind is now commanding the brigade. Without wishing the others any ill I wish that something may turn up so that Colonel Hays may get command of the Brigade,

Everybody is well pleased in the regiment with him. And Col Harlan was never more popular in the regiment than Col Hays is.

Write me about the Post Office. I have not learned anything about it except what Mary and (?) wrote. It has troubled a great deal. It is an unjust and uncalled for on the part of whoever had it done, and I don't believe the people who are interested will thank them for it.

I sent you $20.00 by (Mr. Browne). Hope you have gotten it. I was very much relieved of brother John being in Camp Chase. I had begun to fear that he had been killed as I had not seen his name among the list of prisoners. I am sorry that the Military authorities thought it necessary to prohibit the relations of prisoner from visiting them.

I think he will be confined a long time, as we have such a large excess of prisoners. I am glad he says he is well treated. When did you hear from him. I would like to see him very much, but there is no chance of getting a leave of absence. I suppose he has been moved from Camp Chase. I would have written to him before this, but did not know where to write, and don't know yet. I have been looking for a letter from him. Write me his address. I believe I have not told you yet about our sword presentation. The officers of the regiments made Col Hays and Wharton a present of a nice sword a piece.

The company has also presented me with a very handsome, splendid sword. I feel very much complemented and honored by it, the more so, that after two years service in the field together they have thought me worthy of it.

My love to the home folk, and Dee, My regards to all inquiring friends,

Write soon.

Your Aff son,
Seth

Camp on Elk River
Six Miles South of Tullahoma, Tenn.
July 12, 1863

My Dear Sister,

I have just received your letter sent by Lieutenant Funk, the first word I have had from home since leaving Triune and starting our recent march. I wrote to father from Tullahoma, and since, but have not as yet written to you, having nothing of interest to communicate, save what I have written him. Lieutenant F., so long on the road that my letter was quite old before it reached me yet better late than never.

The boxes started with him have not reached us yet. He could not bring them through with him and consequently had to express them. So I shall have to wait some time yet for the "good things" you have been so kind as to send me.

Well it does seem that the "10th" will never have any hard fighting to do. In the recent advance of the army, Genl (?) selected his old division, ours, and for three days when it was thought that every moment would bring on a general engagement, held it in advance of his whole corps. And for two days before the evacuation of the rebel fortifications at Tullahoma, our Brigade was in advance, and on the morning of the evacuation every man of us from the Major Generals down expected to have had a hard fought battle before gaining possession of the town. But the bird had flown, and we took quiet possession. And the 10th Ky 'was not cut to pieces as I understand it was again reported, it only being on (?) skirmishing.

We have been fasting here for several days, the road being in such terrible condition that our supply trains could not get to us; but it is right now as the cars are running to within five miles of us bringing any quantity of "crackers and bacon."

You would probably have some curiosity to know when we will push on further South and I am sorry I cannot inform you; I would like to be enlightened on that point myself. I think we will move down on the railroad some ten or twelve miles distant in two or three days, and in my opinion, will remain there for at least six or eight weeks and probably longer as I think it impossible to cross the mountains in less time and keep up communication.

I never was in better health or spirits than at present, the only drawback is that you home folks dont write often enough. I should like very much to get a letter from (?) and (wee?) Albert. I would be glad to hear from him again.

I am glad to hear that Dee will be with you so soon, give her my love when she comes and tell her if she will tear up that photograph she has of mine, I will send her a better one. I have one for you and will send it as soon as I think it safe in the mail. They have been so irregular lately that I have thought it scarcely worth while to write at all.

I am glad that you like the (Misses) Carter so well, and are enjoying yourself so much, hope you will see a good (time) at the picnic, or rather have seen for I suppose it is over before this.

You have never said anything (?) Covington leaving town and going back. I have heard through John's letters, I believe. Has anybody heard from him since he left. Write me what you know about him. I want to write to him—what is his address. If you dont know find out from Sue. I know she does. By the by how is Sue. When Mollie was at home I always knew how Sue was getting on, and where she was or had been, for Mollie and she were almost inseperable and if I heard of the one I also heard of the other. Give her my regards.

We have had great jollifications about the good news from Vicksburg and the Potomac. Our batteries have been firing Salutes and the men throwing their hats in the air over the news. Surely there never has been so dark a day for the Southern Confederacy as this. And yet with all of this, how sadly disappointed will this be who carried away by the enthusiasm of the moment look forward to only a few short months of war, think they see beyond the dark lowering clouds of desolation the sunshine of peace already breaking through. No, the end is not yet. But God grant it may come as soon as the most hopeful expect it.

I have heard the reports about Morgan taking Lebanon and passing through Springfield. I am exceeding sorry that Morgan has been able to again make an invasion of the State with safety. I had hoped that such dispositions had been made of the forces of our State that it would no longer be subjected to his raids. And then the papers have published accounts of atrocities committed by his men which I pray may not turn out to be true, and which I cannot believe to be true for with all his faults and crimes John Morgan has won the title of being kind and generous to his prisoners, as I have heard some who have been taken by him testify. And for my brothers sake I hope it may not be true, for as I know that he would scarce to be a party to such treatment and such atrocities as I hear have been committed, I hope that none with whom he is associated have done so. I know he must have been very happy to get home and that you were all glad to see him. I would it were so that I could meet him as I would like to. Perhaps the time may come when forgetful of the past we may again be brothers as we have been. God grant it may. Nothing would give me more pleasure. Thinking of him has reminded me of something you wrote to me about not long since—that it had been hinted to you by some persons that you were not doing your duty to me as a sister by being so decided in your opinions in opposition to mine when I was in the army and by speaking so freely in my presence. No, my sister, if I thought for a moment that you could for one instant believe that I could think the less of you, or love you the less, because you do not think as I do, or because you have been candid enough to tell me so, I would indeed be grieved. I am more generous to my enemy on the battle field than that. Am I to believe that every rebel who marches forth from his home to meet me on the battle field as a bad hearted man who that can (?) dispassionately and without prejudice think about this contest can for a moment think so. AmI to spurn my brother because he has espoused the cause he has, however much I may condemn him in it? Am I to have any the less brotherly affection from him, however much I may regret the action? You have always known how I have felt about this. I shall feel the same about it always. I would be glad if everyone I loved could think as I do. It would give me great pleasure. But whatever difference there may between us, I shall love you and all of you none the less.

I am glad you have come to the conclusion to stop talking. It certainly does no good and has a tendency to estrange you from your friends, and I am not sure should such be the case the fault would be as much yours as any (that's) of your friends.

Say to Dee for me that I want her to convert you to the true faith. Tell father I want him to answer my letters, and give me all the local news, and, indeed, you must write oftener.

My regards to an inquiring friends.

Your (?) Bro.
Seth

Camp Thomas
Near Winchester, Tenn Aug 12th 1863
My dear father,

I have not written to you for some time, and have not had a letter from you for a long, long while. One of Mary's or (?'s) letter mentioned that you had written to me; your letter has never reached me. I wrote you from the camp on Elk River, in last month but have never heard whether you received it or not. So I thought that instead of answering Mary's letter, I would write to you tonight.

We are under marching orders. Will certainly march tomorrow or the next day. Where, I can not tell, though the general impression is that we go in the direction of Bridgeport Ala, which is the point at which the Memphis and Charleston R.R. crosses the Tennessee River. General impressions in regard to the destination our army are as apt to be wrong as right. We are certainly going somewhere in two or three days and when we get there I can tell you with more certainty where we are. For some reason I am loth to leave here and for some other reasons I would be glad to move down further South, at least across the mountains. It is very warm weather now to march, and the roads will be very dusty. But by marching early in the morning, and going into camp at Ten O'clock, we can do very well, and I dont know but what a march and a change of scene will be good for us. We are encamped now in a nice shady woods, about one mile from Winchester. The Boiling Fork of Elk River runs within four or five hundred yards of the camp, affording a fine opportunity for bathing and one that is not neglected. It is very cold water, being fed by large springs. There are innumerable number of springs an along the banks, anyone of which would in our country be called remarkably large. The water is boiling up from these springs all through the Summer. Winchester is on a hill on the opposite side of the river from our camp which rises gradually from the river bank, though in some places so abruptly as to amount to a Cliff. Going in from this direction I think it presents the prettiest most picturesque appearance of any town I have seen in the South. It has been a town of some importance and one of the most pleasant towns in Tennessee. For although now for more than a year occupied by Troops, it still wears an air of refinement that makes me sorry that (?) now so desolated. If we go to Bridgeport it will take us about six or seven days to get there, for although it is only forty miles, we have the mountains to cross.

We have been living very well for the last few days, the sutlers have been supplying us with cabbage and onions. Cabbage @ 20c per head and onions @ 3 cs piece. We shall soon get plenty of roasting ears here.

Genl Rosecrans reviewed our Division today. It is the first time many of us have seen him.

I would have known him from the photographs I have seen of him, though he is rather heavier made than I had supposed. And is very pleasant in his manner. Gent McCook accompanied him, also Genl Jeff C Davis. These Genls and their staff, together with Genl Brannan (our commander) and his staff presented quite an imposing appearance. It was so very warm that two or three men from the regiment fainted and fell from the effects of heat, and one man from the 74th Indiana had sun stoke falling as if he had been shot through the heart. It is not thought he will recover.

Col. Wharton has a letter from his father saying you and he had taken a box to Lebanon for Gabe and I. I am sorry (Jim) could not send them. The honey you sent by Clem had mostly melted and run out of the box, though we had enough for two or three meals, and the cakes Mary sent were all spoiled. We ate the ham.

Col Hays and Wharton are both in fine health. Col. Hays finds some very attractive rebel ladies in Winchester, he goes there frequently.

Say to (?) that I receive the papers he is kind enough to send me every day or two, and am very thankful for them. I have his letter and will answer soon.

Letter from Captain Israel Webster, Company I, to Mrs. Martha Roaler. Letter located in Private Richard Roaler Pension Record.

Chattanooga, Tenn
Sept. 26, 1863
Mrs. Martha Roaler
Dear Martha

It becomes my painful duty to inform you that your son Richard Roaler, that Brave, that Gallant Boy you loved, whom I loved, who we all loved is dead. He was mortally wounded by the enemy at the Battle of Chickamauga Creek Saturday Sept 19th 1863. He died in the Hospital that night at 9 O'Clock. I think it was about 12 O'Clock (noon) when he received the fatal shot. A musket or rifle ball passed through him entering his bowels and passing out his back. He fell instantly. W. G. Gaddis of our Co and one another took him off the field to the rear where he could get such medical attention he required. His friend Hardister Inman helped him off the field and remained with him until his wound was dressed and was taken back to a Hospital where he died during the night. I deeply sympathize with you in your affliction and pray that God may pour comfort on your bleeding heart, and that his friends of every degree may receive consolation when reflecting upon his past life. I only knew him as a soldier under my special command, and I can say, honestly and truly say that a better or more gallant soldier never fell upon the Battlefield, he was fatally hit while defending his flag of his country standing side by side with the foremost.

His record is clean and his friends reap the benefit of his faithful feeling. I have his Pocket Book containing his money all safe and I will send it to the Administration as soon as I learn who has been appointed to settle his account with you. I would suggest that you appoint James M. Fidler to attend to his business, if he will accept the appointment. Ask him to correspond with me and I will respond at once, placing everything connected with his Military History at his disposal.

Please accept my best wishes for your future happiness and peaceful future. Although you are a stranger to me, you have my sympathy. The Mother of a brave and gallant son must receive the respect of all as she certainly does that of

I. B. Webster, Capt.
Com. Co. I 10th Ky., V. I

This letter by Henry G. Davidson, SC 372, is used with permission from the Abraham Lincoln Presidential Library.

Chattanooga, Tenn. Feby 19, 1864
My Dear Aunt,

You no doubt think that I have forgotten my promise to write to you, but I have not. I have thought of you often, and always with great love and affection. Next to my dear mother, of all women, Aunt Mary has been to me the best loved, and how could it be otherwise? Often and often, do I look back to my school boy days with fondest recollections. Happy days were those when Mr. Jones taught us in the old log school house. Carmi and its surroundings are sacred to me—but alas! how may changes have taken place since "old lang syne." The grass grows green over the heads of those we loved most of all on earth. We deeply mourn that they are not with us, but we still fondly cherish a remembrance of their many virtues, and are filled with affectionate recollections of them. Time passes with us too. We stay here but for a while, and when the time arrives for us to go, may we meet them in that land, where there is no grief, nor mourning, and where once having met, there shall be no more parting. May God in his mercy grant that I may again be permitted to meet my Dear Aunt, and her family, not once, but many times. When my duties will allow it, it will afford me the most unalloyed pleasure, to hasten to Carmi, to see you once again. Since leaving your house in August last, my Dear Aunt, I have passed through many dangers and perils, and up to this time unhurt. I found my regiment about twelve miles above on Bridgeport, Ala. on the Tennessee river on the first day of September. Our Division (the 3rd Division, 14th Army Corps) crossed the Tennessee, on rafts, constructed by our own men. A few days we commenced crossing them mountains, on the 14th of the month, we were in Lookout Valley, fourteen miles from Chattanooga completely flanking the enemy. While we were here Bragg evacuated the place, and right here, Gen. Rosecrans committed his first error, instead of marching his army to Chattanooga, taking possession, & making it a base of operations, he divided his forces and went in pursuit of the enemy. The 14th Corps under General Thomas, crossed Lookout Mountain twenty seven miles from Chattanooga, and we found ourselves confronting the whole rebel army eighty five thousand strong. Now Bragg [had] his chance, he could have overwhelmed Thomas, and then turned upon McCook, whose Corps was twenty five miles on our right in the direction of Rome. General Crittenden's Corps, was at Chattanooga, 27 miles on our left. Gen Rosecrans arrived, saw his danger and ordered a concentration of his troops. We staid where we had crossed the mountain boldly confronting Bragg's whole army. McCook was hurried up to us and Crittenden quietly joined us. As soon as a junction was effected the movements towards Chattanooga began, our whole force about fifty thousand men. Bragg immediately took up his line of march, parallel to ours hoping to reach Rossville, before us, cut us off from Chattanooga, and destroy our army and capture all our munitions of war. On Friday the 18th of September, at 5 oclock P.M., we received orders to march, which we did the whole night, the 14th Corps passing the 21st (Gen. Crittenden's Corps). At 7 oclock A.M. on the 19th our Brigade was ordered to attack the enemy, which was done in a most gallant and handsome manner driving them in some confusion a considerable distance. Soon the battle opened vigorously on our right, a short time after on our left, the enemy at this time attempted to flank our Brigade. Our Regiment (the 10 Ky) was ordered to charge them with the bayonet, which we did, driving them back about a quarter of a mile. Upon returning to our place in line of battle, the enemy considerably reinforced, again made a furious onslaught upon us. The whole Brigade stood like a solid wall, and although many a gallant spirit fell, we drove the enemy back not only holding our ground but advancing upon and occupying theirs. Soon a battery was seen getting into position to go to work upon us. Our Brigade (2 Brigade, 3d Div.) was holding an extended line at this time, leaving a gap between the three right, and three left regiments, Col. Hays, of the 10th Ky in command of the 31st Ohio 10th Ky, and 10th Indiana Regiments. He ordered a bayonet Charge, which was performed in a style never surpassed and scarcely ever equaled, there three Regiments, charged, Walker's whole Division of rebel Arkansasians and Misissippians, driving them in the wildest confusion, actually running clear through their lines, capturing many prisioners, and light pieces of artillery. One piece was dismounted, and had to be left on the field. All the artillery horses but one had been killed, forming a line of battle to meet the enemy who had been rallied and were advancing upon us evidently determined to retake their cannon. We determined to keep them or die. A detail was made from each regiment and they went to work with a will, carried every piece off the field by hand. The fighting here was most terrific and bloody, our loss was very heavy at this time. As soon as the cannons were carried away we slowly fell back to our line of battle, where we took position on a small hill, the Rebels attacked us again, and again, but without success, for the last two hours, Gen. Thomas was with us in person—at 2 oclock P.M. we were relieved by Gen. Johnson's division having fought, seven hours, without rest. You can judge how hard we fought, when I tell you that one hundred and twenty one of the brave men of my own regiment were either killed, or wounded, a terrible—terrible thing, but the enemy had suffered far more than we had. We were now ordered about two and a half or three miles to the right, where we bivouacked for the night. The next morning (Sunday) we were placed in position at 3 oclock. Everything was perfectly quiet, until a bout 9 oclock when the enemy attacked Gen. Crittenden on the left, it sounded like the muttering of distant thunder, it came nearer, and nearer, until at last, it reached us. The enemy had massed their entire force and had attacked us most furiously. We held our ground manfully, at this time, a Division on our right was moved to the left, leaving a gap between us and McCook's corps, the enemy taking advantage of this forced us to change our position, and fall back about three hundred yards to a hill, where we hurriedly threw up a small breastwork of logs and rails. About twelve oclock McCook's corps gave way in confusion and now the whole rebel horde rushed on us thinking to achieve an easy victory, again & again they charged us, again & yet again they are driven back. Rosecrans, McCook & Crittenden have left the field, but Gen. Thomas "the noblest Roman of them all" is still with us, cheering us with his noble example & brave" words. Now our ammunition is about to fail, the men silently fix their bayonets without orders, resolved to hold the hill, or make it their grave, in good season Gen. Gordon Granger arrives with part of the reserve corps, the enemy are driven back with great slaughter. Our men have supplied themselves with ammunitions from the boxes of the dead and wounded. In a great many instances, our men would run to a dead or wounded rebel & take his cartridge box and again fall into line. Several prisoners were taken, and their ammunition immediately given out to the men. The Rebels fought bravely and stubbornly, they approached in some instances to within twenty yards of us and in one instance a Rebel color bearer planted his flag within five steps of our rail breastwork, he fell pierced by a hundred balls, in another case a rebel approached so close that one of our men jumped over the works caught him by the collar and dragged him into the midst of the Regiment. The hill was covered with the dead & wounded Rebels. Our own loss was much lighter than on Saturday being protected by the logs and rails. My regiment lost forty four men this day, making a total of one hundred and sixty five killed and wounded out of four hundred and fifty two. It would be impossible for me to give you an accurate description of the battle this day—imagine two hundred pieces of cannon belching forth, and seventy five or eighty thousand muskets firing all at the same time. The grape shot cannister, and bullets fell around thicker and faster than any hail storm you ever witnessed. At seven oclock P.M. when it was quite dark we withdrew quietly, and without being molested by the enemy, and camped for the night at Rossville. The next morning rations and ammunition were served out to the men, and we prepared to renew the struggle, but the enemy were too badly crippled to pursue. On Monday night we retired to Chattanooga.

It may be interesting to you to know that the Brigade to which I am attached was the first to begin the battle, and the last troops to leave the field. All day Tuesday our men worked manfully throwing up intrenchments, on Wednesday the enemy appeared in sight and took position on Mission Ridge three miles in our front. We expected an instant attack. Everybody said let them come we are ready now, but they did not come, and the consequence was that in two weeks time, Chattanooga has simply impregnable—but now a more fearful enemy than Gen Bragg seemed about to attack us. Famine seemed to stare us in the face. But every man determined to hold Chattanooga, it had cost us too much to abandon it to the enemy again. While things were at their worst Gen Grant arrived. Gen. Hooker also arrived with a part of the army of the Potomac, a skillful move gave us possession of the river to within eight miles of the city, from which place we easily hauled our supplies, rations became easier, everything more plenty.

<hr />

Ringgold Georgia March 7th 1864

At this stage of my letter I commence again. I had to leave off on the foregoing page having had marching orders delivered to me while writing, since which time I have again been under the enemy's fire near Dalton, GA.

To resume where I left off. After a month of quiet. Everything indicated that the army was to again be put in motion, and on the 23rd of November, Hookers cannon was heard on our right, the fight on Lookout Mountain had begun. Our Brigade was encamped at the foot of the mountains and about one mile & a half from it so that we had a full view of what was going on. Just a few stragglers were seen, then a column of Rebels turning the point towards us, and then the old flag borne rapidly forward, floated proudly on the breeze—such cheering and shouting, you never heard in your life. The Rebels were driven completely from the mountain. The next evening the 14th Army Corps were moved forward in front of Chattanooga while Sherman attacked the right of the Rebels. The newspapers hardly give you a full account of this fight. Then on Wednesday Nov, 25th we lay quiet until three oclock P.M. when the word to advance was given. No soldiers ever want to battle in such splendid spirits. With one wild, loud, cheer the men went forward, up up, the steep rugged sides of Mission Ridge the soldiers go, each one as best he can. Mounted officers threw themselves from their horses, and climbed the steep ascent. The Rebels made a stand against our Brigade, our men made a furious assault, & the Rebel line is broken. They form again & endeavor to retake the Ridge. We charge then and scatter them to the winds, the fight is ended, the Rebels fly in disorder. The stars & stripes wave over Mission Ridge, and the great victory of the war is won. I am fearful I have tired you, my Dear Aunt, but hope you will be glad to hear from me, although in so long a letter. My health is excellent. We have had a hard campaign for the past two weeks, but are again quiet. Give my love to Tom & Lue, and remember me to all my friends in Carmi. Hoping to hear from you soon I am

Most Affectionately Your Nephew,
Henry G Davidson

<hr />

Letters written by Sgt. Edward Mittler to his wife, Margat. These letters were written in German. They are located at the National Archives in Sgt. Mittler's pension file.

New Marietta, Ga July 2nd 64
My beloved Margat—

Last night, I received your two letters dated the 22nd and 25th of the last month. It afforded me great pleasure, to hear, that you and the children are well, which after all, is the best we can wish for. You seem to be worried yet, on account of my wound, I can assure you, that is not necessary, as every sign of it, has disappeared. God has protected me—for, the ball passed through the filled water canteen of my neighbor to the left before it struck me, had the bullet struck me, without taking the course which, it did, I would surely not be able to write to you now. At the time of the occurrence we were behind a fence, and I was just upon the point of firing, when the bullet—stuck me, having only a black mark, which disappeared in the course of a few days.

We are no nearer to Marietta, as we were 14 days ago, and I think, that Sherman himself is not able to say how long we will yet remain in this position. Our fortifications are only 20 foot from those of the rebels. Last Monday, our whole line, made an attack upon the rebels, but did not gain much by it. We lost about 8–900 men which we buried Wednesday, while under a Flag of Truce. Our regiment was so fortunate as to be on the march,—in order to change position, therefore did not take part in this engagement. This work has been pretty quiet until this morning, when at day-break our artillery opened fire, to which the rebels, however, responded but very little.

It is very hot, down here,—a great many are sick and have to go back.

I will now close this Epistle, Please do not forget to send stamps.

Kiss the children for me—Many greetings and kisses for you dear wife.

I remain yours for ever,
Edward

⁊⁄

Chattanooga, July 7th 1864
My beloved Margat:

You will be surprised on seeing that any letter is dated from here, as my letter from the 2nd was written on the battle field. Saturday night, the rebels left their fortifications and Sunday morning we received marching order—to pursue the rebels. As I had not been here very well for several days, I was brought to the railroad in an ambulance. We were on the road, for two days—and since yesterday I am here in the Convalescent Camp, and I probably will remain here. You must not allow yourself to be worried on my account I am not well, but I hope that I will be alright soon. I do not care, where I am, for the rest of my time. I will write to you again in 2 or 3 days. You must not answer this letter, as I do not know, how long I will have to stay here, I will be able to tell you in my last letter.

Kiss the children for me—

Yours for ever
Edward

⁊⁄

Chattanooga, July 12/64
Much beloved Margat:

I cannot forbear, to write to you a few lines, not withstanding that I do not know of any news, of which I could inform you—I am better, and hope to be entirely well in a short time. My captain, has informed me, through Capt. Riley,—that I will have to go to Bridgeport Ala. where I will have to attend to the Company Books. I expect a letter from Hill, and also other papers—and hope that I will be in receipt of the same in about 2 or 3 days when I leave here, for Bridgeport. I will write to you as soon as I arrive in that place, if possible. I wish I was 4 months older.

You must not answer this letter, as your letter would probably not reach me. I will write to you, as soon as I am acquainted with my place of destination. Until then, farewell. Kiss the children for me, as I kiss and embrace you.

Yours for ever,
Edward

⁊⁄

Bridgeport, Ala July 18/64
Much beloved Margat

I left Chattanooga, yesterday at noon and arrived here, last night. Probably, I will have to stay here, for some time, to rest myself, my legs are swollen, and I am not able to walk about, much at present. I have not received a letter from you, since the 30th of last month, and you can imagine how anxiously I am looking for one. I am out of stamps, please send me some.

Kiss the children for me—as I kiss and embrace you,

For ever yours
Edward

Bridgeport, Ala July 23/64
Much beloved Margat

Notwithstanding, that I have not yet received a letter from you—I cannot forbear to write you, a few lines, hoping that your birthday has found you in the enjoyment of good health.—

Dear wife, there is something which troubles me, namely the Paymaster, has not yet been here and I doubt that we will be paid off before the expiration of our time, which will be on the 21st of November. If you could manage to get along until then, I would be glad, if not I will write to Conrad, to give you some money, therefore, let me know, when you are in need of it.

As far as I am concerned, I can inform you, that I am better, and my knees are almost alright again. I will close, for this time, hoping, to hear from you, soon.

Direct your letter: Sergt Edward Mittler
Bridgeport, Ala

Bridgeport, Ala July 30/64
Much beloved Margat

Last night I received your letter of the 21st. I cannot describe to you, the pleasure it afforded me, to hear, that all of you are well. I see that you are worried on my account. I am well again. All I have to do here, is writing. I have a good rest, and only 12 of our division are here. You say I should try to get to Louisville, in the Hospital, and hope that I will never to go to one of them and if it was but for one day.

In my next letter, I will enclose a few lines for mother.

It is again very warm today and I will go soon, to cool off, in the Tennessee River.

I will now close, hoping to hear from you, soon.

For ever yours,
Edward

Bridgeport, September 17/64
Much beloved Margat

I am writing these few lines in haste. Our regiment will leave here in the morning, for Ring-gold, and I will write to you, as soon, as we arrive at that place. This is my 4th letter to you— Why do you not write?

Kiss our children, as I kiss and embrace you

For ever yours
Edward

Ringgold, Sept 22nd 1864
Much beloved Margat:

Your welcome letter of the 10th inst. I received on Sunday morning, where we were on the point of leaving Bridgeport. The regiment arrived here, last Sunday,—and our loss in the Battle of Jonesboro—Sept. the 1st was not as great as I had imagined. Two members of my company were killed, two wounded, one of them lost a leg, both our lieutenants were wounded, though not dangerously. Our company is stationed between Ringgold and Dalton, and all the duty I have to perform is keep the books of the company.

McKay is well and sends his regards.

We have not yet received any money, therefore, if you are out of money you will have to lend you some. I do not think it will be very long until we get paid off. My dear wife It will not be more than two months until I can again press you to my heart and I am looking forward, to that hour, with excessive desire.

Yours, for ever,
Edward

Chapter Notes

Chapter 1

1. Kent Masterson Brown, *The Civil War in Kentucky* (Mason City, Iowa: Savas, 2000), p. 5.

2. Ibid., p. 8.

3. Nash Hayes, "The Civil War in Marion County," *History of the Marion County, Kentucky, Vol. I* (Marion County Historical Society, 2001), pp. 192–194.

4. John Harlan, "John Marshall Harlan," John Marshall Harlan Papers, 1816–1911, Library of Congress.

5. John Marshall Harlan, An autobiographical letter written to his son, July 4, 1911 (University of Louisville, School of Law Collection).

6. John Harlan, "Some Experiences a Captain of Home Guards," John Marshall Harlan Papers, 1816–1911, Library of Congress.

7. *Biographic Encyclopedia of Kentucky* (Cincinnati, Ohio: J.M. Armstrong, 1878), p. 281.

8. Arthur Kelly, "Hays Family History," unpublished.

9. *Louisville Commercial*, February 23, 1887, p. 1, col. 8.

10. *Biographic Encyclopedia of Kentucky*, p. 65.

11. *Louisville Courier-Journal*, February 23, 1887, p. 1, col. 1.

12. W.H. Perrin, J.H. Battle, and G.C. Kniffin, *Kentucky: A History of the State* (Louisville, Ky.: F.A. Battey, 1887), pp. 919–920.

13. National Archives, Pension Records.

14. "Richard Nash. Died," *Louisville Daily Journal*, February 11, 1865.

15. William McChord, "History of His Life" (Photocopy of typescript, 1923), pp. 40–52.

16. Harlan, Autobiographical letter.

17. "Ancient Letter is of Interest—Communication Found in War Issues of Louisville Journal Refers to Military Activities Here in Civil War Period, October 12, 1861," *Springfield Sun*, 1936.

18. McChord, pp. 40–52.

19. Brandon Slone, Kentucky Military History Museum, personal communication. Not published.

20. Harlan, Autobiographical letter.

21. Regimental Order Book, National Archives, 1861.

22. Regimental Records, Kentucky Historical Society, 1861.

23. Tenth Kentucky Infantry Regimental Record Book, National Archives.

24. *Louisville Daily Journal*, October 1861.

25. Thomas Speed, *Union Regiments of Kentucky* (Union Soldiers and Sailors Monument Association of Louisville, Kentucky, 1879), pp. 367–379.

26. 10th Kentucky Regimental Order Book, National Archives.

27. Thomas Speed, *The Union Cause in Kentucky, 1860–1865*. Foreword by John Harlan (New York: G.P. Putnam's Sons, 1907), p. v–ix.

28. *Report of the Adjutant General of the State of Kentucky, Vol. 1: 1861–1866* (Printed at the Kentucky Yeoman Office, 1866), pp. 806–823.

29. Hilpp Adolph and Freddie Hilpp family records, Lebanon, Ky.

30. "Capt. Hilpp Dead," *Louisville Courier Journal*, April 10, 1908, p. 3, col. 2.

31. "Joseph Adcock. Obituary," *The Historical Encyclopedia of Illinois and History of McDonough County*, Dr. Newton Bateman and Paul Shelby, comp. (Chicago: Munsell, 1907).

32. *History of Pottawatomie County, Iowa, Part 2* (Chicago: Thomas Clark, 1907), pp. 743–46.

33. "War Ills," *Courier Journal*, March 10, 1902, p. 10, col. 3.

Chapter 2

1. Kenneth Hafendorfer, *Mill Springs: Campaign and Battle of Mill Springs, Kentucky* (Louisville, Ky.: KH Press, 2001), pp. 29–32.

2. Ibid., pp. 130–132.

3. Abraham Lincoln, Letter to Orville H. Browning, September 22, 1861.

4. Kent Masterson Brown, *The Civil War in Kentucky* (Mason City, Iowa: Savas, 2000), pp. 47–77.

5. *Louisville Journal*, January 15, 1862.

6. John Marshall Harlan Papers, Library of Congress.

7. Israel B. Webster, *National Tribune*, April 21, 1892.

8. Harlan Papers.

9. Charles McKay, Pension File, National Archives.

10. Hafendorfer, p. 165.

11. Ibid., p. 283.

12. G.B. Crittenden, *Official Records*, Vol. 7, p. 107.

13. Ibid., p. 110.

14. John Marshall Harlan, An autobiographical letter written to his son, July 4, 1911 (University of Louisville).

15. *Louisville Journal*, January 27, 1862.

16. Harlan Papers.

17. Richard Boyle, *National Tribune*, January 24, 1907.

18. Harlan Papers.

19. John Harlan, *Official Records*, Vol. 7, pp. 88–90.

20. *Report of the Adjutant General of the State of Kentucky, Vol. 1: 1861–1866* (Kentucky Yeoman Office, 1866), pp. 806–823.

21. Ibid., pp. 806–823.

22. Thomas Speed, *Union Regiments of Kentucky*, 1879 (Union Soldiers and Sailors Monument Association of Louisville, Kentucky, 1879), pp. 367–379.

23. Harlan Papers.

24. Ibid.

25. James Scott, letter to his parents, Pension Record, National Archives, 1862.

26. 10th Kentucky Regimental Order Book, National Archives, 1862.

27. Mary Kate Atkisson, letter, Kentucky Historical Society, 1862.

28. *Washington County, Kentucky, Bicentennial History: 1792–1992* (Paducah, Ky.: Turner, 1991), p. 250.

29. I.B. Webster, Pension Record, National Archives.

30. Civil War Pension Records, National Archives.

31. Jack Mills, Pension Record, National Archives.

32. John McCauley, Pension Record, National Archives.

33. John Harlan, "March from Mississippi into Kentucky," John Marshall Harlan Papers, Library of Congress, 1816–1911.

34. Ibid.

35. Ibid.

36. Frank Armstrong, *Official Records*, Vol. 22, pp. 827–828.

37. John Harlan, *Official Records*, Vol. 22, pp. 822–824.

38. Armstrong, Vol. 22, pp. 827–828.

39. "A Little Story of Fight and Prisoners of War," Letter from Col. W.L. Curry to Judge Kumpe, January 24, 1916, Columbus, Ohio. *Moulton Advertiser*, February 9, 1916.

40. Don C. Buell, *Official Records*, Vol. 22, pp. 819–820.

41. Harlan Papers.

42. Harlan Papers.

43. Ibid.

44. "Traitor Clergyman Arrested," *Nashville Daily Union*, August 8, 1862, p. 3, col. 1.

45. Doris Kelso, "The Arrest of Dr. Mitchell by Union Forces," *History of the First Presbyterian Church* (First Presbyterian Church, 1968), pp. 30–32.

46. Harlan Papers.

47. Ibid.

48. Kenneth W. Noe, *Perryville: This Grand Havoc of Battle* (Lexington: University Press of Kentucky, 2001), p. 98.

49. James Lee McDonough, *War in Kentucky: From Shiloh to Perryville* (Knoxville: University of Tennessee Press, 1994), pp. 30–60.

50. Harlan Papers.

51. Ibid.

52. Ibid.

53. Gwinn Thompson Hahn, story told by her grandmother, Ollie Crouch Moore, daughter of Martin V. Crouch.

54. Richard Grace, Pension Record, National Archives.

55. John Harlan, *Official Records*, Vol. 29, December 4, 1862, pp. 24–25.

56. Letter by William H. Hays, 1862, Nash Hayes Collection.

57. William F. O'Bryan, letter, 1862, Pension Record, National Archives.

58. John Marshall Harlan, "Battle of Hartsville," John Marshall Harlan Papers, Library of Congress, 1816–1911.

59. John Harlan, *Official Records*, Vol. 29, pp. 47–48.

60. Harlan, "Battle of Hartsville."

61. Harlan, *Official Records*, December 12, 1862, p. 49.

62. Harlan, "Battle of Hartsville."

63. Edison Thomas, *John Hunt Morgan and His Raiders* (University Press of Kentucky, 1985), p. 65.

64. Ibid., p. 61.

65. John Marshall Harlan, "My Pursuit of John Hunt Morgan," John Marshall Harlan Papers, Library of Congress.

66. Arthur L. Kelly, *Crowded Moment: Morgan Brings the Civil War to Springfield* (Springfield, Ky.: A.L. Kelly, 2003), p. 13.

67. John Marshall Harlan, *Official Records*, Vol. 29, pp. 137–139.

68. Harlan, "My Pursuit."

69. Harlan, *Official Records*, p. 141.

70. John H. Morgan, *Official Records*, Vol. 29, pp. 154–158.

71. 10th Kentucky Order Book, National Archives.

Chapter 3

1. Lt. Col. G.C. Kniffin, U.S.V. "The Battle of Stones River," *Battles and Leaders of the Civil War*, Robert Underwood Johnson and Clarence Clough Buel, eds., Vol. 3 (Castle Books, 1985), pp. 613–615.

2. 10th Kentucky Infantry Regimental Record Book, National Archives.

3. John Marshall Harlan, *Official Records*, Vol. 34, pp. 20–22.

4. Thomas Speed, *Union Regiments of Kentucky* (Union Soldiers and Sailors Monument Association of Louisville, Kentucky, 1879), pp. 367–379.

5. William O'Bryan, letter, 1863, in Pension Record, National Archives.

6. James Scott, letter, 1863, in Pension Record, National Archives.

7. John Marshall Harlan, An autobiographical letter written to his son, July 4, 1911 (University of Louisville).

8. "John Marshall Harlan." John M. Harlan Papers, Library of Congress.

9. *Report of the Adjutant General of the State of Kentucky, Vol. 1: 1861–1866* (Kentucky Yeoman Office, 1866), pp. 806–823.

10. U.S. Census Records, 1850–1860.

11. "To Be Brigadier Generals," November 29, 1862, *Executive Journal*, January 22, 1863, pp. 92–93.

12. Seth Bevill, letter in Pension Record, National Archives.

13. Court-martial Record, Capt. Seth Bevill, National Archives.

14. Court-martial Record, Lt. James Sallee, National Archives.

15. Ibid.

16. Court-martial Record, Capt. Charles McKay, National Archives.

17. Court-martial Record. Pvt. Isaac Hicks, National Archives.

18. Court-martial Record, Pvt. Jefferson Perkins, National Archives.

19. Court-martial Record, Pvt. Daniel Richardson, National Archives.

20. Court-martial Record, Pvt. Tandy Greier, National Archives.

21. Court-martial Record, Pvt. James Burnell, National Archives.

22. Ibid.

23. *Official Records*, Vol. 34, p. 216.

24. James Milburn, Pension Record, National Archives.

25. Jerry Korn, *Fight for Chattanooga* (Time-Life Books, 1985), pp. 18–30.

26. *Official Records*, Vol. 34, p. 413.

27. William Rosecrans, "From Tullahoma to Chattanooga," *Battles and Leaders of the Civil War*, Vol. 5. Peter Cozzens, ed. (University of Illinois Press, 2002), pp. 410–421.

28. Ezra J. Warner, *Generals in Blue: Lives of the Union Commanders* (Baton Rouge: Louisiana State University Press, 1964), pp. 42–43.

29. John Brannan, *Official Records*, Vol. 34, p. 451.

30. Ibid., pp. 451–452.

31. Ibid., p. 452.

32. Israel Webster, Pension Records, National Archives.

33. Charles Hardesty, Service Record, National Archives.

34. Seth Bevill, letter to his sister, 1863, Pension Record, National Archives.

35. Henry Cist, *The Army of the Cumberland* (New York: Charles Scribner's Sons, 1882), pp. 172–173.

36. Bevill, letter to his sister.

37. Scott, James. Letter to his parents, 1863. Scott Pension Record, National Archives.

Chapter 4

1. Seth Bevill, letter to his sister, August 12, 1863, National Archives.

2. Ibid.

3. *Report of the Adjutant General of the State of Kentucky, Vol. 1: 1861–1866* (Printed at the Kentucky Yeoman Office, 1866), pp. 806–823.

4. Henry Davidson, letter, Chattanooga, Tenn., to Mary Davidson Brown, February 19, 1864. Abraham Lincoln Presidential Library and Museum. 9 pages.

5. Peter Cozzens, *This Terrible Sound* (Urbana, Ill.: University of Illinois Press, 1992), pp. 103–110.

6. Ibid., pp. 110, 119.

7. Ibid., pp. 122–124.

8. Ezra J. Warner, *Generals in Blue: Lives of the Union Commanders* (Baton Rouge: Louisiana State University Press, 1964), pp. 42–43.

9. Israel Webster, "Chickamauga: Going into Action with Hands Full of Bacon and Coffee." *National Tribune*, July 2, 1891.

10. Cozzens, pp. 125–126.

11. Webster, "Chickamauga."

12. Cozzens, pp. 126–127.

13. Ibid., p. 128.

14. Tucker, Glenn. *Chickamauga: Bloody Battle in the West* (Dayton, Ohio: Morningside Press, 1984), p. 130.

15. Cozzens, pp. 129–132.

16. *Official Records,* Vol. 50, p. 422.
17. Webster, "Chickamauga."
18. Davidson letter.
19. *Official Records,* Vol. 50, p. 422.
20. Cozzens, p. 131.
21. Steve Woodworth, *A Deep Steady Thunder* (Abilene, Texas: Texas A&M–McWhiney Foundation, 1996), pp. 34–44.
22. Webster, "Chickamauga."
23. Cozzens, pp. 136–138.
24. Ibid.
25. *Official Records,* Vol. 50, p. 422.
26. Davidson letter.
27. Daniel Govan, *Official Records,* Vol. 51, p. 258.
28. *Official Records,* Vol. 50, p. 422–423.
29. Davidson letter.
30. "The Battles at Chickamauga," *New York Times,* Sept. 27, 1863, p. 1.
31. Webster, "Chickamauga."
32. Ibid.
33. *Official Records,* Vol. 50, p. 423.
34. Ibid., p. 423.
35. John Brannan, *Official Records,* Vol. 50, p. 402.
36. Davidson letter.
37. Webster, "Chickamauga."
38. Cozzens, pp. 374–375.
39. *Official Records,* Vol. 50, p. 423.
40. Brannan, Vol. 50, p. 402.
41. Adjutant General's Report, pp. 806–823.
42. William Beglow, Pension Record, National Archives.
43. Benjamin Smith, Pension Record, National Archives.
44. Henry Warren, Pension Record, National Archives.
45. James Sallee, Pension Record, National Archives.
46. Brannan, Vol. 50, p. 402.
47. Henry Kingsbury, *Official Records,* Vol. 50, p. 425.
48. Cozzens, pp. 424–426.
49. Ibid., 425.
50. John Bowers, *Chickamauga and Chattanooga* (New York: Harper Collins, 2001), p. 148.
51. Brannan, Vol. 50, p. 402.
52. Davidson letter.
53. Webster, "Chickamauga."
54. Cozzens, pp. 470–477.
55. Gabriel Wharton, *Official Records,* Vol. 50, pp. 423–424.
56. Bowers, *Chickamauga and Chattanooga,* p. 152.
57. "The Battles at Chickamauga," *New York Times,* Sept. 27, 1863, p. 1.
58. *Louisville Daily Journal,* November 3, 1863.
59. William Kelley, Pension Record, National Archives.
60. Henry Dunn, Pension Record, National Archives.
61. Brannan, Vol. 50, p. 404.
62. Ibid., p. 405.
63. Webster, "Chickamauga."
64. Davidson letter.
65. Henry Cist, *The Army of the Cumberland* (New York: Charles Scribner's Sons, 1882), pp. 192–193.
66. Tenth Kentucky Regimental Record Book, National Archives.

Chapter 5

1. 10th Kentucky Regimental Record Book, National Archives.
2. William H. Hays, *Official Records,* Vol. 55, pp. 540–542.
3. Henry Dunn, Pension Record, National Archives.
4. Benjamin Smith, Pension Record, National Archives.
5. Henry Warren, Pension Record, National Archives.
6. James Davenport, Pension Record, National Archives.
7. *Report of the Adjutant General of the State of Kentucky, Vol. 1: 1861–1866* (Printed at the Kentucky Yeoman Office, 1866), pp. 806–823.
8. Andersonville Prison Records, National Parks Service, United States Department of the Interior.
9. Henry Davidson, letter, Chattanooga, Tenn., to Mary Davidson Brown, February 19, 1864. Abraham Lincoln Presidential Library and Museum. 9 pages.
10. Wiley Sword, *Mountains Touched with Fire* (New York: St. Martin's Press, 1995), p. 38.
11. Ibid.
12. Ibid.
13. Davidson letter.
14. Israel Webster, "Missionary Ridge," *National Tribune,* March 10, 1892.
15. Ibid., pp. 42–44.
16. Ibid., pp. 99–104.
17. Columbus Filiatreau, letter to Ray Filiatreau, November 24, 1918, "Descendants of Kentucky," Blandford family papers, unpublished.
18. Josiah Vestrees, Pension Record, National Archives.
19. Peter Cozzens, The Shipwreck of Their Hopes (Urbana and Chicago: University of Illinois, 1994), p. 7.
20. Ibid., p. 4.
21. "Death List of a Day. Gen. Absalom Baird." *New York Times,* June 15, 1905.
22. *Official Records,* Vol. 54, p. 807.
23. Court-martial Record, Pvt. Adam Arnold, National Archives.
24. Court-martial Record, Pvt. Jerry Arnold, National Archives.
25. Court-martial Record, Pvt. Royal Clark, National Archives.
26. Ibid.
27. John Bowers, *Chickamauga and Chattanooga: The Battles That Doomed the Confederacy* (New York: Harper Perennial, 1995), pp. 223–229.
28. Cozzens, p. 248.
29. Ibid.
30. Webster letter.
31. Ibid.
32. Cozzens, p. 265.
33. Baird, Absalom. *Official Records,* Vol. 55, pp. 508–509.
34. Cozzens, p. 265.
35. Gabriel Wharton, *Official Records,* Vol. 55, pp. 547–549.
36. Webster letter.
37. Ibid.
38. Ibid.
39. Baird, Vol. 55, pp. 509–511.
40. Cozzens, p. 325.
41. Thomas Ireton, letter to his brother, Dec. 5, 1863, Thomas Ireton Papers (Pearce Civil War Collection, Navarro College, Coricana, Texas).
42. Wharton, Vol. 55, pp. 547–549.
43. Hays, Vol. 55, pp. 540–542.
44. Cozzens, p. 334.
45. Baird, Vol. 55, p. 510.
46. Davidson letter.
47. Baird, Vol. 55, p. 511.
48. Cozzens, p. 361.

Chapter 6

1. *Report of the Adjutant General of the State of Kentucky, Vol. 1: 1861–1866* (Kentucky Yeoman Office, 1866), p. 806–823.
2. Thomas Speed, *Union Regiments in Kentucky,* (Union Soldiers and Sailors Monument Association of Louisville, Kentucky, 1879), pp. 367–379.
3. Frederick Dyer, *Dyer's Compendium of the War of the Rebellion* (Cedar Rapids, Iowa: Torch Press, 1908).
4. *The Union Army: A History of Military Affairs in the Loyal States 1861–65; Records of the Regiments in the Union Army, Cyclopedia of Battles, Memoirs of Commanders and Soldiers* (Madison: Federal Publishing, 1908), Vol. 8, p. 83.
5. Henry Waller, Pension Record, National Archives.
6. Tenth Kentucky Regimental Record Book, National Archives.
7. George Riley, Pension Record, National Archives.
8. Tenth Kentucky Correspondence, National Archives.
9. Tenth Kentucky Correspondence, National Archives.
10. William H. Hays, *Official Records,* Vol. 72, pp. 816–817.
11. *Report of the Adjutant General,* p. 817.
12. James Champion, Civil War Pension Record, National Archives.
13. Albert Castel, *Decision in the West* (University Press of Kansas, 1992), p. 319.

14. *Report of the Adjutant General*, p. 808–811.

15. Edward Mittler, letter in Pension Record, National Archives, 1864.

16. Ibid.

17. Tenth Kentucky Regimental Record Book.

18. William H. Hays, *Official Records*, Vol. 72, pp. 816–817.

19. Ibid., pp. 816–817.

20. Ibid., pp. 816–817.

21. Andersonville Prison Records, National Parks Service, United States Department of the Interior.

22. Tenth Kentucky Regimental Record Book.

23. Richard Grace, Pension Record, National Archives.

24. Henry Warren, Pension Record, National Archives.

25. George Este, *Official Records*, Vol. 72, pp. 807–808.

26. H.G. Neubert, "Account of the Battle of Chickamauga," *Toledo Blade*, July 23, 1864.

27. Tenth Kentucky Regimental Record Book.

28. Franklin Hill, Pension Record, National Archives.

29. John McCauley, Pension Record, National Archives.

30. Andrew Thompson, Pension Record, National Archives.

31. Court-martial of Pvt. Phillip Brown, National Archives.

32. Castel, pp. 475–480.

33. William Sherman, *Official Records*, Vol. 76, p. 6988.

34. Castel, p. 497.

35. Ibid., p. 499.

36. G.W. Terry, "The Charge at Jonesboro," *National Tribune*, November 4, 1915.

37. George Este, *Official Records*, Vol. 72, p. 810.

38. Castel, p. 517.

39. Terry, "The Charge at Jonesboro."

40. John Green, *Johnny Green of the Orphan Brigade: The Journal of a Confederate Soldier*, Albert. D. Kirwan, ed. (Lexington: University Press of Kentucky, 2002), pp. 152–165.

41. Larry Strayer and Richard Baumgarter, *Echoes of Battle: The Atlanta Campaign* (Huntington, W. Va.: Blue Acorn, 2004), p. 306.

42. Standard Harley, "A Johnny Reb Writes," *National Tribune*, June 11, 1914.

43. Henry Neubert, *Daily Toledo Blade*, September 16, 1864, p. 2.

44. Castel, p. 518.

45. Ibid., p. 518.

46. William H. Hays, *Official Records*, Vol. 72, pp. 817–818.

47. William Beglow, Pension Record, National Archives.

48. William Kelley, Pension Record, National Archives.

49. James Davenport, Pension Record, National Archives.

50. Este, Vol. 72, pp. 812–813.

51. William Carlin, *Official Records*, Vol. 109, pp. 640–641.

52. Henry B. Mattingly, Congressional Medal of Honor File, National Archives.

53. Court-martial of Pvt. Gerald Goodman, National Archives.

54. Court-martial of Pvt. William Goodman, National Archives.

55. Court-martial of Corporal Thomas Jones, National Archives.

56. Court-martial of Pvt. Joseph Uptergrove, National Archives.

57. Court-martial of Pvt. William Lawson, National Archives.

58. Speed, pp. 367–379.

59. Henry Davidson Obituary. *Louisville Daily Democrat*, November 22, 1864, p. 2, col. 4.

60. John Denton, Pension Record, National Archives.

Epilogue

1. Douglas Linder, "Famous Trial Cases," University of Missouri–Kansas City Law School. Unpublished.

2. "Justice Harlan Dies," *New York Times*, Oct. 15, 1911, p. 7.

3. *Biographic Encyclopedia of Kentucky* (Cincinnati, Ohio: J.M. Armstrong, 1878), p. 281.

4. Samuel Wilson, *History of the United States Court for the Eastern District of Kentucky* (Lexington, Ky., 1935), pp. 8–9.

5. *Louisville Courier Journal*, September 7, 1879.

6. "Death of Judge Hays," *Courier Journal*, March 8, 1880.

7. *Biographic Encyclopedia of Kentucky*, p. 65–66.

8. "Col. G.C. Wharton Dead," *Louisville Commercial*, February 23, 1887, p. 1.

9. *Louisville Courier Journal*, February 23, 1887, p. 1, col. 1.

10. *Louisville Daily Democrat*, November 22, 1864, p. 2, col. 4.

11. *Louisville Daily Democrat*, November 23, 1864, p. 2, col. 4.

12. *Louisville Daily Democrat*, November 23, 1864, p. 3, col. 3.

13. W. W. Graves, *Annals of Osage Mission*, 1934, p. 244.

14. W. W. Graves, *Annals of St. Paul*, 1942, p. 345.

15. William Atkisson, Pension Record, National Archives.

16. James Hatchitt, Pension Record, National Archives.

17. "Death of Dr. J.G. Hatchitt," The Frankfort Roundabout, July 18, 1896, p. 1.

18. *Medical History of Michigan*, Vol. II: *Medical Veterans of the Civil War*, Library of Congress Collection, pp. 831–832.

19. Ibid., pp. 831–832.

20. Ibid., pp. 831–832.

21. Charles Stocking, Pension Record, National Archives.

22. U.S. Census Records, 1870, 1880.

23. "Died—Stocking." *Freeport Weekly Journal*, January 26, 1881, p. 8, col. 3.

24. Ibid., p. 8.

25. Charles McKay, Pension Record, National Archives.

26. Henry Warren, Pension Record, National Archives.

27. Ibid.

28. "Grace." *St. Louis Post Dispatch*, September 8, 1925, p. 26.

29. "Major W.J. Lisle Dies Suddenly Yesterday Afternoon," *The Lebanon Enterprise*, June 30, 1911.

30. James Reynolds, Pension Record, National Archives.

31. John Estes, Pension Record, National Archives.

32. John Milburn, Pension Record, National Archives.

33. "Capt. John T. Milburn's Long Illness Ended by Death," *Courier Journal*, March 26, 1891.

34. William O'Bryan, Pension Record, National Archives.

35. John McCauley, Pension Record, National Archives.

36. Robert Short, Pension Record, National Archives.

37. "Capt. Hilpp Dead," *Louisville Courier Journal*, April 10, 1908, p. 3, col. 2.

38. Edward Hilpp, Pension Record, U.S. Department of Veterans Affairs.

39. "Death Takes War Veteran," *Lebanon Enterprise*, October 9, 1923.

40. William Mussen, Pension Record, National Archives.

41. James Sallee, Pension Record, National Archives.

42. "J.E. Sallee is Dead after Long and Patient Suffering," *LaRue County Herald News*, July 28, 1914.

43. George Riley, Pension Record, National Archives.

44. James Mills, Pension Record, National Archives.

45. U.S. Census Records.

46. William Hupp, Pension Record, National Archives.

47. Stephen Dorsey, Pension Record, National Archives.

48. Seth Bevill, Pension Record, National Archives.

49. Andrew Thompson, Pension Record, National Archives.

50. "Andrew Thompson Dead," *Springfield Sun*, October 16, 1899.

51. "The Killing of Funk," *Nelson County Record*, October 23, 1884, p. 1, col. 3.

52. Clem Funk, Pension Record, National Archives.

53. Franklin Hill, Pension Record, National Archives.

54. "Capt. Hill's Death," *Springfield Sun*, October 27, 1898.

55. Benjamin Smith, Pension Record, National Archives.

56. "Joseph Adcock Obituary." *The Historical Encyclopedia of Illinois and History of McDonough County*, Dr. Newton Bateman and Paul Shelby, comp., 1907, p. 808.

57. James Davenport, Pension Record, National Archives.

58. Edward Blandford, Pension Record, National Archives.

59. William Hunter, Pension Record, National Archives.

60. *Washington County, Kentucky, Bicentennial History: 1792–1992* (Paducah, Ky.: Turner, 1991), p. 101.

61. U.S. Census Records, 1870.

62. *History of Pottawatomie County, Iowa, Part 2* (Chicago: Thomas Clark, 1907), pp. 743–46.

63. Henry Dunn, Pension Record, National Archives.

64. William Beglow, Pension Records, National Archives.

65. Ibid.

66. Buford Pendleton, Pension Record, National Archives.

67. I.B. Webster, Pension Record, National Archives.

68. "War Ills," *Courier Journal*, March 10, 1902, p. 10, col. 3.

69. William Kelley, Pension Record, National Archives.

70. John Myers, Civil War Service Record, National Archives.

71. Henry Waller, Pension Record, National Archives.

72. John H. Denton, Dearborn Independent, October 12, 1893.

73. James R. Watts, Pension Record, National Archives.

74. Dick Watts. *Louisville Courier-Journal*, January 18, 1898, p. 3, cols. 1–2.

75. William Tweddle, Pension Record, National Archives.

Bibliography

"Ancient Letter is of Interest—Communication Found in War Issues of Louisville Journal Refers to Military Activities Here in Civil War Period, October 12, 1861." *Springfield Sun*, 1936.

Andersonville Prison Records, National Parks Service, United States Department of the Interior.

"Andrew Thompson Dead." *Springfield Sun*, October 16, 1899.

Armstrong, Frank. *Official Records*. Vol. 22.

Atkisson, Mary Kate. Letter. Kentucky Historical Society, 1862.

Atkisson, William. Pension Record, National Archives.

Baird, Absalom. *Official Records*. Vol. 55.

"The Battles at Chickamauga." *New York Times*, September 27, 1863.

Beglow, William. Pension Record, National Archives.

Bevill, Seth. Letter of August 12, 1863, to his sister. National Archives.

Bevill, Seth. Letter to his sister, 1863, Bevill Pension Record, National Archives.

Bevill, Seth. Pension Record, National Archives.

Biographic Encyclopedia of Kentucky. Cincinnati, Ohio: J.M. Armstrong, 1878.

Blandford, Edward. Pension Record, National Archives.

Blandford family papers. Not published.

Bowers, John. *Chickamauga and Chattanooga*. New York: Harper Collins, 2001.

Bowers, John. *Chickamauga and Chattanooga: The Battles That Doomed the Confederacy*. New York: Harper Perennial, 1995.

Boyle, Richard. *National Tribune*, January 24, 1907.

Brannan, John. *Official Records*. Vol. 34, p. 451.

Brannan, John. *Official Records*. Vol. 50, p. 402.

Brown, Kent Masterson. *The Civil War in Kentucky*. Mason City, Iowa: Savas, 2000.

Buell, Don C. *Official Records*. Vol. 22, pp. 819–820.

"Capt. Hill's Death." *Springfield Sun*, October 27, 1898.

"Capt. Hilpp Dead." *Louisville Courier Journal*, April 10, 1908.

"Capt. John T. Milburn's Long Illness Ended by Death." *Courier Journal*, March 26, 1981.

Carlin, William. *Official Records*. Vol. 109.

Castel, Albert. *Decision in the West*. University Press of Kansas, 1992.

Champion, James. Civil War Pension Record, National Archives.

Cist, Henry. *The Army of the Cumberland*. New York: Charles Scribner's Sons, 1882.

Civil War Pension Records, National Archives.

"Col. G.C. Wharton Dead." *Louisville Commercial*, February 23, 1887.

Court-martial Records, National Archives: Private Adam Arnold, Private Jerry Arnold, Capt. Seth Bevill, Private Phillip Brown, Private James Burnell, Private Royal Clark, Private Gerald Goodman, Private William Goodman, Private Tandy Greier, Private Isaac Hicks, Corporal Thomas Jones, Private William Lawson, Capt. Charles McKay, Private Jefferson Perkins, Private Daniel Richardson, Lt. James Sallee, and Private Joseph Uptergrove.

Cozzens, Peter. *The Shipwreck of Their Hopes*. Urbana and Chicago: University of Illinois, 1994.

Cozzens, Peter. *This Terrible Sound*. Urbana, Ill.: University of Illinois Press, 1992.

Crittenden, G.B. Official Records. Vol. 7.

Davenport, James. Pension Record, National Archives.

Davidson, Henry. Letter: Chattanooga, Tenn., to Mary Davidson Brown, February 19, 1864. Abraham Lincoln Presidential Library and Museum. 9 pages.

Davidson, Henry. Obituary. *Louisville Daily Democrat*, November 22, 1864.

"Death List of a Day: Gen. Absalom Baird." *New York Times*, June 15, 1905.

"Death of Dr. J.G. Hatchitt." *The Frankfort Roundabout*, July 18, 1896.

"Death of Judge Hays." *Courier Journal*, March 8, 1880.

"Death Takes War Veteran." *Lebanon Enterprise*, October 9, 1923.

Denton, John. Pension Record, National Archives.

"Dick Watts." *Louisville Courier Journal*, January 18, 1898.

"Died—Stocking." *Freeport Weekly Journal*, January 26, 1881.

Dorsey, Stephen. Pension Record, National Archives.

Dunn, Henry. Pension Record, National Archives.

Dyer, Frederick. *Dyer's Compendium of the War of the Rebellion*. Cedar Rapids, Iowa: Torch Press, 1908.

Este, George. *Official Records*. Vol. 72.

Estes, John. Pension Record, National Archives.

Filiatreau, Columbus, letter to Ray Filiatreau, November 24, 1918. "Descendants of Kentucky." Blandford family papers, unpublished.

Funk, Clem. Pension Record, National Archives.

Govan, Daniel. *Official Records*. Vol. 51.

"Grace." *St. Louis Post Dispatch*, September 8, 1925.

Grace, Richard. Pension Record, National Archives.

Graves, W.W. *Annals of Osage Mission*. St. Paul, Kansas: published by W.W. Graves, 1934.

Graves, W.W. *Annals of St. Paul*. St. Paul, Kansas: Journal Press, 1942.

Green, John W., and Albert D. Kirwan. *Johnny Green of the Orphan Brigade: The Journal of a Confederate Soldier*. Louisville: University Press of Kentucky, 2002.

Hafendorfer, Kenneth. *Mill Springs: Campaign and Battle of Mill Springs, Kentucky*. Louisville, Ky.: KH Press, 2001.

Hahn, Gwinn Thompson. Story told by her grandmother, Ollie Crouch Moore, daughter of Martin V. Crouch, and passed on to author.

Hardesty, Charles. Service Record. National Archives.

Harlan, John Marshall. An autobiographical letter written to his son, July 4, 1911. University of Louisville, School of Law Collection.

_____. "Battle of Hartsville." John Marshall Harlan Papers, Library of Congress, 1816–1911.

_____. "John Marshall Harlan." John Marshall Harlan Papers, Library of Congress, 1816–1911.

_____. "March from Mississippi into Kentucky." John Marshall Harlan Papers, Library of Congress, 1816–1911.

_____. "My Pursuit of John Hunt Morgan." John Marshall Harlan Papers, Library of Congress.

_____. *Official Records*. Volume 7, pp. 88–90; Vol. 22; Vol. 29, December 4, 1862, pp. 24–25; Vol. 34. pp. 20–22.

_____. "Some Experiences a Captain of Home Guards." John Marshall Harlan Papers, Library of Congress, 1816–1911.

Harley, Standard. "A Johnny Reb Writes." *National Tribune*, June 11, 1914.

Hatchitt, James. Pension Record, National Archives.

Hayes, Nash. "The Civil War in Marion County." *History of the Marion County, Kentucky, Vol. I*. Published by the Marion County Historical Society, 2001, pp. 192–194.

Hays, William H. Letter. Nash Hayes Collection, 1862.

_____. *Official Records*. Vol. 55, pp. 540–542; Vol. 72, pp. 816–817.

Hill, Franklin. Pension Record, National Archives.

Hilpp, Edward. Pension Record, U.S. Department of Veterans' Affairs.

Hilpp family records. Adolph and Freddie Hilpp, Lebanon, Ky.

History of Pottawatomie County, Iowa 1907. Part 2. Chicago: Thomas Clark, 1907.

Hunter, William. Pension Record, National Archives.

Hupp, William. Pension Record, National Archives.

Ireton, Thomas. Letter to his brother. Thomas Ireton Papers, 1863. Pearce Civil War Collection. Navarro College, Coricana, Texas, December 5, 1863.

"J.E. Sallee is Dead after Long and Patient Suffering." *LaRue County Herald News*, July 28, 1914.

"John H. Denton." *Dearborn Independent*, October 12, 1893.

"Joseph Adcock Obituary." *The Historical Encyclopedia of Illinois and History of McDonough County*. Compiled by Dr. Newton Bateman and Paul Shelby, 1907.

"Justice Harlan Dies." *New York Times*, October 15, 1911.

Kelley, William. Pension Record, National Archives.

Kelly, Arthur. "Hays Family History." Unpublished.

Kelly, Arthur L. *Crowded Moment: Morgan Brings the Civil War to Springfield*. Springfield, Ky.: A.L. Kelly, 2003.

Kelso, Doris. "The Arrest of Dr. Mitchell by Union Forces." *History of the First Presbyterian Church*. First Presbyterian Church, publisher, 1968.

"The Killing of Funk." *Nelson County Record*, October 23, 1884.

Kingsbury, Henry. *Official Records*. Vol. 50.

Kniffin, G.C., Lieutenant Colonel, U. S. V. "The Battle of Stones River." *Battles and Leaders of the Civil War, Vol. 3*. Robert Underwood Johnson and Clarence Clough Buel, eds. Castle Books, 1985.

Korn, Jerry. *Fight for Chattanooga*. Time-Life Books, 1985.

Lincoln, Abraham. Letter to Orville H. Browning, September 22, 1861.

Linder, Douglas. "Famous Trial Cases." Unpublished. University of Missouri–Kansas City Law School.

"A Little Story of Fight and Prisoners of War." Letter from Col. W.L. Curry to Judge Kumpe. January 24, 1916. Columbus, Ohio. *Moulton Advertiser*, February 9, 1916.

Louisville Commercial, February 23, 1887.

Louisville Courier Journal, September 7, 1879.

Louisville Daily Democrat, November 22, 1864.

Louisville Daily Democrat, November 23, 1864.

Louisville Daily Journal, October 1861.

Louisville Daily Journal, November 3, 1863.

Louisville Journal, January 15, 1862.

Louisville Journal, January 27, 1862.

"Major W. J. Lisle Dies Suddenly Yesterday Afternoon." *The Lebanon Enterprise*, June 30, 1911.

McCauley, John. Pension Record, National Archives.

McChord, William. "History of His Life." Photocopy of typescript, 1923.

McDonough, James Lee. *War in Kentucky: From Shiloh to Perryville*. Knoxville: University of Tennessee Press, 1994.

McKay, Charles. Pension Record, National Archives.

Medal of Honor File. Henry B. Mattingly. National Archives.

"Medical History of Michigan," Volume II. *Medical Veterans of the Civil War*. Library of Congress Collection.

Milburn, James. Pension Record, National Archives.

Milburn, John. Pension Record, National Archives

Mills, Jack. Pension Record, National Archives.

Mills, James. Pension Record, National Archives

Mittler, Edward. Letter in Pension Record, National Archives, 1864.

Morgan, John H. *Official Records*. Vol. 29.

Mussen, William. Pension Record, National Archives.

Myer, John. Civil War Service Record, National Archives.

Neubert, H.G . "Account of the Battle of Chickamauga." *Toledo Blade*, July 23, 1864.

Neubert, Henry. *Daily Toledo Blade*, September 16, 1864.

Noe, Kenneth W. *Perryville: This Grand Havoc of Battle*. Lexington: University Press of Kentucky, 2001.

O'Bryan, William. Letters from Pension Record, National Archives, 1862, 1863.

O'Bryan, William. Pension Record, National Archives.

Official Records of the American Civil War, Vol. 34; Vol. 50; Vol. 54, p. 807.

Pendleton, Buford. Pension Record, National Archives.

Perrin, W. H., J. H. Battle, and G.C. Kniffin. *Kentucky: A History of the State*. Louisville, Ky.: F.A. Battey, 1887.

Regimental Records, Kentucky Historical Society, 1861.

Report of the Adjutant General of the State of Kentucky, Vol. 1: 1861–1866. Printed at the Kentucky Yeoman Office, 1866, pp. 806–823.

Reynolds, James. Pension Record, National Archives.

"Richard Nash. Died." *Louisville Daily Journal*, February 11, 1865.

Riley, George. Pension Record, National Archives.

Rosecrans, William. "From Tullahoma to Chattanooga: William S. Rosecrans, Major General, U.S.V." *Battles and Leaders of the Civil War, Vol. 5*. Peter Cozzens, ed. University of Illinois Press, 2002.

Sallee, James. Pension Record, National Archives.

Scott, James. Letter. Pension Record, National Archives. 1863

_____. Letters to his parents. Pension Record, National Archives. 1862, 1863.

Sherman, William. *Official Records*. Vol. 76.

Short, Robert. Pension Record, National Archives.

Slone, Brandon. Kentucky Military History Museum. Personal communication. Not published.

Smith, Benjamin, Pension Record, National Archives.

Speed, Thomas. *The Union Cause in Kentucky 1860–1865*. Foreword by John Harlan. New York: G. P. Putnam Sons, 1907.

_____. *Union Regiments of Kentucky*. By the Union Soldiers and Sailors Monument Association of Louisville, Ky., 1879, pp. 367–379.

Stocking, Charles. Pension Record, National Archives.

Strayer, Larry, and Richard Baumgarter. *Echoes of Battle: The Atlanta Campaign*. Huntington, W. Va.: Blue Acorn Press, 2004.

Sword, Wiley. *Mountains Touched with Fire*. New York: St. Martin's Press, 1995.

Tenth Kentucky Correspondence, National Archives.

Tenth Kentucky Infantry Regimental Record Book, National Archives, 1861–1864.

Terry, G.W. "The Charge at Jonesboro." *National Tribune*, November 4, 1915.

Thomas, Edison. *John Hunt Morgan and His Raiders*. University Press of Kentucky, 1985.

Thompson, Andrew. Pension Record, National Archives.

"To Be Brigadier Generals." November 29, 1862. *Executive Journal*, January 22, 1863.

"Traitor Clergyman Arrested." *Nashville Daily Union*, August 8, 1862.

Tucker, Glenn. *Chickamauga — Bloody Battle in the West*. Dayton, Ohio: Morningside Press, 1984.

Tweddle, William. Pension Record, National Archives.

The Union Army: A History of Military Affairs in the Loyal States 1861–65; Records of the Regiments in the Union Army, Cyclopedia of Battles, Memoirs of Commanders and Soldiers. Wilmington, N.C.: Broadfoot Publishing, 1998. Vol. 8.

U.S. Census Records, 1850–1860; 1870; 1880.

Vestrees, Josiah. Pension Record, National Archives.

Waller, Henry. Pension Record, National Archives.

"War Ills." *Courier Journal*, March 10, 1902, p. 10, Col. 3.

Warner, Ezra J. *Generals in Blue: Lives of the Union Commanders*. Baton Rouge: Louisiana State University Press, 1964.

Warren, Henry. Pension Record, National Archives.

Washington County, Kentucky, Bicentennial History: 1792–1992. Paducah, Ky.: Turner Publishing, 1991.

Watts, James R. Pension Record, National Archives.

Webster, I.B. Pension Record, National Archives.

Webster, Israel. "Chickamauga: Going into Action with Hands Full of Bacon and Coffee." *National Tribune*, July 2, 1891.

_____. "Missionary Ridge." *National Tribune*, March 10, 1892.

_____. *National Tribune*, April 21, 1892.

Wharton, Gabriel. Official Records. Vol. 50, pp. 423–424.

Wilson, Samuel. *History of the United States Court for the Eastern District of Kentucky*. Lexington, Ky., 1935.

Woodworth, Steve. *A Deep Steady Thunder*. Abilene: Texas A&M–McWhiney Foundation, 1996.

Index